THE DILYS POWELL FILM READER

Dilys Powell was born in 1901 and was educated at Somerville College, Oxford. She was *Sunday Times* chief film critic from 1939 to 1989, and has been on the Board of Governors of the BFI and the Cinematograph Film Council.

Christopher Cook is a writer, broadcaster, and documentary film-maker.

The Dilys Powell Film Reader

Edited by
Christopher Cook

Oxford   New York
OXFORD UNIVERSITY PRESS
1992

Oxford University Press, Walton Street, Oxford OX2 6DP

Oxford New York Toronto
Delhi Bombay Calcutta Madras Karachi
Petaling Jaya Singapore Hong Kong Tokyo
Nairobi Dar es Salaam Cape Town
Melbourne Auckland

and associated companies in
Berlin Ibadan

Oxford is a trade mark of Oxford University Press

First published 1991 by Carcanet Press Limited
First issued as an Oxford University Press paperback 1992

British Library Cataloguing in Publication Data
Data available
ISBN 0–19–283082–1

Library of Congress Cataloging in Publication Data
Powell, Dilys.
The Dilys Powell film reader / edited by Christopher Cook.
p. cm.
Originally published: Manchester: Carcanet Press, 1991.
Includes indexes.
1. Motion pictures—Reviews. I. Cook, Christopher. II. Title.
791.45'75—dc20 PN1995.P69 1992   92–12538
ISBN 0–19–283082–1

Printed in Great Britain by
Biddles Ltd.
Guildford and King's Lynn

Contents

For M.M.

Preface

> [In the early days] people didn't appoint people as film
> critics because they knew anything about the cinema or
> were thinking seriously about it. It was just somebody who
> hadn't got a job who could put three words together in
> roughly the right order . . . Most of the popular film critics
> just happened to be the people who were . . . around and
> hadn't got a job.   – Dilys Powell

Dilys Powell wrote her first column on the cinema for *The
Sunday Times* in 1939. And she continued to review each week's
newly released films for that newspaper until 1976, when she
moved to *Punch*, while still previewing films on television for
The Sunday Times. The cinema is just short of its hundredth
birthday and Dilys Powell has been writing about it for over half
of this century. That in itself is a remarkable record: to have
attended the press screenings of *Citizen Kane*, *Les Enfants du
Paradis*, *Bicycle Thieves* etc., to have midwifed the very first
London Film Festivals and to have encouraged two and possibly
three generations of readers to share a personal enthusiasm for an
art which, more than any other, has held up a mirror to the
twentieth century. But longevity, or simple staying power, or
enthusiasm are not enough to sustain a reputation. Dilys Powell
is also a scrupulous critic. Or should one say reviewer? And here
we arrive at the nub of the problem in measuring Powell's
achievement in over fifty years of writing about the cinema.

It is thirty years now since a fault-line first opened between
film criticism and regular reviewing in newspapers and
magazines. And as film criticism has gradually achieved a kind
of academic respectability in this country, with French theorists
in the vanguard, so the reputation of serious film journalism of
the kind practised by Dilys Powell has declined. In passing, one
might note that this cultural shift has paralleled the continuing
decline of the cinema as a popular medium when measured by
the number of people of all ages who pay to watch films, but that
is another subject. (Clearly it would be naïve to assume that it is
the Semiologists and Post-Structuralists who have driven a mass
audience out of the movie theatres.)

The point is that for twenty years or so there has been a growing tendency to dismiss film journalism as lightweight, ephemeral, pabulum for Sunday morning breakfasts and little more. A reassessment of the worth of critics such as Dilys Powell and C. A. Lejeune, her fellow reviewer on the *Observer*, may help to redress the balance. But in reconsidering Powell's career it is not a question of either/or, of Althusser or Powell. This revaluation is part of a larger project, already underway wherever Cultural Studies are taught alongside Film Studies, which is exploring how the cinema in all its aspects operates within a culture. To put it in another context, it would be a foolish cultural or design historian working in the field of twentieth century British ceramics who ignored the mass production of stoneware in the 1950s and 1960s and devoted his or her attention exclusively to Bernard Leach, Lucy Rie or Hans Coper.

Dilys Powell grew up on the South Coast in Bournemouth, in the years before and during the First World War, and her earliest memories of the cinema stem from that time. Westerns were an early favourite, and that genre has continued to afford Powell the greatest pleasure in the cinema. 'I still think the Western is the basis of the cinema: action, background, quick movement. I thought it was wonderful.' Buster Keaton was admired, too, and much preferred then to Chaplin, though Powell has generally liked Chaplin's full-length features. However 'when I see a Keaton film I think he's really superior to all of his contemporaries. He's a real cinema maker and I think he is . . . not only funny but a really serious filmmaker. I became an addict of Keaton at the beginning of the First War.'

From Bournemouth High School Powell went up to Somerville College, Oxford, where she chose to read Modern Languages. She continued to go to the cinema without necessarily taking films very seriously. 'There was a little cinema around at the back of Somerville College and you saw a film which had its sequel next week. It went on and on and it was just something one enjoyed.' After Oxford Dilys Powell joined the literary staff of *The Sunday Times*, but her early career as a book reviewer was slightly curtailed in 1926 when she married Humfrey Payne, who was appointed Director of the British School of Archaeology in Athens. She continued to write for the newspaper while dividing her time with her husband between Oxford and Athens.

Powell resumed a full career on *The Sunday Times* after Humfrey Payne's death in 1936, but it was three years before she was appointed as the newspaper's film critic. 'I got the job simply because I was there. I was just told "Here's the job, get on with it." I didn't *know* anything about the cinema. Goodness knows I know little about it now . . . It takes a lifetime to learn about the cinema and I tried very hard to know as I still try. But no, nobody was told anything. I succeeded somebody who really didn't know the difference between a film and a sponge. I don't think he *cared*, you see.' Powell's recollection of her appointment might seem to confirm the low esteem in which the cinema was held by the editors of serious newspapers in the 1930s, doubly confirmed, perhaps, by giving the job to a woman. On the other hand, another woman, C. A. Lejeune, was already writing about the cinema in the *Observer*, and Graham Greene had contributed some of the best film criticism of the 1930s to the *Spectator* between 1935 and 1940.★ It would seem that if the editors of magazines and newspapers rarely encouraged their reviewers, they did not actively discourage them from taking the cinema seriously.

Hardly had Powell begun her career as *The Sunday Times* film critic than Britain was at war. As she consolidated her critical reputation in the 1940s, she came to regard herself first and foremost as a writer who must establish a particular rapport with her readership, and then as a film critic.

I did want to entertain and amuse my readers. I mean if you're a professional writer you want to be read and you want to be with your readers. And if people would sometimes enjoy a joke I'd made – well, I'd enjoy it myself you know. [But] I hope I always thought I was being serious. Not only serious but truthful. I may have had lapses, but I really think I always wanted to explain why I thought *this* film was good . . . I suppose in a kind of impertinent way I did want to educate my

★ In an interview recorded by the BBC in 1979, on the occasion of Greene's 75th birthday, Dilys Powell told Philip French: 'One was terribly grateful that somebody of his literary genius . . . should care so much [about the cinema] as he did, and with such deep and original feeling about it – care so much about a medium which was not literary [but] which was partly visual and partly literary. I've always admired him absolutely passionately and I think that, in a way, we should all model ourselves – if we could – on Graham Greene.'

readers. I probably thought I must persuade people to go and
see this film which I liked very much, which moved me.

These simple precepts were to guide Powell through her
thirty-seven years on *The Sunday Times*. Having embarked upon
a conversation with her readers (and conversation in the real sense
of that word – witty, knowing, informed, teasing even, but never
gossip for its own sake and rarely judgemental – seems the most
apt description of Powell's particular style), it was her responsibility
to hold the reader's ear while also delivering a verdict on the
particular film under review and encouraging readers to pit their
own judgement against hers. There's a democratic spirit about
all of Dilys Powell's reviewing; hers is the opening gambit in the
conversation, the first and therefore privileged view of a new
work, but it is never intended to be the last word. In this sense
she can be described as a 'reporter', using the traditional meaning
ascribed to the word, since she intends to encourage you into the
cinema by recording as accurately as language will allow her own
reactions to this or that film.

It would be a mistake to suppose that such evenhandedness in
the relationship which she strives for with her readers precludes
judgement and a consistent attitude to the practice of criticism.
'I don't think I can really think of anybody whom I think of as a
good critic who isn't a moralist. I think in a way it is the basis of
criticism.' How to be a moralist while refusing to moralize is the
underlying tension in all of Powell's writing. It is also the true
mark of her 'Englishness', since it is irony that allows the English
liberal humanist like Powell to point no obvious moral to adorn
a tale.

The extent to which Dilys Powell shares the values of the high
English literary tradition is readily apparent when she writes
about adapting literature for the cinema. And it was also Powell's
determination to hold faith with her belief that the critic was
nothing if not a moralist which caused her difficulties in the
1970s. Her dislike of Sam Peckinpah's *Straw Dogs* is well
documented, and it is clear that she disapproved of many of the
new directions which world cinema was taking twenty years ago.
But Powell never lacked the courage to swim against the tide of
critical fashions and as a consequence a younger generation of
readers and professional colleagues, who ought to have known
better and who might have been expected to understand if not
agree with her position, were thought to have deserted her.

Re-reading Powell's reviews from this period, one sees that what at the time was presented in some quarters as a clash between ancients and moderns now seems clear evidence of the general confusion which surrounded all manner of cultural debates at the close of the 1960s.

Thirty years earlier, Powell had already established the way in which she would undertake her week's reviewing.

Just before the war one would probably see nine films a week. I would go, so far as I recall, on Monday and Tuesday and Wednesday and perhaps Thursday mornings and afternoons and see films. My copy had to be in by Friday and, as I recall, my husband [in 1943 Dilys Powell was married for the second time to Leonard Russell, literary editor of *The Sunday Times*] and I used to take the car down to *The Sunday Times* and leave it about the middle of the night, about three in the morning. And the printers, who were always very good and kind to me, would send up my proof and I would correct it. My husband was a very good judge of – what shall I say – the truth of writing. And so he would make suggestions and I would complain bitterly and say, 'Nonsense, nonsense, it's all right as it is.' But he was nearly always right. It's a very great help to any writer to have just one person you trust.

Powell made a point of trying to review each of the week's new films, which became easier during and after the war when nine new releases became four or five. There was always the difficult decision about which film should lead the column, and here it seems pragmatism was the rule. 'It gives the film more interest to start with it. It looks as if you might have something more to say about it and perhaps it might be more important. I often made mistakes but one tries to think quickly about which should have most emphasis on it; that's all, I think.' At one level it's remarkable how few mistakes Dilys Powell made in choosing which film to lead with; at the same time, it has to be said that our present sense of which films are significant in the history of the cinema has to a great extent been determined by reviewers like Powell. But a simple test of the sureness of Powell's judgement is to remind ourselves that in the 1940s she invariably gave a favourable place in her column to the films of Powell and Pressburger which, twenty years later, when the Archers reputation was at its lowest ebb would have seemed a decidedly idiosyncratic judgment.

If Powell felt that she failed to do justice to a particular film, then she would try to see it again the following week and record her second opinion. A notable example of this occurred when *Citizen Kane* first opened in London. Why did Powell write about Welles' film at such length in two successive columns, having seen the film at its British press show? Was it that she was immediately aware of its importance in the developing aesthetic of the cinema? The answer is altogether more human. Powell, who was doing war work in 1941, was prevented from reaching the press show on time; having missed the opening sequences of the film, she was puzzled by the references to 'Rosebud' and thus the significance of the sledge which is consigned to the flames at the end of the film. It was only at a second viewing the following week, once the film had opened to the public, that she was able to fit together all the pieces of Welles' narrative jigsaw puzzle. Given that she has cultivated a relationship with her readers so carefully, it comes as something of a surprise to learn that Powell would always prefer to see a film at its press show, or even better, on her own in a small viewing theatre. 'I don't want other people's coughs and laughter and slight applause, if there is any. I just like seeing it alone as I like to read a book by myself. I don't want to be interfered with!'

The analogy with reading a book is significant: further proof that Dilys Powell brings a literary sensibility to her appreciation of the cinema, an interest in narrative and character first, and then the action and the visual aesthetic of a movie. Her concern with the craft of writing reinforces such an interpretation. Twelve hundred words was by and large the length of her weekly column in *The Sunday Times* for all of her thirty-seven years on that newspaper. Latterly, critics elsewhere have been granted a great many more column-inches (Pauline Kael, say, in the *New Yorker*), but Powell liked the discipline imposed by a limited amount of space. 'I think it's very valuable. You learn not to waste your memory or your energies, such as they are. I think the discipline is . . . enjoyable in a way.' In Powell's hands the short column can become a miniature essay, and that would seem to be the ideal, even if five films are to be 'noticed' in the space of the twelve hundred words. Once again it is literature which provides the model.

In certain critical quarters it has become fashionable to descry the literary roots of so much English criticism, and to argue that the Anglo-Saxon tradition, American as well as British, is blind to visual subtleties, that we read our culture with our ears not our eyes. The evidence for this diagnosis is at best circumstantial, and at worst pure prejudice. What is required is a proper understanding of what we might mean by the term 'literary', and an examination of how it determines the critical practice of the so called 'literary' critics as they respond to predominantly visual media. I believe that a careful examination of Dilys Powell's writing about the cinema is an important step along that road.

At the same time it would be quite wrong to read Powell only in an attempt to answer to these questions. She is much more than a cultural curiosity, she is a living and a lively critic, by which I mean that there is a freshness about her judgements that jumps across the decades in which they were first shaped to the present day. She measures her response upon the pulse of her own sensibility, and encourages us to do the same. Naturally her work helps us to understand the cultural context in which cinema was viewed from the 1940s to the mid-1970s, and to participate in the developing debate between criticism and reviewing that I touched upon earlier, but what makes Powell's writing so distinctive is her delight in cinema itself. And it was ever thus, each week in *The Sunday Times* from 1939 to 1976.

There are two sets of choices facing an editor when presented with so large and so varied a body of writing on a single subject as Dilys Powell's complete film criticism. The first is what to include in a selection and what to omit. Here I have been guided by three criteria: what might interest a serious reader in the literature of the cinema; what best conveys Powell's particular qualities as a critic; what helps our understanding of her place in the wider context of British film culture since 1939. The second choice is whether to arrange the selection chronologically or by theme. Generally, as should be clear from my chapter headings, I have plumped for themes rather than chronology. Within each chapter or section of a chapter, however, I have usually followed a straightforward chronology. In making both of these choices I have been guided, inevitably, by my own preferences, and, I daresay, prejudices. It was Dilys Powell's weekly column in *The Sunday Times* which first alerted me to the pleasures of the cinema thirty years ago, and I responded then, as I still do, to the implicit invitation in all that she has written to join her in a personal dialogue.

In making my selection of individual pieces I have not confined myself to *The Sunday Times*, although the greatest amount of Dilys Powell's work was published in that newspaper. Powell was a regular broadcaster about the cinema, particularly on the BBC's Third Programme and later Radio Three, and I have included a talk on film directors she first gave for the BBC. She also contributed to magazines such as *Sight and Sound*, a number of publications which have long since disappeared, and after leaving *The Sunday Times* in 1976 she was the film critic for *Punch*. I have chosen material from all of these sources, but unless otherwise indicated at the end of each piece, everything in the book was first published in *The Sunday Times*. All of the quotations in my preface are from an interview I conducted with Dilys Powell in 1991.

My principal debt in editing this selection is naturally to Dilys Powell, who endured my peripatetic appearances at her home, unceasing questions and insatiable curiosity with grace and humour. I am also greatly indebted to Philip French, who first suggested that I might care to work on this material. Furthermore, without Philip French's continual encouragement during his time at the BBC as a producer for Radio Three, and the example he sets in the *Observer* and elsewhere to anyone who would write about the cinema, I might long ago have been left on the cutting-room floor of film criticism.

My thanks are also due to Michael Schmidt at Carcanet, who watched successive deadlines sail by with perfect equanimity, or so it seemed to me. And to Robyn Marsack, who saw this book through the press with the minimum of fuss. The responsibility for all that follows is of course mine and mine alone.

Christopher Cook
London and Lewes, summer 1991

1 BRITISH CINEMA 1939–1967

'British Cinema should express the national character and not some fiction of the box office' is the concluding sentence of Dilys Powell's review of Carol Reed's film *Bank Holiday*, which she much admired. And a concern for a national cinema located in Britain and speaking about Britain, but to a world as well as a local audience is a continuing theme in Powell's criticism. She understood that the Second World War had brought about an aesthetic sea-change in British cinema, that the wedding of the documentary tradition of the 1930s to that of the British feature film had produced a particular kind of cinema and she was concerned to support this marriage as it matured. Therefore in the late 1950s and 1960s there is praise for 'Free Cinema', *Room at the Top* and later *Poor Cow*. At the same time, Powell understood the economic difficulties that have always attended the making of a British cinema and came no nearer than any other critic in prescribing a course of treatment – outright government subsidy in some form or other, say – that would guarantee full health for a national industry.

Last Sunday, writing of the success of French films and the remarkable effects achieved by the use of regional character, I suggested that British producers and directors might well follow the example and use the regional material at their disposal in this country. Readers in Sussex, Dorset, and Montgomeryshire have welcomed the suggestion, each advocating the claims of his own county to be filmed with a partisanship at once ferocious and exclusive. And indeed there really seems no reason why pictures should not be made distinguishing between, let us say, the gossips in a Sussex pub and the groups of men standing about the streets in a Welsh market town, as clearly as the French distinguish between the northern poacher and the hunter going out with his gun in Provence. Even the BBC, standardized English notwithstanding, occasionally introduces a touch of local character into its programmes. The film industry leaves it to an American to make a film of *Wuthering Heights* with a synthetic Yorkshire and Californian heather.

We in this country have as yet evolved no style of our own in films. The French have their own style, the Russians have theirs; so, once, had the Germans (whether they still have it there is, with the disappearance of German films from the British market, no means of judging). We need producers and directors and script writers to translate English life into terms of the cinema as the French are all the time translating French life. Occasionally, of course, someone brings off a good translation. **Bank Holiday** for instance, with a script by Rodney Ackland and Hans Wilhelm gave a beautiful impressionistic picture of the tragi-comic miseries of an English seaside holiday. But one picture doesn't make a tradition, and, like Dr Johnson when asked if he was not satisfied with the evidence for the immortality of the soul, we could wish for more.

Carol Reed, who directed *Bank Holiday*, is modest about the director's part in the success of a film. 'The really essential thing,' he insists, 'is a good script. With that, the rest is easy.' But what so often seems to be lacking in British films is visual imagination, the imagination which sees the emotional effect of certain lighting, certain shots, certain angles, which unifies the mood of the whole picture, and lets nothing appear that does not bear, however indirectly, on its theme.

The English are less accomplished in the visual arts than in the arts of literature. They are, however, not blind, and have at some periods in their history produced domestic architecture and landscape painting – well, not wholly negligible. The producers and directors of British films, who are presumably alive to the emotional impact of the visual, will not have failed to observe the lovely vigilance of a deserted city street, with the lamps shining on the wet black mirror of the road; or the way in which a farmhouse, with its barns and sheds, composes itself in a hollow of the downs. Yet such scenes rarely intrude into our pictures, which present us rather with the smart nondescript interiors of flats in Maygravia.

We have, surely, the writing and producing and directing talent in this country; we have the actors, too. 'Men and women in the great crises of their lives show very little emotion in their faces. Whenever I can I go to the Old Bailey and watch,' says Carol Reed; 'a man will accept the severest sentence with an almost expressionless face. That is how much emotional acting for the cinema should be done.' English stage actors who used, when in a film, to pass a tea-cup as if it were a death-warrant, have learned the value on the screen of the tiny gesture, the hardly perceptible flicker of the face. So now all that is wanted is backing from someone who believes that British films should express the national character and not some fiction of the box-office.

1939

The emotional impact of **In Which We Serve** was immense. The experiences of civilian and fighting men were presented as essentially one, bound together by the ties of human love and devotion; nobody but felt he had a stake in this drama. But if we look at the film with a detached and critical eye we must recognize the technical skill, the command of the medium which has gone to its making. The authority with which the complex strands of the narrative are handled, the mastery of simple unemphatic dialogue, the easy unobtrusive use of camera angle and movement – all are here. And the acting was pretty near faultless. Not all critics have praised Coward's own performance as the captain; there is, perhaps, a trace of self-satisfaction in it. Yet in the emotional climaxes of the film – the colloquy between captain and dying sailor, the last good-bye between captain and crew – there is no self-consciousness. The film brought prestige also to many players not, till then, recognized as first-rank film performers. To Celia Johnson, for example, a polished stage actress, who now brought an easy technique to the part of the captain's wife; to John Mills, everlastingly English as the naval rating; to Bernard Miles as the petty officer and to Richard Attenborough as the frightened boy. Coward, during the rest of the war, directed no more films, though he was the author of more than one. But *In Which We Serve* had set a new standard in the English cinema.

There is nothing experimental, certainly nothing revolutionary, in the style of *In Which We Serve*. What makes it historically important in the British cinema is its use of two significant motives: documentary background and the native theme. The film opens with a purely documentary sequence presenting the building of a warship; and throughout the story is underpinned, as it were, by fact, the fact of the sailor's life. But even more important at this stage was the emphasis on a subject germane to the experience of every man, woman and child in the audience. I have said that before the war the British cinema had no tradition. One might go further and say it had no subject. Looking back at the history of the cinema in Europe and America, one detects, beneath the superficial variety of themes, something which might be called a national theme. The French, a people with a deep and tender feeling for the under-side of life, the shadowed pavement of the street, the human unfortunate, have made their best films on the theme of undisciplined life. Renoir, Carné, Duvivier, René Clair, have shown us the crook, the vagabond, rather than the established citizen, the raffish boarding-house rather than the *bourgeois* home; the picture has been translated into a kind of poetic realism which found beauty in the smoky confusion of the railway viaduct, the quayside, the murky back-street. In the great days of the Russian cinema, the theme was revolution, the protagonists were the infantryman in the trenches, the half-starved sailor, the suffering worker in farm and factory; and once more a savagely dramatic handling of pictorial values translated the realistic scene into poetry. The American cinema at its best, on the other hand, has dealt with the brilliant surface of life. The poetic overtones of D. W. Griffith's great films were lost in the work of his successors: and the American cinema became a representation, fast-moving, sometimes ironic, always realistic, of the face of America: the face of the crowded city, the face of the enormous landscape. Always, one sees, the concentration on native material. It is when the French producers, or the Russian, or the American, venture outside their own national experience, that they most obviously fail. This is not simply because the cinema, however poetically handled, must rely on a basis of realism. Superficially realism can be acquired; an Englishman can learn the factual background of life in, say, New York. It is a thousand times more difficult for him to acquire the rhythm and cadence of American life. The film, in its natural dependence on material native to producers and directors, does not differ from the other arts: Tolstoy uses his immense genius on Russian subjects, the Great English novelist, Dickens, builds up his superb tragi-comic picture of life from the London and the England he knows.

This concentration on inherited and contemporary experience was almost completely lacking in the British cinema of the 'twenties and 'thirties. Subjects were to hand; for Britain in its small compass holds an infinite variety of ways of life, of types, from the factory-worker in the Northern and industrial towns to the fisherman of the Scottish coasts, from the shepherd of the South Downs to the steel-worker, the coal-miner, the railwayman, the shipbuilder. It took a war to compel the British to look at themselves and find themselves interesting. This did not mean, as I hope I have made clear, anything resembling isolationism. The British remained indefatigably curious about the outside world from which war had cut them off. But the circumstances of war, the total effort of the country, narrowed the physical circle in which the creative imagination could work; intent on the business of daily survival, the national conscience began to dwell more than ever before on its local problems. Noel Coward in *In Which We Serve* took a handful of typically British men and women and made from their stories, ordinary enough in themselves, a distillation of national character. The films of the same period, or of the years which followed, may have been uneven and faltering. But at least they showed a movement towards a national subject, in the sense in which I have just used the phrase.

From: 'Since 1939'(1948)

In the appraisal of the regional film the critic of nondescript provenance is at a grave disadvantage. He cannot say, with the assurance of the native, that this is or is not a fair rendering of scene. He cannot even, in ninety-nine cases out of a hundred, claim the remotest acquaintance with the original; for no matter how mobile the journalist, he gets around less than the camera. The best he can do, in fact, is to decide whether or not the film conveys to him personally the strong flavour of earth and water, and leave it at that.

It is, then, not for me to discuss the accuracy of the new Powell-Pressburger piece, *I Know Where I'm Going*. This story of the storm-swept Hebrides may or may not speak to the Islander of his home; I can say only that to me it communicates an overpowering sense of place.

Regional films have not been common in our cinema. *The Edge of the World*, *Owd Bob* – before the war they were a handful and no more, if we exclude the documentary pieces. The sensuousness of the French regional background, the fervour, in turns romantic and savage, of the Russian rendering of landscape and man in relation to landscape, were almost entirely lacking in our own films. The war, indeed, narrowing the physical horizon, turned the eyes of producers and directors in on the native scene; from this constriction there emerged at last a native subject, obvious enough in all conscience, yet not grasped before: English character. The setting has been slower to find than the theme. Films of English character (I speak again of fiction films) have dwelt chiefly on urban character without a corresponding emphasis on its pictorial background. There has been nothing to compare with the Frenchman's poetic handling of the back street and the scabrous alley, or the American's rendering of the confused movement of subway and pleasure park; only the documentary worker has composed the dramatic lights and shadows of the tenement and the playground. And only within the last year or so have country character and the country scene begun to play a considerable part in the entertainment film.

When last year Michael Powell and Emeric Pressburger made *A Canterbury Tale*, the justice and beauty of the rural setting were not balanced by any equivalent strength in the narrative, and the film's argument for the traditional ways of life was lost. In *I Know Where I'm Going* the thread of plot is much stronger, and though, reduced to its structure, this is just another story of a girl engaged to a prosaic rich man and deserting him for a poor one, the mood and treatment swell this cinema stock-in-trade to something curious and memorable. The stark sudden hills, the dark waters, the island seen through veils of spray and mist – landscape and seascape here are handled as if they had personalities of their own; one feels the presence of wind and shore in a manner for which I can think of no English parallel except in Brian Desmond Hurst's early film of Synge's *Riders to the Sea*. The shots of the furious sea, the sullen curtain of the approaching storm, the whirlpool in whose gulf the little boat which plies between the islands is nearly lost, are as good as anything of their kind I can remember. And over and above the feeling of the physical setting there persists the feeling of a way of life too, remote and self-contained as the life of Jean Epstein's *Mor Vran*. No doubt parts of the picture have been romanticized. But, whether or not *I Know Where I'm Going* is true to its original, it has an imaginative truth which holds fast in the mind. Not always an agreeable truth; to me indeed there is something a little sinister about these people, this landscape, this self-sufficient farawayness. But I shall remember the piece as I do not remember many films, for a power of suggestion which atones for the cheapjack narrative tricks of the last sequence. The acting of Wendy Hiller, Roger Livesey and Pamela Brown strikes no false note; and many, I am sure, will share my enjoyment of the performances by Captain Knight and his golden eagle as himself, itself, and themselves in a style endeared by many an hour's lecture-hall bird-watching.

December 1945

Last Tuesday a throng of beaming film executives and less receptive newspaper types learned that a British film company, Associated British Picture Corporation, were to join with an American company, Warner Brothers, in producing in this country six films 'similar in quality to the best now produced in America'; above the sounds of hospitality I heard that Warners would supply their leading stars, directors and producers 'to ensure that these pictures are of the highest quality, suitable for world markets.' The following day I saw **Odd Man Out**. The director and producer of this film is English; the players are English, Irish and Canadian; the director of photography is Australian-born. The piece is not, indeed, if we are to judge by the work which reached us during 1946 'similar in quality to the best now produced in America'. It is not similar because it is better.

Odd Man Out, from a novel by F. L. Green, is the story of a young Irish revolutionary leader who kills a man in a hold-up planned to get money for 'the organization', fails to escape clear with the rest of his party, and, badly wounded, is tracked through the city from afternoon to midnight. Superficially, in fact, it is a story of pursuit; and Carol Reed, who has more pace than any other director working in this country, has given to the scenes of chase a brilliance of action which dazzles. The hunt is threefold: while Johnny the leader hides dazed in the air-raid shelter, two of his companions are cornered at the house of the smiler with the whisky bottle; his friend, trying to lead the police off the main scent, races through alleys and across roof-tops, doubles through crowds. The fast-moving images are in themselves beautiful: erratic shadows spinning along lamp-lit walls, children playing in the shining dark night streets; but amid the poetry of light and shadow, the drama of the tumbling elaborate fights which Mr Reed handles so surely, the central movement is never lost from sight. Sound is used with unusual descriptive effect: the alarm bell, the dog yapping after the wounded man, the musty silence in the air-raid shelter with the children's voices shrilling in the distance and the small hollow thump as the little girl's ball bounces in. But again the whole complex of sound is directed towards a single narrative end: the clock striking the quarters, the ship hooting, delicately remind us of the shortening of time, the impossible margin for escape.

And while so much of the action leaves the central character hidden or lost, the audience never forgets him; and in the constant concern for him underlined by the asides of the people of Belfast, the crowds and stragglers of the film, there is evidence of the success with which the story has been constructed and balanced. One passage excepted. I find in *Odd Man Out* the warmth and human bizarreness which I missed in so correctly and indeed finely made a piece as *Great Expectations*. But there is one character whose bizarreness strikes false: the drunken artist who carries the half-conscious fugitive off to his studio to paint the lineaments of pain and dissolution. Is it perhaps that Robert Newton plays the part in a style over-reminiscent of Ancient Pistol? At any rate the scene in the studio, with Johnny's delirious visions, is the least achieved in the film; for once the director seems to be attempting something not yet within his grasp.

Yet one would not wish him to have evaded it. Last week, writing of Fritz Lang's *Cloak and Dagger*, I said that in the genre of the thriller the British cinema still did not attain such certainty. But with *Odd Man Out* it is creating beyond the reach of simple nervous tension. I should be doing the film no service if I exaggerated its scope. It is first of all a film of action; and its probings into conscience are only hesitant. But it has undertones: undertones of loyalty, guilt, cowardice, defiance. And it has human beings. As the wounded leader, James Mason has little to do but stagger and suffer, which he does very well. But the development of secondary characters is more detailed. The seedy jackdaw of the streets; the shiftless, self-excusing young gunman; the crinkled old woman remembering the flavour of life – these, as played by F. J. McCormick, Cyril Cusack and Kitty Kirwan, are at once fantastic and solid. Kathleen Ryan's cool girl, the priest of W. G. Fay, the policeman of Denis O'Dea, the pitying Samaritan of Fay Compton would be outstanding in a cast less generally accomplished.

On the evidence of such work as *Odd Man Out*, and in the present state of the American cinema, the importation of directors, producers and stars from America to England can scarcely benefit us aesthetically. What it can do is to benefit us financially, by persuading American audiences to pay to see so-called British films – which I suspect will be really American films made with American gloss in British studios. No doubt in our present economic straits there are good arguments for the deal. But it is, I feel, a deal in the long run dangerous to the growing British cinema, which must surely win its reputation – and its markets – by developing in its own way.

February 1947

So the Government propose to finance the independent producers of films in this country. On the face of it the plan is admirable. But who is to decide which producer, and which idea, is worth helping? The Government say that the proposed Film Finance Corporation shall advance money, not direct to producers, but to distributors, who in their turn will pass it on to the film-maker whose ideas they approve. The distributors, in fact, are to decide:

a provision by which the Government undo with one hand most of the good they are doing with the other. For the job of an independent film producer is to be independent, and here he is dependent once more on distributors who, before he has begun to make his film – and this is the danger – can sterilize his idea.

Surely a system by which the creative mind in the cinema must always begin by convincing the wholesaler of the commercial value of his idea – which is what the present financial scheme means – is likely to result in unadventurous and repetitive films. I trust I am not being unfair in suggesting, for instance, that had Michael Powell and Emeric Pressburger been talented beginners instead of established names, they might have had quite a bit of bother persuading a wholesaler to let them make **The Red Shoes**. I am not implying that the Government's money should necessarily be put into films such as *The Red Shoes*; I am not even implying that *The Red Shoes* is all good. But if, as I take it, the intention of the Government is to encourage commercially successful cinema, the Government ought to begin by encouraging good films; and you don't get good films without fresh ideas, fresh talents and imagination.

Fresh ideas: well, perhaps the theme of *The Red Shoes* is scarcely new. The ballet which gives the piece its crux is a rendering of a Hans Anderson story (a particularly brutal one): the tale of the girl who insisted on going to church in red shoes and whose feet thereafter would not stand still; even when they were cut off they went on dancing in their red shoes. And round the ballet has been constructed a story faintly echoing Hans Andersen: the central figure of the film is a young dancer who cannot give up dancing, and who rather than choose between her husband and her career prefers to kill herself. I would not deny that a masterpiece might be written for the cinema with this theme. The Powell-Pressburger tale, however, has been shaped showily rather than tragically; its frequent falsities make the story (as so often in the work of this gifted team) the weakest part of the film.

But if one accepts the story, talent becomes a small word for the quality of its handling. Once more an extraordinary audacity informs the screen; as in *Black Narcissus*, as in *A Matter of Life and Death*, the medium is handled with a command for which no elaboration of description, no excursion into fantasy, is too difficult. Let me say again that, in this matter of enjoyed authority and daring, Powell and Pressburger have in my opinion no rival anywhere, either in America or in Europe. And in them we see a producer-director team who, even when their basic story is banal, are not afraid of imaginative decoration.

It was, after all, not a commonplace idea to make ballet the motive of a film. And in *The Red Shoes* we enjoy for once a ballet written and composed for the cinema in the first place. For this pleasure – and it is an extreme pleasure – we must thank Brian Easdale, whose music brings so sharp an excitement to the film; Robert Helpmann, the choreographer as well as dancer and actor throughout the piece; and Hein Heckroth, to whom we owe the designing of the whole production, but whose composition in form and colour is, naturally, most free and most beautiful in the limitless world of cinema ballet. The sense of space, of motion through imagined worlds and suggested terrors, is strong enough in the whole of the central ballet sequence to make the occasional emphasis on symbols of size and movement – the sea boiling suddenly in the auditorium as the ballerina whirls across the stage, the dancers translated into flowers, birds, clouds – seem intrusive and even vulgar.

And the dancer herself? Moira Shearer gives a performance which, while she dances, is all delight; and the fragments from old and famous ballets in which she appears testify to her technical range. It is, perhaps, too much to expect that as an actress also she should excel. She is, after all, in competition with players of experience: Anton Walbrook, admirable except in an overacted last scene, as the impresario who demands complete devotion of his dancers; Marius Goring as the young composer with whom she falls in love; and the great Massine himself, a genius of mime as well as dancing, whose every gesture can still bring tears to the eyes. It is to her credit that in such company she conveys without embarrassment to anybody the impression of a nice girl who happens to be a brilliant dancer.

July 1948

From the moment it opens, even from the flash-by of the impudent credit titles, *Hue and Cry* goes with a swing; the young heroes sport against a background warmed by everyday life, the situations multiply in a whirl of fancy, Georges Auric's lively music suggests a general caper. There was a time a year or two ago when one began to fear that the British cinema would be another case of arrested development. The war films were fine: the admirable democratic principles, the reticent characterization, the new solidity of background, the group-heroes. But even reticence can harden into a convention; the group-hero, so laconic, so impartially dialectal, so much the common man, can become as much of a cliché as Errol Flynn winning the battle of Burma; one longed for the cinema in this country at any rate to do what is expected of any art and stretch out into fresh themes and new fields for experiment. In isolation *Hue and Cry* doesn't mean much. But taken together with say, *The Rake's Progress*, *Dead of Night*, *The Overlanders*, *Great Expectations* and *Odd Man Out*, it means a great deal. It means that the British cinema can get along without its war-time formula, that there is a chance of establishing a tradition without forming a habit, that yesterday's adventure needn't necessarily grow into tomorrow's boredom.

What is wanted, of course, beside the major virtues of the creative imagination, is vitality of invention. *Hue and Cry* is nothing to pull a solemn critical face about. To say it breaks new ground would be pompous as well as false; but it takes a commonplace and discovers fantasy; it has the air of having been thrown off by an art which has time and energy enough to make a youthful joke. Looking at the film, one is reminded of the German *Emil and the Detectives*, which also told the story of a thief caught by a variant of the Baker Street Irregulars. But the new piece scores by building on a familiar dream-world; in T. E. B. Clarke's excellent screen play, the boys who read a serial and then find themselves playing a part in it do more than bring a crude fiction to life; their adventures give a touch of witty caricature to the tuppenny blood. The elementary code in which the boss, through the medium of a boys' weekly, sends orders to his gang; the password and the rendezvous; the mocking laugh of the villain as he dodges round the walls and up the stairs of the wrecked warehouse and heaves half-a-brick at Joe the hero – it is at once serious enough to be exciting and ironic enough to be funny.

The story, while ingeniously using the natural skeleton of the ordinary – the games among the rubble of the old bomb-holes, the child collecting car-numbers, the pair mending the bicycle tyre in the mean street – imposes its own gay decorations of comic incident and narrative fancy. The young sleuths, feigning interest in a shop window, find themselves exchanging grimaces with a battle-axe doing invisible mending; as they tussle with the night watchman in the stores, a machine announces their collective weight; a police car parks on the manhole lid through which, in flight from the law, they are trying to get out of their disagreeable refuge in the sewers.

And the background has the curious charm, so rare in English films, of the recognizable. Hordes of yelling boys tear down real London steps, across a real London bridge. The bombed site is a real bombed site, empty, flattened; the camerawork sharply conveys the desolation of rubble and dust. Occasionally I felt that the timing of action would have been the better for tightening; with a little more precision in direction, passages good as they are might have become first-rate. Charles Crichton's direction of the playing, however, is remarkable. This is not to deny the quality of the players. With the exception of a few names such as Jack Warner, Alastair Sim and Jack Lambert (of *Nine Men*), the cast is almost unknown on the screen; many of its members have never acted professionally before. Yet the Blood-and-Thunder Boys play with the sureness, the easy communication of character, of the Dead End Kids at their first astonishing appearance. I will mention only the eager blundering Joe of Harry Fowler, Ian Dawson's more sophisticated adolescent, Douglas Barr's adventurous nipper and Stanley Escane as the cynic of the party. But to be strictly fair one would have to give the entire list of the young players who have brought to the cinema a fresh stratum of London life.

February 1947

When the *The Criminal Life of Archibaldo de la Cruz* was shown at the National Film Theatre a reader wrote, most interestingly, to reproach me with taking the film too seriously; instead of sitting whey-faced, palms sweating with fright, I should have been enjoying as a *comédie noire* Buñuel's story of a murderer whose murders never came off. Or rather he reproached me with taking it seriously in the wrong way, for he went on to point out that *comédie noire* is important in its own right. I still find Archibaldo's criminal career too *noir* to be comic. But I am glad that the appearance of **The Ladykillers** (director Alexander Mackendrick) allows me to return to the genre.

The Ladykillers is, I fancy, the first black comedy to be made in this country since *Kind Hearts and Coronets*, a film, also from

Ealing Studios, to which it bears a superficial resemblance; that is to say, it rattles off a series of murders and treats them as jokes. But in *Kind Hearts and Coronets*, which as you may remember was about a man engaged in wiping out the relatives who stood between him and a dukedom, the joke consisted in murder. In *The Ladykillers* the murders are incidental. The joke lies in a situation expounded during the first ten minutes, when a vague but indomitable old lady, much given to fanciful reports to the police, is seen welcoming as lodger a shady customer who presently uses her roof as cover for planning with his confederates an armed robbery.

William Rose, author of story and screenplay, has brought to his intricate tale charm as well as resource. The piece opens rapturously with old Mrs Wilberforce trotting round to the police station to correct a friend's report that a space-ship had landed in the garden, then returning to show her home to the sinister individual with the strawy hair, the Brer Fox teeth and the faintly demented eyes. Everything here is right: the seedy little street, the trains smoking and shrieking past under the back windows, the horrid reconnoitring shadow of the visitor; above all the furnishings, the photographs, the shell ornaments, the chimney-piece loaded with a hundred Victorian objects whose collection must have brought joy to the ingenious heart of the art director, Jim Morahan. And Tristram Cary's wittily devised musical accompaniment nicely underlines the ironic situation.

The acting is triumphant. As the Professor, brains of the conspirators, Alec Guinness gives – I will make the claim high – the best of his comic performances I have seen: shabby-sinister, teetering on the edge of mania, yet in its lightning changes from urbane to savage cunning gloriously funny. As the other members of the gang Herbert Lom, Peter Sellers, Danny Green and in particular Cecil Parker do well. But a large share of the triumph belongs to Katie Johnson, an actress on the far side of seventy, whose portrait of Mrs Wilberforce is to the life: the precise speech, the gentle good breeding, aged frailty drawing itself up, in moments of crisis, into resoluteness. I last saw Miss Johnson, I think, in a tiny part in Ealing's *I Believe in You*; to have cast her in this new, long part, for which her presence and gifts so beautifully fit her, was an inspiration.

The beginning, then, is faultless; the end is satisfyingly mischievous; and the middle? After the robbery I find a tiny slackening of grip, though not enough to affect the general success of a well-mannered, captivating film. Indeed, I should hesitate to mention it were not this the point at which the comedy darkens.

Darkens: it does not turn quite black. In *Kind Hearts and Coronets*, in *Monsieur Verdoux* we are invited to laugh when some innocent though not necessarily attractive character is knocked off; for the essence of true-black comedy is that the comic crime or disaster shall have no moral justification. With *The Ladykillers* moral scruples are satisfied by the sacrifice of the undesirable, and the innocent escape. When Buñuel makes a joke about murder he makes it so wholeheartedly that it shocks – and for me, at any rate, ceases to be a joke. Artistically, I suspect, *The Ladykillers* needs a shade more of the macabre; it would be a better film if it were blacker. But I am beginning to find that I can see a joke better in twilight than at midnight.

December 1955

'FREE CINEMA'

It has been a pleasure this past week to be wrong. Constant though my addiction to the cinema, fond though my enjoyment of even bad films, I have lately fancied that the whole affair might be running down for want of ideas. Technical revolution we have had, and I am all for it. But what about new creators? The young directors who appear come from the commercial cinema and use their gifts in the commercial cinema. Nothing against that; only the need of any art, if it is to keep alive, for explorers and experimenters who practise because they must, for love.

In 1952 the British Film Institute received from the British Film Production Fund a grant to encourage experimental cinema, and set up a committee to advise on the use of the money. This evening and for the next three days the National Film Theatre is showing two pieces, *Together* and *Momma Don't Allow*, sponsored by the committee, and one, *O Dreamland* made independently.

The trouble with experimental films is that they are often so unalluring. I remember seeing a piece in which the main, possibly the only, character after a few minutes dwindled into the distance and vanished into a mud puddle; since I have no X certificate I will not describe what happened to the heroes of the other works in the programme. The films at the National Film Theatre (which are called, by the way, 'free', not 'experimental') are not trick films or symbol-films. Two are comments, one angry, one affectionate. *O Dreamland* is about a seaside fun-fair: a ferocious picture of the meagre and dragging pleasures of a tripper from London.

Indeed, I was startled by a savagery foreign to the director, Lindsay Anderson (who made *Thursday's Children*). But the attack is against not the visitors but the kind of fun they are offered; and Mr Anderson and his cameraman and recordist, John Fletcher, are giving an individual view, and giving it brilliantly in acid pictures and mocking jungle sounds (recorded at the fair).

Come to that, I am thankful for a bit of savagery in the genteel British documentary cinema; just as I am grateful for the friendliness of *Momma Don't Allow* (directors Karel Reisz and Tony Richardson; cameraman Walter Lassally), an account of an evening at the Wood Green Jazz Club. The players and the dancers, the couples weaving their hypnotic repeated figures, the excited onlookers and the tepid visitors – observed with unforced sympathy, the film is infectious with high spirits. I have seen it twice, and I like it more and more.

Both these films are at once professional and personal; but they are descriptions, not inventions. *Together* is a short fiction, set in London's East End; story by Denis Horne, music by Daniele Paris, direction by a young Italian artist, Lorenza Mazzetti. It is about two deaf-mute dock-labourers, played with miraculous command by a painter, Michael Andrews, and a sculptor, Eduardo Paolozzi: their life together, cut off from other lives, the landlady who hates them, the children who run jeering behind them. Into a series of uneventful episodes shown against a background of bomb-sites, warehouses, strutted narrow streets and the sad river, Miss Mazzetti has contrived to infuse deep pathos and a warning of tragedy – and without a word of dialogue. *Together* goes back to the true basis of cinema: visual narrative, human relations. My question about new talents is hopefully answered.

February 1956

A decade has gone by since the burst of creative activity which at the end of the war suddenly made the world conscious of the British cinema. That was the period of *Dead of Night* and *Great*

Expectations, Hamlet and *I Know Where I'm Going, It Always Rains on Sunday, The Way to the Stars, The Rake's Progress, A Matter of Life and Death, Odd Man Out, Brief Encounter*. The successes of those post-war years may have been multiplied in imagination; we forget that even then there was always a *Jassy* to counter a *Hue and Cry*. But at least they were years of independent native promise. Years, I admit, of too much self-felicitation; I remind myself of the financial crisis which succeeded them.

Since then we have seen an endless struggle for recovery. The Rank Organisation has austerely set its house in economic order. Government intervention to shore up the industry has steadily increased. Yet today there is once more the sense of a crisis in production. Studio after studio goes over to television; interesting talents are unemployed; with Korda's death a source of imagination has vanished. And once more the old Anglo-American question repeats itself: Who is to invade whom?

Of the chief films to be produced in Britain this year, it seems likely that over a third will be made wholly or partly with American money. Olivier is to make *The Sleeping Prince* for Warner; Litvak is directing Ingrid Bergman in *Anastasia* for Twentieth Century-Fox; all Ealing films are to be backed and distributed by M.G.M. And while Rank promises £3 million for twenty films this year, Columbia announce through Warwick Films, an American group established in this country, £6 million for nine in the next three years.

Nothing wrong with that so long as the result is indigenous. American money has often helped British talent to make British films; some of the early work of Carol Reed, for instance, had American backing. But there is always the danger of denationalisation. The Warwick productions – *The Red Beret, Hell Below Zero, Cockleshell Heroes*, to name a few – have, I am told, been successful. They are everywhere accepted as British. But they are no more British in feeling than Salt Lake City.

It is only natural that a company putting its money into cinema should want to put its stars in too, and more and more American players appear in the films made in British studios. Again, nothing against this. It is delightful to think of Marilyn Monroe appearing with Olivier in *The Sleeping Prince*; Katharine Hepburn does us honour by working here. In any case, acting is one department in which America has been importing far more from us than we from America. Hollywood is full of English players; there is a kind of British invasion.

Not quite, perhaps. Hollywood take our promise and turns it into performance. Richard Burton was never properly advanced in the cinema until he went to America; nor, for that matter, was Olivier himself. Again and again a player who has made little headway in this country is enlarged in reputation by working in America. Especially is this true of actresses. I can contain my admiration for Joan Collins; but she has certainly improved since she went to Hollywood. It is, I fear, less of a British invasion than – by our own fault – an American annexation.

For the American-financed British cinema to invade America may be comparatively easy, and some will say that this is a gift-horse not to be looked in the mouth. But one cannot quite renounce hope that the independent, the genuinely British film may still make money in the United States. For every day it grows clearer that if the indigenous British cinema is to survive it must be either subsidised or exported. In the so-called art houses of America it already wins applause. But art houses are not enough.

Unsophisticated American cinema audiences, no doubt, are with difficulty converted to British films. One cannot always blame them. The Rank Organisation, I know, has sold a considerable number of its productions to American television. So far so good; but it seems to me that too many of our cinema films are essentially television films: little comedies which will drag nobody from the fireside, over-domesticated, over-genteel, under-sexed and understated. Certainly there are times when in contrast with Hollywood braggadocio our underemphasis looks lifelike as well as admirable. But understatement can in itself become a kind of exaggeration.

Gentility and British phlegm: to these America adds inaudibility. Our players, she says, move like snails and talk like machine-guns. American audiences simply can't hear what is being said.

Yet when one looks back over the past fifteen years one can think of scores of British films of exceptional quality, films which have earned the enthusiasm of serious critics on the Continent as well as in the United States. There is a great reserve of talent in this country, players, directors, writers, technicians, who deserve to be used in producing cinema which is their own and not a copy of Hollywood. But without help the British industry, with its small native market, cannot go on indefinitely. And now it seems that we stand between self-help and American help, between foreign infiltration and Government subsidy.

Government intervention has long been accepted as a fact. The trouble is that it has always worn a temporary air. Finance corporations are set up, funds levied, but always in a short-term fashion. The cinema is a long-term business, making its plans for production far ahead; it needs to feel safe. At the moment it has no guarantee of continuing help.

And surely the time has come for it to be accepted as a force not wholly frivolous. Entertainments tax, I suppose, we must endure. But the cinema says with some justice that authority, in discriminating between what should be taxed and what exempt, deals harshly with the film. And I for one still cannot see why cutting off King Macbeth's head on the stage is educational, while cutting King Richard's throat on the screen is a highly taxable depravity.

July 1956

After weeks of mediocrity, with half the best minds in the business idle and the British cinema apparently settling down to the production of endless romps on the promenade deck, suddenly a film which is violently in earnest. After months when one had begun, against all one's instincts, to think that the best hope lay in coproduction, with directors and players and writers from other countries eking out not so much the talent – there really is plenty of that – as the creative courage of this country, suddenly a film which succeeds by being native. **Room at the Top** directed by Jack Clayton and produced by John and James Woolf, speaks from the word go with consummate authority.

Perhaps I ought to have expected it. Mr Clayton, after all, showed what he was capable of when he directed *The Bespoke Overcoat*. But I have had my disappointments before now, and it was with a shock of pleasure that I watched the confident opening of the new film: the young man arriving in the northern town and taking stock of the local government offices where he is to work; the eyes of the typists and the girls at the counter suddenly arrested, fixed on him as he comes in, then, conscious of detection, hurriedly averted; the first meeting with the condescension of a boss who can imagine no goal above the heights of his own position. Nothing over-emphasized, everything given value; the detail closely woven to form a comment on the narrative theme.

The novel by John Braine from which the film is adapted is about a smart young man from a working-class family who is destroyed as a human being by his ambition; and it is about class – class and money. Only too often one is obliged to admit that translation to the screen has coarsened or blurred a novel or a play. It is all the more a pleasure to be able to say this time that the film is an improvement on the original. I will confess that I have been puzzled by the admiration lavished on Mr Braine's novel, which, with allowances made for the current fashions in social level (and a bit of commitment), strikes me as today's equivalent of *The Green Hat*. But Neil Paterson's screenplay, sharpening and defining the characters and the motives, has turned ambiguity into decision and strength.

Not that the plot has been altered. The structural characters are all there; and there has been no attempt at a romantic finish. Joe Lampton (Laurence Harvey) is still driven by his sense of social inferiority and his desire to attain the world of expensive cars, well-cut clothes and deferential club servants. He still wants the innocent goose (Heather Sears), carefully guarded daughter of the rich, self-made factory owner, less for herself than for her money and her finishing-school gloss. And he still falls in love with a married woman (Simone Signoret) older than himself, and for her sake considers abandoning his cold plan to marry brass and class.

Yet on the screen scripting, direction, production, playing and editing give this not particularly subtle plot an exceptional subtlety of mood. Now and again the overbearingness of the moneyed has a note of caricature; but for the rest one is smoothly made to understand the young accountant's touchiness and his fox-gnaw scheming. Ralph Brinton's sets – the grandiose mansion, the borrowed love-nest with its upright piano and its flossy theatrical photographs – beautifully stress social barriers; and I must not overlook the camerawork, directed by Freddie Francis, and the ferocity of its stare at the scabrous alleys of the town from which Joe Lampton has managed to escape.

Subtlety, in fact, is married with an emotional directness not often found in a British film. The love-scenes are quite unlike the usual dormitory charade; a quarrel has the savageness of people who are still in love. There is a splendid performance by Simone Signoret as the unhappy wife with her consciousness that she is ageing, her promiscuous past, her besotted surrender to the present. Heather Sears suggests cleverly and with a touch of irony in her sweetness the conventional nature of the shielded little rich girl. And as the central figure in the trio, calculating but not heartless, astonished by his own capacity for devotion. Laurence Harvey executes a series of brilliant variations on the themes of love, desire, envy and vulgar ambition.

Smaller roles are played with distinction by Hermione Baddeley (rousing as the theatrical friend), Donald Houston, Beatrice Varley and Donald Wolfit. But then this is one of the rare films in which even the anonymous half-minute appearance made in long-shot is acted as carefully as if it were a leading part. It gives one faith all over again in a renaissance of the British cinema.

January 1959

Well, one says, there was *Room at the Top*, wasn't there; and what about *The Angry Silence*, and *Saturday Night and Sunday Morning*, and *The Entertainer*, and – one pauses – of course there was *Room at the Top* . . .

As you may guess, I am putting myself in the position of the critic challenged to defend the British cinema, and doing his best to take up the challenge. It is a defence in which I engage far more often than some readers give me credit for; more often, perhaps, than I should, for it is difficult to resist wanting one's own side to do well. And yet when one considers the international field the position isn't easily tenable, or hasn't been these last few years. It isn't that good, well-made British films don't appear. Of course they do; and at the end of the year one can usually scrape up a title or two for one's list of favourites. It isn't that they don't turn up in larger numbers. I don't see great numbers of good French films either, or good American films, or good Italian or Japanese films. It is that when one comes to pick not merely the pleasing but the everlasting flowers, so few of them have grown in the soil of this country.

The films which ten or twenty years later are instantly remembered, which become part of history, which belong not merely to a national but to an international cinema: we don't produce enough of those. Not that I have always cherished our everlastings. *The Private Life of Henry VIII*, one is always being told, put the British cinema on the American screen; I thought it vulgar. *Brief Encounter* entranced fastidious Continental audiences, and many distinguished judges would include it among the best films ever made; I found it dreadfully damp. Yet vulgar or damp, these two films count; and Carol Reed's dazzling *The Third Man* counts; and Olivier's three monumental Shakespearean films count. But it is a long time since *Richard III*; and struggle as I will I can't discern many monuments in the interval.

I have been trying to recall the contribution which, the films just mentioned apart, this country has made to the screen since the end of the war. The decent thriller – sometimes, as in the best work of Carol Reed, rising to the level of creative imagination: most people would grant us that (though when Hitchcock went to Hollywood we let an irreplaceable gift slip through our fingers). Comedy, too, and in particular Ealing comedy: applauded by sophisticated America, occasionally delighting everybody with, for example, a *Kind Hearts and Coronets*; much attacked in its declining years, perhaps deservedly; and yet I fancy that when the next batch of histories comes to be written we may find that Ealing comedy is suddenly being regarded as the intellectual's treat. We can claim satire in the Boulting manner; erratic bursts of unclassifiable virtuosity from Michael Powell; a respectable standard of documentaries – but I won't go on. It isn't a bad contribution. But it isn't brilliant either.

And yet we have assets: devoted directors; first-rate technicians; fine actors – Alec Guinness, Peter Sellers, Trevor Howard, Peter Finch, and a glittering new generation appearing with Albert Finney, Peter O'Toole and James Booth. (With actresses we are, I admit, less generously provided.) One would think we might be able now and then to throw up a *Hiroshima, Mon Amour*, or even a *Don't Shoot the Pianist*. But we don't manage it. We don't invent; we follow. We follow the inventions of our own stage (*The Entertainer*); we follow the styles of other people's films (it is years since a stylistic innovation came from this country).

And there is something depressingly medium-sized about the British cinema. About, I was going to say, its material; but that would be to suggest that the remedy lay in choosing some overblown theme. Far from it: the enormous film, enormous, I mean, in emotion, can draw its life from the most tenuous of human situations. But a universal situation: often a passionate situation. The trouble is that even the best of recent British cinema is inclined to shrink from passion of any sort, and especially from the relationship, the simple relationship, between a man and a woman. There is class-anger in plenty; but precious little love.

Perhaps that is why one raised so loud a cheer over *Room at the Top*, which indeed admitted the existence of love. It is intensity of feeling, whether in tragedy or comedy, which distinguishes the lasting from the transitory film. To turn away from it is to stick at the point the British cinema has reached: the level of the promising second eleven.

January 1961

A deathly event, a long look at the emotional conflicts which led up to it, a short look at the consequences: that is Joseph Losey's *Accident*. The initial event – the squealing brakes, the figure running out of the darkened house, the silent upturned car – is splendidly done; and the handling isn't the handling of simple action; you are immediately aware of some jarring element which has nothing to do with the fact of the accident itself. But the heart of the film is in the personal animosities and treacheries revealed in the long flash-back – which is really an act of memory: a flash-back itself containing minor flash-backs and transpositions. Memory, after all, doesn't work in strict chronological order.

Joseph Losey's film, I say. But it is also Harold Pinter's film: Losey as producer and director and Pinter as screen-writer working together to adapt a novel by Nicholas Mosley. Within the film, three characters who are active, two who are passive, one who is a catalyst; simply by being herself, beautiful, sensual, calculating, the girl (Jacqueline Sassard) changes the others without being herself basically changed. She is an Austrian student at Oxford; three men are attracted to her – a young aristocratic undergraduate, his philosophy tutor and a second tutor. Both the older men are married; the wives see what is happening without doing or being able to do much about it. And the camera gives a curious impression of being an intent observer: watching the cool laconic girl and the wife who, though she says nothing, is herself watchful as her husband betrays himself; especially watching the two men as their hostility towards one another smoulders and spurts.

Amazing how little is said and how much is told. Harold Pinter's dialogue – the long pauses, the interchanges which glance along the surface of a scene – is a kind of shorthand of talk; yet its elisions and abbreviations give you the character, the emotion, the situation. Sometimes it is used with ironic effect (there are wickedly funny passages reflecting on the preoccupations of a Senior Common Room). Once, in an interlude in which the don who is the central figure revisits an old flame, it is a duologue superimposed on the action and heard not as conversation but as if the two people were thinking aloud; extraordinary how Delphine Seyrig without apparently speaking a word is enabled to convey the nature of a former bedfellow, easy, sexy, elegant.

But in general the dialogue is used, and Losey's infinitely subtle direction of playing and timing is used, to show character changing with experience and unhappiness. The tutors are natural opponents: the extrovert (Stanley Baker) who is a novelist and a television personality and a triumphant Casanova; the philosophy don (Dirk Bogarde) who is conscious of retreating youth, ashamed of his thoughts of infidelity, jealous of the other man's success. Their conflict is played out against the background of hazy sensuousness which Oxford at its best can provide: the dreaming river, the sound of summer afternoon cricket; at the end, as the result partly of the working of the catalyst, partly of the accident with which the film opens, their positions are reversed. Now it is the extrovert who is left shaken and uncertain and the introvert who is sure of himself, capable of living with a painful and discreditable secret.

Into this complex the director has woven the theme which was major in *The Servant*. 'All aristocrats are made to be killed,' the tutor says to the undergraduate. The boy's rejoinder is significant: 'Yes, I'm immortal!' I asked Losey about this; the fact of lineage, he said, made the aristocrat feel immortal; the name always lived on. Nevertheless the gay handsome boy has in him the seeds of self-destruction; he is the doomed one.

This theme of defeat – defeat in which once again a woman is instrumental – is made poignant in *Accident* by the performance of Michael York, a young actor with a presence and a resource which can stand up to formidable acting competition. Certainly the competition is formidable: Stanley Baker with his mesmerizing compound of arrogance and defenceless bewilderment; especially Dirk Bogarde with the physical composure beneath which you can see the movement of suspicion, recognition, rage, misery, resolve, a range of thoughts and emotions; it is a superb performance of a character forced into self-realization.

And I must not forget Vivien Merchant as the observant wife or Alexander Knox's economical sketch of the Provost – or, indeed, the music of John Dankworth and the colour photography of Gerry Fisher. Everything in the film seems to me precisely matched – except perhaps the morning scene in which the two dons bound confidently up the female college stairs into the girl's bedroom. But that, Mr Losey assures me, is in order nowadays. Oh well, Oxford is no longer the home of lost causes.

February 1967

For a study of the change in the mood, the pace, the general attitude of the screen during the past few years a visit to the London Pavilion just now is to be recommended. The change has come tardily. For years the novel and the theatre have been rejecting the conventional storyline and carrying on about middle-class corruption; only recently (if one excepts the great anarchists, Buñuel for example) has the cinema begun to blow off about bourgeois morality and traditions. But now everything comes with a rush: in France, in Italy, even (for whatever the qualities of the British cinema it has not been noted for daring and experiment) in this country. Orgies are adumbrated. The heroics of the war film are assaulted. Why, there have even been jokes at the expense of James Bond.

And now, at, as I said, the London Pavilion, **Poor Cow**. The film arrives trailing shreds of notoriety from the printed page and the domestic screen: the script is by Nell Dunn (from her novel) in collaboration with the director Kenneth Loach, who was the television director of *Cathy Come Home* and (Miss Dunn's original again) *Up the Junction*; both productions brought fame to the actress here, Carol White. Fair to say that this time the cinema is learning something or at any rate picking up something from its young relation; *Poor Cow* might not have been made were it not for the success of those television programmes. Still, its attitude to society – the anti-sentimentality, the absence of moral judgements – is characteristic of the new cinema. So is the setting: the house-breaker's pad, the alley echoing to the bawl of pop music. Look back to the factory-worker home of *Saturday Night and Sunday Morning* seven years ago and you are already in another world. Look back to Nöel Coward's self-respecting family in *This Happy Breed* and you are in another universe.

Absence of moral judgments: Joy, the girl who is the central character, accepts as a matter of course that her husband should live by stealing and that the man with whom she later enjoys what to her is an idyllic love-affair should do the same; when an old woman is, according to the judge in court, half-blinded by the violence of a robbery, that is all part of the game. For Joy lives on the frayed edges of society. She warms to a job as near-nude model for bogus amateur photographers. Protesting her fidelity to her lover in prison, she sleeps enthusiastically with all offers. During a faint show of divorcing her husband, she makes a pass at her solicitor. The film with its fashionable chapter-headings and its abrupt changes of scene faithfully reflects a disjointed existence; it is often very funny, often bawdy, always miraculously fluent, as apparently spontaneous as if lived, not acted.

With the increased tendency to improvisation this kind of performance grows more frequent on the screen; even so the playing and its direction here are exceptional. There is an ease which is a pleasure to watch in the portrait of the husband by John Bindon (a newcomer); of the lover by Terence Stamp (who has never done better): of the solicitor by Ellis Dale; of slack-laced relations and friends by Queenie Watts and Kate Williams; above all of Joy herself by Carol White. Seven years ago I noted a performance by Miss White in a modest but well-made film called *The Man in the Back Seat*. Today she has complete command of the screen; whether her range extends beyond the sub-world in which she at present appears remains to be seen, but within that sub-world she can stir sympathy and even liking for the most hopeless character. For Joy really is a hopeless character. Yes, she loves her child; but she shows no sign of trying to get him out of her sub-world. Perhaps, though, to try would be, by the code of the new cinema, in itself a submission to bourgeois values.

When a quarter of a century ago Nöel Coward appeared in his war-time *In Which We Serve* – and Celia Johnson gave her incomparable performance as the captain's wife – there were growls about the upperclass atmosphere; the British cinema, people used to say, was obsessed by drawing-room society (whether or not that society was well portrayed seemed to be a matter of indifference). Today the recommended background is the slum; the favoured action is rape or robbery; the heroes are dingy seducers or layabouts. The drawing-room is out, and its inhabitants, as far as serious cinema is concerned, are pariahs. The cinema, in fact, is as class-ridden as ever, and a new snobbery has been substituted for the old.

All the same *Poor Cow* is supremely well done.

December 1967

Never, say the tribe of correctors, judge a film for failing to do what it did not set out to do. Agreed – but there is the other side: a film ought to make up its mind what it intends. **Privilege**, now: is it in the category of *Elmer Gantry*? Or *A Face in the Crowd*? Or is it warning us that we are victims of those famous Hidden Persuaders? A little of all three, I should say – and more.

First, the contributors. The director is Peter Watkins, who gave us the enterprising but overpraised exercise in the minatory, *The War Game*. Nothing like a bit of banning for sympathy (and publicity); many people have been curious to see what Mr Watkins would do next, and it was sensible to let him forge ahead with an unconventional subject (in colour too). *Privilege*, the first feature-length piece he has made for the cinema, is a beginning also for the leading players, both of whom are making their first appearance in a feature film. One of them is Jean Shrimpton – famous for her appearances as a model but now overshadowed, if that is the word, but the even more insubstantial Twiggy: Miss Shrimpton, making a nervous dab or two at a discreetly concealed canvas, plays a painter. The other is the pop singer Paul Jones, who plays a pop singer, hero or victim of the plot (screenplay based by Norman Bogner on a story by Johnny Speight). Whether a pop singer is the best choice to act a pop singer is open to doubt; he may, however, be the best at singing the pop singer's songs – for there is no intention here of guying the pop style. The satire is aimed in other directions.

It is aimed at some future Establishment (I had hoped never again to use that word, but fate has been against me); aimed at other forces too, but let us begin with the Establishment. The singer is being mercilessly used. It is not merely that his managers and backers control for commercial purposes his every move; he has become a political pawn as well. At the start he appears in a repulsive number as a manacled prisoner beaten up by the police and begging to be set free; the commentary which runs through the film tells you that he has a prison record which has proved valuable for exploitation and that the idea is to provide a release for the violent instincts of the public (who are shown sobbing and flinging themselves at the performers).

After some talk about resisting the forces of Communism and anarchy the plan changes. Commercialism, looking for a new trick, decides to set the prisoner free; now the ostensible aim is to 'subdue the critical elements in the youth of the country' – and that needs the co-operation of the High Establishment. The Church is called in, and the pop singer becomes the centre of a revivalist campaign with pop parsons, pop hymns, an ecclesiastical juke box jury and a Nazi-type rally sporting Olympic-type torch-bearer, marchers, slogans, maniac speeches, Hitler-style hand-shakes for the troops and what looks uncommonly like a Ku-Klux-Klan fiery cross.

The Establishment, then – a corruptible Church and, though it is no more than an invisible presence, a reactionary Government – allows itself to be used by commercial interests. But it also sides with them; *Privilege* is an attack on authority. There are some good sour jokes – the revivalist meeting comes off well as a savage political parody. But many of them, for instance the burlesque of a television commercial, are enthusiastically rather than pointedly made; indignation gets the better of Mr Watkins. And again one asks: indignation about what precisely? Not only the Establishment, reactionary politics, religious time-serving; for Mr Watkins and his able team (and they really are able: design, costumes, photography and editing make their effect) seem to me distractingly confused about the target; the gun wavers alarmingly in the hand. Sometimes advertising or commercialism is the enemy, sometimes the pop star or the pop audience. The general public is hysterical, vicious and glad to be led by the nose; the joint, in fact, is ready for Fascism.

With the attack going on in all directions it is understandable that the central figure, the pop singer, should become a kind of automaton for whom it is difficult to feel any deep sympathy. Paul Jones is personable and may well be gifted. But when he is not belting out a song he is being directed to underact to the point of extinction. The life is provided instead by the supporting players (Max Bacon, William Job, Mark London) – and, to be fair, by the talents, here disseminated but never without promise, of that indignant young man Peter Watkins.'

April 1967

Looking back, one sees the cinema always, like a political commentator at the cross-roads. It was at the cross-roads when the two-reeler gave way to the long feature film; when Hollywood began inviting European directors to come over and help; when sound arrived; when colour became manageable; when the screen took to growing wide and voices to coming from the sides instead of the middle. And in its subjects, too, the cinema has always been making right-angle turns; from domestic affair to minatory orgy-films to gangster films, to song-and-dance films, to problem films, to sandal-and-tunic films and back again. It is making one now.

I do not mean simply the new freedom in sexual morals. Though that is a change sharp enough: until quite recently something in the mind of the audience, far more than the Johnston Code and all the other censorships, said that sex was a bit off. To go as far as the seduction in *A Kind of Loving* – or even the hilarious frustrations of *Only Two Can Play* – would have been unthinkable in a British film ten years ago; while the love-scene in *Les Amants*, the rape in *Rocco and His Brothers* and the orgy in *Viridiana* would have been out of bounds to even the far freer Continental screen.

But I am thinking of something less obvious. The cinema has not merely observed what the public is ready to accept. (Only in Russia has the screen offered moral exhortations: in the West it has never led opinion, only followed it.) For once it has been keeping pace with the change in form of the novel and the stage play. I was about to say the reaction against form; but even from the improvizations of the young French directors something emerges which time, I fancy, will show to be the form of its period.

Certainly the new generation of critics recognizes the new form. For criticism, too, takes turnings: from the brisk social pamphleteering of the Grierson period to the invective and aesthetics of *Sequence*; from Lindsay Anderson and commitment to anti-commitment and the beauty of wrists bleeding into buckets. And once again the cinema is the home of enthusiasms. The film magazines multiply. It seems not so long since *Sight and Sound* stood monumentarily alone. Now *Film*, the magazine of the Federation of Film Societies, has become a regular quarterly to be found on the bookstalls, and very informative it is; while *Films and Filming* appears in a smart new shape.

The universities are active. I have yet to find more illumination on François Truffaut (whose *Jules et Jim* should be reaching us soon) than there was in the Peter Graham interview which appeared last autumn in *Granta*. *Motion: the University Film Magazine* includes in its third issue analyses of works by Claude Chabrol, Jack Clayton, Nicholas Ray (of course) and Robert Aldrich ('*Kiss Me Deadly* is the best crime fantasy since *The Testament of Dr Mabuse*'). And the former *Oxford Opinion* group are preparing a new magazine to be called *Movie*, which should give us all a good talking-to next month. For the stirring thing about the new voices is their insistence on the importance, sometimes of films which the distributors haven't even bothered to show to the critics, sometimes of once-admired directors whose work, in the opinion of the old lot, has deteriorated to the point of idiocy. And I really mean stirring. The new voices may be right or wrong or merely modish; but they make you look again.

Yet neither new nor old lot is inclined to cry Hot Dog over British cinema. An occasional piece – *Saturday Night and Sunday Morning*, for instance – is hailed by one side or the other; but the general climate is one of damp disapproval. And yet the talent is here: directors, writers and, goodness knows, players. I believe the trouble is that the British cinema hasn't quite made up its mind to take the turning I have been talking about. It produces some pretty good films, and any critic who isn't the prisoner of his own prejudices ought to have the sense to say so. But there isn't the feeling that it is leading the way anywhere.

April 1962

No denying that it can be a struggle to get through White Papers and Government reports; the last time I felt rewarded for the effort was when a witness remarked that I was not a critic who could be bribed. Not that anybody had ever tried. Today, of course, nobody could afford to bribe anybody.

Nevertheless one does read, and I have been reading the Report of the Prime Minister's Working Party on the Future of the British Film Industry. Indeed nobody could ignore the stir the Report has created. Newspaper letters, newspaper leaders; last week the magazine *Screen International* was busy with complaints and recommendations. And though the timing may have been accidental, the other day at the British Academy of Film and Television Arts a large and distinguished audience of directors and writers and technicians debated the question: Do We Need a Film Industry in Britain?

Do we? Of course we do, as everybody at the Academy evening agreed. The problem is how to get it – or rather how to keep it. Of course we have a film industry. But the number of films we nowadays produce looks meagre. There is unemployment. Creative people leave this country and go to work in Europe and America. John Schlesinger makes *The Day of the Locust* in the United States; I know it is an American subject, but there must be themes here which could engage his attention. Dirk Bogarde has not acted for years in a film made in England. Directors from other countries sometimes settle here to work, but they don't always stay; Joseph Losey we thankfully have, but it is elsewhere that Roman Polanski, for instance, makes *Chinatown*. And one asks what we have done to drive talent away – or what we have failed to do to keep it here.

Looking back, I think regretfully of the years when Michael Powell was active in England. I think of the best of the Ealing period – and though people tell me that Ealing didn't make much money and add that we need to please a foreign audience as well as our own I can't help recalling a night in New York when I watched crowds pushing into a late night show of *The Ladykillers*. Sixteen years ago the British cinema was discovering the British working people, and Karel Reisz was directing *Saturday Night and Sunday Morning*. But last year we watched *The Gambler*; and Karel Reisz made that in America. If these were isolated instances we could shrug them off – and after all the cinema is and should be international; admirable and desirable that the Americans should sometimes work here and the British sometimes work there. One still hopes for a cinema with its roots in this country – as, say, *The Conversation* and *The Candidate* and *Dog Day Afternoon* have their roots in the United States.

So what ought the British film industry to be doing? Not, I suggest making *The Bawdy Adventures of Tom Jones*, not wasting time and talents on *Mr Quilp*, a limp musical version of *The Old Curiosity Shop*. Go on Carrying On, by all means; make money if you can out of cheerful and sometimes rich vulgarity. But a national cinema can't live without the support also of an intellectually demanding and discriminating audience. One wants – the American film industry wants – *The King of Marvin Gardens* as well as the routine gangster stuff.

One turns to the Working Party Report; give the British film industry some money, it says, urging the Government to cough up once more; as usual the magic sum of £5 million is mentioned. Establish a British Film Authority to replace the two Government Departments at present responsible. Link cinema production and television; improve distribution; revise taxation; help cinemas to smarten themselves up. But above all (I simplify I know) give them the money, Barney. And in principle, despite the denigrators of the Report, it is all quite sensible. Nevertheless the essential question, it seems to me, as it seems to many others remains unanswered. Give *whom* the money.

I have been reading a book about Hollywood, or to be precise about the Metro-Goldwyn-Mayer Studios in their glamorous days: *Mayer and Thalberg*, by Samuel Marx. In Hollywood they gave the money to Irving Thalberg, and Thalberg understood something beyond the popular and the commercial cinema. *Anna Christie, Hallelujah, The Big Parade, The Crowd, Flesh and the Devil, Camille, A Night at the Opera*, Stroheim's *The Merry Widow, Romeo and Juliet*; one may not have liked all the films, but giving Thalberg the money to make them wasn't such a bad idea. We have never had a Thalberg in this country. The nearest we got was Alexander Korda, and though one recognizes his extravagances, his mistakes, that wasn't such a bad idea either.

We still have great creative talent. Lindsay Anderson, for instance; or the erratic Ken Russell – and if you don't like *Lisztomania* or *Tommy* there is still *Mahler* with Robert Powell as the composer. You may not take the James Bond films very seriously; but with Sean Connery as 007 they had the bravado, the dash which America finds gloomily lacking in British movies. Nicholas Roeg possesses extraordinary gifts; think of *Don't Look Now*, with Donald Sutherland and Julie Christie. But his gifts and other people's aren't correlated. There is no continuity of creation. And if I say there is no control I am not thinking of the kind of control implied by censorship or boardroom management. I am thinking of the advice, the support, the sympathetic criticism which all but the greatest artists need. Give the money, the control, to a body – presumably the Working Party has that hypothetical British Film Authority in mind – and and it evaporates. What the British Film Industry needs is an Irving Thalberg.

February 1976

2 NINE PARTICULAR DIRECTORS

From 1939, when she first began to write about the cinema for the *Sunday Times*, Dilys Powell took it as a first critical precept that the best films were made by good directors. Nearly twenty years before *Cahiers du Cinema* proposed a 'cinema des auteurs', Powell presumed that a film was authored in much the same way as the novel, or a painting or a piece of music. Furthermore she noted similarities from one film in a director's career to his next. These are generally stylistic rather than thematic – this is pre-eminently the case when Powell reviews the work of Alfred Hitchcock, whom she never quite forgives for having left England in the late 1930s after the success of *The Lady Vanishes*, which for Powell is one of the best films of that decade. In this chapter there are reviews of the work of nine directors who Dilys Powell particularly admired: Hitchcock, Bresson, Chaplin, Disney, Renoir, Buñuel, Fellini, Antonioni and Jansco. However Powell's admiration for their work is never uncritical: praise for success co-exists with reproach when things go wrong, though whenever a favourite director is censured, Powell is always eager to understand the reasons for the failure of a particular film.

The Director

A few weeks ago I was looking at the Victorine Film Studios just outside Nice. It was a brilliant hot day, and to my inexperienced eyes there seemed to be a couple of thousand people on the set: extras in peasant dress, visitors in dress not exactly peasant, but just as fancy; official visitors taking a swig of Pernod, a few mahogany-coloured types in berets playing pelota, a star in striped petticoats, carpenters running up a church, electricians fixing up a submarine, and, just behind me, a young Englishman explaining to his friend why French-women's legs were too short: as babies they were allowed to walk too soon. But where, in all this, was the director? Was he the handsome young man with golden legs, scurrying about with a megaphone? Was he the character superintending the shifting of one of the huge metal reflectors which intensified the already dazzling sunlight? Was he the disembodied voice which from time to time urged us to get out of the way of rehearsal – or just to step up and have a drink? Nobody seemed to know.

But somewhere or other on the set the director's always there. Sometimes he's the cool young man in a pullover saying to the African dancers: 'Let's try it once more.' Sometimes he's the smooth type rehearsing, with an air of inexhaustible patience, the comic in a woman's petticoat. Sometimes he's the rugged type urging the star to put more into it this time. Sometimes he's one of those two men high up on the crane, swinging over the mob of exasperated extras. But what can he do in this – this factory of lights, action, sound, the carpenters, the electricians, the arc lights, the actors – and invisible in the background, the producer, the backer, the box office? How can one man leave the mark of his personality and his talent on this hugger-mugger? But he does. Don't take me to mean that the work of every little director can be recognized. There are plenty of nonentities making films, just as there are writing books: plenty of directors who are content to take somebody else's shooting script, and go straight on the floor with it, and turn out a film to pattern – a film in whose composition they've had no part. But if you consider the cinema as a whole – a great straggling phenomenon of commerce and art – here and there names, talents, creative talents, stand out. Talents whose expression is both individual and national.

People like talking about the cinema as an international art. But moving pictures can be very national too – and I don't mean just that they have national, or nationalist, themes. The visual image on the screen, the lighting, the rhythm, the very shape of action, can be national: it has the impress of the land which produced it. When it hasn't, you're surprised. Critics said about an early Preston Sturges film that it was like a French film. Why? What was it about *Christmas in July* which reminded us of the French cinema – to be exact, of René Clair? To begin with, I think, something in the rhythm of the crowd scenes: a shindy starting in the street, the crowd throwing every available missile, the whole moving almost like a ballet, with the speed, the precision, the comic emphasis of the scrimmage over the hero's coat in the last part of *Le Million*. Then there was a kind of French irony in the handling of types: the hero and heroine a rather insignificant little pair, two little ninnies picked up by fortune, then dropped on the seat of their pants: two poor boobies who think they've won the huge prize in an advertising campaign, then find they haven't – then, at the very last opening of a door find, yes, they have won it. But there was something else in the film. Something that was pure Preston Sturges: something individual added to the rhythm and the speed: a kind of contempt for the public which was to become almost the principle of Sturges's later work. Something which says: a spoonful of honey, a spoonful of vinegar, then the honey triple strength to send the boys and girls home happy. If you look at the work of Preston Sturges today – say *The Miracle of Morgan's Creek* or *Hail the Conquering Hero* – you'll find a brilliantly sustained rhythm, a speed in cutting, calculated to a hair's breadth: this is jet-propelled comedy. But always, a kind of insolence: ruthless farce, and then the honey: they'll swallow it.

The American directors are generally concerned with the human being in relation to his own kind: man in the crowd. Take Capra, for instance. Capra has a kind of warm feeling about human relationships: sometimes perhaps a rather sentimental feeling. Capra likes putting a mixed bunch of people together in a bus, or gaol, and saying: look how well they get on. He likes showing the individual winning his battle because he has popular feeling behind him: in a way Capra is the most American of the American directors because he plays on the American notion of democracy: all men are buddies. But of course there's romanticism in the American cinema too: the romanticism of John Ford, for instance. Ford has experimented .

in a variety of subjects: the romantic Western, such as *Stagecoach*; problems of loyalty, as in *The Informer*; the courage of the poor and dispossessed – *The Grapes of Wrath*; the drama of simple character – *The Long Voyage Home*. But Ford always looks at his subject with the eye of a romantic. He looks beyond the immediate, the realistic, to the mystery of the solitary human soul. Even *The Grapes of Wrath* – that terrible indictment of a gimcrack civilization – even *The Grapes of Wrath*, with its emphasis on individual heroism, was a romantic picture. No matter how much it insisted that it spoke for the masses, it spoke in those terms of pity and love which it is fashionable nowadays to reject. And pictorially it was romantic: in its tender emphasis on the solitary figure, the head and shoulders silhouetted against light, the features touched gently and lovingly by a shadow. Ford, like Capra, deals with human beings in the group. But also he likes to show man against the natural background; the stage-coach scurrying across the plain between the cliffs, the ship setting out on her lonely course over the trackless waters. And he likes to emphasize the isolation of the human being: the sailor trying to escape, running up the path of light between the dark ship and the dark shore, the man dying alone amidst his shipmates.

How different this is from the Russian approach! Russian films have presented both the group and the individual; but always in relation to the State, whether a hostile or a friendly State. In the great revolutionary films of the silent period the State was generally hostile: in Eisenstein's *Potemkin*, in Pudovkin's *Storm Over Asia*, the conflict is between human beings demanding their natural rights, on the one hand, and a traditional tyranny on the other. In later films the revolutionary impetus has gone: the later Russian cinema is concerned to build up the authority – and the benevolence – of a State created by revolution. In the days of the silent cinema we used to say that Eisenstein was concerned with men in the mass, and Pudovkin with the individual. Eisenstein showed us collective action: mutiny in the battleship Potemkin, the lovely elegiac scene of the mourners crowding along the mole at Odessa to weep before the body of the dead sailor. Pudovkin showed us the consequences of the individual action: in *Mother* the woman innocently betraying her son, in *Storm Over Asia* the terrible scene when the victim is led away in the misty light to be shot in the back, and his body left to topple into the mud of the river far below. That was the grand period of the Russian cinema; we've had little or nothing to equal it since. We've seen little of the work of Pudovkin in the talking cinema: the only piece of importance I can recall is his historical study *General Suvorov*. We've seen more of the work of Eisenstein: here again, curiously enough, the work has been historical: *Alexander Nevsky* and the latest piece *Ivan the Terrible*. It seems that Eisenstein himself has been moving more and more towards the analysis of the individual: Alexander the individual battle-hero, Ivan the individual political leader, creator of the Tzarist state. But aesthetically the most remarkable thing is Eisenstein's attempt to orchestrate the cinema: to create a film in which the visual image, and the spoken word, and the music, are interwoven, so that each plays its part as if it were an instrument in an orchestral score. *Ivan the Terrible* is probably the most intellectual film we've ever had, for this very reason. It's the very antithesis of romantic cinema: it has the precision, the calculated movement, of classical drama.

The Russians have not concerned themselves with the private relations of human beings. The French, on the other hand, have concerned themselves with very little else. The French cinema is a very adult cinema in that it deals with deep and bitter human problems: love, treachery, passion, hatred. Perhaps its weakness is that it never, or scarcely ever, ventures into the even deeper problem: man in relation to the mystery of life and death. A Russian director, Marc Donskoy, tackled this ultimate problem in one of three films he made from the autobiography of Maxim Gorky: the film called *My Universities*. The French directors have been content with the poetry of the angry human heart. Within those limits the major French directors have made wonderful films. Of course, I'm not forgetting the foundation of irony which has given the French cinema much of its glitter. But to my mind there is something more important: the poetic seriousness of the work of, say, Jean Renoir or Marcel Carné. We are still waiting to see in England Carné's famous *Les Enfants du Paradis*. But we know from *Quai des Brumes* and *Hotel du Nord* and *Le Jour se Leve* what strange poetry this director can draw from life in shadow. One recalls from his films lovely scenes where the tawdriness of the everyday has been transformed into formal beauty: the railway bridge with mushrooms of smoke rising from the trains passing below: the squalid shack on the sea-shore, the factory standing like a skeleton against the dawn sky.

Marcel Carné prefers the urban scene: Jean Renoir has found poetry in landscape as well as townscape. The basis of Carné's cinema, I think, is pictorial composition. The basis of Renoir's cinema is rhythm. In his early film *Toni* it is the slow, deliberate rhythm of natural life: a man walking across the fields, sunlight on the vines, men sleeping by a bonfire in the woods. In *La Bête Humaine* it is the mechanical rhythm of the train, the railway siding: in this terrible story of a man poisoned by his heredity, the drama of human suffering is punctuated again and again by the roar and rattle of engines, the vision of fields, telegraph poles, railway platforms flashing past the moving train.

During the war Renoir went to America; and there he refuted the critics who believe a director is never at his best outside his native country, by making one superb film, *The Southerner*. But I think this is the exception which proves the rule; in general a director works best among his own people, against his own background, and with his native material.

From: 'Film Directors', a talk for the BBC's
Third Programme, October 1946

1 *Alfred Hitchcock*

Often have I said to Mrs Harris: What an educational force the cinema is! During the past fifteen months a receptive public has been introduced to such authors as Zola, Emily Brontë, Victor Hugo, and A. E. W. Mason. Journalists have been found in corners, sheepishly reading, in the interests of film criticism (or again, maybe not), *The Light That Failed*, *The Swiss Family Robinson*, *The Wizard of Oz*, *The Hound of the Baskervilles*, and *Gone with the Wind*. (It is an exhilarating thought that some day, who knows? the standard of public education may be raised still higher by films of *Piers Plowman*, *The Mysteries of Udolpho*, the *Critique of Pure Reason*, and the *Mahabharata*.) I am all the more at a loss to explain why I have not opened Miss Daphne Du Maurier's *Rebecca*.

As a result of this negligence I am unable to judge how far Hitchcock has been affected in making *his* **Rebecca** by adherence to the original. The story, as every circulating library subscriber knows, is about an unsophisticated girl who marries a hag-ridden widower, is taken to the ancestral home built, apparently, on the scale of the Colosseum and in the style of Keble College and the Oxford Museum, and finds herself haunted by the name of his first wife: the beautiful Rebecca, the witty Rebecca, Rebecca whose initial is embroidered on every napkin, every blotting-pad, Rebecca whose hairbrushes still wait in the titanic bedroom.

Now, frankly, this does not look at all like Hitchcock's pigeon. Hitchcock has shown himself a master of melodramatic detail, the kind of detail in which each little harsh fragment, like a clue in a murder story, gives a tiny shock to the audience, and the multiplicity of shocks creates a state of tension into which action bursts like a bomb. In *Rebecca* he had to use a different kind of detail; he had to create atmosphere, a sensation of undefined malevolence. The picture begins slowly, with a rather tired emphasis on palm courts and marble halls. But as it goes on it gathers terror. Hitchcock has, one feels, been hampered by the ornateness of the setting in which he had to work; not a knife, not a revolver slowly levelled in the concert hall is the point of menace, but a pair of doors which might be Hollywood's idea of the Doge's Palace. Yet the atmosphere menaces; and a sharp climax of fright is reached in the scene where the girl enters the forbidden room, with its great veil of curtains and the sea booming outside: so sharp, indeed, that when in the silence the latch clicks I started in my seat.

From this point the film collapses. One might have thought that when blackmail and murder were out Hitchcock's feeling for quick explosive action would show itself. Oddly enough he seems instead to lose interest. Perhaps the exquisite silliness of the story was too much for him. It was, apparently, too much for the cast, who, playing admirably so far, suddenly dwindled to automata. In the first half of the picture Judith Anderson as the housekeeper gives a remarkable portrait of malevolence. Laurence Olivier is good as always in the part of Maxim de Winter. As the wife Joan Fontaine, who was so touching in *The Women*, has a delicate naturalness rare in film actresses; her range does not appear to be wide, but within that range she shows singular talent. It remains to be said that many sequences in the picture are extremely beautiful to look at; unfortunately many others are extremely boring.

June 1940

'Blank is smart,' said one director about another. 'He uses a lot of chases. He has them in most of his pictures, just as De Mille used to put in bath-tubs.' This was not said about Hitchcock, but it might have been. Hitchcock is smart. When he has a chase it is, like the March Hare's butter, the best: the chase of chases. The chase in **Foreign Correspondent**, now: the white-haired statesman walking slowly up the steps through the rain and the crowds, the Press photographer, the shot, the statesman's face seen, in a horrifying flash, agonized and shattered, the shrubbery of umbrellas fantastically agitated as the murderer burrows through, and then, *prrrt*, figures scurrying and doubling through the trams, the struggle on the running-board, the following car, shots at the windscreen, cars and motor-bicycles whizzing round the bend in the street where the man waits with a jug in his hand to cross, starts out, shrinks back, starts out again, scrambles back, and at last, since the chase, it seems, will never end, shakes his old head and shambles indoors with his jug. So, you see, there is no need to be put off by the dedicatory caption about the far-sightedness of foreign correspondents, nor, indeed, by the solemn appeal of the final speech, made in a broadcasting studio darkened by falling bombs: 'America! Hang on to your lights, they are the only lights left in the world!' This is not a hortatory picture; the message is only a postscript (and frankly, America, the lights over here are holding out better than you had ventured to hope). This is genuine Hitchcock, the kind of chiaroscuro of sinister and jolly which Hitchcock handles better than any other living director.

He has, of course, been excellently served by his cast. Joel McCrea, as the American crime reporter sent to report Europe: George Sanders as his polished English helper; Albert Basserman (you remember him as Koch in *Magic Bullet*?) as the kidnapped statesman – these are all first-rate. Herbert Marshall is suitably gentlemanly as the man of peace, Robert Benchley as the inert London correspondent gives possibly the best and certainly the funniest performance in the piece, and there is a delicious sketch of almost maniac good will by Eddie Conrad. The dialogue is amusing throughout. There are one or two moments when the tension of the plot is allowed to slacken more, perhaps, than it need. But with so much that is brilliant – the realism of the wrecked plane, the beautiful scenes in the darkness of the windmill amid the turning wheels, the superb melodramatic shot of the torturers' faces seen by the victim under the arc-lamps – I scarcely noticed the blemishes. This film is worth fifty Rebeccas.

October 1940

What are the elements in the thriller which thrill us? The problem is always engrossing; and it is always changing, for what seems almost unendurably exciting to one generation becomes a joke to the next. In the second half of the twenties everybody rushed to the theatre to see *The Bat*, a play containing, so far as I can remember, little to stir the fancy except the occasional passage across the darkened scene of a small green nightlight (though I have to admit that a companion piece, *The Beetle*, in which an Oriental was reincarnated in the shape of a gigantic clockwork cockchafer, fell rather flat). I doubt whether similar entertainment would have the same success today. Even Edgar Wallace, were he alive now, might have to modify his trap-door technique.

The odd thing is that the cinema, which so many people think of as cruder than the theatre, has reacted against this kind of melodrama. Or perhaps it is not so odd; on the screen, where everything is expected to be clearly visible and convincing, you have to be sparing with tin beetles. And Alfred Hitchcock, whose new film **Strangers on a Train** has just appeared, was already demonstrating in the late twenties that you didn't need a body in the cupboard to frighten your audience: a bread-knife lying on the table would do just as well. As far as I am concerned it will do far better. For me the effective elements in the thriller are the matter-of-fact ones: the commonplace object which is not quite right, not in the right place, perhaps, or not in the right focus. And it is on just these elements that Hitchcock has insisted in his best work: in *Blackmail*, in *The Lady Vanishes*, in *Shadow of a Doubt*.

Strangers on a Train, then, is most exciting when it relies on the matter-of-fact, the almost ordinary. There is an exhilarating start in which we watch two men arriving at a station and taking a train; or rather we watch their feet; one pair of shoes isn't quite right: too black-and-white, too flash-Harry, moving a bit too sleekly. And there is a brilliant sequence in a fun fair, with the girl ogling the smart stranger who follows her party round with such flattering attention, showing off his strength with the hammer, pushing after her through the turnstile to the Tunnel of Love: the circumstances are ordinary, only the pursuing figure is not quite right.

Unfortunately the character himself is not quite right: not right in the head. In an earlier Hitchcock film, the famous ten-minute-take *Rope*, Farley Granger played a young man who was party to a murder. Here he plays an innocent young man accused of being party to murder by the murderer himself; the murderer being one of the fashionable society maniacs. Robert Walker, a good actor long misused, gives a suave, plausible and fluent performance. But once you admit a lunatic to a film the whole thing is likely to go off the rails; and that is where *Strangers on a Train* goes. In particular the ending, with a chase on a merry-go-round taking the place of Hitchcock's favourite rooftop chase, is wildly over-complicated; one feels that the director has been distracted from his job of creating suspense by the fun of handling the trick setting.

All the same the film (based on a novel by Patricia Highsmith: script by Raymond Chandler and Czenzi Ormonde) is enjoyable enough for one to wish it were longer. I don't mean simply that it has the Hitchcock pace and the Hitchcock touches of virtuosity (for example the shot of the murder, reflected in the victim's spectacles as they lie on the ground). I mean that the direction of the players has the old authority; note the shading in the character of the murdered girl (Laura Elliott) and the irony in the portrait of the murderer's mother (Marion Lorne). Granted that lunatic behaviour is not confined to lunatics in the story, I still think *Strangers on a Train* is the best thing Hitchcock has done for a good many years.

August 1951

Looking for a reason why Alfred Hitchcock's **To Catch a Thief** is only moderate Hitchcock, I reflected that the distinguished hair-raiser needs, to be at his best, the smell of blood. He needs death, I was going to say, death and murder. But once again it was brought home to me that generalizations are more trouble than they are worth. I remembered that one of my favourites, *The Lady Vanishes*, does not hang on murder, and I was paid out for contemplating a round statement by having to search every Hitchcock film for a motive. At the end I came out with a feeling instead of a fact. *The Lady Vanishes* indeed does not depend on death. Its excitement comes from fear, the suggestion of some unexplained horror. I repeat: the smell of blood.

The new film (screenplay by John Michael Hayes, based on the book by David Dodge) smells not of blood but of Grasse. It is set amidst the corrupt desirable elegances of the Riviera, and it is about one of the Riviera's chief industries, jewel-stealing. The woman who rushes on to her balcony yelling blue murder is merely advertising the loss of a bracelet or two. The prowler on the roof is after diamonds. And the reformed thief, setting out to catch the imitator of his technique, never gives the impression of risking anything much worse than sunburn. Even though somebody else is killed by mistake there is no chill in the air. Techincally this may be blood. To me it looks more like plasma.

To Catch a Thief is a comedy-thriller in which not only is the emphasis on the comedy; the comedy lays a veneer over the action. Excitement breaks through now and then: in a car-chase over the Grand Corniche, magnificently photographed from, I take it, a helicopter; in the final shemozzle on the roof. Occasionally there is a Hitchcock joke: the rich American mother stubbing out her cigarette on a fried egg; the screams of the robbed punctuated by shots of a black cat padding unhurriedly back and forth over the roof-tiles; the shadowing police in the wrecked car trying to explain that they came to grief avoiding a hen. But the old start of horror is replaced by the cool surprise of sophisticated comedy. The composed, insolent, deliberately overdressed American beauty belongs to the cinema of Lubitsch rather than Hitchcock; indeed the cross-cutting of amorous invitation, flashing jewellery and fireworks display might come from Lubitsch in his more obvious moods.

It would be absurd to imply that *To Catch a Thief* does not entertain. Among the films shown in ten years of Royal Film Performances few choices have been as blameless. It is competently played by Cary Grant as the ex-thief and Grace Kelly as the beauty; Jessie Royce Landis gives the mother a lively warmth; John Williams as the insurance man makes his points urbanely; Charles Vanel looks better than his part, and Brigitte Auber shows herself an impudent little enchantress. All that does not ward off a slight disappointment. Hitchcock's talent is here; but not, I think, his mischievous blood-sniffing heart.

November 1953

They have never had it so tough, not all at one go. In the Pearl White days the cliff-hanging stuff was parcelled out, one insurmountable peril to each instalment. In Hitchcock's **North By Northwest** it is continuous. A moment comes when you think sadly that it must be over. You are underestimating the Old Indefatigable, not to mention his screen writer Ernest Lehman. Off it goes again.

I must not give away the development of the plot, but perhaps it will do no harm if I say that the hero (Cary Grant), like Hannay in *The Thirty-Nine Steps*, is on the run from both police and anti-police. Like the character in *The Wrong Man* he is, though less lugubriously, the wrong man: like the hero of *The Man Who Knew Too Much*, he knows too much. The trouble, I might add, is that, like the killer in *The Trouble With Harry*, the right man never – well, perhaps not; better to stick to the enigmatic style. There is, however, no need to be inscrutable about the setting: New York, the Plaza Hotel, Grand Central Station, the United Nations Building; Chicago and the splendours of the Ambassador East; South Dakota, Mount Rushmore and the enormities of the presidential heads carved in the mountainside. And, of course, the railway. As in *Strangers on a Train*, the hero strikes up a pretty risky friendship on a train.

North By Northwest has a masterly opening: masterly not only in the way it starts the plot working, one tiny, ticking cog setting in motion another wheel and another, but in its lightning sketch of the man's type: experienced drinker (not easy, then, to put him quite out even with an undiluted bottleful of bourbon); fast thinker (he had better be fast if he is to talk himself out of the trap in the auction room), impudently resourceful (if you can grab one man's taxi it isn't surprising when you snatch another man's lorry – or commandeer the keys to another man's hotel room). Not that one has a chance to reflect on the ingenuity of the preamble; not, I mean, until the end of a film running two hours and a quarter.

For the hero wastes not a minute. Dumped half-conscious in a car headed for a cliff; attacked by a knife-thrower; chased by a crop-spraying plane; caught in a road-smash; shot at point-blank range; left hanging by one hand (the other is gallantly supporting his partner) on a precipice while somebody stamps on his knuckles – his experiences almost distract one from ticking off the Hitchcock themes: the civil villain with his bland everyday household; the murder in the heart of a crowd; the mountaineering on a monument; the body plunging from a height – but I won't go on; students of Hitchcock will enjoy making up the catalogue.

In the past one has occasionally felt that the director was losing, in the hugeness and wealth of the United States, his own sharp self. Not this time. The crimson-lined hotels, the trains full of lollers in armchairs, the empty, whistling, ochre plains – in *North By Northwest* he has taken pleasure in filling the screen with the extravagance of America, but he has used the extravagance without ever subordinating to it his own wicked ingenuity. In the middle of all that size he has made the absurdities of the adventure seem almost possible.

The other day someone asked Cary Grant, who was in London for the launching of the film, whether stunt men were employed for certain of the exploits. No, no, said the star, you do them yourself; and he went on to tell us how, in the crop-spraying scene, he would be made to run for dear life with the plane roaring down at his back, while Hitchcock, from the camera-trolley tracking ahead of him, would give a signal just in time for him to fling himself full-length and allow the aircraft to

miss him by a few inches. 'How many times did you do it?'
Mr Grant turned on the questioner the handsome tigrine head
and the coppery complexion we have known for a quarter of a
century. 'Eight times,' he said coolly. And perhaps the insistence
on risk and discomfort has its value. Somehow the presence of
courted danger can be felt in the film; that, and a subterranean
Hitchcockian violence.

But *North By Northwest* is never brutal. Mr Grant calls it
a comedy; I would agree that it is consistently entertaining,
its excitement pointed by but never interrupted by the jokes.
Among the cast Eve Marie Saint, James Mason, Leo G. Carroll
and Jessie Royce Landis must not be forgotten. But it is on Mr
Grant's own performance, intent, resourceful, witty, as always
beautifully timed, that a large part of the pleasure depends.

October 1959

'In New York,' said Mr Hitchcock, grinning at me across his
Hollywood office, 'I have Pinkerton's men outside the cinemas
to see that people don't get in after the beginning. Even,' he added
with a touch of delighted malevolence, 'people who've already
bought their tickets.' It was a month ago. We were talking, of
course, about **Psycho**, and agreeing that going to the cinema
ought to be an occasion, not a matter of dropping in half-way
through a film. It never entered my head that so soon after I got
back to London I should have to make an occasion of it myself.

The problem last week was to get in to the Plaza, where
Hitchcock's new film is now playing. (Playing, I mean, to people
who are on time; as you have doubtless all read, not even the
manager's brother will be admitted late.) The trouble was that I
was prevented from going to the Press show. How to see *Psycho*
('My first horror film,' said Hitchcock) in time to report on it?
Normally the critic can slip in later to a public showing. Not this
time; not with this Hitchcock. The Press show had been expressly
set late in the week. And the alarm went round: there could be
no earlier view of the blood in the bath, no other admission, not
for reviewers, to the cautionary tale about the consequences of
wrapping forty-two thousand dollars in the *Los Angeles Times*
and spending the night in a motel full of stuffed birds.

Why, you may ask, not just go and buy a ticket and see what
happens to Janet Leigh under the shower? 'People who've already

bought their tickets': that unveiled threat muttered in my ears. I saw myself, ticket in hand, protesting vainly that I was the manager's brother, fighting just too late through the crowds round the Plaza (and believe me, there are crowds). No, there must be some other way to discover why the sheriff was sceptical when John Gavin and Vera Miles woke him in the middle of the night to tell him about the disappearing private investigator.

And of course another way there was. By the kindness of the distributors a seat would be found for me. But I must be sitting in it early. Early! By now mere punctuality seemed inadequate. Telephone messages, reassurances, warnings: the household was in a ferment. Perhaps I ought to take my passport. My driving licence might come in handy. Or, if necessary, I could rustle up a certificate of vaccination. Anxiously we sychronized our watches.

I managed to reach the Plaza in time for an organ recital, a series of advertising films, the newsreel and a cartoon. When at last Saul Bass's harsh, green-tinted titles for *Psycho* forked across the screen I was in a frenzy lest the occasion should not justify the preliminaries.

The quiet start – it is, come to that, a quiet horror film; punctuated by silences or small sibilant noises, by rain or a shower left running: only now and then, cunningly, the huge eyeballs and the scream.

You might say that the screenplay which Joseph Stefano has drawn from Robert Bloch's novel has a plot manifestly absurd. You might say that it is full of deceptions, false trails, dark glasses which mean nothing, car numbers which mean nothing; that the cross-cutting between the two amateur detectives, both inviting murder, is old hat, almost flippantly done. And I dare say you would be right. But from these lunatic situations Hitchcock has created something persistently compulsive. From his players, and especially from the duel between the brilliant Anthony Perkins and Martin Balsam (the detective) he has drawn frightening, sombre comedy. And when you come out to the foyer where his recorded voice exhorts you not to betray the story's end, to the street full of people drawn to a film a bit difficult of access, you feel still under his spell. At least I do. For, to my relief, this is the felicitous, the mischievous, old-style Old Master Hitchcock. Though you, of course, may say I am loco about *Psycho*.

August 1960

Everything in a film, Hitchcock says, should advance the story, point in the single right direction; shot from the wrong angle, the best-written scene can fail. Casting, then, becomes enormously important. It always is important, of course; every year films are wrecked because some unsuitable star is foisted on the director. But nothing and nobody can be foisted on Hitchcock, the Great Contriver. His choice of players, then, in itself should advance the story, strengthen the mood. And looking at his new film, **Marnie**, I find the casting of this psychological thriller about a compulsive thief extremely cunning.

Not looking for the first time. The first time, when I am lucky enough to have a first and a second time, I prefer to give in to a film, let it carry me: delightful not to have to bother with mental notes. And *Marnie* certainly carried me – which goes to show that Hitchcock really does insist on pointing in that single right direction. I think he likes introducing one character who seems diversionary, a kind of irritant in the smooth flow of action and enigma. The sinister cop who interrupts the flight of Janet Leigh in *Psycho* is an example, and in *Marnie* there is another – the intruder who on the racecourse claims to recognize the heroine-thief.

You may assume, since by then the girl's system of false names and dyed hair has been established, that he does in fact recognize her. But he never reappears. He remains an odd man out, disturbing. And that is his function in the film: to disturb. Just as the cop in *Psycho* drives the grit of apprehension under the skin, so the accoster on the racecourse leaves the audience anxious, unsettled: receptive, in fact, to the tale of obsession which is to follow. He is a means of strengthening the mood.

I must not forget that Hitchcock and his screenwriter, Jay Presson Allen, are working from somebody else's original: a novel by Winston Graham. I have not read it and I can't say which scenes have been added or altered. But that the emphasis and the slant are Hitchcock's there is not much doubt. And at a second look, detaching myself from the seductive flow of narrative, I recognize the craft with which the psychological clues to the thief's make-up have been introduced. The first employer, fooled and robbed, gives his minute, angrily lecherous description of the missing clerk, so good-looking, especially so stand-offish. Back at home with her disguise thrown off, the girl wakes from her recurrent nightmare; it is the shadow of her mother which slips down the staircase wall. The sexual trauma and the puzzle of the unresponsive, dominant mother-figure – within the first few minutes they have been hinted; and presently the persistent thieving is linked with the rest of the clues and the story drives on to its solution.

A high-temperature solution; but a thriller, after all, is meant to boil over. There is one moment when the heat is turned on confusingly and unfairly: a moment when the girl's dream is suddenly presented as if it were fact. And there is one moment which I find painful: the accident to the horse. For the rest, clear cunning, and especially – for I must get back to my beginning – in the casting of the two stars.

In a film such as *Marnie* Hitchcock doesn't need stars of great range. He needs players who can be employed as symbols of a certain attitude, a certain mood: players whose whole make-up can be pointed in one single direction. For the resourceful, fastidious, frigid thief he needs a cool symbol: and there is Tippi Hedren, burnished, elegant, with the tiny pout of the small amused mouth: not by any means a frozen symbol, capable on the contrary of flashes of desperation (in the riding-kit of the final scenes she has exactly what the script demands, the air of a desperate child), but still fixed in coolness. For the man who falls in love with the girl and means to save her Hitchcock needs a sardonically masculine symbol; and there is Sean Connery, trailing Bondish clouds of sexual arrogance, a man who can afford to bide his time.

July 1964

Only too often as I reflect on the cinema I am appalled by the extent of my own insensibility. Other critics discover alarming psychological depths in films which to me have seemed perfectly straightforward. Scenes which I have regarded as purely narrative are dissected and turn out to be full of phallic symbols. Even as I come away from a Press show I can hear a buzz of disquieting technical comment: the lethargic editing, the deplorable colour matching, the perfectly dreadful travelling matts. And all the time I have been sitting there actually enjoying the damn thing.

Whether Hitchcock's fiftieth film, **Torn Curtain**, will reward with psychological profundities its more perceptive critics remains to be seen. I doubt it; but I have been wrong before and may well be wrong this time. As far as I am concerned

Torn Curtain is fun. Not one of the grand Hitchcocks. It hasn't the character-detection of *Shadow of a Doubt* or the shock effects of *Psycho*, the inexorable mosaic of detail of *Rear Window* or the disturbing psychological shifts (psychological: now you have got me talking that way) of *North by Northwest*. If the director were to adopt Graham Greene's method of dividing work into novels and entertainments, solid and light, he might call *Torn Curtain* an entertainment. Well, mostly entertainment.

A thriller about a defecting American nuclear physicist who isn't really defecting, only shamming defection in order to prise out of an East German scientist a fragment missing from his own calculations: had the film been made in the mood of *Vertigo* (a story, to put it in its briefest and therefore crudest terms, of a changing identity) we might have been invited to watch the face of the scheming physicist turning into the face of the sham defector and back again. But it hasn't and we haven't, and the face is just the face of Paul Newman from whichever side of the Iron Curtain the camera looks. And after a few scenes of initial puzzlement (the inquisitive German colleague at the Copenhagen Congress; which side is he on? The bookseller releasing his package to unwarranted hands; whose agent is he?) you can settle down to an adventure in four parts: one, escape to East Germany and the brake put on the operation by the American's fiancée (Julie Andrews), a tenacious innocent who hasn't been let into the secret; two, amateurism and its dangers in espionage; three, confrontation with Eastern European scientists; four, the chase.

In the course of the adventure you may recognize some Hitchcock favourites; for instance, suspense in a theatre scene, the climax on the stage and the climax in the auditorium; cross-cutting between a man playing a game against time and, miles away, an action which if completed may destroy him (in *Strangers on a Train* lawn tennis was the game; here a game of mathematical wits). The script (by the novelist Brian Moore) has both ingenuities and slack passages; now and then the escapes seem too easy for fiction. In life, of course, people escape all the time, from prison, from working parties, from this and that; possibly the director wanted not only to emphasize the amateurishness of his spy but to give a touch of realism to the picture by stressing the incompetence of the professionals, too.

As for the weaknesses; last Sunday I quoted Hitchcock as saying that on the screen things had to fit. Now comes *Torn*

Curtain with a scene in which the American confers with a Western agent on a tractor in the middle of a field; as the tractor appears to move some of the field appears to recede, but not all of it: a bit here, in fact, which doesn't fit. But I don't find myself greatly perturbed. The real flaws strike me as lying rather in the two leading performances: in the absent air of Mr Newman, in Miss Andrews's brisk house-prefect manner even when in bed with her fiancé (yes, I know it is a cold war, and we are told it is a cold climate and the heating has been switched off; but does it have to be as cold as all that?). Luckily or cunningly the rest of the cast make up for them: Gunter Strack as the suspicious professor, Ludwig Donath as the mathematician, especially Lila Kedrova (who gets the best of the script too) as a Polish countess stranded by the tide of Communism: a miraculous portrayal of wreckage, pathetic, absurd and admirable, a flutter of scarves, veils and earrings on a rigid framework of aristocratic distaste. And Wolfgang Kieling as the German security escort with his American partner: I was sorry to see him knocked off so early in the film, though I must say that the manner of his death is the finest Hitchcock.

In BBC's 'Twenty-Four Hours' programme (which I hate missing) the director said that he was interested in using visual images to create emotional effects, and you don't have to look far in this film to see him doing it: the composition of the passage in which the defector, just arrived by plane in East Berlin, is hemmed in by interviewers and photographers, his liberty already lost; the repeated freezing of action in the theatre scene, so that each time the pirouetting ballerina whirls towards the two escapers in the audience she is immobilized for a fraction of a second, her face grotesquely fixed in recognition and hostility. Myself I don't think the frozen-frame trick quite comes off; but it has an emotional effect all right. The death of the security escort, however, prolonged, savage and desperate, is more than a camera trick or an essay in composition. It is a statement about murder. Hitchcock is exciting not simply the horror which belongs to an 'entertainment', but the horror of realization; killing a man, the images say, with your hands, a knife, a shovel is a squalid, a sickening, above all a slow business, and don't think it is easy.

And the scene is horrible; and one longs for it to end. But it is the only moment when I don't want *Torn Curtain* to go on and on.

August 1966

2 *Robert Bresson*

For more than eight years I have been waiting for one of Robert Bresson's films to be publicly shown in this country. There are three of them: *Les Anges du Péché*, which I saw in Paris at the end of 1944; *Les Dames du Bois de Boulogne*, which has been shown here by film societies only; and *Journal d'un Curé de Campagne*, based on the book by Georges Bernanos. The last now appears, under the title **Diary of a Country Priest**, I had almost given up hoping for its arrival in England; so, no doubt, had the readers who have written to ask why a film which two years ago I called a masterpiece was nowhere to be seen. But then to show this beautiful film takes courage. I for one should like to thank the Curzon Cinema for the service it is doing us.

Courage is needed because *Diary of a Country Priest* makes no concessions to an audience's desire for emotional comfort. There is nothing comfortable about the story of the young priest, dying of a terrible illness, who finds grace in the acceptance of pain, solitude and the injustice which the world has heaped on him. It never relents: its devotion is absolute. And yet it leaves one with a sense of triumph. I have seen numbers of films which claim to be religious. Many have seemed to me to degrade as well as sentimentalize religion; here is one for the austerest taste. Or so I should imagine. Not for me to prescribe; nor can I insist that from an aesthetic point of view anybody must like the film.

Much of my time is spent assuring worried enthusiasts for the cinema that they need not agree with every word I say; criticism, I write in answer to some agitated inquiry, is not an exact science. But now and again I see a film with which an audience, I feel, should take trouble. *Diary of a Country Priest* is such a film: difficult, severe, but with rewards which I will venture to call pure. I have seen it three times. At each fresh visit I find it more exquisite, more powerful, more moving, its images stronger, its figures and shadowed faces full of an intenser feeling. I can find no praise too high for the playing of Claude Laydu (the young priest), André Guibert (priest of a neighbouring parish), Madame Arkell (the Countess) and Nicole Ladmiral (her daughter). In the version shown here an English voice speaks the priest's personal narrative. The voice is well chosen and the discrepancy with Laydu's own voice, heard in dialogue, is easily forgotten.

April 1953

In **Mouchette** the movement is deliberate, the black-and-white photography harsh, the gaze inexorably concentrated on the sad central figure. I say inexorably, for in his studies of solitude and human heartlessness Bresson does not admit pathos; he did not admit it in *The Diary of a Country Priest* or *The Trial of Joan of Arc*, and if it crept into the beautiful *Au Hazard Balthazar* that may have been because the central figure there, the sacrificial symbol, was a donkey, and a donkey looks pathetic anyway.

The central figure in *Mouchette* is a village girl brought up in poverty and wretchedness; she is young enough still to go to school but she has no friends, she is old enough to lend a hand at the local bar but she is still innocent, natural victim of a drunken rape. Bresson has drawn from his young actress, Nadine Nortier, an extraordinarily expressive performance; the face under its screws of dark hair barely changes, and yet you have the impression of sullenness and resentment and joy, the gleam of hope, the cloud of resignation. In the squalid setting of the hovel where her mother lies dying and against the pitiless background of village callousness her story, echoed by the cruel trapping of birds and the hunting of animals, has a elegiac quality. I know I should have more resilience than to long as well for the kind of elevation one experienced at the end of *The Diary of a Country Priest*.

March 1968

3 Charles Chaplin

War, says the voice of the commentator as **The Great Dictator**
opens, war on the Western Front, war in 1918; and 1918 it is,
with Chaplin as a German soldier chased by a mad shell, Chaplin
dropping a hand grenade down his own sleeve, Chaplin flying
a plane upside-down; the photography is 1918, the make-up
is 1918, the fun is 1918, everything is 1918 except – Chaplin
speaks. He speaks in a normal English voice; an agreeable but
not a memorable voice; the voice not of a comic, but of a pleasant
little chap worried rather than scared by the incidence of mad
shells, elusive hand grenades and recalcitrant planes. But not for
long. The years whiz by; and now it is nearer 1940 than 1918,
and Chaplin as Hynkel, Dictator of Tomania, is driving down an
avenue embellished by the statuary of the New Order, statuary
in which even the Venus de Milo has an arm for giving the Nazi
salute; he is conferring with his gallant Garbitsch and his stout
Herring, he is addressing his loving people in a crazy German-
sounding gibberish, he is shouting and screaming and frothing
and wheedling about the Jews and the British and democracy
and the inalienable rights of the heroic and suffering Tomanians.
And somewhere in the city Chaplin as a little Jewish barber, the
same little man who suffered the unwelcome attentions of the
mad shell, is returning to his shop in the Ghetto after years in
a hospital where he has heard nothing of the glorious march of
the new Tomania.

After nearly thirty years, then, of playing one character in one
set of clothes, Chaplin takes on a double role. The subject of the
film is thus new to him, or shall we say it is a new and advanced
branch of his old subject, the dictatorship of the powerful and
cruel over the humble and the dispossessed? He delivers his assault
on the mighty not indirectly only, through the medium of the
comical oppressed, but directly as well, through the medium of
the comical oppressor; the attack is a split attack. In another way,
too, the film is a split film; it darts between satire and realism;
at one moment the comic Chaplinesque fight, at another the
wholly uncomic sadism of the Storm Troopers, at one moment
the Dictator robustly ridiculed, at the next the burning Ghetto,
the sobbing women. Only the presentation, both of satire and
of realism, is not new; the camerawork, though it emerges from

the primitive simplicity of the first sequences, never reaches the standards we have come to expect today. Chaplin is still the Great Dictator in the cinema; he makes his own laws; the film is his own film, connived, elaborated, controlled by his single imagination.

But how superbly he does the things which lie within the compass of his comic genius! The screaming dictator tearing off Herring's decorations (down to his trouser-buttons), or posing for an infinitesimal second to despairing sculptors and painters before stamping off to strum on the harmonium; the little barber attending to a customer to the rhythm of a rhapsody from the Tomanian radio, and straightening his tie at the mirror of the man's bald head; the dictator dancing a parody of a bubble-dance with the world, the little barber drawing lots for the task of blowing up the palace, finding the fatal coin in *his* piece of pudding, surreptitiously swallowing it, taking a confident second mouthful of pudding, finding a coin in that too, swallowing again, swallowing coin after coin until as he hiccups the cash chinks treacherously together. But it would not be just to imply that Chaplin is a one-man band; the touching charm of his scenes with the Jewish working girl (very well played by Paulette Goddard), would be refutation enough, and so would the farcical interplay with Napaloni, the rival dictator (Jack Oakie). Indeed there are moments when Jack Oakie, loud, beaming, the very portrait of a cheerful, boisterous ruffian, holds the screen, and deserves it.

All the scenes between Chaplin and Oakie are brilliantly contrived and played: the train drawing up at the wrong end of the platform, Napaloni bawling from the window, 'You gotta de carpet, you puttema down!'; Madame Napaloni arrested by the police for trying to get into the same car with her husband; the two dictators, while waiting reporters are assured of the cordiality of the meeting, brawling at the buffet and throwing the nearest thing to a custard pie. The comic invention throughout has the old Chaplin touch. The serious interludes, the domestic scenes in the Ghetto, even the moments of brutal realism, though there are poor and dull patches, did not offend me by their contrast with the satirical farce of the rest of the story; in deed, I was moved by much of this as I have not been moved by the more ambitious horrors of the straightforward propagandists. But for me the film contained one major error: the final speech in which the little barber, mistaken for the Dictator, speaks to the people in the serious tones of an orator appealing for humanity and brotherly pity. This finale is so blatantly out of harmony with what has gone before as to nullify much of the effectiveness of the preceding two hours.

December 1940

It is a good many years since arriving confused and late at a house distinguished for its literary afternoons, I was introduced to a guest whose name I failed, as usual, to catch. A man of middle age, greying, with dark serious eyes, he was talking with his hostess about the letters of John Keats. I took him for some professor; though the University ambit seemed somehow hardly to suit him, and I was vaguely conscious that a respect generally denied to the life of research was being readily accorded, by a company including such figures as Augustus John and Lytton Strachey, to this urbane character. Presently he got up from his chair, folded his arms, and gave an impersonation of Winston Churchill; and at that moment the face, the hair, the eyes took on their proper name. Crikey, I said under my breath (Harold Nicolson had already sanctified the word in *Some People*), crikey, it's Charlie Chaplin!

Anybody who arrived in the middle of **Monsieur Verdoux** without having been warned might recognize Chaplin with the same shock. Not that the familiar Chaplin, Chaplin the clown, has remained unalterable since he appeared on the screen in February, 1914. In his first film, as a matter of fact, he played a down-at-heels toff in silk hat and monocle. And when the costume and make-up we all know had been established, the character itself was to suffer changes as time went by. The early Chaplin was a lady-killer, a drunk, a city slicker, an unprincipled little tough. The underdog with the mournful spaniel eyes was a later development; and though there were touches of social satire as early as *The Immigrant* in 1917, it was only with *Modern Times* in 1936 that his attack on the structure of society, oblique in the great middle period of the twenties, became direct.

Monsieur Verdoux makes a complete break with tradition so far as dress is concerned; the suave wife-murderer of the new film is a spruce little man with a waxed moustache and a trilby. Only occasionally is there a trace of the old Chaplin: once, in the boating scene where he ignominiously fails to tie a millstone round the neck of Martha Raye, we see the famous

ogle and the clasped knees; twice a bit of slapstick – a wild
fall with a cup of tea, a back somersault through a window –
disturbs, regrettably I feel, the delicate style of the rest of the
performance. The character itself, however, is not quite out of
line. The superficial heartlessness links it with the short films of
1914-16. On the other hand, the insistence on social criticism is
in direct descent from *The Great Dictator*. In any case, Chaplin
is only following the example of most of the great humorists in
coming out with a message.

Of course he was right to abandon his old character of the
tramp, a character by now too restricted for what he has to
do. The bitterly, perhaps naïvely, pessimistic moral of *Monsieur
Verdoux*, which argues that in a world bent on massacre a bigamist
can hardly be blamed for murdering a few wives, can be dismissed
as incidental. Easy enough to deride the moral; no doubt it is
un-English as well as un-American. The point is that an artist
may set out to preach; but what he says as an artist, what in fact
he creates, swallows up his text. Chaplin by his performance
as an actor – a performance which in my opinion outdistances
anything he has ever done – has created a living figure, ironic,
exquisitely funny, in the end touching. It is a mannered figure
with its precise movements, its little starts and lip-pursings, its
dandyish gestures; to take its morals at face-value is about as
sensible as to accept Restoration comedy for a model of social
behaviour, or solemnly to consider the practical consequences of
Swift's Modest Proposal for keeping down expenses by boiling
the children of the poor.

I admit that there are in *Monsieur Verdoux* one or two dull
passages and one or two moments of incongruous sentiment.
The rest is written and played with an incomparable sense of
irony, of drama and of character; of character which, developing
with the plot, attains at the last the dignity of pathos.

In fact, Monsieur Verdoux is a new character, a character
created, no matter how much it may be based on Landru and
Wainewright the poisoner. Chaplin, starting, apparently, from
an idea of Orson Welles, has given us a piece written, produced
and directed by himself; for which he composed the music; in
which he is scarcely ever absent from the screen. He had the
help of two associate directors (Robert Florey was one); the
'artistic supervision' was by Curtis Courant, cameraman of
La Bête Humaine; the director of photography was Roland
Totheroh, who has photographed every Chaplin film since

1915. But the result is pure Chaplin; and his genius alone has perfected the astonishing central portrait, among the few which, owing nothing to stage or fiction, belong entirely to the cinema.

November 1947

As a professional critic I must by now have attended at a rough guess five thousand films, but I do not recall one after which the spectators showed the slightest inclination to harness themselves to the star's carriage. Not, that is, until last week and the Press show of *Limelight*. There had been occasional applause throughout the film – a manifestation common enough at the Venice or the Cannes Festival but almost unheard of here. But when at the end of the performance Charles Chaplin came downstairs towards the foyer the crowd pushing from the stalls burst out clapping and cheering. For a moment I thought I was at last to witness that vehicular scene indispensable to nineteenth-century fiction about opera-singers.

There was a shade of relief in my own delight. I had been afraid that I might not like the film: afraid not of finding myself missing the old Charlie, but of finding that the new Mr Chaplin with what he calls his first dramatic role was venturing into fields of solemn pseudo-philosophy. Then after all the miracle had happened. The ageing clown and the young, beautiful dancer saved from suicide who loves her elderly rescuer and denies herself the love of a younger man – it is one of the oldest bits of cheese in the business. But with Chaplin writing, directing and playing the piece, something happens which I have never seen on the screen before: the story comes true. It takes on not the persuasive excitement of drama, not the stare-in-the-face of fact, but a truth independent of time and place. It becomes an abstract, at once funny and pathetic, of human behaviour.

Chaplin himself plays an immensely varied part, ranging from the resourceful drunk of the opening, through drama, music-hall song-and-dance, philosophic argument, clowning and comedy of character to the composed, dying figure of the close. To say that the role is based on personal experience might suggest that it is partly autobiographical. Obviously the actor's knowledge of the English music-hall and of the stratagems and tragedies of its people has been drawn on for the picture of backstage life in London in 1917. But the part is much more than a revival of experience. It is experience and observation lighted up by imagination and feeling. The whole film is deeply felt. And since the emotion is the emotion of one man and, Chaplin being sole arbiter in his own work, has not been submitted to the judgment of others. *Limelight* is quite different from any film, good or bad, which you may see nowadays. It has the personal errancies of a work of art untouched by the machine.

The danger with emotion of this kind in novice hands – and Chaplin, in spite of the rhetoric of *The Great Dictator* and the angry irony of *Monsieur Verdoux* comes new to directly serious dialogue – is that it may become embarrassing. Chaplin wants to express what he feels about living, about growing old, about loneliness, about youth drawn to death and age clinging to life. He implies his views throughout his story; he also explains them in speeches sometimes a phrase too long. And yet every time you begin to think he is moralizing too much or relying too much on some mannerism, a monotonously repeated shake of the head perhaps, in the delivery of an emotional passage, at that moment he breaks clear into irony or self-denigration. An extraordinary tact enables him to make violent changes in mood. On his knees behind some carpenter's spar, praying aloud during the performance for the success of the dancer, he is discovered by a stage hand: 'I've lost a button,' he says hastily, and you are dissolved into sympathetic laughter.

Laughter is lying in wait all through the film There is the laughter which we enjoy at a fragment of comedy such as the scene at the bar with an unwanted acquaintance or the impudent coaxing of a sullen landlady. And there is the laughter which doubles us up during at any rate one of the music-hall turns: the one in which Chaplin is accompanied by Buster Keaton, wearing as brilliantly as ever the impassivity of a man for whom everything, especially the inanimate world, has gone too far. I will not say I lost my heart all over again to Mr Keaton, for to tell the truth I have never since I first saw him recovered it. As for Chaplin in this passage, he taught me at last the full meaning of laughing till you cry, the tears being not merely those forced out by the contortions of guffawing, but tears of joy, too. A great deal of the fun, by the way, is produced by his ability to shorten either leg at will, the fugitive limb vanishing vertically into the pants. Another time there should be less fuss about fixing up an actor to play poor Toulouse-Lautrec.

It says a great deal for Claire Bloom that in such company

she holds her own. This young actress does more: her playing, sincere and passionate, establishes itself securely in the memory, making me feel more strongly than ever that her delicate Juliet at the Old Vic deserves to be judged seriously as a piece of acting, not dismissed as the flight of a shooting star. Sydney Chaplin is pleasantly modest as the composer, and there is good playing from Nigel Bruce and from Marjorie Bennett as the landlady; the dancers are André Eglevsky and Melissa Hayden. All the cast are fortunate in appearing in a film which from now on must be counted one of the great works of the cinema.

October 1952

First, what kind of film and what kind of character. *A King in New York* is Charles Chaplin's first film to be made in England. Superficially it looks different from the American series. It has scraped off some of the shaggy finish which was so charming in, for instance, *Monsieur Verdoux*; the sets (and even the London Streets which occasionally stray into the New York scene) have a smooth, clean air. Basically, though, it is not so very different; not, that is, from the last three films.

Of course it is no use going on looking for the out-at-elbows figure in the big boots. Chaplin gave up being Charlie after *The Great Dictator* in 1940 – though it is a proof of his genius that all these years later we still carry that image in our hearts.

As a matter of fact the last real Charlie film was *Modern Times* in 1936. Already in *The Great Dictator* Chaplin was splitting himself off from Charlie, playing Hitler (though a farcical one), delivering messages and saving humanity. With *Monsieur Verdoux* he created an entirely new comic character, a natty murderer who made us consider our own guilt. And with *Limelight*, as the ageing, philosphizing clown, he was sloughing off disguises. *A King in New York* brings him right out into the open. This is a Mr Chaplin film: no trick moustaches, simply a middle-aged man with white hair, an active figure, a face which is alive and makes you look at it, and nothing to be entertaining with except his own perpetually astounding gifts.

And his own experience. The new film is Chaplin's retort to McCarthyism. It begins lightly. A dethroned European monarch arrives in New York with laudable plans for the peaceful use of atomic energy; he finds himself penniless, he is lured into television. So far straightforward enough. Some of the elements in American city life which distress the royal visitor – the roar, the rush, the vulturine publicity – in their proper setting are not necessarily displeasing (personally I find the mad, electrifying activity of the great country entrancing). But Chaplin makes them brilliantly funny. The King having his fingerprints taken while he delivers into the microphone a message for the American people about liberty; the rock-'n'-roller biting him devoutly in the ankle; the crooner's recorded voice bawling over the Broadway crowds 'When I think of a million dollars tears come to my eyes' – the jokes are made airily and at speed; and the full-dress satire on television advertising never seems too long.

The kernel of the film, however, is disclosed when the hero befriends a boy whose parents are ex-Communists and is hauled before the Un-American Activities Committee. And here what Chaplin amidst all the gags is insisting is that to force a man to inform against his friends is wrong, and to bring up children in the belief that betrayal is praiseworthy is bad for them.

I cannot see that this is an unreasonable thing to say. Chaplin may be mistaken in his faith in the plain, serious statement sandwiched in farce. His most faithful admirers, among whom I count myself, may feel that the turn in the narrative by which the boy (played by young Michael Chaplin) is introduced is ineffective, and that the film never quite recovers its pace or its unity. But the political retort does not strike me as ill natured or even angry. On the contrary, it is soft, it is sentimental. The awkwardness which some critics have found in the recent films proceeds from a kind of ingenuousness. Through all the vicissitudes of his life Chaplin has retained an essential innocence.

In one respect, I admit, A King in New York differs from its predecessors: it has no real tears. It has the other Chaplinesque elements: a pretty girl (Dawn Addams); good supporting acting (from Oliver Johnson); incomparable miming (Chaplin's demonstration to a waiter who can't hear above the noise of the band that he wants some caviare is in the great tradition). But it has no pathos. Never mind, it has the heaven-sent gift of making you laugh uncontrollably. A King in New York is, as I say, a Mr Chaplin film. But the ghost of that old reprobate Charlie keeps on looking over Mr C.'s shoulder.

September 1957

4 *Walt Disney*

Walt Disney, who died untimely last week, is reported to have said that he made films for the family, not for egghead critics. All the same there were plenty of egg-heads among his admirers. Eisenstein, for instance, referring to his pioneering work, spoke of him in the same breath with D. W. Griffith and Chaplin. For the fact is that Disney introduced a new dimension into the cartoon film; or rather he took the simple, uncomplicated line-drawing of his predecessors and gave it depth, colour, a voice and a capacity for the poetic. Before him we laughed at the humble slapstick of Mutt and Jeff and the stratagems of Felix the cat. But it took Disney to show us, with *Flowers and Trees*, what could be done on the screen with imagination, music and pure, clear brilliant colours.

The whole astonishing enterprise began in 1928 with *Steamboat Willie* – a cartoon in black and white, but for the first time using sound. Its resourceful little figure, gallantly steering his boat, was to become one of the world's heroes: Mickey Mouse; and his adventures, presently in colour, were to create a new kind of mythology. Mickey was followed by a family of other grotesques: Donald Duck, frustrated, irascible, with his nervous tics and his furies; Pluto the dog, the engaging bumbler who when taken out on a hunt would stay motionless while the game-birds perched all over him; Goofy with his rich fruity voice, cheerful victim of the mechanical inventions of the modern world. Together they formed a gallery of characters whose activities were as mesmerizing as the activities of any of the established creatures of fairy-tale or folklore.

And parallel with these inventions there were Disney's own versions of literary fiction and fairy-tale; the full-length films of *Snow White and the Seven Dwarfs*, *Pinocchio*, *Bambi*. A few years earlier it would have seemed impossible for audiences to sit by the hour enthralled by the adventures of a set of drawings. But sit they did. It was the Disney miracle: the discovery that not only laughter, but excitement, sympathy, fear, a whole catalogue of emotions and feelings could be stirred by the composition, rhythm and pace of drawings which moved.

In his ceaselessly busy life there were other kinds of film-making, not all of them from an aesthetic point of view as successful. There were the live-action films from *Treasure Island* in 1950 onwards; sometimes – for example with *The Absent-Minded Professor* – they struck a vein of amiable fun, but they did nothing for Disney's serious reputation. There were the nature films, from the tarantulas and scorpions of *The Living Desert* to the domestic players, the dogs and the Siamese cat, of *The Incredible Journey*; astonishing, many of them; but looking back I feel that other observers in the cinema have taken a less anthropomorphic and a more authentic view of the perpetually mysterious creation in which we live. And there were the films which attempted to combine cartoon and live action – always, in my opinion, an uncomfortable marriage, and I have never been able to bring myself to think of the popular success *Mary Poppins* without shrinking. Impelled by a driving energy, Disney always had some new thing in hand: the establishment, for instance, of his famous Disneyland Park; and commercial reasons, naturally enough, forced him into ventures outside the cartoon, which was expensive to make and might be slow in earning its keep. But the unencumbered cartoon film, that was the area of his genius; and it really was genius.

I must not be taken as saying that all the cartoons are to be admired. In the worst of them – and among those I number *Peter Pan* – the ideas grow arch and the images are vulgarized. Even the best are flawed now and then by sentimentality and a desperate quaintness. Even *Pinocchio* has its Brothers-Grimm cuckoo-clock-style woodcarver; even the incomparable *Dumbo* has its mawkish mother-passages. In *Fantasia* Beethoven provides an accompaniment for some deplorably cavorting baby centaurs; and somewhere or other a Dopey or his like usually manages to sneak in.

But against Dopey and the centaurs one must set the original inventions. One must remember Dumbo and his dream of pink elephants – a marvel of pattern-making; one must remember the submarine scenes with their brilliant darting fish; and those huge seascapes – Pinocchio washed up from the belly of the sea-monster – in which the cartoon film achieved a kind of grandeur. Not least there is the portrait-gallery to be remembered: not only Pluto and Donald and Goofy, but the more sinister figures. I have often thought that the Fox in *Pinocchio* – J. Worthington Foulfellow, to give him his full name – has a Dickensian quality. A little more and he might have been a Montague Tigg.

Since Disney's period of triumphant supremacy in the 1930s and 1940s the cartoon has changed and developed. Other artists, other styles have made their mark. There was the contribution of the UPA group with the myopic figure of Mr Magoo. A new kind of satire was discovered in the films of Ernest Pintoff. The Europeans, the draughtsmen of Yugoslavia for instance, gave their cartoons political undertones; and in this country the work of Halas and Batchelor and the sardonic Richard Williams has put fresh life into the genre. The cinema, like the cartoon film itself, has to move fast; and it has a short memory. In recent years there has been a tendency to think of Walt Disney as a sentimentalist, a dealer in popular whimsy. That is to forget not only his great pioneering work, but the enduring quality of his comic creations.

I fancy that when more sophisticated cartoons have long been forgotten the name of Mickey Mouse will still be remembered.

December 1966

Walt Disney has sometimes shown a tendency to move from pure fantasy to fable; the comic and poetic inventions of the Silly Symphony – the spider playing on its web as on a harp, the flowers making an elaborate toilet at daybreak – sometimes gave place to figures pointing an Aesopian moral; the frugal and industrious ant, the busy little hen it was which won the day. In his second full-length picture, **Pinocchio**, Disney has moved from fairy-tale to morality. For really the story of Pinocchio, the wooden boy-puppet who strays into temptation after temptation but in the end wins by his bravery the reward of becoming a human boy, is nothing else but a modern child's morality. Pinocchio is Everyboy; with him goes the cricket, Conscience; he has a guardian angel (who warns him that liars grow long noses decked with foliage and birds' nests); he is tempted by the fame of the stage and lured to a Pleasure Island complete with such deadly sins as cigars and snooker. The responsibility is not all Disney's; after all, the author of the original story has to be remembered; but there it is, to some people the didacticism of the picture may seem a bit overpowering.

But how marvellous the invention is throughout! The beginning of the film it is true, is a little slow. And the setting of the first part of the story, the old woodcarver's house, encourages the quaintness into which Disney sometimes descends rather than the fantasy of which he is so brilliant a master. Geppetto the woodcarver is a stock quaint figure; Disney, who makes his animals such marvellous caricatures of human beings, has not yet found a way to give individuality and life to his human characters (except, of course, when these are themselves caricatures as in such cartoons as 'Mother Goose Goes Hollywood'). But with his central character he has been much more successful than in *Snow ·White*, for Pinocchio, being a puppet, calls for none of the attempts at realism which disfigured much of the first picture. And the second part of the film, when the action moves with growing speed, has a quality of size new in Disney – the Pleasure Island scenes, with the fun fair still rumbling in the background as the wretched boys, sprouting donkeys' ears and tails, cower under the monstrous shadow of the coachman with his whip; the submarine imagery, always beautiful in Disney pictures, but here more lovely than ever, with the striped gorgeous fish hovering and darting, the sea-horses goggling at the intruders, the sea-anemones blazing from the boulders; most terrific of all the pursuit of Pinocchio and his friends the great whale leaping and thrashing like Moby Dick, the waves curling and breaking, the wash, white-frothy, carrying in the bodies, sliding over the rocks, draining away, leaving them at last high and dry. Much of this is so superb in colour and rhythm that it makes me wish more than ever for one Disney cartoon conceived and executed in complete seriousness.

Pinocchio has some excellent burlesques; best of all are the Fox and the Cat, hangers-on in the Montague Tigg and Chevy Slyme manner, urging the advantages of the actor's life. An agreeable wit, too, has given Conscience the fruity voice of a rich uncle who feels that any sum over half-a-crown at half-term will ruin a boy's character. But this kind of thing has been done better before by Disney and his collaborators; what have never been done so well are the grand-scale designs of the last half-hour of the picture.

March 1940

SHORTS

How often, my Grizeldas, have you and I sat out that film about the tough – maybe a gangster, maybe just a cowboy or a garage hand – prepared to risk all for his little brother? Sometimes the boy is at college; sometimes he is composing a symphony; sometimes he has embezzled from his employers and sure needs dough bad to put back in the safe. Whatever the circumstances, his big brother will save him. He will see him through college; he will corral him an orchestra; he will sell Brooklyn Bridge and go up the river for him. There is, as the incomparable Hermione Gingold used to sing in her catalogue of cinema emotions, love of crippled brothers; there is also love of younger brothers.

Walt Disney, third of the creative geniuses of the American film, drives this home in a new way in 'The Little Whirlwind', one of his latest batch of shorts. Mickey Mouse is the hobo sweeping up leaves for the promise of a meal; as he sweeps, a baby whirlwind comes hopping and spinning down the path, hides for a flash behind the clothes-line, then skips into the basket. The battle is on: industry against mischief, Mickey against whirlwind. For a moment industry seems to be getting the best of it, and mischief scurries up the path and vanishes over the hill. But here the ethics of the cinema take a hand. Younger brothers must be rescued; the little whirlwind has merely gone to fetch help; and as he hurries back we see at his side the shape, black, menacing, enormous, of the adult, the big brother whirlwind. Once more the Disney mixture of caricature, fantasy and mad slapstick has supplied the perfect, the unanswerable comment on the realistic film. There's love of younger brothers.

Several times in the new group of Disneys the banalities of the conventional realistic film appear in caricature. In general, however, the little pieces are pure comic fantasy: Pluto, in 'The Pantry Pirate', hampered on a marauding expedition into the kitchen by a surfeit of soap-flakes; Donald Duck big-tree-felling in 'Timber' and fire-fighting in 'The Fire Chief'. 'Goofy's Glider' is Disney's retort to the instructional film: 'Should unforeseen emergency arise do not allow the craft to get out of hand,' Goofy reads from his handbook as the recalcitrant glider swoops empty into the barn. All this is enchanting. But for the pleasure of the critic, whose lips are so often sealed by civility and the libel laws, Disney might spare five minutes now and then for the kind of caricature which he alone can do: the caricature brilliantly executed, for instance, some years ago in 'Mother Goose Goes Hollywood'. What would we not give, as the hours drag on and the five o'clock whistle never blows, for his comment on the mammoth film, the family serial, the epic of the north-west! It need not distract him from his major inventions: and the hero-worshippers among us would still follow with the old, breathless attention the adventures of perhaps the only characters created in the last decade, Pluto, Mickey Mouse, and Donald Duck.

May 1941

Some years ago Disney made a short film called 'Band Concert'. It was the first coloured Mickey Mouse (it is still one of the best); Mickey, grandiosely engaged in conducting the 'William Tell' overture, is interrupted by Donald Duck, who breaks in at every pause with a brisk tootle on the penny whistle. *Fantasia* is Disney's personal Band Concert; only this time it is not the one and only Donald who keeps breaking in, but the other Mr Disney. For there are two Disneys, just as there was a Dr Jekyll and a Mr Hyde. There is the Disney, master of moving design, genius of fantastic invention; and there is the Disney of cheap whimsy who can dress his centauresses in striptease brassières and make of his Bacchus something off a seaside comic picture postcard. The first Disney it is who created *Fantasia*; but even in the great Pastoral Symphony the second Disney persistently interrupts.

Briefly, *Fantasia* is a long, varied, brilliant, and often astonishingly beautiful ballet performance, with music by Bach, Beethoven, Tchaikovsky, Stravinsky, Schubert, Moussorgsky, Dukas, and Ponchielli, conducted by Stokowski, and with choreography and décor by Disney. The *corps de ballet* is various. In the Bach D Minor Toccata and Fugue the dancers are abstract shapes, fountains and sprays and stars, great heaving, rolling bands of colour. Let me say without more palaver that Len Lye used to do this kind of abstract decoration better, and that in any case I found it merely exasperating, after the initial delight of the tuning up of the orchestra, to be expected to look at a lot of bubble and squeak while listening to Bach. The Beethoven ballet, again, was a trial; partly because of the vulgarity of the centaurs-and-centauresses episode, partly because the invention of the rest, though in itself enchanting, was inappropriate to the music. Disney has never done anything better in the way of pretty invention than the Pegasus family, but these little tumblers have nothing to do with Beethoven. Ponchielli's 'Dance of the Hours' gets a *corps de ballet* of ostriches, hippopotami, crocodiles, and elephants, which is about what the piece deserves; the Stravinsky *Rite of Spring* as the worthy compére, Deems Taylor, points out, instead of being treated as a series of primitive dances (I have not forgotten the Diaghilev performance in the early twenties, and the ballerina, lovely Sokolova, if I mistake not, leaping about as one possessed of the toothache) is used as a demonstration class in antediluvian history. This, with its bellowing volcanoes and its race of lumbering, imbecile monsters comes somewhere near success; it is consistently interesting to watch; and, with a few lapses, its grotesqueries communicate a kind of mindless ponderous horror.

I have left the best till last. Moussorgsky's 'Night on Bald Mountain' is treated to an exhibition of devilry at once grand and horrifying in conception and design; and with Mickey Mouse as the Sorcerer's Apprentice, Dukas's piece becomes the source of a fine comic exuberance of design. Here and with the 'Nutcracker' Suite Disney's command of moving design is superb – best of all, perhaps, in the 'Nutcracker' ballet, with its arabesques of flowers and whirling leaves, its petals and bubbles drifting into an exquisite submarine world, its thistledown floating on the wind with the proud, melancholy gesture of a Sylphide. *Fantasia*, in short, is Disney sometimes at his worst, often at his very best; and the best is on a level which no other cinematographic designer has reached. It takes over two hours, but somehow or other I'm afraid you will have to find the time.

July 1941

Bambi is to be the last long Disney until after the war; the producer has, apparently, resolved to make his farewell appearance in a blaze of inoffensiveness. Were there nightmarish passages in 'Snow White' which might scare the children? There should be none in *Bambi*. Was the moral story of *Pinocchio* told with a display of grand and ferocious imagery apt to an adult theme? None of that either. Did the artist, elated with the lovely moving designs of parts of *Fantasia*, hold up the story of *Dumbo* while he saw what could be done in his infinitely exploitable

medium with pink elephants? Not this time. No frights for
the nursery, no asides for the cynic, above all, none, or hardly
any, of the adventures in technique, the dazzling experiments
in elaborate comic and romantic form and rhythm which in the
past have lifted the work of Disney out of the fun fair into the
sphere of visual art. The very colours have been toned down.
It is, we are told, the first time oils have been used in a Disney
film, which makes it all the odder that so many of the characters
should appear in what, I believe, are known as pastel shades.

This said, and the first disappointment, due no doubt to over-
anticipation, worked off, it must be admitted on the other hand
that the film is pretty and enjoyable. The story is taken from
Felix Salten's book, which I remember only faintly; in Disney's
hands it becomes graceful, sentimental, a nature study rather
than the fantasy we have come to expect, a wild life piece in
which every animal pleases and only man (off-screen) is vile.
No, I am forgetting the hounds, baying and crimson-mouthed,
which are allowed for a few minutes to disturb the peace of the
forest ruled by the Great Stag, Bambi's Landseerish Victorian
papa. For the rest no tooth or claw is red in the thicket where
the fawn first receives the congratulations of rabbit, quail, and
mole, first hoists himself on to intractable shanks, first walks,
runs, jumps, talks; the owl is the friend of mice and such small
deer, and should hoof be lifted in anger, it will be nothing more
than a couple of stags fighting according to the Queensberry
rules.

There are, of course, comic characters – Thumper the young
rabbit, skater, leader in reckless exploits, incorrigible object of
parental sermons; the owl himself, indulgent mentor of the
young. But the whole of the first part of the film is varnished
with tenderness, and Bambi is exquisitely and affectionately
observed in his childhood. It is worth noting that much of
the fun proceeds not so much from the drawing as from the
voices: the rabbit speaking with the toothy note of an urchin,
the owl, sagacious in the tones of the shrewd old gentleman
from the next allotment. The drawing, indeed, lacks the vitality
of *Dumbo*, as it lacks the grandeur of *Pinocchio*, substituting
for both a wistfulness which sometimes verges on the insipid.
There are some beautiful Monet-like reflections in water, and
the effects of dark and half-light in the forest are often indicated
with astonishing success. But there it is: the film, charming and
touching as it can be, belongs more to the Disney of whimsy

and sentiment than it does to the creative artist; and those who remember the Schubert in *Fantasia* will know what I mean when I say that a good deal of this tale of a forest deer is in Disney's Ave Maria manner.

August 1942

5 Jean Renoir

'But why,' said the eminent critic, bustling out at the end of *La Bête Humaine*, the first film to be shown at the new cinema, the Paris, 'why give only half the picture? What happened to Cabuche? Did they guillotine him? What happened to the husband? Did they guillotine him? The French always think that once the woman is killed the story is over!'

La Bête Humaine is in many ways a superb picture, sombre without flatness, a human darkness illuminated by the forked lightning of passion and terror. Based on Zola's novel, it makes little attempt to evade the Zolaesque gloom and none to satisfy the popular clamour for orange-blossom. With one exception the major characters are finely acted. The direction by Jean Renoir is for three-quarters of the film strong and imaginative, rising at moments to a terrible excitement. The opening scenes – the train roaring across fields and bridges; the driver and the fireman working with a kind of laconic urgency; the engine snatching up water, shrieking through the deserted station, flying blindly through the tunnel towards nothing, towards the pinprick, towards the growing livid circle of daylight – this is a masterly rendering in moving-picture terms of the age of the machine, this is the cinema doing something it should do and doing it excellently.

The doom which overhangs the characters is ineluctable. Lantier the driver (Jean Gabin), with his accesses of animal savagery is condemned by heredity to murder what he loves; Roubaud, the station official (Ledoux), must kill out of jealousy; his wife Séverine (Simone Simon), out of terror must be his accomplice in the murder of her elderly lover, the innocent Cabuche (a moving little piece of acting by Renoir himself) is rested; and the development of the film up to its violent climax shows the reversal of roles – the jealous husband grown complacent, the terrified wife grown murderous, Lantier, for a time free from terror of himself, become her lover. Individual scenes are memorable: Lantier tenderly questioning his mistress about her emotions at the moment of the crime; Roubaud, with the dead man's watch dangling from his hand, standing in tears before his murdered wife. And yet – true, it is only half the picture, it is only half the novel.

Half the novel, not only because it does not tell us, as Zola tells us, that Cabuche was set at liberty but rearrested for the murder of Séverine, not only because it leaves us wondering if Roubaud still went free, but because it fails to give those links in the development of character, those gradual stages of disintegration, those comments and analyses which are an essential part of nineteenth-century psychological fiction. The actions, the changes of character, appear sudden, unexplained. Why, we ask, does Roubaud, just now mad with jealousy, turn complacent? Simone Simon is as lost amidst these abysses as a kitten playing with alligators in the Everglades; but even were the part acted in tone it would still be incoherent and patchy. In the days of the silent films a caption could knock off in a single sentence the passage of time and the growth of a character. When the films took over the human voice they took over also some of the disabilities of the theatre and lost some of the advantages of the novel. The novelist can slip in an explanatory aside; the playwright, the talking-film director, can't.

I do not, myself, sympathize with the people who suffer when a novel is inaccurately reproduced by a film (I do not even share their anxiety about the effect of films on the study of history, which seems to me little more hampered by an American accent than by a Whig, Tory, Marxist, Fascist or Carlylean accent). No work of literature, obviously, can be clapped straight into another medium, and the best thing the film directors can do is to rewrite and remodel until they have a film and not a novel. The problem is to decide what is a subject for a film and what is not. The cinema has liberties denied to the stage. It can range over the earth; to ask how far it can probe into the recesses of the human heart is not to belittle its possibilities. And if anybody hastens to say that the stage can explore all those recesses and is *therefore* superior to the film, let me ask whether a play has yet been written which conveys, for instance, the strange psychological flavour of Proust?

Zola's *La Bête Humaine* has two themes: the menace of the machine, the beast in the man who wants to kill so that he may completely possess. Renoir's *La Bête Humaine*, too, has both themes, but the emphasis is on the second. It seems to me that, remarkable as his film is, it would have been more remarkable had he emphasized rather the first. With the psychological, the pathological theme, he can do no better in his medium than the novelist in his, and is likely to do less well.

With the machine-theme, which after all does not exclude the human element but shows it in relation to non-human forces, he has all the resources of the cinema to help him. And yet it is Zola, not M. Renoir, who ends his story with a picture of the runaway train, without driver, without fireman, flying through the night 'like a blind, deaf animal set loose in the midst of death'!

April 1939

Those of us who looked on the French film, in the years just before the war, as the most consistently interesting contribution to the cinema which came our way, were glad to think, after the fall of France, that one or two of the major directors and players were to work in America. Duvivier and Renoir among the directors, Gabin among the players – that was at least something to be going on with; a kind of insurance policy, perhaps, which might some day pay a small bonus. We had not reckoned with the notorious reluctance of film directors, and particularly French film directors, to flourish in alien ground. We had a warning the other day in Duvivier's *Lydia* – though we should have known by now that Duvivier is not at his best when transplanted; well, here is a sadder disappointment: *The Man Who Came Back* a way down, backwoods, all-God's-critturs piece directed by none other than Jean Renoir. Hollywood, no doubt, did its best for the eminent visitor. Renoir (who is the son of the painter) made when in France films distinguished for their pictorial beauty; you remember the tunnel scenes in *La Bête Humaine*, and the rain splashing into the water-butt outside the shed where the lovers lurk? Mindful of this, perhaps, the producers gave him a cameraman of some standing in the person of Peverell Marley. Again, in France Renoir had been served by writers, shall we say not undistinguished? Very well then, if in Hollywood they could not find him a Zola, at least his screen-play should be written by Dudley Nichols, who did as much for John Ford in *The Informer* and *The Long Voyage Home*.

As for the story itself, did the producers perhaps base their offer on an examination of the director's native choices? *Toni* was a regional film, a story set in the south-east fringes of France that sunny, violent, brooding district, with its sandy wastes and its overlooking hills; what about setting M. Renoir to direct a piece about the swampier side of life in Georgia and an extensive bog called, believe it or not, Okefenokee? *La Grande Illusion* (which, I might as well say here and now, I find overpraised) dealt with the desperations of prisoners of war shut in on themselves; what about a fugitive from justice (Walter Brennan in his old-timer's beard would do) living alone in Okefenokee with the snakes and the skeeters? *La Bête Humaine* presented us with murder, adultery, the infamies of the heart. Why not a couple of backwoods toughs who fill in the intervals of murder with pig stealing from Marty's old shack down by the crick? Why not a village siren with two strings to her bow and her golden hair hanging down her back? Why not a bit of false evidence before the sheriff (doggone it, let's give Eugene Pallette a serious part) and a bit of gunning in the swamp? Do I embroider? Very well, then, I embroider. The instigators of *The Man Who Came Back* thought of none of these things, but merely of a job for M. Renoir. The result is the same: a banal, confused, crime-and-rehabilitation piece to which Renoir's grave, harsh talent contributes precisely nothing. The best moment of the film was for me an echo of the past. I remember cheering madly as a child when, in a silent and early version of *Lorna Doone*, Carver Doone stepped into the bog. There was a suspicion of a cheer at the present film when the First Murderer plumped into the mud of Okefenokee, and after some seconds spent like a coal-heaver in a manhole, expostulating with an incompetent rescuer, ducked neatly and left no trace but his derby.

Directors, I say, do not readily flourish when uprooted from their own soil; and here in Renoir is an illustration of the fact. Yet when we look at the circumstances of a film director's work is that surprising? I have always held that the director's is the mind which makes a film good or bad. But his mind and imagination cannot work efficiently without material native to them. A writer writes in his own, not a foreign language; and the language of the cinema is something more than the mere technique of the camera. A good film is a composite expression of an idea: the work of actors, scenarists, art directors, cameramen, technicians, given unity by a single controlling imagination. Renoir, like other foreign directors before him, is working now with alien collaborators, alien material: what is more, with alien ideas. The strength of the best French films lay partly in their restriction to French character and background; just as the best that has come out of Hollywood has always been the result of essentially American thoughts and ideas. The cinema is regarded as an international art; well, international in its appeal, perhaps, but in its expression national to the core. It is no bad thing that the war is forcing us in this country to make films on rigidly national themes.

April 1942

Opening with a fine flourish of marquees, national costumes, and pathfinders in oil driller's hats, the London Film Festival gave us on its first night Jean Renoir's *The Vanishing Corporal*; after this successful start the film (with an A certificate) is now to be seen at the Academy Cinema.

The Vanishing Corporal is a war film: a second-war film. Not a nationalist film, for though the central character has a Parisian's nostalgia for Paris, though he nurses an obstinate prejudice against remaining a prisoner, though he is punished to the point of exhaustion for his attempts at escape, the Germans are not held up to hatred as the enemy; they are regarded merely as victors and captors and therefore the legitimate target of ruse, defiance and occasionally ridicule. And it is not an anti-Nazi film. The Gestapo and the concentration camp don't come into it, and Hitler is no more than a figure in the newsreels who receives a capitulation. The horrors are no concern of the corporal, who from the Stalag sees the second world war as a challenge to his personal independence. As he says, he hasn't signed an armistice. And out of a mixture of impudence and self-respect he escapes and, repeatedly caught, repeatedly escapes.

The comedy – for *The Vanishing Corporal* is a comedy which shades sometimes into farce and once into tragedy – will inevitably be compared with the high sobriety, the grief and the hope of another war film by Renoir: *La Grande Illusion*, made a quarter of a century ago and about a different war. Both stories of escape: both treating of the loyalties engendered by the stresses of war. And both hinting at reconciliation. In *La Grande Illusion* one of the fugitives plans to come back some day to the German woman who has sheltered them; in *The Vanishing Corporal* it is a German girl ('I do not,' she says, 'like slaves') who finds civilian clothes for the escapers, and on their way to the frontier they come across a French prisoner who has no intention of ever leaving the humble, widowed peasant for whom he is working.

But that is the end of the resemblances. In the new piece the mood, except in two of three scenes, is deliberately light. It is as if, ready in dealing with the long, sombre tunnel of the first war to stress the concept of sacrifice (in *La Grande Illusion* the aristocrat gives his life to help the escape of the two companions alien from his world, the Jew and the man commissioned from the ranks), Renoir had felt after the moral cataclysm of the second the need to reassure by laughter, to point to the tenacious gaiety with which a man will sometimes uphold a quixotic principle.

The film is based on a novel by Jacques Perret. But the script is by Renoir himself in collaboration with Charles Spaak (his co-author in *La Grande Illusion*) and Guy Lefranc; and as usual with a Renoir film you feel the personality of the director throughout. Interesting to watch the performance, as the persistent escaper, of Jean-Pierre Cassel: allowed in only a few moments of farce to indulge his gifts of effervescence and extravagance, the actor here expresses a resource at once desperate and irrepressible; melancholy may settle on the large-eyed aquiline face, but vigour is always there, and besides the vigour the warmth, the sympathy with which Renoir infects those he directs. An excellent portrait of a dull-witted, sou-saving farmer by Jean Carmet; and as the escaper's friends Claude Brasseur and Claude Rich give a good account of themselves – though in his final scene M. Rich is permitted or perhaps invited to offer too operatic an apology.

The scene itself, come to that, seems to me out of key with the rest of the film. And yet I find it forcing its way back into memory; and I wonder whether a Renoir film will once again prove much more durable than I had at first sight supposed. That is what happened recently with *Déjeuner sur l'herbe*: something in the way Renoir holds out, as it were, a hand to his players and his audience makes the film breathe and persist. Looking the other evening at *The Vanishing Corporal* I thought it attenuated: the fun dissipated by repetition, the emotion too thinly drawn out over incidents too shallowly defined. But next morning I woke up thinking about it: and thinking through it about Jean Renoir himself, about the formidable delight with which this artist son of an artist watches the gestures of life.

For Renoir the cinema has become, as he says, a means of showing human beings. Sometimes he uses it with romantic or with elegiac melancholy – in *The River*, in the wonderful *Partie de Campagne*; lately, and now, with a rattle of comedy – and this is not, I admit, the Renoir I admire most. But then I recall a remark he made not long ago: you should judge a work of art – it was, he said, something he learned from his father – as you judge a friend. 'A bad conversation with Mozart, if you like him, is much more interesting that a good conversation with a composer you don't like.' And I like Renoir.

October 1962

Twenty-three years ago Luis Buñuel opened a film with a view of a bisected eye, and went on to show a pair of dead donkeys rotting beneath the lids of grand pianos. Since then the surrealist has turned to realism, and in place of the fantastical symbols of *Un Chien Andalou* Buñuel offers us the true images of human wickedness and decay. **Los Olvidados** is a film drawn not from the subconscious but from the police files.

Everything has changed – and nothing has changed. Buñuel in his advanced-guard days proceeded by a series of shocks; all was rage, rebellion, anarchy. Today, though the reflection of existence is direct and not refracted, though the film is a plain story about the external life of human beings, it is still a film of protest; the shocks are still there. What *Los Olvidados* has to tell us about the breeding of a criminal makes Hollywood's gutter children, our own essays on rat-nurseries and what I can remember of the over-praised Russian *Road to Life* look like a sequel to Fauntleroy with Louis Quinze fittings.

This Mexican film is about a group of neglected boys in Mexico City who wander in the streets stealing and even killing. The images of violence multiply: a blind street singer is attacked by the gang and stoned as he strikes out aimlessly at his tormentors; a cripple without legs is dragged from his trolley and left helplessly gesturing in a deserted street; the blind beggar tries to assault a little girl, who retorts by drawing a knife; a boy stuns another with a rock and beats him to death as he lies. And there is no redemption; the end, savage and brutish, accuses us all.

And yet there is a change since Buñuel first shocked the cinema. When I saw *Los Olvidados* at last year's Cannes Festival it seemed to me to be ruled by hatred. I think now that I was wrong. What Buñuel communicates is horror of the things lonely human beings do and suffer; and underlying the horror is pity for those driven to wrong. The children of the story are victims – even the boy who robs, seduces and kills without compunction; and his death, solitary as the life in which he remembers no father, no mother, is deeply pathetic. The whole film is magnificently acted. There are only two professionals in the cast: Estela Inda as the mother of the innocent boy, a splendid study in limestone; and Miguel Inclan, whose performance as the blind beggar has the terrifying malignancy of a nightmare; the rest are not shamed by comparison. The story, Buñuel says, is based on fact, and the characters are taken from real life. It is life in the lower depths, heartbreaking and dreadful. I shall not put *Los Olvidados* among the films I have most enjoyed; but I am far from sure that it should not go among the monuments of the cinema.

May 1952

This week at the Dominion and the New Victoria two interesting films, one of them of exceptional interest, are being shown in the same programme, and the readers who write to me complaining of the vagaries of programme-planning are for once, whether by luck or cunning, answered.

What the name of Luis Buñuel means to an educated cinema audience in this country I have no idea. Perhaps it stands for the pity and terror of *Los Olvidados*; perhaps some will recall the revolt long ago of *L'Age d'Or*, the deliberate savagery (and the slit eyeball) of *Un Chien Andalou*. Certainly nobody bearing in mind those films and a later one, the extraordinary study in jealousy and madness called *El* shown at Cannes a year ago, could fail to be curious on hearing that the director was to make a version of **The Adventures of Robinson Crusoe**. Let me add that now I have seen the new film, made in Pathecolor in Mexico, I for one am not disappointed.

I am told that there have been four versions of 'Robinson Crusoe', all silent (I am not including Fairbanks's *Mr Robinson Crusoe*). I saw none of them, but it is easy to imagine what a version made today might have been like: the exaggerated tension, the too-frequent fauna.

Buñuel in *El* and now in the new film is developing a matter-of-fact style which breaks out into abnormalities the more frightening for their suddenness. His *Robinson Crusoe* begins coolly; long lines of breakers, a man struggling ashore, looking desperately at the green wilderness, climbing to the fork of a tree to sleep. True, nothing sentimental or irrelevant is introduced into the opening passages. But the Crusoe (Dan O'Herlihy) bears himself at the start much as any young Hollywood star might; the wreck to which he swims next morning looks much like any of the craft inhabited in film after film by Errol Flynn and Burt Lancaster; and for one faithless moment I feared that we were going to see a piece not only conventional but lacking in what are sometimes the redeeming vulgarities of Hollywood tosh.

I soon forgot my doubts. Buñuel and his collaborator on the script, Philip Roll, have simplified Defoe's story: the arrival of Friday's father and the Spaniard has been omitted, and the tale closes with a shortened version of the encounter with the mutineers. In fact instead of interpolating action Buñuel has abbreviated action, and at the end one asks oneself how, with such austerely shaped material, he has managed to give his film the feeling of time passing, danger passing, life persisting.

To begin with he has allowed his central character to harden, grow crotchety, take on the nervous vigilance of a wild creature; the Crusoe whom Dan O'Herlihy, in a carefully developed performance, shows us rescuing Friday is a very different man from the Crusoe who came ashore from the wreck. The Friday, nobly played by James Fernandez, has been given the apprehensions of a beautiful, gentle animal. But what I find most interesting is the way in which, by small invented episodes (Crusoe's rage when Friday puts on a woman's dress), by savage details erupting amidst smooth narrative (the killing of the rats, the horrible, mad little incident with the ant), the director has pointed for us the terrors and degradations of solitude. His humane sympathies come out in his handling of the character of Friday. But the angry Buñuel grimly opening his eyes on images of disgust is still there. *The Adventures of Robinson Crusoe* may seem on the face of it like a simple film of adventure. Look again, and you will see something far less amiable, no doubt, but also far stranger and more exciting.

August 1954

It was enterprising of the National Film Theatre to arrange a season of films by Luis Buñuel, and the organizers deserve their luck in being the first to show in Europe his latest piece, *The Criminal Life of Archibaldo de la Cruz*.

Of all living directors, Buñuel strikes me as the strangest, the most personal, the most idiosyncratic, and the selection of his work to be seen on the South Bank underlines the strangeness. I am not thinking of *L'Age d'Or*, whose savage revolt against social conventions belongs to an historical movement, the surrealist movement of the twenties and early thirties. I am not thinking even of *Los Olvidados*, though the realism of this picture of outcast children has a quality of ferocity which I believe to be peculiar to Buñuel. It is when the director is dealing with a subject which at first sight looks straightforward that a terrible perverseness stares out from the smooth surface. There are three films in the National Film Theatre programme which have for me this ability to frighten, and from a clear sky. *The Criminal Life of Archibaldo de la Cruz* is one of them.

The new film (finished this year in Mexico before the director came back to Europe to work in France) is a story about a madman, and a madman whose superficial behaviour differs very little from that of the stock madman in the stock thriller – *House of Wax*, for instance, or *The Lodger*. For some reason Buñuel has chosen to let the story end softly, to say in fact that the madman is not mad after all, but just fanciful.

In another study of obsession, *El*, which opened the season, there is no such relenting; a terrifying physical quirk leaves no room for doubt that the madman is still mad. The new film gives us every reason to expect a similar twist of the tail, for in other respects it is very much like *El*; the same smooth social stream, the same undercurrents of vindictive rage. In any case the softening is in vain; once a tale has been told it belongs to its hearers or readers, and for me, and I imagine many other admirers of Buñuel, Archibaldo de la Cruz will remain a murderous lunatic.

But what I find most interesting is Buñuel's ability to bring the feeling of genuine savagery and irrational hatred into a story which in other hands would have been a commonplace thriller; to use a boring social setting to sharpen the horror of the lunatic passions it frames. When I saw *El* (at Cannes two years ago) I thought its descriptions of well-to-do society merely dull. After looking at *The Criminal Life of Archibaldo de la Cruz* I can see that in both films the enervating how-d'you-do passages have their purpose. And in the new film, as in *El*, Buñuel has not only given a frightful reality to melodramatic obsessions; he has created, in place of the grimaces, by now laughable, of the conventional madman of the screen, a whole repertory of erotic and deathly gestures which chill the flesh. I cannot forget the pantomime of the substitute-murder in which the killer, cheated of his victim, trundles to the furnace the wax model he has been fondling and watches its mechanical convulsions as it burns.

It may be said that horror should be expected in these two

films about madmen. But it is present in a third film, too, one which wears a look of directness and simplicity: *The Adventures of Robinson Crusoe*. Beneath the surface of this version of a classic terrifying ideas lie in wait. Buñuel's deeply sensitive nature has understood the meaning of solitude; Crusoe's life turns sour and crooked, the island is full of madness. And once more there is the sense of perverseness; nothing is quite as it should be, or as we accept that it should be, everything slants away from the straight.

Buñuel has declared his liking for 'the instinctive and the irrational'; this predilection I suppose it is which helps to mark his work with a disquieting individuality. Nearly all directors, even those who start in rebellion, conform as time goes on; they preserve, perhaps, flavours of style or of sentiment, but they make films in the way laid down for them by common practice. Buñuel, like Cocteau, goes his own way, no matter what the material he is handling; whether he is adapting a literary classic, or telling a story of morbid obsession, or drawing a realistic picture of a city's social disgraces, he is himself. Of a novelist one expects that; one expects a painter to go on using the same pair of eyes. In a maker of films this constant vision is at once reassuring and exciting. It is manifest, as I say, in *The Criminal Life of Archibaldo de la Cruz*, a work not as overwhelming as *El*, but strange enough, mysterious enough. I am grateful for the chance I was given to see the film before its public showing.

July 1955

On the table the dead man's trinkets are spread out. Cynically indifferent to the whimpering of his mistress, who is preparing to go to bed, the heir turns them over: a chiming watch, a tiny mesh purse. He fingers a crucifix; and gently, deliberately, he clicks it open to reveal a knife.

There is the moral (if one can use the word of so anarchistic a piece) of Luis Buñuel's ***Viridiana***, which was made in Spain and is now banned there – every print in that country and even, I am told, the original negative having been seized and destroyed – and which has just arrived at the Curzon with an X certificate but no cuts, a fact greatly to the credit of the British Board of Film Censors. True, it would be impossible to trim the film without ruining it; but there was a time (I am thinking of what happened in 1948 to *Le Diable au Corps*) when that would have been regarded as no deterrent. You have either to take *Viridiana* or leave it; either let anti-clericalism, anti-Catholicism, come to that anti-Christianity have the floor or apply the total gag. The censor has gone out for free speech (and it certainly isn't only speech which is free in this film).

Not that free speech is ever really free: freedom, I mean, always ends up as freedom to be intolerant about somebody else. Buñuel's film, and it is an extraordinary film, a superb film – revolts against the authority of the Church in Spain. Viridiana is the name of the principal character, a girl taking, as she thinks, a last dutiful look round before entering a convent; but life traps her, she feels herself responsible for the suicide of her only relative, and in penitence she stays in the outside world and devotes herself to oppressively sanctimonious good works. The rest of the film is concerned at first with the undermining, at last with the brutal annihilation of her beliefs.

Buñuel goes far beyond attacking professional religion and the practices of celibacy and self-mortification. He assaults the very basis of a creed which he sees as upholding a callous and decaying society. The Christian myths are savagely parodied. A band of the maimed, the halt and the blind, recipients of Viridiana's charity, drunkenly re-enact the Last Supper and after it fall to coupling behind the sofa, while a repulsive outcast puts on the veil and crown of the Bride and, scattering the feathers of the murdered Dove, joins in dancing to the Hallelujah Chorus. This is not the simple derisive reaction against the forms of religion which many inquiring minds go through in early life (and from which many permanently adolescent minds never emerge). It is the expression of a hatred which has developed, which has matured. For Buñuel the Church is anti-life.

Viridiana repeatedly contrasts the negations, as he sees them, of the religious existence with the positives of the worldly. The hands of the would-be nun recoil from milking a cow: it is the sinner who takes pity on the drowning insect, the mocker who, in an ironic little scene, rescues the ill-used dog; while the believer is leading her vicious and lecherous protégés in *al fresco* prayers the atheist is getting a move on with the spring sowing. For a moment one is reminded of Lawrence's rejection of Christian ethics. But the difference is clear enough: Lawrence's passion to affirm life, Buñuel's rage to crush the enemies of life. And here the rage to crush becomes itself a denial of life. The attack on intolerance becomes itself intolerant.

All the same the intolerance is in itself magnificent: one can see why this release of wolfish ribaldry, this long harsh cry of blasphemy shared the highest awards at Cannes last year. It is pure Buñuel as *L'Age d'Or* thirty-two years ago was pure Buñuel; today the director has replaced the fantasy-images of the early work with the painfully real images of deformity and disease, rape and murder, but the fury against authority is the same. Of course Buñuel can make a routine film if he is put to it. But nobody can more piercingly present human cruelties, nobody can hint more appallingly at human perversities.

And nobody can make the approaches with more deceptive mildness. The first scenes of even *Viridiana* look harmless enough; it isn't until the bearded recluse begins trying on his deceased wife's stays that you see where you are heading. And then there is no drawing back. The control over pace and the timing of the shock-moment are infallible: infallible, too, the direction of a notable cast: the madonna-faced Silvia Pinal as the pale duped girl, Francisco Rabal as the practical-minded cousin. Fernando Rey as the uncle. And the hideous rabble of beggars truly terrifies. In fact all through this film Buñuel has you by the scruff of the neck.

April 1962

'What interests me is the inner drama, the moral conflict; it is the masochistic character of her motives which I want to examine . . . the obsessions which come and go . . .' Quoted in Raymond Durgnat's recent monograph, Buñuel is speaking of his new film **Belle de Jour**, which, fresh from its triumph at Venice and benevolently left untouched by the hand of our censor, is now to be seen at London's Curzon.

In the analytical pause after a second look (after the first I was too deeply spellbound to enquire) what interests me is the extent to which this is a Buñuel creation rather than a version of the novel. Joseph Kessel told a story about a well-to-do young woman who is happily married, who dearly loves her husband, but who is driven by irresistible impulses to spend her afternoons in a brothel. It is a seriously-intended though rather hot-breathed novel; the moral conflict is there, and together with that Buñuel has accepted much of the framework of the plot. Everything else he has turned into Buñuel: Buñuel references, Buñuel suggestions, superbly, devilishly devised Buñuel images.

Not the deliberately squalid and disordered images of, say, *Viridiana* or *The Exterminating Angel*. Once there is a memory-image; as Séverine nervously and hesitatingly climbs the brothel stairs to her first experience of self-degradation, the director cannot resist a blasphemous reference to another sacrifice of the body; she sees herself as a child at her First Communion, shrinking away from the offered Host. The rest are day-dreams, all the more disturbing for the contrast between their revelations of the young woman's hidden longing and guilt and the bright, clear, almost pre-Raphaelite style in which Buñuel presents them. Joseph Kessel's heroine has dark and chaotic fantasies. The visions supplied by Buñuel are of a more flattering masochism: bound by one wrist, wearing pure white, Séverine is spattered with filth; flogged by her husband's servants, she is unmarked by the blows; or like some Burne-Jones innocent she is roped to a tree while defender and traducer fight out their romantic duel.

And the other images, records not of sexual fantasies but of sexual experience: these too are sharp, clear and, in the case of the three most notable (and funniest), contributed by the film and not by its original. But Buñuel and his co-adapter Jean-Claude Carrière have preserved from the novel the first brutal encounter in Madame Anaïs's cosy little establishment and, later, the threatening and indeed fatal affair with the young gangster – and here I must say that Pierre Clementi makes of this character a memorably dangerous, dandyish, Byronic figure. Indeed all the leading players serve Bruñuel well: Catherine Deneuve as a Séverine who manages to look both chilly and subterraneously debauched; Michel Piccoli as the cynical Husson, first guide to infamy; Geneviève Page as a faintly Lesbian Madame Anaïs; only Jean Sorel as the husband is left with little to do except look a thoroughly decent fellow. And there is some brilliant hinting, and more than hinting, in the performance of the subsidiary episodes – the Buñuel episodes: the titled gentleman who invites participation in a rite involving a coffin and a dress composed with simple elegance of nothing except a chaplet and a transparent black shroud; the Asiatic type, fussy about erotic zones and their exposure or concealment, who produces a mysteriously buzzing decorated box ('it won't hurt you'); the quiet professional man humbly crawling about on all fours – but I must not be so precise as to spoil the wicked jokes.

And I hope I shall be spared the usual plaintive requests for elucidation: elucidation, I mean, not of the arcana of eroticism (what was in that box?) but of narrative enigmas and seeming contradictions or the puzzling juxtapositions of fact and fantasy. Why does Séverine daydream about the open carriage and the uniformed lackeys before the actual experience (and surely it is an actual experience) in which they are concerned? Why in that same daydream does she echo, in calling out to her husband about the cats, a phrase used by the butler to the Duke in that same experience? Why, in the final shot, is the carriage, lackeys and all, shown driving away empty? Does it mean that the tragedy which has struck her husband has exorcised her obsessions? Frankly, I was thinking of asking you. One expression of opinion, however, I will risk. The tendency of modern criticism is to take everything, from Lewis Carroll downwards or upwards, tragically; and Buñuel, rightly recognized as one of the most important directors in the cinema today, is sometimes subjected by admirers to the kind of critical analysis which might be accorded to Freud. Agreed, he is a revolutionary figure – a revolutionary moralist. But he is also a joker: a delighted deviser of gigantic black jokes. I find *Belle de Jour* a brilliant film. I find it also a brilliantly funny film. And I fancy that some of the puzzles are joke-puzzles.

November 1969

When the alarming film *El* was first shown we all – well, some of us – were in raptures over the psychopath's final zigzag walk. Brilliant, we said; the repeated visual expression of madness gives a frightening indication that the man is still crazy. Some time later somebody asked Buñuel about it. 'Oh,' he is reported to have said, 'I just thought it looked rather nice.' That was a warning against reading too much into startling images.

The new Buñuel film, **The Phantom of Liberte**, is composed of startling images and enigmatic scenes. It begins during the Napoleonic invasion of Spain: a statue biffs an invader on the head, a man about to be executed cries Down With Liberty. Then without interval we are in the present day, a nursemaid is reading aloud to a friend while her charges are being accosted by a smooth plump stranger who slips them a batch of dirty postcards. When the children are questioned by their parents (Monica Vitti and Jean-Claude Brialy) the postcards turn out to be – but why spoil the joke?

Everything in the film is reversed, upside down, inside out, In the middle of the night birds and animals prowl through the bedroom, and the postman looks in to drop the mail on the bed. Parents (no, not Vitti and Brialy – they are never heard of again) are summoned to a school to discuss the disappearance of a child who is visibly present, answering the roll-call. At a sociable evening the guests withdraw to a small room with a lock – not to excrete but to eat. The pretty nurse played by Milena Vukotic asks permission from the doctor played by Adolfo Celi (how nice to meet the pair of them again! We saw them last week in *Black Holiday*) to visit her ailing father, but after an evening spent at an inn frequented by poker-playing monks, a young man trying to lay his ageing aunt (Hélène Perdrière) and a commercial gent (Michel Lonsdale) nattily dressed for flagellation she vanishes from the story and we are off on another tack.

Nothing, in fact, is connected with anything else in the film – or perhaps one should say that nothing is connected with anything except Buñuel. One knows these incongruities: the bizarre sexual practices, the inversions of the social code, the animals irrationally joining in human activities. They all belong to Buñuel's recurrent interior vision of the world; and they do indeed reflect a revolutionary attitude, a desire to undermine existing institutions, among them the bourgeoisie (on whose patronage Buñuel depends for his living; I doubt whether his films are much attended by what are called the workers). But first of all the incongruities are instinctive: realist in expression, the photography bright and clear, the playing briskly matter-of-fact, but surrealist in feeling; and surrealism is not to be reduced to logic. Pressed about *The Exterminating Angel*, Buñuel obligingly wrote a short introduction. 'Perhaps,' he said, 'the best explanation . . . is that, rationally, there is none.'

One can, of course, extract fairly obvious significance from what seems irrational in *The Phantom of Liberté*. One can say that the postcard scene satirizes middle-class prudery, that the poker game is yet another anti-clerical crack, that the whole film exposes our enslavement by social dictates. Surrealism in a film isn't the same thing as surrealism in a poem or a painting. The poem is privately composed, the painting executed in solitude, but in the production of a film other people are concerned, and the personal vision is bound, with the loss of privacy, to harden, to acquire a sharper definition; and the definition encourages an audience to ferret around for the symbols, the meanings it longs for. *The Phantom of Liberte* looks like a case for ferreting. It is comparatively easy Buñuel – easier anyway than *The Exterminating Angel*, less complex than *The Discreet Charm of the Bourgeoisie*; it is, also extremely funny. I think, though, that one should beware of taking the jokes too seriously. Buñuel may just have thought they looked rather nice.

March 1975

7 *Federico Fellini*

Ever since **La Strada** was shown during the 1954 Venice Festival one has been hearing about this Italian film. It has won prize after prize; Italy adores it; France is crazy about it; the young director, Federico Fellini, has given a new lease of life to Italian neo-realism; his wife Giulietta Masina, the star, is the toast of the Continent, and even in England I have heard sober elderly men remark that the girl has something. At first the applause surprised me, for when I saw the film at the Italian Festival in London I thought it lugubrious and disagreeable. But surprise dwindled to curiosity, and it was with a desire to learn what I had missed that I hurried off for a second look.

La Strada is the story of a half-witted girl from a starving family who is bought as an assistant by a drunken brute of a street entertainer. His methods of instruction are simple: he beats her. The pair wander the roads; they join a travelling circus, but the man is thrown out for fighting with an acrobat who makes fun of him. The girl, at first dimly resentful of her master's animal indifference to her feelings, is presently persuaded that he needs her – a conviction which does not prevent the association from breaking up, after a bit of murder, in desertion and a rather spiritual type of delirium tremens.

The film is admirably played, and the fact that the two leading actors, Anthony Quinn and Richard Basehart, are Americans and that their voices are consequently dubbed, never destroys illusion. But it is on the portrait of the girl that the film depends. Giulietta Masina plays her with an urchin cut, a tomboy walk and four expressions; interest, injury, gratification, ecstasy. It is an effective performance. But pathos, I take it, is intended, and I have difficulty in finding pathos in a performance so reminiscent of Harpo Marx. Though melancholy is there all right, not only in the playing and the story (by Fellini himself), but in the setting of forlorn beaches, rainy towns, empty plains under snow.

I begin to think that one of the reasons for the success so far is the fairground subject. Continental audiences, especially intellectual ones, find in the circus a mystical significance which escapes me; they like to think of the performers as victims of sexual torment and *Weltschmerz* instead of the hard-working people I have always imagined packing up at the end of the day for a hearty meal of garlic sausage or stewed scrag end. One must not underestimate the lure in this case of the recurrent and to me, I fear, peculiarly mawkish musical theme. Nor must one underestimate Fellini, whose direction powerfully evokes squalor, deformity, mournful destitution. A gifted man; but it seems to me that his gifts are rightly seen not here but in *I Vittelloni*, which, I am glad to hear, is coming to London next year.

November 1955

Where Federico Fellini is concerned I am subject to violent oscillations. I admired *The Swindlers*, *I Vitelloni* I thought the most telling study of aimlessness I had ever come across in the cinema. But the adored *La Strada* left me untouched. Now what *La Strada* did for many respected friends **Cabiria** does for me. I come away drowning in sympathy for its principal character, and the admiration for Giulietta Masina which I failed to experience with *La Strada* quite overwhelms me with the new film.

Cabiria (*Notti di Cabiria*) is about a street-walker. The cinema usually feels itself called on to go to moral extremes about the prostitute. There was a time when she was always presented as a victim driven by need and a sick baby to trudge through the, snow; then she was known as The Woman or An Unfortunate. Latterly she has got mixed up with Paris bars, the drug traffic, the mackerel and the free use of knives, and has come to be called Forbidden Companion or Shadow on the Pavement. Fellini's heroine has nothing to do with either viciousness or romantic pity. She is a scruffy little creature, absurdly dressed in ankle-socks and mangy fur, who is buying her house, a dreary quadrilateral of masonry on the outskirts of Rome, who is born to be bilked and puts a brave face on it. Matter-of-fact and comically truculent, her exercise of her job is observed against the background of professional gossip and the faintly sinister farce of professional rivalry.

And a varied but logically linked series of incidents shows her true nature. A farcical contretemps with a high-class client; a passage of naïve religious fervour and disillusion; a dreadful public humiliation inflicted by a hypnotist – one of the cruel jokers who infest the stage in Fellini's world: impudent or cowed, childishly gloating in a moment of triumph or pathetically crushed by treachery, Cabiria betrays her deep helplessness. The plot is not a catalogue of things which happen to her, it is a catalogue of things which happen because she is what she is. The story does not draw a character; the character is the story.

Stylistically the whole film with its dejected setting and its riotously fluent movement is brilliant. And the acting is superb: Amedeo Nazzari's handsome, arrogantly self-absorbed, heavily indifferent film star; Franca Marzi's big plump prostitute, wobbling across the waste lots in high heels and a transparent negligée; especially François Périer's mysterious stranger, so persuasive, so ingratiating, yet somehow suggesting to all eyes except Cabiria's that he is up to no good (how delicately induced the tiny flicker of apprehension when one notices that he has put on dark glasses!).

But Cabiria is the one we know, the one we mind about. I have heard it said that Giulietta Masina's portrait is monotonous, and I should not deny that the little self-depreciatory grimaces are, in the early scenes, repetitive. Why shouldn't they be? Human beings behave repetitively; only actors change their tune. What Fellini and Masina give us is not a realistic portrait, not a piece of romanticizing either; it is the essence of the immortally hopeful, eternally cheated, indestructible human sparrow. The figure is desolating, but it is funny too, for it recognizes – as we should all of us recognize if we were honest – that the ridiculous lurks in the heart of tragedy. And Masina – like Chaplin, like nearly all the grand comics – shows it blossoming there.

April 1958

But don't you think it's too long? people ask, speaking of *La Dolce Vita*. Never too long, I say, for me.

Perhaps what the questioners are getting at is that Federico Fellini's latest work has no sharply limited plot: no obvious terminus. An episodic film? The adjective suggests a broken movement, and I find that the action has on the contrary a strong single direction. Yet I don't know what other word to use to describe a piece so varied in its incidents, its scenes and its people. It is the story of one character, a cynical young journalist who supplies a newspaper in Rome with the baser forms of gossip.

Yet it isn't the story of the character which gives the film value, it is the nature of the character's encounters. And 'story' is too hard, too precise a word for this panorama of a man's progress through a corrupt society.

The journalist pleasures a nymphomaniac in a room hired from a tart; pursues a gnat-brained, exhibitionist film star; observes the hysteria of crowds deluded by the lying claims of two children to a miraculous vision; ventures into self-conscious intellectual company and into the macabre gaieties of a decaying aristocratic household; leads a party of wealthy riff-raff in an orgy of violence and vulgarity.

There is satire, there is attack, but Fellini says he is not concerned with making social criticisms, he is concerned with communicating something he has known, something which demands to be communicated. It is the attitude of the true artist: rare enough anywhere, especially rare in the cinema. Fellini has not forced his material into a neat shape. He uses it in huge bold chapters, each chapter independent enough to make a film on its own.

And rich enough. The striptease at the party to celebrate a divorce, the lunatic whims of the film star in the deserted, dark streets – these Roman nights are filled with phantasmagorical shapes, complex patterns of movement, sad, funny, menacing, beautiful. And they are followed by chill ghostly dawns. The call to the house of the suicide; the father's ill-starred visit to the city (how affectingly composed, on the wide screen, the shot of the old man sitting, defeated and ill, in the cabaret-girl's bedroom, his coat off, his back to the camera!) – these are the tragic signposts on the road towards the collapse of the journalist's remaining convictions. There is, you see, a shape; but so dazzlingly accompanied that for a moment one does not recognize in it that old-fashioned thing a plot.

I find two scenes where a faint monotony of pace gives the effect of pause: the opening of the miracle-episode, the opening of the orgy. For the rest I am not conscious of the passage of time, and scarcely conscious of the presence of professional performers: Marcello Mastroianni, Anouk Aimée, Yvonne Furneaux, Alain Cuny, Anita Ekberg and scores of others, all extraordinary. I am conscious only of the passage of life: of a world created.

La Dolce Vita could not have been made twenty years ago; you might say it could not have been made before *Citizen Kane*. It belongs to a new, restless, self-analytical age and a new generation of artists.

December 1960

Like Resnais, like Antonioni, Federico Fellini has set himself to explore memory, dream, the country of the vagabond mind. The cinema has often played surrealist games, often delighted in the display of technical make-believe; but today's directors are doing something different: translating into visual images the fantasies of the half-conscious, the submerged. In $8\frac{1}{2}$ Fellini's subject was a nervous and psychological crisis in a man's life. The man was a creator at a loss, a film-maker in whom the failure to find a subject had provoked a journey through the emotional maze of his past; reflected in the theme you saw the director's own artistic and psychological problems. *Juliet of the Spirits* is about a crisis in a woman's life. The woman (Giulietta Masina) is at a loss, too. But whereas the Guido of $8\frac{1}{2}$ wanted to disentangle himself from tenacious women, the Juliet here is frightened by the thought that she is losing her hold on her husband; she suspects him of infidelity, she fears that he is planning to leave her. It is, in fact, the reverse of the coin. I admit that I find the choice of the immediate source of crisis conventional. But not the treatment.

A superb opening: the woman – not young, not by the standards of her society smart, surrounded by idiotic acquaintances in idiotically modish clothes – is prevailed on to join in an evening's table-turning. It is a moment not yet of crisis in her life but of emptiness; and, as Fellini has no doubt been taught by the Church which constantly revisits his scene, where there is a vacuum the devils take possession.

She begins to have visions. Sitting on the sands, a plump, pale little body in white, she watches a party of bathers setting up an awning; the women wear the extravagant capes and head-dresses seen in fashion photographs rather than on the beach; the awning has an eastern shape, as if Genghis Khan were about to pitch camp. Suddenly the reality fades. Instead there is the figure of a man in red – cardinal's red – wading in from the sea; he is pulling on a rope; he hands it to her. The landing-craft which she hauls in has a hostile look; for a flash the occupants are revealed, invaders from a primitive past, savage, glaring. Then the vision is gone and you half-wonder if you ever shared it – or if what you took for the reality was itself a day-dream. Flesh and blood put on the dress and shape and colour of fantasy; waking and dreaming become indistinguishable.

It is this border country – the landscape of a mind beset by uncertainties – between the real and the imagined which is the creation of *Juliet of the Spirits*, as it was of *8½*. I say imagined, not imaginary, Juliet's visions of the past are not baseless. They are solid events transformed by a memory which blurs their sobriety, exaggerates their grotesqueness.

The woman resurrects the ghosts, benevolent or imprisoning, of her childhood: the convent school and her own appearance, a stumpy garlanded child, as a Christian martyr in a play; the grandfather who protested – and who ran away with a circus girl. Now she sees the nuns as hooded faceless gaolers and the grandfather as the pioneer, the liberator who vanishes into the skies in a Model-T plane. But the present too is transformed: a visit to some fashionable quack, an aged gnome attended by oriental seconds and creaking out apophthegms from the Kama Sutra, becomes a trip through an Apocalypse. As the crisis intensifies, the woman grows less and less capable of distinguishing between fact and the translation of fact offered by her disturbed eye and mind; and looking with her you see the house of some no doubt modest courtesan as flanked by stone eagles with bulging breasts and nipples, furnished with the trappings of the Grand Turk's harem, and revealing in every nook a couple coupling.

This structure of erotic imagery is both startling and funny. And it is not only a structure of visual imagery, not only the sets and the costumes and Gianni di Venanzo's camera-work; Nino Rota's music serves, everything serves to create an effect which is erotic and at the same time deliberately absurd or even repulsive. The colour (this, with the exception of an episode in *Boccaccio '70*, is Fellini's first colour film) underlines the psychological conflict: pale, sweet, ice-cream tones for the childish, the puritanical past, fierce hot glittering greens and purples, yellows and reds for the explosive present. And a remarkable use of white: the woman wears red for her explorations of the erotic, red to her stands for fire and deviltry, but in white she is herself; and when at last she dismisses her visions and welcomes solitude it is in white against the soft greens and browns of the pine forest that you see her. By then, like Guido at the end of *8½*, she has made an act of acceptance and submission; if I may borrow a bit of the current jargon, she has found her identity.

The journey has been long, sometimes brilliantly entertaining, always dazzling to watch; the companions, especially Sandra Milo as the courtesan, have often been cruelly amusing. And Masina herself as the woman overwhelmed by memories and suppressed desires – the bewildered, enquiring face with the hopeful eyes is expressive as ever. But I can't help feeling that the actress here is diminished by her setting. She is a prisoner in the fantasy-world of parakeet-voices and tropical colours; she is forced into a role so passive as to deny the character interest and life. And I can't help feeling that Fellini runs a risk of trapping himself in his own inventions. Sometimes the fantasy is too rich, too extravagant not only for the little figure at its centre but for the theme itself; certainly it overpowers the moment at the end when Juliet, rid of her spectres, alone and free, returns to the ordinary world. The moment itself is a dream of another kind; the solution is too easy. But the pleasures which have gone before make me forget that.

February 1966

It is hardly possible to make a dirty film today. Pornography is old-fashioned, obscenity wears an ageing hat, everything is public, everyday, and because not hidden not dirty. And that, no doubt, is morally to be applauded, though one may have moments of nostalgia for the time when a copy of Ars Erotica Veterum, that learned German compendium of antique indoor sports, was a treasured possession to be kept at the back of the bookshelves.

Or perhaps what I should say is that nowadays what we have is clean dirt. Anyway it is dreadfully boring.

A good deal of Federico Fellini's adaptation of Petronius' Satyricon – **Fellini Satyricon**, as it is oddly entitled – is boring, or so I thought at the end. Not at the start. At the start my spirits, always friendly to Fellini, rose sharply. One had the feeling that the great wayward Italian director was bringing to life on his wide screen the figures of some Pompeiian wall-painting, one of the kind which zealous custodians used to conceal and perhaps still do conceal from the eyes of modest female tourists. And the feeling persisted for a good while – through a scene in a hideous clownish theatre-show, through nightmare brothel-visions, through Trimalchio's feast; though towards the end of that famous gathering one was already flagging, sated with supping not on horrors but on greasy squalors. I should almost have welcomed a steaming human hand rather than the dishes of sausages and liver and lights, or as the translator of Petronius has it, black puddings, which were extruded when the belly of the pig cooked whole was carved.

In this passage Petronius and Fellini astonishingly meet – astonishingly because the film captures with such terrifying richness of disgust the sense of its antique original. Perhaps this is the moment for me to admit that I find Petronius boring too. But then I know the Satyricon only in translation; I miss the admired qualities of style, the contrast between the elegancies of the author and the vulgarities of speech of the people he presents. What I get is an ancient-world picaresque novel, interrupted by erudite literary disquisitions, illuminated by descriptions of the rich profiteering society of provincial Italy under Nero, and punctuated by references to such contemporary celebrities as poets and gladiators – but too fragmentary (after all we have only a bit of it) for the narrative, such as it is, to hold one's attention. It is a work for scholars.

Certainly, though, it gives one some characters: the narrator Encolpius (played by the English actor Martin Potter) and Ascyltus, the false friend with whom he quarrels over Giton, the pretty boy they both desire; Trimalchio gorging at his extravagant feast; Eumolpus the wandering poet. And it gives one some good anecdotes, for instance the one about the readily consolable Widow of Ephesus, which Fellini incorporates, and the one about the guest-tutor and the complaisant but demanding boy, which he omits but which I was happy to rediscover during a tussle with a passage or two regarded by the 1913 Loeb edition as too indecent to render into English.

'The decent obscurity of Latin' – I must say that sounds deliciously absurd today, especially after the film. For what Fellini, with the help of his designers, has done is to turn the Satyricon, and the Satyricon really is a cool customer of a tale, into a fever-house peopled with personified obsessions and repulsive figures far more obscene, I should have thought, than anything on the printed page.

Two other names are listed as screenwriters, Bernadino Zappone and Brunello Rondi, as well as that of the director himself. But those of us who have watched the development of Fellini from *La Dolce Vita* through *8½* to *Juliet of the Spirits* will see in this Satyricon the familiar hand of the dream-bound artist, slave and creator of disturbing fantasies. He has discovered in Petronius a release for his own obsessions with the monstrous and the grotesque; and taking the ancient work as basis he has rearranged, simplified, magnified, elaborated, borrowed, always struggling to clothe the antique shapes with the riches or the putrefying rags of flesh seen through the veil of dreams.

The new Satyricon too is picaresque, leaping carelessly from scene to scene; and fragmentary as well, ending on an unfinished sentence with the characters, as if in a transfer pattern, frozen, plastered into wall-painting on broken masonry. Fellini, though, has given the narrative some kind of forward movement. After Trimalchio's feast Trimalchio's projected funeral is mimicked, not merely imagined. After the enigmatic sea-voyage, enigmatic, goodness knows, in both print and celluloid, there is a series of added adventures made possible if not plausible by an interpolated fragment about the murder of a Caesar. A patrician couple commit suicide rather than face the judgment of the new régime (is Fellini perhaps in this tranquil episode, which anachronistically quotes Hadrian's 'Animula vagula blandula' poem, recalling the story of Petronius's own suicide in face of Nero's disfavour?). As a result the deplorable heroes of the film enjoy an encounter with one of the household's slave girls. They are murderously involved in the abduction of a hermaphrodite, pale, naked and worshipped as a god. There is a fight with a simulated Minotaur. At last the story, vaguely linking up once more with Petronius, ends with the cannibal funeral meal implied in the original.

At last, I say; for excitement has long since vanished, and for the final half-hour and more bewilderment has set in. Yes, it is boring all right, boring because it is not only long but disconnected, allowing no sympathy for its characters, admitting no development of anything. Well, you say, that's Petronius for you, and this time that's Fellini too.

Nevertheless when one has escaped from the cinema something strange happens. In the cinema, *Fellini Satyricon* grows wearisome. But in retrospect the film suddenly isn't boring. It hasn't the deadly, clinical cleanliness of the modern sex-film; it is a brilliant curiosity. People may say it is not a film at all but a long strip of gross and nauseating images, anti-erotic too with its succession of blubbery bodies and gross lewd poses. I can't see why the powers of the cinema shouldn't be used in a hundred styles. Fellini has used them to present a personal vision of a mortal decadence which at once fascinates and appals him. The result is a phantasmagoria, inhuman, horrible. It is totally unrealistic. All the same it says something about the filth and cruelties of the ancient world, and perhaps of some other worlds too.

Anyway if you want orgies here they are.

September 1970

Thank heaven for a Fellini, even if it is only a sketch rather than the fantasia on human behaviour which we have come to expect. *Orchestra Rehearsal* runs for no more than seventy minutes; it is, on the face of it, just what the title says, a rehearsal. The hall is empty; then an old body wanders in with an air of preparation and recalls the glories of the past. One by one the musicians appear. They are to be interviewed for a television documentary. They argue, grumble – will they be paid for their interviews? – and little by little disclose themselves. They talk – the cellist and the tuba-player, violinist and flautist, the performers on the trombone, clarinet, oboe, trumpet, harp – about themselves, about their relations with the instruments they play.

Everybody, of course, is against the conductor. And he, when presently he appears, is against them, their egoism and what he regards as their indifference to the object of their meeting, the music itself. During a break and in his temporary absence – for he too must be interviewed, must speak his mind, release his grievances – dissension among the players grows. They don't need a conductor. A metronome would do as well. Up to this moment – one remembers a campaign in this country for the conductorless orchestra – the action may have seemed extravagant, but you could say that it still reflected some kind of reality.

But here Fellini shows himself. True, in the past he has based his work on his own experience, on his observation of the life around him. But again and again he has heightened reality with fantasy. And at this crisis in *Orchestral Rehearsal* fantasy breaks in. It allows the director to draw a parallel. It allows him to use the orchestra as a symbol.

In its narrative content, as far as it has narrative, the film is unlike anything Fellini has done before. The obsessive themes are absent: the anti-clericalism, the circus, the clowns. Nevertheless it is unmistakably Fellini. He intended it, one is told, as a kind of stop-gap. A television piece to keep work going during delays on a major project. But it grew; and what it has grown into is a social, even a political comment. Don't be put off. It is serious, as all works by great directors are serious even when making a joke. But it isn't solemn. When in the quiet after the storm the conductor reclaims his orchestra – we are all musicians, he reminds them – there is a shudder of emotion. But the essence of the film is its declaration of life. Its figures seem to speak not from a script but from within themselves. Whatever else it may have, *Orchestra Rehearsal* has the sense of a world irradiated by imagination. And that has always been the achievement of Fellini.

Punch, February 1980

Within three weeks, a second look at **L'Avventura**: one approaches with excitement and a pencil and paper. The first time one simply watched, ravished. The second time – perhaps the second time there will be a chance to analyse, to mark the elements of the bold freehand style. Anyhow, one tries. One drags one's eyes away from the screen and makes, as one thinks, notes. But at the end of nearly two and a half hours there is nothing on the paper but a straggle in which a few words recur. 'Landscape,' they say; 'architecture'; 'figures'.

The richness which defeats one is not in the plot of Michelangelo Antonioni's film. *L'Avventura* is about just that, an adventure: an affair. A man whose fiancée has disappeared and the girl who was her close friend: those are the characters. In a corrupt society he is corrupted, a destroyer, though not a wilful one; in a sophisticated society she is a sophisticated innocent, and she is betrayed.

A steel thread of story, no more; the elaboration is in the human setting which produces such figures and such a plot. To speak of background characters is misleading. The idlers in the yacht – the princess with the gigolo whom she repulses out of mere indolence, the pin-headed girl (brilliantly portrayed by Dominique Blanchar) who is publicly derided by her husband – the people who weave about the central pair are drawn in detail and in depth, and it is only gradually that two figures move into the foreground. Even the minor attendants – a woman in a shop, electric with jealous hate; the predatory boy with whom the despised wife takes a vulgar revenge – are alive, their faces looking out of the screen in naked defiance.

Something about this tight pattern of characters reminds me of *Les Liaisons Dangereuses*; though Laclos would not have left, as Antonioni leaves, an important member of the company without destiny. The unfinished history of the disorientated, dissatisfied girl (played with a fine capriciousness by Lea Massari) who talks of solitude to the lover she can't bear to be without leaves one, I suppose, questioning.

But mystery is of the essence of *L'Avventura*. Incompleteness is part and parcel of the errancy of the human creatures who are the subject of the film. That the story should sometimes break off and leave only a fragment deepens the sense of the insecurity in which they live. And the adventure is set down against a scene of sexual disharmony. The girl and her lover provoking and taunting one another, the quarrelling married couples, the very crowds who form a tapestry behind the figures – the mob yelling for the publicity-hunting actress, the loafers in the Sicilian town wolfishly, silently eyeing the girl waiting outside the hotel – all imply a savage, almost an animal restlessness.

There is, then, a pattern of characters and a pattern of crowds, the whole superimposed on a background – for I must get back to my scrawled words – of landscape and architecture: Aeolian and Sicilian landscape, Sicilian architecture. On the island, one of the Aeolian archipelago, where the yacht puts in the members of the party group themselves in a perspective which is exciting without theatricality; the tiny figure on the distant cliff above the sea, the man turning insultingly away from the chattering girl and walking over the stony slope towards the camera – the disposition, the changing disposition of the characters in relation to one another and to the background has a powerful narrative and dramatic effect. In relation to the background: Antonioni uses space with a command which can fill with emotion a simple shot of a woman against a blank, peeling wall in a waiting-room: against, come to that, one end of a blank wall.

And he uses architecture, whether it is the blind, masked, cold face of an untenanted village or the generous baroque of a Sicilian provincial capital. The graceful and passionate buildings of Noto, of Taormina, enclose the penultimate scenes of the adventure. Antonioni dwells on the monuments with a communicated delight; they are not merely an adjunct to the tale, they are part of its life. But then *L'Avventura* is a film all of one piece: landscape and architecture, the sound of the sea and the eloquent asides of Giovanni Fusco's score – and the playing; for now I find that I have come to the end of the affair with scarcely a word said about the cast. The man is played by Gabriele Ferzetti, the girl by Monica Vitti: he with a delicately gauged rendering of the born rover's persistent, urgent appeal, half-sincere, half-false; she with a desperate reluctance turning to a transfigured consent. She has gay moments of comedy; she has elegance and beauty; and she brings something far rarer – the quality of love – to this complex, difficult, splendid film.

November 1960

At a first view Michelangelo Antonioni's **La Notte** floats by at the deliberate pace of a dream at dawn; one is transfixed. At a second view one tries to grasp it, but this time it flashes past: still a dream, but a dream in which the images of life shift with bewildering speed. As in one of the toys, a zoëtrope perhaps, in which the cinema began, the figures and the background stir and merge, then hesitate, slow down and break up once more into their separate forms and meanings. I can find no other way to describe the hallucinatory movement of this story (written by the director in collaboration with Ennio Flaiano and Toni Guerra) of a marriage which is dying: the dazzle of the narrative, the slow finale, and the emergence of the themes of solitude and impermanence. Only, of course, the images here are not flat, mechanical silhouettes; they are human beings, true, living: you might say desperately living.

The Night: during a circle of the clock a climactic moment in two lives is reached – though to put it like that might imply a sharp sequence of events, and there are next to no events. The story is told through the negation of action; it is precisely because nothing is done that the characters arrive at a crisis. Nothing is done: I must not say nothing happens. But as in Antonioni's *L'Avventura*, the crisis is precipitated by an event off-screen. In the earlier film the unexplained disappearance of the girl leads to the affair between friend and fiancé. In *La Notte*, it is the telephoned news of another kind of disappearance – the death of the friend who in the first scene is visited in a nursing home – which forces the novelist and his wife to recognize that their marriage is moribund. Meanwhile between first scene and last a series of gestures and intentions rather than actions has made the emotional situation clear to the audience.

There is some finely expressive playing: to begin with, a superb performance by Jeanne Moreau as the wife faintly essaying to revive desire in her husband; if Marcello Mastroianni as the novelist presents a portrait slightly more blurred in its detail, that may be because Antonioni gives the woman quicker apprehensions and greater honesty. Bernhard Wicki plays the dying friend with tragic point; as the brilliant, wilful girl who for a moment seems to offer the husband a break-out, Monica Vitti sparkles coldly, sadly, proudly. But the performances are only part of the story. The wife, ignored at a party in honour of her husband's new book, leaves and wanders through the streets; glances with a shadow of invitation at a man sitting in a window;

watches boys letting off rockets in the melancholy outskirts of the city; interrupts a brutal fight between young men one of whom, still bleeding, makes to follow her. In the encounters, in the faces of others even more unmistakably than in her own, you can read her frustration.

And the roaring, vertical architecture of Milan plays a role as important as that of the Sicilian baroque in *L'Avventura*: dwarfing the human figures, setting them against blank walls, enclosing them in cold glass and steel. Figures are reflected and duplicated in glass, watched through glass, distorted in rain-swept glass; at the industrialist's swimming-pool party with its night-long, febrile diversions where the drifting couple come at last to a stop you begin to feel that the whole aimless company of the film exists without air in a glass cage.

Antonioni has said that he hates 'message' films, and it would be a crude simplification to take *La Notte* as an attack on a myopic, materialist society. Social criticism might, I suppose, be detected in the dilemma of the central characters, victims of a boredom and lack of purpose which they share with the world they live in. But there is no anger, only the bitter delight of the artist in translating and interpreting what he sees. And what Antonioni sees is the terrible isolation of men and women drawn together by impermanent desire. This is a film of supreme, of ferocious elegance: a film belonging in its rejection of the traditional forms of narrative to the new worlds of fiction. I do not myself feel as passionately involved in it as in *L'Avventura*: not yet. But I shall; I think I shall.

January 1962

Everything in Michelangelo Antonioni's **The Eclipse** casts the shadow of destruction. The rooms in which people move have a deathly abstract *chic*; the pictures, the chairs, the lampshades, the ornaments are coldly designed and designing, un-lived-with. The houses, the shells which enclose this modish décor, are angular, knife-edged. A window at night opens a wide strip of brilliance in a blank, black wall; along the wide Roman streets the balconies of the rich new blocks repeat themselves in a long perspective of rectangles. And everything is mechanical. In the gray dawn room where in the opening sequence the girl breaks with her lover, the only background stir comes from the electric fan –

until, interrupting his protests, the man goes next door, and you hear the buzzing of an electric razor. For a moment you have the sense of alienation to which Brecht has accustomed us.

·The action is played out in a Waste Land from which the girl, alone in recognizing the sterility of the society which surrounds her, is struggling vainly to escape. At the start she breaks free from an affair which has grown meaningless to her, only to become entangled in another which – though the film leaves it unconcluded – carries its own doom. But by some acuteness of feeling, some special spring of vitality, she has so far withstood the destructive forces (in the trilogy of which this film is the third part, it is always the woman who is the resistant, the live creature). Again and again you see her stretching towards release: delighted by the spatial freedom of an empty airfield, eagerly questioning a friend about the world symbolized by photographs of Africa, bursting out in a mischievous parody of a tribal dancer.

She is in fact the non-conformist: her very gestures – holding a shawl in front of her face, playing in the dark with a stray dog, running her fingers over the cruel, clumsy relic of an elephant's foot – create bizarre shapes, defiant against the background of her own uncertainty and melancholy. Behind her, around her, a desperate activity. In particular the desperation of the Stock Exchange: a shouting, gesticulating, jostling, scurrying complex of figures which, under masterly direction, fragments itself, re-forms, dissolves again into images of expostulation, indifference, despair, impassivity.

Here, and in the view of a crowd fascinated by the human débris of an accident, Antonioni presents a scene which one can take as realistic. Indeed the world he shows is always the normal, visible world: a garden with a hose playing, a nurse wheeling a perambulator, a man driving a trotting pony, a street with lamps, a corner with a derelict building. But for much of the time that world is so lighted, so quieted, so echoed as to seem a kind of limbo. Especially quieted. At intervals all movement is stilled: the telephone bells impiously ring while the Stock Exchange stands in silence for a dead colleague, in the night breeze there is a faint, unearthly clashing and tinkling of the flagpole-cords round the stadium; and life waits for the Eclipse.

The first time I saw the film I thought it magnificent but chill, played glitteringly – Monica Vitti as the lost girl, Alain Delon as the young stockbroker – but with a distant glitter. At a second visit the passion breaks through. It is not simply that the reflecting, deeply expressive performance of Monica Vitti with her quick-silver responses illuminates this arctic Waste Land. Suddenly the ice burns you. And with better acquaintance – for tenacious, exciting though it is this is a difficult film – the progression from *L'Avventura* through *La Notte* to *The Eclipse* seems perfectly logical.

The narrative shape of all three is similar. In *L'Avventura* and *La Notte*, the relationship between a man and two women, a near-break with the more stable of the two, and a reconciliation which one knows won't last: in *The Eclipse*, the relationship between a woman and two men, the second of whom one knows will be as impermanent as the first. In each film, an emotional shock which precipitates or influences the progress of an affair: in *L'Avventura*, after the disappearance of the fiancée, the encounter with the dead, deserted village; in *La Notte*, the news of a friend's death in hospital; in *The Eclipse*, the spectacle of the man drowned in the stolen car. And in each the part played by architecture in the emotional development: the rich, baroque, sensual architecture of Sicily; the airless glass cages of Milan; the empty, self-duplicating box-houses of the suburbs of Rome – and, on the verge of the city, a lunar building with a threatening, a prophetic outline: a mushroom-shape.

But in *The Eclipse* the fragility of human affections is much more directly associated with the climate of society. One must not, with an artist as refined, as elegant, as aristocratic as Antonioni, talk of drawing morals, All the same, in the last minutes, when a series of objects in themselves commonplace appear in a juxtaposition which powerfully suggests finality, when trivial incidents are repeated in the curiously noiseless, darkening air which accompanies a true eclipse, the menace is unmistakable. And one's reactions, inevitably, are different. I still – no doubt because it is the easiest, the least remote from ordinary experience of the three films – feel most intimately in touch with *L'Avventura*. But *The Eclipse* is the grandest.

January 1963

Why, one sometimes asks, why not an enclosed set? There are plenty of occasions when the sense of claustrophobia or of solitude which it can induce would be valuable in the cinema. True that the camera with its gift of mobility is naturally impelled to use that gift: to stare in a character's face, open a door, scurry down the street, climb to the rooftop; the ability is one of the advantages it holds over the theatre, though now that stage performers have taken to tramping through the auditorium perhaps the benefit is dwindling. True also that when the enclosed scene has in fact been used it has rarely been a success; even Hitchcock with *Lifeboat* (I know I hold a minority view here) didn't get the effect of isolation which was needed to emphasize the situation of the shipwrecked survivors in their cockleshell in the Atlantic.

But this week there is a splendid example of the enclosed scene, and I am ashamed to think that when I first saw the film, nearly a year ago now, in Budapest, stunned as I was by its tragic impact I did not recognize exactly what the director was doing. **The Round-Up** (director Miklos Jancso) is said to be based on a fragment of history. The period is almost exactly a hundred years ago; Kossuth's revolution in Hungary has long since been defeated, but scattered in country districts there are still rebellious stragglers from the movement. Authority needs to find and destroy them; and the method chosen is to arrest all the outlaws of the peasant community and by threats, bribes and confrontations, by the encouragement of informers, by trickery of the most merciless kind to discover which among them are not simple criminals but ex-members of a famous revolutionary band.

A multiple murderer is promised a pardon if he will point to any prisoner who has killed a greater number. In order to force a man to identify himself his girl – one of the black-shawled women who bring food and lay it obediently on the ground outside the prison – is stripped and made to run the gauntlet between two lines of gendarmes. A father and a son are invited each to save himself by testifying against the other. Everything is done patiently, coldly in a gradual, pitiless erosion of resistance. Each step in the interrogation leads logically to another identification and another until the final scene of self-betrayal is reached.

It is an unforgettable denunciation of a police inquisition – and the setting is an enclosed scene. One might not immediately recognize it as enclosed. Beyond the prison yard with its high walls and its purgatorial cells, beyond the whitewashed interrogation buildings the plain endlessly stretches. Sometimes a man walks out, or the women who have brought food take fright and scatter like a flock of rooks. But the man is shot in the back as he walks, the women are herded by mounted police; the plain itself, the huge distance without hiding-pace, that is the prison. The interrogators and the peasants are locked in a psychological battle; and the isolation of the men under arrest is intensified by the view of the empty world beyond the bars and the gates. Every passage in the film is designed to emphasize the denial of liberty: the contrast between the measured, official movements of inquisitors and guards and the shambling walk of the shackled prisoners; the alternation of long shots looking into an infinite distance and close shots of passive faces against bleak white walls. Outside the walls the wind whistles remotely and the larks sing; there is no accompanying music. In this magnificently composed work you never notice the absence.

October 1966

When Miklos Jancso's *My Way Home* was shown in London I was surprised to find it less popular than *The Round-Up*, for though it has not the obvious brilliance of the second film it is more comprehensible, more humane and to me more likeable. Somebody offered a reason. *The Round-Up*, he said, was a kind of detective story.

I suppose he was right; the terrible tale of the prison on the Hungarian plain and the cat-and-mouse tactics of the authorities after the 1848 revolt does have something of the excitement of detection. *The Red and the White*; a study of civil war in Russia after 1917, had other qualities; there Jancso was analysing with controlled horror the simple brutalities which revolution produces on both sides. Now, with **Silence and Cry**, he returns to a theme related to that of *The Round-Up*; but without the element of detection. The new film, set in 1919 after the overthrow of the Bela Kun régime, is about the persecution of the defeated Communist revolutionaries.

Once again the immense plain stretching desolately out of sight, interrupted only by occasional whitewashed farmsteads – or by the sandhill where at the opening of the film the mood is set by an execution; to order a prisoner to be taken to the town 'over the sandhill' is to sentence him to be shot in the back as he climbs. The 'silence' of the title is the silence of despair. Suspects are kept under humiliating supervision, made at fixed hours to stand motionless in the yards of their farms, obliged to see their womenfolk summoned to sleep with the gendarmerie. Jancso simply sets the incidents before you: the first execution; the old woman who tries to curry favour by sending her daughter to be debauched; the political suspect Karoly (a portrait of desperate subjection by Jozsef Madaras) terrorized into incriminating himself in the death of two men who have presumably been shot by the police.

Sometimes you really need a bit of help if you are to understand what is going on. Istvan, a wanted revolutionary (Andras Kozak, hero of *My Way Home* and *The Red and the White*), is in hiding; his reluctant host is the unfortunate Karoly, whose wife (Mari Töröcsik, remembered from Fabri's *Merry-go-Round* years ago) and sister-in-law are both in love with the fugitive. Gradually, as the game of hide-and-seek goes on, you realize that something else is in progress; the two women are slowly poisoning the old mother of the household – and the husband too. Why? Perhaps because the victims are beaten, incapable of dealing with the new, frightful conditions of life; the women feel they are the rightful successors.

But Jancso assumes that you will know about the wave of poisonings which, we are now told, swept through Hungary after the first world war. He never bothers to explain this women's revolt, nor does he offer more than the most cursory reference to the relationship – the same school, a shared childhood – between Istvan and the officer (Zoltan Latinovits) who tries to protect him. All this certainly contributes to the elusive, broken quality of the narrative. There is nothing elusive, though, about Jancso's own view. He sympathizes, of course, with the persecuted. But he never idealizes them. They can be cowardly and self-seeking; they abase themselves; they murder. And on the other hand authority itself can show decent feeling. Once more this director is on the side of people, not of politics.

And more and more clearly he sets his signature on his films. Unlike Hitchcock, he doesn't make a personal appearance; but the style – the rare breaks, the long takes – is unmistakable. The camera travels in curves round the figures on the screen, and they in their turn circle as they hesitate, reflect, confront one another. It is a kind of dialogue in movement, often without speech. And the final cry of defiance after the silence of humiliation, that too is voiceless, a mere gesture.

But it is a gesture which ferociously redeems the abasements which go to make up this strange, haunting, memorable film.

July 1969

Bliss was it that dawn – well, was it? When I first saw Miklos Jancso's *The Confrontation*, I felt that in spite of the undertone of menace the film was essentially jubilant, a reflection of the fervour of a revolutionary generation. That was at the première in Budapest last spring. Now I am not so sure.

Gaiety is there, of course; compare the brilliantly circling crowds with the isolated figures of *Silence and Cry* or the prisoners trapped in the immense spaces of *The Round-Up*. Jancso has moved forward in time; after the nineteenth-century persecutions and the horrors which followed the first war he deals now with seeming liberation. Hungary in 1947 – the scene, with girls in anachronistic miniskirts, is in a way symbolic. The Communists have taken over, and there is a moment of delirium. A party of students, boys and girls, jovially waylay a group of Communist police; horseplay is no crime among friends. Then they go singing on their way to invade a Catholic college; the boys educated in the old tradition must be converted – but by debate, by persuasion. The pacific assault on the hill-seminary, the storming of the gates, the amiable round-up of the Catholic students – it is an explosion of generous high spirits and good feeling. It is what revolution ought to be.

Jancso has translated this epitome of the ideal revolution into images of stirring action. The invaders break into song or folk-dance; linking arms, briskly reversing direction in obedience to what might be the cry of a games team, with mock-discipline they herd their undrilled, hesitant opponents. The weaving movements familiar in Jancso's work – the camera looping round the player or following his curving course – are more marked than ever before but also more significant; the camera deliberates with the character. And for the first time abandoning black-and-white the director has used colour – the red banner flung round the crucifix or mischievously draped over the embracing couple – with sharp dramatic effect. The sense of a new spirit of freedom grows with the ceaseless flowing movement.

Then suddenly the face of things alters, or rather the feeling alters. The stir of the restless crowd persists, the scene in the splendid courtyard looks the same; but the reality of revolution has intruded. The policeman who earlier had submitted to the horseplay of his friends has come to make arrests; there is division among the students, a call for terrorist methods; finally the democratic procedures of the enthusiasts are overruled by authority. True, the film ends in an outburst of rebellious joy. It may leave you entranced by its visual beauty, its choreographic elegance – and by the extraordinary vitality of the playing: Lajos Balazsovits as the persuader, Andrea Drahota as the terrorist girl, Andras Kozak as the policeman, Andras Balint in a fine cool performance as a Jewish student. But beneath its exhilarating surface there is the shadow of things to come. *The Confrontation* doesn't seem to me to controvert Jancso's basically pessimistic view of history.

April 1970

Probably one should take a course in the work of Miklós Jancsó – begin with the comparatively easy narrative films and work up to the later pieces with their complex patterns and rites. Work up, in fact, to **Red Psalm**. Not that it would be anything but magnificent without preparation. But preparation helps, and I feel myself fortunate in having begun years ago, and in Budapest itself, with *My Way Home* and with *The Round-Up* – though even that with no English titles, no warning, and a friend, also I fancy a bit flummoxed, murmuring improvised translations into my ear, I found pretty bewildering at the time.

Red Psalm is the full flower of Jancsó. He is, I know, a director who doesn't give foreign audiences much help. Only the other day I was reproached with failing to tell readers what *Agnus Dei* was about (though I did think I had pointed to its picture of a demoniacal Hitler-type paganism). So what is *Red Psalm* about? It takes place in the vast Hungarian plain which is Jancsó's favoured background, and it is about a farm-workers' revolt (in the 1890s, one is told, though I don't find that indicated in the film, not unless a quotation from Engels is a clue).

The farm-workers, the resolute men and the bold beautiful girls, are sitting around singing the Marseillaise; all through the film singing goes on, playing goes on, revolutionary songs, folk songs, even, unexpectedly, 'Charlie Is My Darling'. And dancing. If you saw *The Confrontation* you will remember the rows of boys and girls, arms linked, dancing for the Liberation. Here the patterns are more complicated – the dancing lines forming into circles, breaking into groups, a trio of lovely naked girls detaching themselves from the crowd, riders (horsemen are the symbol of oppression in Janczó's work) circling as if herding the revolutionaries; the straight lines and the elliptical movements which, set on the horizontal plane of the landscape, are so much a part of Janczó's work weave and intersect until at the last, with workers and troops mingling, they are merged in a moment of joy.

A moment only. Sometimes in the film one is reminded of Wordsworth and that famous dawn when it was bliss to be alive; nobody like Jancsó for communicating the excitement of revolution. But he too knows that the bliss doesn't last; and here it is the prelude to massacre. Not the kind of massacre to which the cinema is addicted; no screams, no blood, everything remote, everything symbolic. This is a director who moves farther and farther away from realistic violence – and from realism itself. Wounds, in the first, almost festive part of the revolt, turn to scarlet flowers; an officer who refuses to shoot the insurgents and is killed by his own side rises from the dead; only the church, when in a wave of anti-clericalism it is set on fire, really blazes. Revolution itself turns to ritual, and a kind of Church ritual at that. The farm-workers recite their own litany; a convert from the service of the oppressors, the estate-owners, makes a general confession and is confirmed in his new socialist faith; in the most pacific of deaths an anti-militant sacrifices himself for his people.

For *Red Psalm* really is a psalm, a hieratic chant, a rite. The appearance of players we know from other films, from *Agnus Dei*, from *The Confrontation* – Andrea Drahota, Lajos Balázsovits, Andras Bálint – strengthens the sense of a consistent vision of history. And in the mood which is engendered the elements in the director's work which have sometimes begun to look like mannerisms, the circling, the restless movements to and fro, fall naturally into place. One surrenders to the rhythms of action and music. One accepts, shall I say, Jancsó's affirmation of life.

March 1973

3   TRYING TO LIKE . . .

It was Dilys Powell at the end of her review of *The Boy Friend* who first minted the phrase that has clung to the director Ken Russell's career in the cinema, 'an appalling talent'. It is a telling judgment, both in pinpointing in three words what has become a commonly held view of Russell's work and in revealing Powell's attitude towards certain kind of cinema. She freely admits that certain film-makers have particular gifts, although she dislikes their work. At the same time she is determined to find qualities in that work which she can admire, or at the very least explain to her readers why talent has gone astray or been squandered in the course of the film she is reviewing. In this sense Powell is always that unfashionable kind of critic in an age that likes its judgments in black and white, a 'judicious critic'. She would like to think better of Fritz Lang's American movies, the work of Ingmar Bergman, or Jean Luc Godard and Ken Russell, and is full of regret when a director she likes, such as Robert Altman, fails her.

1 *Fritz Lang*

Among the many questions which nag at the fretful cinemane is the question of the development of the individual worker in the film medium. In literature or painting the critic traces with love and delight the growth of the artist, watches the succession of phase on phase, sees the moods of life and experience reflected in the moods of creation. But not in the cinema, at any rate not often. A Chaplin, a D. W. Griffith grows and develops indeed; but as a rule a film is an act of creation too composite for the free unfolding of the individual talent to be easily apparent.

That is not to say that the individual talent is without influence. Obviously the imaginative director leaves the mark of his style on what he directs; you don't take a John Ford film for a William Wyler film, or an Orson Welles film for either. But it would, I fancy, be difficult to deduce from the work of any one of them a process of development or expansion, however erratic. Welles's second film was as a matter of fact less sure and complete than his first. Where, except in certain lovely and confident strokes of style, is the connection between Ford's *Stagecoach*, *The Long Voyage Home*, and *How Green Was My Valley*? From Wyler's *Dead End* or *The Little Foxes* to *Mrs Miniver* is certainly not an advance; it is not even a move backwards along the same track. The fact that in every one of these films (except the first Welles film, *Citizen Kane*) the director was working with somebody else's material, whether story, novel or play, does not explain this isolation of one piece from another. Shakespeare does not cease to be Shakespeare because he is doing up a bit of Holinshed.

I am driven to these melancholy reflections by the appearance of a new film by Fritz Lang, **The Woman at the Window**. This is a good bit of craftsmanship on the theme of unpremeditated murder and tallyho, with a nicely judged use of realistic detail: the accomplice, fearful of betrayal, lurking in doorways, always watching; the dead man sitting up with disinterested stare in the back of the car; the murderer puffing through the dripping woods with a dreadfully recalcitrant corpse. The story, after a pompous start, is neat and taut, and the film as a whole (played, by the way, Edward G. Robinson and Joan Bennett), though it isn't nearly as good to my mind as *Double Indemnity* or *The Maltese Falcon*, looks distinguished by comparison with the general run. And that is all one can say; and this is a film by Fritz Lang, who made *Metropolis* and that odious but brilliant study in savagery, *M*.

I have never liked his work in his German period, before he left Europe for Hollywood, but I have always admired it; at least it said something which, however brutal and sickly, was consistent, at least it was going somewhere. In Hollywood, too, he has done remarkable things; even within the last few years his use of colour in *Western Union*, his handling of macabre detail in *Man Hunt* and *Hangmen Also Die*, stand out. But if one asks in what direction this director, who began with such decision, is travelling, the answer is Nowhere; and if one asks what this director, who spoke once such horrible half-truths, is saying, the answer is Nothing.

The case of Fritz Lang, a man transplanted from his own soil and obliged to conform to the rules of an alien industry, is perhaps peculiar. Yet there are dozens of cases of directors who, working in their own region and capable of stamping mind and personality on single films, still fail to create sequence and consistency in their work as a whole. The remedy, I suppose, is in more freedom for the director to choose and shape his material.

February 1941

Last week's revival of a famous Hollywood film, **You Only Live Once**, is in a sense saddening, for it offers no evidence of a subsequent advance in the American cinema: on the contrary, if one looks with a comparing eye at this piece, made in 1937, and at the general American output of 1946, the result is singularly flattering to the past.

The revival, however, is of particular interest at the present time, since it allows us to see a creative talent in some kind of chronological perspective. Fritz Lang is fortunate among directors whose films have been produced over a longish period in that the film societies have combined with the commercial cinema to keep his work in circulation. Others with a claim to critical consideration have not been so lucky. Hitchcock, for example; though the latest Hitchcock piece is always sure of a large audience, though the last Hitchcock but one or two is probably to be tracked down in the repertory cinemas, the early Hitchcock has almost vanished, and you can whistle for a sight of *The Lodger*. But the work of Lang can be illustrated in almost all its periods. Quite lately members of the New London

Film Society saw his first important film: *Destiny*, an essay in the expressionist manner with one of those fairytale themes, set against an overpowering architectural background, so popular in the German cinema of the early twenties. *Metropolis*, again with an emphatic architectural setting, again with a fantastic theme, but with an added element of the savagely macabre and an undertone of social criticism, is familiar in all film society programmes. From *Metropolis* in 1926 it is an easy step to *M* in 1933; a terrifying study in pathological crime, crammed with vivid narrative detail but marked, or so it seems to a present-day audience in this country, by an oddly German brutality.

By 1936 Lang was working in America; and from this time onwards there is, or has been, little difficulty in following his development. *Fury*, which was re-issued a few years ago, and *You Only Live Once* belong to the time when he was applying the lessons learned in Germany to a new set of circumstances and questions, when he was elaborating the theme of the relationship between society and its victim, guilty or innocent. The experiences of his life in Europe, perhaps, sharpened his recognition of the problem; for however effectively he has absorbed American ways and American feelings (and his success in handling American themes has been phenomenal), he has never, to this very day, quite accustomed himself to the idea of a society in which the individual is a willing and welcome partner; his most significant films have been concerned with the outlaw in society, with the mob's cruelty to the fugitive.

A group of films with a social subject was followed by a pair of films on Western or pioneering subjects; it is worth remarking that one of them, *Western Union*, contained some of the best colour passages encountered up to that date. Then a pair with a Nazi background, *Hangmen Also Die* and *Manhunt* (again, you see, the notion of the hunted hero, or victim, or prey), which show a return to the emphasis on macabre detail of Lang's German period; and so to the latest manner, the deliberate, rather cold, circumstantial manner of *The Woman in the Window* and *Scarlet Street*. And today we can look back from *Scarlet Street*, with its economical, oppressive narrative, to the sharp excitement, the beautifully controlled tempo of *You Only Live Once*; and I cannot but feel that nine years ago Lang showed a clearer understanding of the strength of the cinema medium than now. The mounting pace of the prison break, with Henry Fonda's set face turned towards the warder and his hands struggling secretly to twist

the tin mug, and the blood-drops falling on the floor of the cell
at last to show that a vein has been cut in those hands with that
mug – again and again we find in this film what can only be
described as camera style, the use of the pictorial image, singly
and in combination, to narrate with the maximum of emotional
impact.

Lang's last two films have, indeed, been in their way exciting.
But I miss in them the startling image, the breathless pace broken
by moments of recollection and pause, which he could command
in his early American films. And I miss, too, the social attack; for
whether or not one agrees with his criticism of society in *You Only
Live Once*, the moral attitude lends an extraordinary interest to
the piece.

April 1946

2 Ingmar Bergman

Few would deny that **The Seventh Seal**, provides a pretty sobering occasion. Certainly its director, Ingmar Bergman, meant it to be sobering. He meant it, in spite of its medieval setting, to frighten you and me about here and now. In fact, it has what, for want of a couple of longer words, I will call contemporary application.

The Seventh Seal takes its title from Revelation, its opening words from the chapter which, beginning 'And when he had opened the seventh seal, there was silence in heaven about the space of half an hour,' announces universal destruction: the sea turned to blood, the star Wormwood falling, 'burning as it were a lamp.' The film is an allegory, but an allegory much of which is in realistic terms; when Mr Bergman cries Woe he intends not some vague alarm but physical agony before your eyes.

And he has set his story in a period when there seems, at any rate to those of us who are not devoted medievalists, to have been a pretty general addiction to agony. A Knight and his Squire come back to Sweden from the Crusades. They find their world changed. The Black Death rages; corpses on the seashore, in the farmyard, in the forest. There is a frenzy to avert the anger of heaven; flagellants drag themselves whining through the villages, witches are blamed for the plague, tortured and burned. The Knight himself has altered in ten years of fighting and wandering. He is no longer certain of anything; he broods, he doubts, he questions. Over everything there hangs the menace of some still huger, some final disaster.

To nobble Saint John the Divine as a handy guide to a modern situation is not as new as some appear to think; one recalls without indulgence how a lot of well-meaning people wore out, by applying it to the conflict of 1914–18, the word Armageddon. But I must not suggest that Mr Bergman is merely battening on the Book of Revelation. What he has done is, drawing on the figures of medieval religious painting – Death, the Holy Family, the Crusader – and using a mixture of historical imagination and, as I say, allegory, to make a film about fear of the H-bomb.

The soldier back from the wars, loss of belief, pervasive fright – the analogy is clear enough. And it is splendidly illustrated. Most of those who are accustomed to looking with attention at the cinema will admit the force of the images of cruelty, squalor and beastliness. And they will recognize the quality of the facial types, seeing in the exhausted, Gothic lantern-head of the Knight (Max von Sydow) the gnawing disquiet of the unsatisfied agnostic, in the stubborn, sardonic grimace of the Squire (a fine performance by Gunnar Björnstrand, and the only *character* in the film; the rest are wall-paintings) the endurance of the honest materialist. *The Seventh Seal* is a notable film, let me make no bones about that; and since notable films are rare we were happy as well as lucky to be able, in the London Film Festival last October, to give it a first showing in London.

And now, the honours done, perhaps I may be allowed to add that I find it repulsive.

When I first saw the film I thought my nausea was a simple reaction from the emphasis on the deformed and the tortured; the crippled flagellants, the young witch howling as, waiting for execution, she comes back to consciousness (whenever the Scandinavian cinema has five minutes to fill in it burns a witch). It is an emphasis in which from the start I saw not the pain of the sensitive artist forcing himself to record a hateful truth but the watchfulness of the inquisitor. But now that I know *The Seventh Seal* better I find my revulsion going much farther. The magnificent craftsmanship, of course, I admit. But beneath the surface of the high-class, bony morality which has understandably attracted so much admiration there lurks what to me is a dreadful squashy sentimentality, the kind of sentimentality which goes hand in hand with obsession by the dark and the cruel. On the one side the executioners and the hysterical self-indulgers, on the other the naïve dreamer, the loving fair-haired wife in a low-necked blouse, the chubby baby. And it goes almost without saying that the dreamer is a strolling player. Innocence in the circus-tent and the caravan; it is the oldest hat in the business.

Death playing chess on the sea-shore – it would be consoling to be able to say that the magniloquent symbols conceal something bogus as well as sentimental. But they don't; Mr Bergman, I am sure, has a midnight, Arctic-winter sincerity; the violence of my dislike of his film is probably evidence of that. Did I say *The Seventh Seal* was sobering? On me it has the impact of one of those spiked iron balls chained to a club, so popular in films about goodwill in the Middle Ages.

March 1958

'Lay,' says our old friend Sub-Title – always a helpful soul – 'a hot wooden lid on his stomach.' No, the source is not some Peter Sellers lark, nor even Bootsie and Snudge; it is *The Virgin Spring*, a Swedish film based on a medieval folk-song; and such is the mesmeric power of the director's name that nobody (well, hardly anybody; I must not count myself) ventures to smile.

The original folk-song deals in the subjects which served to brighten dull days in the Middle Ages: rape, murder, revenge. A young girl takes leave of her father and mother and rides to church in her best silk dress (yes, for once I am going to tell the story; stop now if you don't want to hear it). On the way she is ravished, killed and stripped by three herdsmen who then incautiously offer the dress to the mother and are killed by the father; he repents and promises to build a church, which presumably makes everything O.K.; anyhow, on the spot where the girl's body lay, a spring of water appears.

The film, written by Ulla Isaksson, extends the theme. A struggle between Christianity and paganism is introduced; one encounters a character, endemic in the Scandinavian cinema, who is given to runic rumblings ('However well a day begins it always ends in woe'); and the scene is littered with symbols – raven, dead bat, and some unidentified sacrificial object strongly resembling a turd. It may be a disappointment to addicts of the pitchy Nordic screen that it hasn't been possible to pack in a witch-burning, and I am afraid the censor has cut a chunk out of the rape; but cheer up, there is still a toad in the bread.

Medieval subject, Nordic setting, unremitting solemnity and unlimited horror – equipped with these you can frighten an audience into admiring anything. The images which *The Virgin Spring* offers are either sentimentally sunny (flaxen-haired girl riding towards dappled woods) or heavily squalid (tusky Odin-worshipper fingering mummified hand, witness of murder vomiting picnic lunch). I have nothing against horrors: what about Goya? But here scenes and actions in themselves repulsive are not translated, they are photographed naked.

The barbarisms which are the themes of legend are acceptable in folk-poetry because the narration reflects the attitude of the times towards the events narrated. *The Virgin Spring* sets its barbarisms against a background which is false-naïve; the climax of atonement has no force because one cannot believe in the religious basis of the life portrayed. And because one can't believe one has leisure to observe the ponderousness of the goings-on in which the gifted performers – Max von Sydow, Gunnel Lindblom, Birgitta Pettersson – are involved; the effect is of silent-cinema miming. When I first saw the film I thought it merely nauseous. At a second view I find it generally tedious, occasionally absurd, and always rétrograde.

June 1961

In the train it is stiflingly hot. From the room in the town where the journey is broken the windows look out on a street haunted by bleak preoccupied crowds and a junk-cart drawn by a skeletal horse. The hotel corridors are deserted. When the waiter answers the bell a sign-language must be used, for this is a foreign country; nobody can communicate. And one of the travellers is mortally ill. Everybody, in fact, is isolated from everybody else; the Ingmar Bergman scene is set.

Long before **The Silence** arrived in this country, indeed before there seemed a chance of its ever being exhibited here, scraps of news about it were circulating. It had shocked audiences in its native Sweden – and won a national award. Germany had labelled it positively beneficial. France had first totally rejected it then partially relented. New York had taken the precaution of nipping out the best part of a minute. But nobody told us what it was about. Now that the film can indeed be seen in London the time has come for a simple statement. It is about a sort of Hell.

There are five characters: two sisters; a little boy, child of one of them; a waiter; and a barman, who never speaks, for the simple reason that speech in his exclusively libidinous circumstances is redundant – and anyhow in the unknown tongue his words, like the old waiter's vague mumblings, would be incomprehensible. The sisters are caught in an enclosed scene: the physical enclosure of the hotel; the enclosure of language; and the enclosure – an imprecise menace – of war with something or sombody: the sound of planes breaks the afternoon nap, a tank grinds through the street at night. And they are caught in an enclosed relationship. The air between them vibrates with hatred and rejection. One of the two suffocates in her own illness. The other struggles to escape into sexual promiscuity. And in that, too, there is hatred.

Inside this narrative frame Bergman has contrived extraordinary emotional shades. The little boy would like to live enclosed with the others. Instead, when his mother is not fondling him (and for a moment I fancied there might be something suspect in that relationship too) he is left to himself – or pushed outside while the two exchange taunts. Half the time he spends in his own limbo of hotel passages, watching with the same incurious interest his mother embracing a complete stranger, or a workman attending to the chandeliers. And in the vast spaces of the establishment with its single picture – an erotic one – there is an accented barrenness which becomes a kind of richness.

It is tempting to look beyond the personal story for impersonal symbols. All those dwarfs, now, frolicking with the child or greeting with grave civility the woman drooping outside the sweaty bedroom; surely they must stand for something more than Bergman's infatuation with the deformities of the circus? And the floor-waiter (played with a delicate mingling of the sweet and the ogreish by Hakan Jahnberg) – a cherished correspondent in Germany is convinced that this is really the figure of Death; and why not? The old man is the only one to sit solicitously by the bedside of the agonizing woman. Death is everywhere in the film; when to beguile the child the waiter opens a wallet the snapshots produced are of guess what? A corpse on a bier.

The seconds, meanwhile, tick loudly in the dying woman's room, or pound with her struggling heartbeat. You could say the film was about time, or come to that about silence itself, the silence of loneliness (I think I am right in saying there is no background music, only music natural to the action – a radio playing, for instance). Bergman himself says it is about love: 'a despotic love' which, according to him, is 'the beginning of death.' He denies a lesbian intention in the relationship between the sisters. All the same something uncommonly like lesbianism betrays itself in the words and gestures of the elder sister. A good many other cinema rarities have somehow crept into the film: masturbation, for example, and, in the bedroom scene with the barman, what I can only describe as anal interest. The one element I fail to detect is the simple element of simple love.

The whole film is splendidly made: the lingering views of the impersonal, soundless hotel corridors; the savage close shots of the self-torturing women; the rhythms of editing which emphasize the drag and the urgency of time. And splendidly acted: Ingrid Thulin alternating between cool intellectual control and a disgust, which she insists is not jealousy, with her sister's life; Gunnel Lindblom trolloping around with a defiant, deliberate slut's air. One question: whether for its impact *The Silence* depends on the audacity of its sexual scenes. Partly, of course, it does depend on them. But without them the quality of Bergman would surely persist. I should still detest the film, as I detest the whole world of vomiting and death – a medieval world in more senses than one – which Bergman always creates. (In fact something in my dislike of *The Seventh Seal* has now been clarified: just as in the new piece the element of love seems to me absent, in *The Seventh Seal* the simulacrum of the Holy Family is without conviction; Bergman, opposing it to a plague-ridden society, still makes it a sickly fake.) But *The Silence* would always force my admiration. The film now being shown in London is an abbreviated version of the film I saw privately a month or two ago; some of the shock has been taken out. But I still find the piece brilliant: repulsive but brilliant.

Which brings me to the enigma of censorship. The copy I first saw I understood to be Bergman's original untouched; but that version itself, I was told later, had been slightly trimmed. Now the three most desperate scenes have been further lopped – but scarcely at all by the British censor, who admits to no more than excising a couple of peculiarly explicit English sub-titles and trimming a few frames from a bedroom scene already cut: for the rest the film, he says, is as it reached him.

Whether I personally should have detected any hiatus had I not seen the fuller version I doubt. But since I did see it, I can, from a critic's point of view, only regret the cuts – though it is possible that uncut *The Silence* would have provoked too much uproar to survive in this country. The one thing certain is that in none of its versions is the film pornographic. It strikes me as on the contrary deeply puritanical. Bergman's world with its cries of pain, rage and hatred is one enormous sex-deterrent.

Meanwhile darkness thickens. In answer to a *Sunday Times* telegram asking whether he had authorized abbreviation of *The Silence*, Bergman cables: NO CUTS MADE IN SWEDEN. THE WHOLE QUESTION UNINTERESTING.

April 1964

They are a race apart, the women of the Ingmar Bergman cinema, which now offers us in **Cries and Whispers** a film I admire deeply – but with shrinking.

Perhaps Bergman's men, too, are a race apart. Often, after all, they represent the artist as a being isolated from the everyday world. But Bergman is speaking from the artist's point of view. The women may be regarded with sympathy, admiration, alarm or simply amusement. They may be schizophrenics or holy virgins, they may be howling in childbirth or recognizing a gigantic spider as God, they may be destructive forces or merely appendages to a man (you remember *Now About These Women*?). But they are always treated from a distance and as a separate class of creature. Bergman, one is sometimes told, understands women. Perhaps it is because he is so superbly endowed as an artist that the claim (with a light-weight one could ignore it) seems such bosh. Understanding women? Understanding men? The best one can hope for is to understand a bit about one man, one woman, or come to that one horse, dog, cat.

Cries and Whispers is about four women. One of them, Agnes (Harriet Andersson), is dying. 'It is early Monday morning, and I am in pain,' she writes in her diary; no music, no sound except the ticking of the elegant clocks; only in the park outside her windows the slant of first light through misty trees. Bergman asks a great deal of his actresses. Again and again the camera fixes its cruel gaze on a face and stays there motionless, for what seems like minutes. And the actresses respond. Not only Miss Andersson, retching in agony as the pain strikes or relapsing into quiet on the bosom of her maidservant (a loving portrait by Kari Sylwan). There are the two who have come to their sister's death-bed – the easy-going Maria (Liv Ullmann) whose infidelity once brought her husband to attempt suicide; and Karin (magnificently played by Ingrid Thulin) who one night mutilated herself sexually to avoid the marital bed.

Not an easy film. Easy enough, as the hushed house reminds the women of their story, to follow; but not easy to accept as shame and misery whisper from the past. Loneliness whispers too. The dying woman – unmarried, in childhood the outsider of the family – is the only one of the three sisters to experience affection and the unspoken happiness of unity with other human beings. The other two are incapable of a lasting relationship with one another. There is a short passage of communication, then they withdraw again into coldness, even dislike; Bergman is always conscious of a distance between his people.

The distance is expressed in images more beautiful than anything he has done before. The child spying on the mother who loiters in the park in her long turn-of-the-century white dress; Karin and Maria in their white robes moving round the sick-room with its crimson walls; all three sisters, in white again, running through the park with the maidservant – white for joy and solicitude, crimson against white for death and the blood of suicide and mutilation; the handling of colour is unforgettable. But is the whole film the masterpiece it has been called? Will its horror – for it is a film of horror – compose with time into a durable reflection of life? True that at the end Bergman lets himself come nearer than even before to a kind of reconciliation with living. But I can't help suspecting that his women, monumental creatures, will stand outside the human race.

February 1973

If you want to see two great cinema performances, go and watch Ingrid Bergman and Liv Ullmann in **Autumn Sonata**. Since performances grow or shrink in relation to the direction I must urge you to go also for the work of Ingmar Bergman. Whether you respond to him with rage or with veneration he is a great director, and since a great director needs material which deeply expresses concern with life you should consider with gratitude the quality of the writing. You have the chance of a superb film. I know people too much moved by it to endure a second view. My own feeling is different (yes, I have seen Autumn Sonata twice), but more of that in a moment.

I suppose that by now most people know the film is about a mother and a daughter. Eva, the daughter (Liv Ullmann), is married in friendship but not love to a country pastor; she lives in memories of her lost child and of her own childhood. The mother (Ingrid Bergman) is a concert pianist, a woman of the world wearing a social mask, which enables her to move in a few instants from tearful reminiscences of a dead lover to thoughts of what to put on for evening in a country parsonage. After a long separation she comes to stay with her daughter.

The two women (the cinema is hooked just now on the two-women theme) look forward excitedly to their reunion. And at first their relationship seems fond. Then it disintegrates. The dialogue is composed with extraordinary acuteness; yet for once you almost forget the titles as you watch the faces. The mother, visibly disconcerted by the news that her second daughter is in the house, puts on an act all sweetness as she visits the helpless crippled girl. It is with an expression hardening into censure that Eva watches her mother correcting her amateur interpretation of a Chopin Prelude, then playing it herself with professional self-regard.

In the end all their encounter does is to expose pain and bitterness as the daughter unleashes the disappointments of a childhood sustained by maternal feeling. Her mother, she cries – the resentment of years exploding – abandoned her and disappeared on long concert tours, or came home to twist her personality into shapes for which it was never intended. In the long night colloquy the daughter emotionally destroys her mother.

Only at two points can I quarrel with the masterly handling of the theme. In the argument over Eva's frustrated youth there is a reference to an abortion; the abortion seems to me unnecessary, put in to strengthen the case against a mother who has ventured to live the life of an artist – a choice with which Bergman, himself an artist, should surely sympathize. And there is Eva's final monologue and its promise of reconciliation. I just don't believe in it. Ingmar Bergman understands the human heart: but he doesn't like it. He says that *Autumn Sonata* is about 'love . . . deformed love and love that is our sole chance of survival'. I think it is about hate. And I find detestable its judgment of the mother for her decision to pursue a career. Nevertheless I find myself profoundly admiring the film: the best that Bergman has made or is likely to make.

After all he cannot with greater skill, with more appalling assurance, go on saying that whatever is, is wrong.

Punch, March 1979

Having been progressively lowered in spirit by a quarter of a century of Ingmar Bergman, I had expected to be totally extinguished by **From the Life of the Marionettes**. In the past we have had plague, fruitless childbirth, the collapse of religion, the disgraces of war and the vacuum of marriage. We have watched the despair of the artist and the abysses of nervous psychosis, the melancholies of masturbation and the indignities of anal intercourse. It has been a desolate two-and-a-half decades, scarcely enlivened by Bergman's excursions into comedy; as a matter of fact I have sometimes felt that the director was at his glummest in his dismissal of the devoted harpies of *Now About These Women*, and the new film offers the darkest view yet of the human condition.

But somehow the total denial of hope is almost exhilarating.

Superficially this is the story of a murder and an investigation of the background of murder. Not, of course, an ordinary murder. No matter how much one may shrink from the Bergman analysis of life one is forced to admit that his approach is wholly original, his conclusions unthinkable without the support of his powerful genius; impossible that any pre-Bergman cinema could have explored such depths.

This, then, is a murder forced on the murderer by an encircling destiny. Played by Robert Atzorn, he is a presentable young man, good family, good job, devoted but prehensile mother, beautiful but self-willed wife (Christine Buchegger) – whom he desperately longs to kill. The woman he does kill is not his wife but a prostitute with the same name, Katarina. He is shut in with her, emotionally and physically: he can't get out of the hot, locked, empty brothel, just as he cannot get out of the society which engulfs and uses him. He dangles on the strings of a malignant life-force.

But everybody in this closed circle of figures is helpless – the wife, the mother, the psychiatrist who wants to seduce the wife, everybody is shut in with desire, frustration, pain. Especially the man who assists the wife in her fashion establishment, the homosexual (Walter Schmidinger). Like the others, he had desires he cannot satisfy. He wants to win the husband away from marriage, he wants to possess him. And in a stunningly written exposition of his condition, his place in the world, he expresses the abysses of depression. I am inclined to find the true heart of the film in this character – or perhaps that is because the performance is so superb. The murderer suffers, can't sleep, dreams (there is usually a dream in a Bergman movie), but when it comes to the point he can let go. He embraces the prostitute, then the embrace turns to a snarl; he bites. The homosexual is locked in with himself.

The film begins with the murder; goes back to examine the warnings of murder – the visit to the psychiatrist, the overheard colloquy between wife and psychiatrist, the quarrel between husband and wife; goes forward again to enquire of the witnesses;

at last watches the killer in his barred room, playing chess, tidying his bed, sleeping with a teddy bear. And really he is the luckiest one. He has achieved something; he has achieved death. And in its unalloyed pessimism, its complete negation of hope, the film, stripped of the incidents, the excitements which have illumined the director's earlier work, is the purest of Bergman. He can go no farther.

Or can he?

3 Jean-Luc Godard

Under the brim of a hat tilted ferociously forward the face with its dangling cigarette looks out in a mixture of the foxy and the dangerous. Why not? it thinks; and no sooner thought than done: a parked car chosen, the engine by some professional sleight of hand started, an importunate girl-friend brushed aside, and off along the dizzying highroad to Paris – fields, trees, traffic, speed, the hand discovering the gun in the glove-compartment, the face, still thinking aloud, committed to nothing but the next chance, and the next, and the next.

Breathless (*A Bout de souffle*): tells the story of the thief's zigzag course – bolting from cover to cover, here a mouthful snatched, there an hour's sleep or an hour's love – a course which must in the end leave the runner out of breath, out of invention, out of will to run.

It is the handful of money stolen from a mistress; it is the stranger in the lavatory knocked out and robbed; it is the friend who is never there when the telephone rings, the cheque that can't be cashed, the stolen car that can't be sold; the police, the tell-tale newspaper photograph – and yet no fear, only a kind of feckless resource; no desire, only a vanity which takes a poster of Humphrey Bogart as mirror; no belief except fatalism, no feeling except a stubborn reluctance to do without a certain elegant little giraffe of a girl. She is the American skimming Paris, the hesitater, the experimenter; pity has not touched her, and as the clear conscienceless eyes reflect her debate whether to run with the fox or shake him off one can't help admiring the skill with which the cool, crop-haired grace of the actress has been used (it is Jean Seberg) – and thinking how extraordinary it is that a few years ago somebody should have expected her to play Joan of Arc.

This is the crest of the New Wave; incalculable, violent, self-expending. The film is the work of a triumvirate: Jean-Luc Godard as director, François Truffaut as writer, Claude Chabrol as technical and artistic adviser; perhaps one should add the photographer, Raoul Coutard, for the rectangle of the screen compellingly frames haste and repose, the skitter of lights in Paris streets and the circling and eyeing and long, irritable premating colloquies of the pair in the girl's bedroom. The central figure turning and doubling in sudden movement to which the camera, following quick as a shadow, gives an unpremeditated air; the sense of absolute egoism, the sense – as if there were no controls, no rules – of a being who acts entirely on impulse – it is dazzling; and it is dazzlingly played by Jean-Paul Belmondo.

Belmondo is an actor whom we don't yet know well in this country; but we shall. In the space of a year or two he has become a golden name in France; one can see why. The movements are as unselfconscious as a young animal's; the face, long, triangular, with its curving mouth and blinkered eyes, is a rubber mask which can change its contours at will. In *Breathless* it is the mask of urban lawlessness; the wide boy's face, the face which doesn't think beyond now, doesn't care either.

And yet in a film which lays such claims to realism we at least ought to care – care, I mean, about the creatures of the screen: feel involved, one way or the other, in their destiny.

The sentimental cinema of right and wrong, good and evil, is derided today; often rightly. What the sentimental cinema does is to simplify the underlying emotions and bring them naked to the surface – where they may die of exposure. All the same that is a way of trying to be truthful; the emotions, after all, exist. The new, unsentimental cinema looks only at the cold and brutal surface of life; and that is a way of telling lies. The more honest about appearances, the more truthful superficially, the more deeply untruthful; that is what I begin to feel. The young generation of French film-makers is occupied in a process of disengagement. *Breathless*, for instance, insists that one shall draw back, avoid entanglement in hidden emotions. And so, in spite of the undeniable brilliance of form and style, it remains no more than a superb pattern; a pattern of dried leaves cast on the surface of water. There is a closer approach to human truth in the nonsense of *The Singing Fool*.

June 1961

There are directors who make films which present to the world different aspects of the same face, which in fact belong together: Griffith, for instance, Clair, Antonioni, Bresson. But – leaving aside for the moment the obliging craftsmen who will turn their hands to anything – there is a second group whose work is in two compartments. Hitchcock seems to me to belong to this group; and I am inclined to add Jean-Luc Godard. Not that the marks of his cinema in either compartment are easily mistakable: one recognizes the deceiving flatness of statement, the infectious obsessions, sometimes the fascination by violence. All the same his work strikes me as dividing itself in two, with violence, in one of the compartments, shrinking or vanishing altogether – as it vanishes in *Une Femme Mariée*.

'A Married Woman', not, as when the film first appeared, 'The Married Woman': the change of title has quieted a French censorship which suspected a generic slur on the sanctity of France's marriage bed. For in this triangle it is the woman who changes partners, shuttling with cheerful lack of self-reproach between husband and lover, and who claims the right to infidelity which, according to the popular Gallic myth, is exercised by every paterfamilias in Paris; and not for the first time Godard shows himself in what, if the adjective had not a faintly forbidding shade, could be called a feminist mood. The film begins and ends in the bedroom. The hand caresses the naked body: it is a canticle to erotic love. But the film itself is not erotic. The gestures of love which the wife (Macha Meril) exchanges first with her lover (Bernard Noel) and a few hours later and less enthusiastically with her husband (Philippe Leroy) present something of the passionless quality of marble. Everything has an unflawed look: the rooms, the white walls, the uncrumpled sheets, the elegant naked body of the heroine herself – it is all too cool to be erotic.

Certainly Macha Meril is a dish; and the camera dwells on her, complete or in segments, legs, shoulders, belly, navel, with devoutness. But one still has the feeling that it is the woman's point of view which is being studied; the film seems to look with her more than at her. Wherever it looks, it looks with sly or ironic liking. It is extremely funny: in its bland statements of the thoughts and attitudes of the characters; in the playing, from the confident little boy to the doctor whose pauses, during an interview about contraception and the relation between physical pleasure and the incidence of pregnancy, are so speaking; in its poker-faced use of advertisements, page after page, for belts, brassières and all the controllers of the female figure (there was a moment when I reflected with admiration that here in *Une Femme Mariée* was the true pop art).

'A film,' says Godard, describing the piece, 'in which the cinema is happy and free to play at just being itself.' In this mood of comedy the flashes of bravado which sometimes, for instance in *Bande à Part*, have seemed a director's self-indulgence become perfectly appropriate. *Bande à Part* belongs to the arrogant Godard of *A Bout de Souffle*. *Une Femme Mariée* comes from the other Godard, the Godard of *Une Femme est une Femme* and *Vivre sa Vie*. I don't, I confess, like *Une Femme est une Femme*, and with its melodramatic ending *Vivre sa Vie* for a minute breaks out of its group. But *Une Femme Mariée* is all success.

April 1965

No time for exaggeration: on the contrary let us, while allowing enjoyment to be unconfined, keep our heads, remove our shoulders from the wheel, leave some stones unturned and neglect to pull up our socks. In short don't let's go overboard. I like the latest Jean-Luc Godard film, **Alphaville**. Some of it I like very much – but with reservations.

Alphaville has a sub-title: 'A Strange Adventure of Lemmy Caution'. Peter Cheyney's hero is a special pet of the French: the tough private eye of dozens of tough films in which, as here, he has been played by Eddie Constantine. Jean-Luc Godard, writing his own script, has put this rather seamy figure into a film which is half science-fiction and half salvation-hunt. Lemmy Caution arrives in Alphaville, capital of some remote star-system, with a mission: to find out what has happened to the other agents despatched from Earth, and to destroy the giant computer, Alpha 60, which controls the city and the lives of the local inhabitants but which has been created by an ex-terrestrial scientist, rather pointedly called von Braun.

No explanation about how Lemmy Caution reaches Alphaville, no space-travel stuff. He just drives up to his hotel. For this isn't an essay in material science-fiction: nobody with a triangular tin head. It is an essay in moral and emotional science-fiction: everybody with a tattooed number, built-in responses and no heart. Everybody who is allowed to live, that is. For those who feel, weep, mourn the dead or regret the disappearance of freedom there are public executions, much applauded. For less spectacular nonconformists – drinkers of alcohol rather than swallowers of the regulation tranquillizers – there is the resort of suicide in some shady hotel.

So far so good: the ideas not startlingly new (*Brave New World* had some of them thirty-four years ago), but there is excitement, there is enigma, there is the occasional shudder. You could say that *Alphaville* reverses the moral of *The Red Desert*. In Antonioni's film the heroine is lost because she can't adjust to the industrial, scientific world; and Antonioni says that one must adjust, that it really will be a brave new world. In Jean-Luc Godard's film the non-adjusters are right; they have resisted the mutation which dehumanizes men and women. But Godard goes farther. The individual in this world of non-individuals, he says, can find salvation through – guess what? through love. Painfully the heroine (beautiful Anna Karina) enunciates the phrase 'I-love-you'. And she is saved.

Now nobody, I hope, wants to denigrate individualism or deny the force of human emotions. What unsettles me in Godard's film is the tender of such a very old dramatic hat. In the heartless society of Fritz Lang's 'Metropolis' (and Lang is among the French cinema's favoured sources of quotation) what was the great reconciling power? Love. What, in Karel Capek's study of mechanical monsters, *RUR*, averted universal destruction? Love. Okay, like Dryden we are All for Love. But when we reach the saving syllables in *Alphaville* there is no new life in them. They awaken no echo.

The film is a treasury of author's marks. The name of Godard is stamped everywhere: in the violence, in the infatuation with the American thriller and strip-cartoon, in the literary references – and in the time spent hanging about waiting for an incident or an idea. Lemmy Caution – played by Mr Constantine with what I suppose is his accepted impassivity – savages an intruder into the hotel room; but he quotes Pascal. Interrogated by the computer, he is ready with intellectual answers; but when he finds one of the missing Earth-agents (memorably played by Akim Tamiroff) it is about another 'missing person', Dick Tracy, that he inquires. Homage to Eluard is mixed up with homage to Flash Gordon.

Maddening, sometimes, these exercises in the disconnected and the idiosyncratic. But here – and now I come to my liking for the film – there is a connecting brilliance of style. Godard has used as the setting for his science-fiction world the offices and boulevards of Paris. It is a Paris almost entirely of the night, a Paris which, with the help of Raoul Coutard's superb camerawork, threatens and glitters. Neon-light arrows point the way to nobody knows what; feet climb mysteriously up skeleton stairways; through plate-glass windows you see baleful traffic in the streets. Blurred and distorting and swivelling lights; strange transparencies; the reversal, sometimes, of the normal, as when the figures entering or leaving an Alphaville building are suddenly seen in negative, dark with white shadows – everything is alienated from the everyday. But not as a rule widely alienated. One surrenders to an experience which is the more disturbing for being so near the recognizable normal.

The background to the problem, in fact, is sharply alive; I find in it a constant delight. Only the solution falls dead.

March 1966

At a press conference in Venice last year a young Frenchman, almost genuflecting with reverence, asked Jean-Luc Godard when he thought the public would recognize his work; to which Monsieur Godard replied that he thought the public *had* recognized it. Fair enough. Wherever films are seriously talked about there is talk of Godard; whenever awards are given Godard gets one. It seems to me that with **Pierrot le Fou** he has reached a stage at which self-confidence and self-indulgence join hands to lead him into a disaster area.

In Karel Reisz's extraordinary film *Morgan, a Suitable Case for Treatment*, the tragi-comic central figure hides in madness from a world which is too much for him. In *Pierrot le Fou* the characters surrender deliberately to a cold lunacy, a denial of reason and purpose. The action is concerned with the flight from Paris to the Mediterranean coast of a young married man (Jean-Paul Belmondo) and a girl (Anna Karina) who is unmistakably giving him the old runaround. The pair, shadowed by some mysterious criminal organization but glacially unmoved by the corpses which spatter their path, pursue a ferocious course: stealing cars, wrecking cars, beating up garage hands; finally they join a gang war in which the man is cast for the part of poor Muggsie.

Put like that, the film sounds no worse than some atrocious American thriller (I intend no reflection on Lionel White's novel *Obsession*, on which it is based but which I haven't read). But then I have merely articulated the skeleton. There are all the inconsequences, all the pretentious conversations and repetitions to be taken into account: the references to Conrad and *Paul et Virginie*, the meaningless impersonations – (Belmondo offers

an amateurish one of Michel Simon and an unrecognizable one
of an American gangster star, possibly Bogart); the portentous
correlation of the festering society in which Velasquez painted
with the admass civilization from which the man and the girl
are presumably escaping – but which they themselves degrade.
The director (who is also the screenwriter) fills in the holes in
the narrative with anything handy: a bit of song-and-dance, a
deplorable scrap of savagery about Vietnam, a turn (in itself
brilliantly funny) by the comedian Raymond Devos. Nothing
is continuous, everything is splintered.

The rejection of logical form is of course calculated. That does
not save it from producing stupendous tedium. One might credit
Pierrot le Fou with a mood of despair were there not at the centre of
the dislocation two characters in themselves null and unworthy of
despair, interesting only by their setting of sunlight, trees and sea:
in fact by the magnificent colour photography of Raoul Coutard.

April 1966

Two negroes are talking in the train about Bessie Smith;
belligerently staring at the white boy opposite, one of them
insists that her singing is an expression of racial defiance. A
prostitute sitting at a restaurant table with a German taxes him
with the concentration camps and he bursts out in ineffectual
exasperation: too young to have been guilty, is he never to
hear the end of it? Outside an official building an American
car draws up; while one young Frenchman engages the driver in
talk another paints a slogan: US Go Home. A boy watches two
men kissing in a public lavatory; with contemptuous authority
one of them orders him off. A young woman discussing sexual
attraction insists that it is a question of skin; a boy tells the girl
he desires that he admires her 'style de poitrine'; she accuses him
of regarding himself as the centre of the world; he admits it.

Masculin-Feminin: unmistakably a Jean-Luc Godard film;
anybody else would feel impelled to make the narrative more
emphatic than the fragmentary encounters and not *vice-versa*.
Godard has used two stories by Guy de Maupassant as his
starting-point, but you might be excused for failing to notice that;
what you find is a series of scenes, conversations, monologues,
interviews which create the feeling of a life lived at a particular
moment. Certain characters appear and reappear, two of them

provide perhaps not a plot (Godard moves farther and farther away from the conventional story-film) but a beginning and an end, a meeting and, off-screen, a death. What is important is not the love-affair of the girl (Chantal Goya) and the boy (Jean-Pierre Léaud, the rebel-victim of *Les Quatre Cents Coups*) but the world they live in and their relation to it. One might go farther and say the subject is the relation of their whole generation to the world.

'Children of Marx and Coca-Cola', Godard calls them in one of the titles which, like chapter-headings or sometimes slogans, he uses for emphasis, for clarification or just for pleasure. The girls are the Coca-Cola children; they have scarcely heard of Vietnam, but the name of Sandy Shaw is familiar to them; and they all talk about the Pill. The boys, on the other hand, though persistently concerned with sex are deeply involved in the political struggle; the chief figure among them, you feel, resents his distracting dependence on the girl with whom he has fallen in love. One can't, he says, live without tenderness. But tenderness evades him; and everywhere he sees violence; the most casual encounter in the street is the prelude to a terrible, politically-protesting suicide.

Godard, then, presents a world of fragments, questions without answers; the boys ask the universal questions, the girls, preoccupied with the frivolous and the personal, are uninterested. When one emerges from the cinema the argument turns transparent. But during one's experience of it the film is mesmerizing. Godard's mastery of the medium makes the most unlikely passages interesting, and one is carried unresisting through a recording of a pop song or a documentary inteview shot by a stationary camera; the succession of disparate scenes – a parody of a sex-film, a poem, a wrangle about CinemaScope projection, a minimal sexual invitation from a girl who postulates 'No hands!' – creates a world which for the moment is completely persuasive.

Yet in spite of the emphasis on sexual problems this is an a-sexual film. The boy desires, wins, feels jealous – but you suspect that he and the rest of the group are playing at sex; sexual passion is a pretty rare element anywhere in the Godard cinema. Come to that, passion of any sort is pretty rare; there is gaiety or the sense of danger, but not passion. The rejection of traditional narrative forms, of course, helps to shut the spectator off from emotional involvement; Godard, after all, belongs to the Brechtian age. No doubt we shall all learn to live without involvement. All the same I can't help remembering gratefully that even so notable a forerunner of the detachment method as *Candide* allowed one to care what happened to its hero.

June 1967

Bourgeois to the bone, a young couple set off to drive from Paris to the home of the wife's parents. We know that they are bourgeois because they are so nasty and have an open sports car; though to be honest their conversation on intimate matters (the girl offers some instructive details about triangular goings-on) is scarcely what one would expect from the burghers of, say, Cheam. Each is planning to ditch the other; but first they must get their hooks on the money which the wife's father, whom they have been optimistically poisoning, is expected to leave.

Their departure is marked by a fracas with a parked car; blows and shots are exchanged. Once outside the capital the pair join a traffic jam whose other inhabitants are whiling away the time with chess and ball-games – or rather, they don't join it, they pull out into the unoccupied lane and, hooting, drive indifferently past the smashed cars and the mangled bodies which litter the verges. Further encounters are conducted on a lethal level; blood stains the highways; the trip leads to a family murder. I must not spoil the happy atmosphere by going into narrative details, but it would be difficult to convey the flavour of the expedition without remarking that in the end the characters, those who have survived the warfare of modern transport, take to cannibalism. Swift's 'Modest Proposal' is extended and put into practice in a big way; everybody is cooking and eating somebody else.

Well, there is Jean-Luc Godard's **Week-End** for you. It is in colour, but not, though red comes in handy for the human butchery scenes, colour of a savagery to match the satire; in fact the light and the landscape, elegantly muted, by their moderation accentuate the ferocity of the action (the cameraman is Raoul Coutard). The leading parts are played by Mireille Darc and Jean Yanne. Jean-Pierre Léaud appears for a moment or two as a man in a telephone box singing his message into the instrument; it is one of the fragments, jokey, irrelevant, arbitrary, which Godard likes to cut in, possibly because the material is to hand and he likes using it.

And Godard himself: *Week-End* could not be the work of any

other writer or writer-director. The fantasy of violence: once or twice its extravagance made me think of Genet, but though sexual implications are present nearly all through they aren't, as they are in Genet, the main story. And of course the chapter headings or rubrics or whatever you like to call them – the sudden flashing on the screen of Eisenstein-like titles bawling 'Analysis' or 'The Exterminating Angel' or 'The Class War' – they are the Godard signature. Years ago, in *Vivre sa Vie*, they had a narrative point; by now they have degenerated into a self-indulgent flourish.

But then increasingly Godard's work interrupts itself: a character in vaguely Napoleonic costume stands reciting in a field; a Negro delivers a monologue about the inefficiency of non-violence, then stolidly listens to the harangue of his Algerian companion, while the travelling couple, by now left with neither car nor money, beg a bite of sandwich. True that *Week-End* has cohesion of a kind, though it is the cohesion of something which threatens to tear, which finally does tear. At the start the film is even funny: the violence propagated by that dangerous toy the motor-car is funny; the exasperated reactions of the human creature to impediment and delay are funny; the nervous tension itself is funny. But the violence grows steadily more monstrous. At last, in this political parable, it becomes uncontrollable. Society breaks apart.

Five years ago Godard directed a parable of war, *Les Carabiniers*, in which the combatants, pausing from their executions and their joyless essays in rape, wrote drearily home about their prowess in massacre. That was the depressive half of his cinema; *Week-End* is the manic half. He is appalled by war, by the savagery in a society which nurtures war. Of course: we are all, even while we are engaged in bashing one another about, appalled. But he is also, or so this film suggests, fascinated by violence. There is a scene – it accompanies the triumph of cannibalism – in which a pig has its throat slit and a goose, decapitated, is left flapping. I think it unlikely that these exercises were carried out simply with the practical intention of providing a square meal for the cast. I think also that horror at violence can be roused without resort to actual violence; that the essence of a work of art is the successful translation of physical reality; and that here Godard has neither attempted nor wished to attempt that translation. In short I distrust the pacifism of people who make their protests by violence.

By the end, in fact, I find *Week-End* a pretty unpardonable film.

July 1968

In an unguarded moment last week I went to a Godard film I had seen before.

No, let me correct that. The moment was not unguarded simply in sending me to a familiar Godard film. I should be perfectly happy to see *Le Mépris* again, or one of the earlies, *Vivre sa Vie*, for instance. A dogged curiosity about other people's tastes (always, as I am sure you'll agree, unaccountable) made me watch *Pierrot le Fou* three times. I might even sit through *Week-End* again; it is repulsive but it is brilliant. But remember Groucho Marx. 'They say,' he remarks somewhere, 'I never forget a face, but I'll make an exception of yours.' My trouble was that I had made an exception of **Two or Three Things I Know About Her**. I felt I had seen it, but I couldn't recall a thing about it.

Before I once more erase the film from my mind I might as well share with you the fragments which I still retain.

There is a scene in which a little boy is relating a dream to his mother. I dreamed, he says, I was on the edge of a cliff with a path wide enough for only one person when I saw two twins ahead of me. I couldn't think how they would manage to pass one another, but when they met they merged and became one – and I knew they were North and South Vietnam. Come off it, Little Mao Fauntleroy, one thinks; and personally I am not mollified when I read in Richard Roud's book on Godard that after being refused a permit to enter North Vietnam the director resolved to mention the war in all his future works. All right, *Two or Three Things I Know About Her* is a political film. But it isn't that sort of political film; the reference, totally out of place, merely illustrates a complacency in Godard, a conviction that his admirers will swallow any old thing.

For the piece at the Paris Pullman is about domestic, not international politics. It was made in 1966, before *La Chinoise* and *Le Gai Savoir*, both of which in its method of proceeding by flat statements or discussions it resembles. It has, however, a central character, or at any rate a central figure (Paris itself is the true subject), a kind of window-dresser's model who can be done up in social theories.

Juliet (Marina Vlady) is a housewife living on the outskirts of the capital with a husband who has a modest job and is happy with it – a state of mind which Godard appears to deplore; the film deals with one day in her life. The background is the new city – cranes at work, featureless new blocks – which as in all great capitals today is replacing the old place; a Paris of advertisements, lures to spend money on luxuries, to keep up with a materialistic society. And following what Godard has said is a common practice among wives in the new suburban districts, Juliette goes out for the day, leaves her little girl with a baby-minder and by prostituting herself picks up a little extra money for a new dress. Early in the film there is a direct attack on the Gaullist régime. But really *Two or Three Things I Know About Her* expresses a general disapproval of capitalist urban life – disapproval without suggestions for reform. It would be interesting to know whether Godard thinks his symbolic housewife ought to renounce the luxury of seeing Godard films, or at any rate to avert her eyes from their advertisements.

In describing one tries to clarify, to make connections. Probably I have given the impression of a film with a plot and an easy sequence. On the contrary, on the screen you are offered a collection of comments and pretensious semi-philosophic musings; it has the dislocation, the inconsequence, which in writing one fights to overcome. If it were an imaginative work one would gladly accept dislocation. But here Godard rejects imagination. The creative element persists in the beautiful coloured images which the cameraman, Raoul Coutard, has drawn from the urban spectacle of street and traffic and building site. The film itself is a bit of pontifical journalism, a column and a half, interviews and all, about housing estates, the cost of living and the decay of family life. It is 'Panorama' on an off evening.

November 1970

Films about musicians come in three styles. There is good old Hollywood, in which Beethoven, let us say, after a lover's quarrel goes for a country walk, gets soaked in a thunderstorm, comes home and writes the Pastoral Symphony. There is the method adopted by Jean-Marie Straub, who in *The Chronicle of Anna Magdalena Bach* induced a number of people in wigs just to sit down and perform the music. Perhaps since **The Music Lovers** is produced and directed by Ken Russell one should not be startled to find that a third method has been employed. He has taken off into fantasy.

Generally described as Ken Russell's film of Tchaikovsky, the piece has a screenplay based by Melvyn Bragg on a book, *Beloved Friend*, by Catherine Drinker Bower and Barbara von Meck. This, I learn (I have failed to get hold of it), contains extracts from the letters between the composer and Madame von Meck, the rich widow who during nearly fourteen years gave him an annuity, wrote to him in tones of passionate though spiritual devotion, and never, the records say, set eyes on him except at a distance. Mr Russell's film pursues Tchaikovsky through intimations of homosexuality, disastrous marriage – 'marriage of a homosexual to a nymphomaniac', Gerald Abraham calls it in his biography – to Antonina Milyukova (Glenda Jackson, rather under the weather, or possibly the role), and the bizarre, suddenly interrupted relationship with Madame von Meck (Izabella Telezynska, an agreeably aristocratic figure).

There is a good deal of music, rather loud, including of course some of the B flat minor Piano Concerto, which to my surprise I found presented rather as if it had been a beginner's work. And there are passages where one recognizes even more clearly that Mr Russell is letting himself go. Ready though I always am to surrender to the image on the screen, I did feel it unlikely that the composer had conducted the 1812 Overture while standing on one of the Kremlin domes. Again, I wondered whether his wife, during return from honeymoon in St Petersburg, had really stripped herself stark naked, very stark, and swung orang-utan-fashion to the motion of the sleeping compartment.

But there, one never knows; and remembering the trouble I have sometimes got into with erudite readers I had a shot at checking a few facts – with the result that the element of fantasy seemed even more pervasive than I had at first suspected.

Frankly, once I have recognized that the barrier between fact (and there is quite a lot of fact) and fiction or fancy has been deliberately abolished I don't mind. With Mr Russell's version of D. H. Lawrence's *Women in Love* I was bitterly conscious of caricature in the figure of Hermione, who is based on someone I knew well, Ottoline Morrell. In *The Music Lovers*, on the other hand, I am not really put out when Madame von Meck creeps into a room where Tchaikovsky is sleeping and platonically stretches out beside him. I don't boggle over the suggestion that she not only cut off his annuity (a fact) but on learning of his homosexual tendencies locked him, without warning, out of her country house and set the fields round the joint on fire. I admit, though, to a certain idle curiosity about his death from cholera. Did they, I mean, in an attempt at cure actually *boil* him?

But these are people I don't know, and I can sit back unconcernedly and enjoy the elegances, the extravagances, sometimes the splendours – the lyrical passages of slow motion in the forest, the suggestion of ballet when the child dances out-of-doors, the beautiful use of white dresses against leaves and branches; I can even admire, though perhaps not enjoy, the savage fantasy of the lunatic asylum where the wife ends. I can appreciate the Byronic fervour, not I fancy particularly true to its original, in Richard Chamberlain's playing as Tchaikovsky. Mr Russell, after all, is entitled to give his own interpretation of a famous figure and to express it in his own flamboyant terms; he is entitled to write his own fantasia on a theme. As long, that is, as the audience is warned; one really has to know what one is in for. Well, you have been warned.

March 1971

There are plenty of directors who have no talent and make unbearable films, there are a few who have great talent and for that very reason make unbearable films. Ken Russell is one of the few.

Don't get me wrong. I am not saying that **The Boy Friend** is all unbearable. Some of it – but let's leave that for a moment. To begin with it has Twiggy and Twiggy not only has a grace which is more than physical. Her appearance as the heroine has an air of genuine innocence quite different from the professional innocence which one remembers from performers on the stage. I say her appearance rather than her acting; as a player she needs a great deal more of the professionalism which stands the stage performer in permanent stead. Her acting looks agreeable but amateurish; only when she sings and dances do the earnest face with the big round eyes and the Modigliani stick-insect figure make their effect. She is no Ginger Rogers. Any one of the other four girls in the story, in particular Antonia Ellis as the pushing Maisie, has better technique (so of course has the elongated tap-dancer Tommy Tune). But Twiggy is the one who enchants.

So far, then, one up for Mr Russell (and hooray for Glenda Jackson's unheralded appearance); but now to say what he has done with the rest of the play on which he has based his film. Sandy Wilson's work was part pastiche, part affectionate joking about the stage musical comedy of the 1920s. It was tongue-in-cheek; it was pretty; it had songs which can still give pleasure. Mr Russell has made *The Boy Friend* what the cinema used to call colossal. Ostensibly the story of the heiress at the French finishing school who falls in love with an errand boy (Christopher Gable) is still set in the twenties. But the director by giving it a double framework, presenting it first as a brutally guyed provincial rendering of the play, then as the vision of a film tycoon whose imagination transforms the tattered performance into a glittering spectacle, shifts the show into the thirties. And he achieves a double aim. He erases his original. And in its place he puts the enormous ghost of a Hollywood musical with borrowed songs and with dancers, prostrate as they wave arms and legs, offering a hawk's-eye view of the changing patterns of a glass paperweight. A Busby Berkeley musical in fact.

I won't say there wasn't the germ of a good idea in the double vision of the play. It is even possible that Mr Russell may revive the decaying fortunes of the screen musical (perhaps I ought to say the mammoth musical). What I find unbearable, for now I must get back to my beginning, is that his talent should be so destructive. His touring company becomes a collection of vulgar caricatures. What was indulgent becomes grotesque; directed in exaggeration, the players themselves are destroyed. Aware that the spectator watching from a box is a power in Hollywood, the cast up-stage their partners and play to him alone; some of the best songs are ruined by farcical business. And Busby Berkeley is out-Berkeleyed. Once or twice, for instance in a dreadful pixie-Disney number, the intention is (at least I hope it is) to ridicule. But usually the result is not satire but satiety. Early in the film the school chums, pouting and ogling, overpowering in close-up, seemed to push their faces so near to mine that I almost shrank out of the cinema.

The talent is there all right. But somehow it is an appalling talent.

February 1972

Useless, I find, to resist. One battles with the joke, one suffocates under the weight of its vulgarity. But vulgarity so self-confident, so unrepentant wins a kind of horrified respect. I need hardly say that I am speaking of Ken Russell, and in particular of a passage in his latest study of a composer, *Mahler*.

A hallucination, perhaps, rather than a study; one mustn't take the whole of Mr Russell's interpretation of Mahler's life literally. And here and there in the film you find superb passages; they could be achieved by only an exceptional talent. Consider the imagery of the first ten minutes or so: the quiet lakeside cabin which for no immediately comprehensible reason blazes into a furnace; the stone head in the wilderness and the white-shrouded recumbent figure, a human chrysalis struggling to free itself from its web – no mediocre creator could bring that off so triumphantly, and for a moment I had a start not of respect but of delighted admiration.

The delight cannot last, though it recurs; the splendour of the opening is succeeded by comparatively routine biographical scenes – and by scenes in which the well-known Russell self-indulgence streaks in. The narrative is enclosed in the framework of a train journey. Mahler (played with a fine mixture of austerity, irony and cold rage by Robert Powell) after a season in New York is travelling back to Vienna with his wife (Georgina Hale, in a performance of considerable range). He dreams of his childhood, his family, his friends, his work, his fears; his music crashes about – I was going to say in the background, but really it is in the foreground; Ken Russell is genuinely passionate about music. This is the moment to say that I shall not try to judge the film's handling of the facts of the composer's life and character. One could do a little mugging up, but the result would be beside the point; the director (who is also the screenwriter) is concerned not with facts but, as he puts it himself, with 'some of the things' he feels when he thinks of Mahler's life and listens to Mahler's work.

The knowledgeable may well be infuriated by the visions and the fantasies and by the way they are made to relate to the music; and it is true that the extravagances are frequently a bit off. Nevertheless I am bound to say that, vulgarity and all, the fantasies it is which offer the most satisfying parts of the film. The re-creation of the childhood – the blunt-edged Jewish family, the brutal father, the lonely boy (Gary Rich in a persuasive sketch) – I find of no more than remote interest, though I suppose it does something to explain the obsessions of the adult life. The treatment of the early days of marriage, again, belongs to the convention of composers' biographies, though the young wife's efforts to muffle disturbing rural sounds stray into fancy, and arch, jokey fancy at that; the most devoted of partners would be unlikely to scuttle off, skipping in D. W. Griffith style, to remove cowbells from their wearers and scare off the songbirds. Such cheerful comedy, however, is rare in the film – though one appreciates an impudent reference to Visconti's *Death in Venice*. One must be ready to brace oneself for the sick joke to end all sick jokes.

As a Jew Mahler feels that he is handicapped in his career. Cosima Wagner, scarcely a pro-Semite, is a power in the world of music; and Mahler decides on conversion to Catholicism. A long phantasmagorical passage shows the composer faced with a Cosima, done up as a female Storm-Trooper in Nazi helmet and Nazi boots, who struts in front of a crucifix on a mountain-top and orders the shrinking candidate to jump through flaming hoops, eat pig's flesh and perform a variety of other distasteful or humiliating tasks. Presumably it is a caricature of the obstacles which face a prospective convert; and no doubt a good many people will find it offensive. Looking back, I find I can't help, as I said earlier, respecting Mr Russell's nerve. All the same one prefers to remember less thumb-biting passages. Sometimes the imagery is painful: devoured by jealousy, Mahler dreams of cremation, a living death, and a glass-fronted coffin in which he soundlessly screams as his wife dances lasciviously overhead. Sometimes, on the other hand, a mood is conveyed with extraordinary delicacy. At an applauding reception for the composer a figure in black, black-veiled, top-hatted like a mute at a funeral, follows in the crowd; it is the wife who, her own musical ambitions stifled by the successes of her husband, complains that she is his shadow.

But there is no pinning down the qualities of Ken Russell. Ultimately one is driven to say that he stands on his own, a mixture, at once frightening and preposterous, of Benjamin Robert Haydon, Hieronymus Bosch and the propaganda-poster artists of the Third Reich.

April 1974

5 *Robert Altman*

Robert Altman has never been among my idols, and perhaps even now I should have reservations. But certainly **Nashville** has brought me round.

Since this long film – two hours and forty minutes – has no central cord of plot and no stars it is reasonable to begin by asking what it is about. It is about America: provincial America, local-capital America. To pare that down, it presents a country-music beano. Unlike the characters, who though many of them look identifiable are described as fictitious, the setting is real – Nashville, capital of Tennessee, where the piece was shot. We have seen films about the big American pop festivals, *Woodstock* for example. *Nashville* looks much truer than *Woodstock*, much more real; fiction has this advantage over fact, that it can eliminate the boring and emphasize the believable.

Altman's film strikes an English observer as the purest, possibly the simplest Americana, the kind of thing which it takes an American to know about, which nobody else can understand so well. And the American cinema has a genius for telling other people about America. The British have never had the same gift with their own scene, at least to us it doesn't look as if they had, whereas Americans can believe their own picture of their own country. One can see why *Nashville* has had an enormous success in the United States.

Not that the American scene is all there is to *Nashville*, far from it. There are the songs – all, I think, new, and many of them written by the performers themselves. They begin with an effective passage, full of old-fashioned American confidence, with one of the festival's visiting stars (played with cool conviction by Henry Ginson) recording 'We must be doing something right To last two hundred years'; they end with one of the would-be stars, a hanger-on, belting out 'They tell us we ain't free But that don't worry me.'

Again, when I say that *Nashville* has no stars I mean that there are no star-parts. Well-known names are there: Karen Black appears as one of the applauded singers. There are visiting non-performing celebrities, Elliott Gould, for instance, and Julie Christie. She's a big star, somebody explains; for Nashville can't be expected to know about a famous English actress, even if she did appear in Altman's *McCabe and Mrs Miller* (many of the lesser names in the cast, too, have worked with Altman before).

But well-known or not, every player is absorbed into the complex of society, nobody holds the screen for more than a few minutes. A black singer, a pop group, a gospel singer, they appear, they perform; sometimes behind the performance a fragment of life is discovered. A plane brings in a popular singer (the admirable Ronee Blakley): recovering from an accident, radiating love of her welcomers, she advances, faints, is for the time being out of the show, can't endure listening to her replacement. When she tries a comeback she misjudges her audience, breaks off her song to tell folksy anecdotes, is hurried off the stage. A girl (Gwen Welles) with ambition and no talent is induced to do a strip-tease. Amateurish though it may be, it is better than her voice; but she won't believe she hasn't a future as a singer.

The satire which occasionally creeps in at the expense of the successful turns is delicate. The singers believe in themselves, the audience believes in the singers; the tiny exaggerations never destroy the sense of reality. Behind the festivity and its shifts from small enclosed setting to huge open arena you watch from time to time a scene of personal emotions unconnected with the non-stop entertainment. A man (it is Keenan Wynn) learns that his wife is dead. A husband listens to his wife's telephone calls; the girl finishes teaching her deaf children – then hurries to an assignation with the caller. A woman in the audience complains about anti-Catholicism in Tennessee; she worked, she says, for Bobby Kennedy, she loved him. And in the background somebody is carrying on a political campaign; a car with a loud-speaker patrols the streets, a vast banner stretches behind the arena stage.

Non-communication, say the advertisements. *Nashville* is about many kinds of communication but the people don't communicate. I disagree. Once at any rate somebody communicates in the fashionable transatlantic way with a couple of bullets. From where I sit the single failure in communication is the role of the BBC girl, courageously played by Geraldine Chaplin with a refined English accent. Miss Chaplin is called on to guy the BBC. Engaged in preparing a documentary, she darts with her tape-recorder from star to star, leaving some humbler participant in mid-sentence; she asks naive and tactless questions, she rehearses idiotic high-flown commentaries. And I must say

I recognize the style of the commentaries; Mr Altman and his script-writer Joan Tewkesbury have something there. Otherwise I don't think the joke comes off; the BBC doesn't, I fancy, despatch eager ignoramuses on that kind of assignment, and Miss Chaplin's performance, itself lively, seems false in relation to the sharp native intonations of the others.

But no doubt Americans will enjoy it. And I can see, of course, that the director needed some kind of agent to elicit information from some of the figures concerned. As for the rest, anyway, it communicates with me all right. The sound, the images have the veracity of life. Was it really two hours and forty minutes? It seemed to me rather a short film.

November 1975

Rather heartlessly, I feel, Robert Altman declines to give any guidance on the narrative, significance, even the nature of his new film **Quintet**. No help, then, from the synopsis, and the critics, struggling for an interpretation, are left to make fools of themselves.

Synopsis? I must blow the gaff. The recapitulation of the plot or the identification of the second assistant focus-puller which you find in reviews is not the result of superhuman attention or dexterity in note-taking. It is due to the synopsis, which lists cast and credits and tells the critic what the film was about. In these days of difficult movies the synopsis is indispensable – but Mr Altman, making his enigmatic film – a fable? a parable? – about a lethal game and creeping dissolution will have none of it. He wants, he says, to give audiences 'the rare opportunity to see and experience a film without preconceived ideas or advance conditioning.'

That lets me out; don't expect any ideas from me. I might try, though, to give some indication of what Quintet looks like. It begins in a kind of nothingness: the screen pale, empty; gradually a foreground which might be swamp water, still, with fringes of land, but which turns out to be snow: everywhere snow. Presently two figures, muffled against the cold, advance from the far distance, a man and a woman who mildly rather than meekly follows him; and as we turn to look with their eyes we see, half-submerged in the snow (it is, by the way, real snow, Montreal snow) what looks like a elegantly decorated gasometer.

It is the city which the two figures are seeking; it houses a remnant of humanity (Bibi Andersson, Nina van Pallandt, David Langton) obsessed with the game of quintet. 'Games,' Altman says – this much he vouchsafes – 'always fascinated me. They are reflections of their cultures.' And this is a game where the players who lose will sooner or later meet a violent death. In the meantime they have alcohol – and little else. They live in fear and suspicion. The city is a labyrinth of wreckage, debris of some catastrophe. Nobody buries the dead; dogs, small bands of black dogs, eat the corpses. And even this half-life won't last: everybody knows that. Apocalypse tomorrow.

One might suppose that the Kafkaesque atmosphere – the unidentified period and place, the unexplained violences which punctuate the passage of time – would fail to hold the attention. On the contrary. One is snared by uncertainty; one asks questions. Why is the northward flight of the goose, bright-hued against the colourless sky, hailed as so startling? Why is the apostle of doom (Vittorio Gassman) called St Christopher? Unless, of course, in view of his fate, it is to suggest that the guardian of travellers can no longer guard. Ominous sounds as of cracking ice encompass the city. Nevertheless there is a hint of hope. That north-bound goose was a good augury. The traveller (Paul Newman) in a society which lives on chance and the anticipation of extinction still refuses to accept the gloomy prediction of the adjudicator of the games (Fernando Rey). 'You may know,' he says; 'I don't.'

A parable, then, for our times: I would settle for that. I find it mysterious, exciting, tenacious. And once again you are reminded of the astonishing range of Altman's work. *M.A.S.H.* and *Images*, *Brewster McCloud* and *Three Women*, *Buffalo Bill and the Indians*, *Nashville* and *Quintet* – one never knows what this extraordinary director will do next. And thank heaven for that.

Punch, June 1979

D. H. Lawrence was given to saying that he was a failure as a man in a world of men. I am a failure as a critic in a world of critics. I don't get the point of Robert Altman's **Popeye**.

A world of critics: today everyone is a critic of the cinema. An acquaintance with medical affiliations was indulgent. He could, he said, (I hadn't asked him) sit and watch a Western in spite of the objections of members of his family. Anyway if somebody somewhere enjoys a film, well, that was enough, wasn't it? That, he said, was what he said. It is a precept which I must bear in mind the next time one of the descendants of *The Texas Chain Saw Massacre* shrieks into view. *Ordinary People?* Yes, he had queued to see *Ordinary People*; some spectators saw more in it than was there, didn't they? And we went through the current programmes in a spirit of similar forbearance.

A taxi-driver was less tolerant. It was a long drive and it gave him time to tell me why films which had seemed so good when first seen thirty or forty years ago were really so bad; they were badly acted. *Little Caesar*, now: Edward G. Robinson really had no gift for acting. With John Wayne (everybody has views on John Wayne) he took a more general line. Wayne of course couldn't act. But he played the kind of man, fearless, resourceful, we should all like to be: that was what made him a success. There was one film, however, which he thought wasn't bad. He had seen it, he thought, at that cinema on the South Bank: the film was called *The Grapes of Wrath*. Perhaps I shouldn't have interrupted with my own views on Ford's masterpiece. I gave him what I thought was a decent tip; but from the look on his face I knew he felt it wasn't enough for an assessment of the cinema covering the best part of half a century.

Nobody, however, was prepared to guide me on *Popeye*, and I am left to try to explain what goes on in the movie.

As of course you know, Popeye the Sailor was the hero of a cartoon series popular between the 1930s and the 1950s; it was the creation of Max Fleischer. Its central figure had a grumbling gravelly voice, a girl-friend named Olive Oyl, and by eating spinach was enabled to defeat the most formidable enemies. One recalls him with affection; he was, as Mr Altman has said, a folk-hero. Now Jules Feiffer, a screenwriter as well as a cartoonist, has taken the themes and characters of the Popeye cartoons and made a screenplay out of them, a script for a feature film. But the figures are played by living people: by Robin Williams as a Popeye engagingly armoured against slights; by Shelley Duvall as an Olive Oyl whose purposeful stride is belied by the indecision of feet pointing backwards and sideways; by Paul Smith as the villainous Bluto, Ray Walston as the Commodore and Paul Dooley as the hamburger-eater.

The movie opens with a storm. Popeye, who is searching for his lost Pappy, appears rowing in a realistic boat over a realistic sea. But he lands in a Disney-type sea-port, an extravaganza, all whimsy architecture and tipsy stairways. The people, too, are inhospitable, and new arrivals are heavily taxed. Olive Oyl is engaged to Bluto but takes off from the engagement party; on the point of returning she mysteriously becomes the possessor of a baby (a charmer); and little by little some kind of narrative takes irregular shape.

Popeye finds a Pappy who declares that as a child his son wouldn't eat his spinach; the baby is kidnapped; Olive is trapped in a detached nautical ventilator; there is hidden treasure, there is an octopus. The plot, thickening, achieves a Feiffer consistency, and for a few moments the uneasy union between human beings and fantasy settings solidifies. The final adventure, all shipwreck and screaming captives, succeeds because there is action, a chase, a rescue (also because Miss Duvall gives so heartrending a performance of a black-backed gull in a pulpit).

I still don't see that to reach these modest results it was necessary to employ the magisterial talents of the distinguished Robert Altman.

Punch, April 1981

4   THE FRENCH

When Dilys Powell began writing about the cinema in 1939 it was the work of the French directors of that period, Jean Renoir, René Clair and Jean Vigo in particular who provided her with a touchstone against which the best cinema should be judged. She admired the 'Frenchness' of French cinema, that it expressed the essence of national character with grace and wit and irony. Powell's enthusiasm for a certain kind of French cinema never deserts her. She may dislike the work of more radical spirits working under the catch-all category of the *nouvelle vague*, most notably Godard, but the qualities she likes in films by Truffaut, Chabrol and Rohmer are the very virtues which shone through the work of an earlier generation of French directors, Becker and Autant-Lara for example, dismissed by the Truffaut/Godard generation as academic film-makers. Leaving the cinema after a first viewing of *La Nuit Americaine*, Powell writes, 'It has been a pleasure; one is sorry that it is over and I . . . come out feeling positively good-tempered.' The implication is clear – Powell has spent a morning or an afternoon with an old friend. The talk has been intelligent, conversational, and from life; no baffling theories, no clash of ideologies, civilized and liberal.

Those who regard the cinema as nothing more than a cheap drug are apt to parry the claim that it can be also an art with the question: Where, then, are its artists? A few people in London last Sunday were privileged in seeing work by one of the truly creative artists of the screen, Jean Vigo's *L'Atalante*. Privileged, because the film has not been seen since its presentation over seven years ago by the Film Society.

L'Atalante is the product of an imagination truly cinematic in that it creates exclusively through the moving pictorial image. The film was made in 1933, and is therefore not silent; I must admit that its French dialogue, largely no doubt through my own fault, a little perhaps through the age of the copy, was almost unintelligible to me. But the lovely rhythm and flow of the narrative were perfectly intelligible. The story is, reduced to its bare bones, simple enough: a provincial girl marries a barge-hand, longs to see Paris, is prevented when within reach, runs away, is stranded, at long last is found again and brought back to the barge and her distracted husband.

On the realistic plane the film makes ravishing use of the strange, deliberate, isolated life to which it introduces us: the barge moving slowly down canals and rivers, nosing through fogs, hauled past locks, under the spans of great bridges, the crew stopping only for a night's roistering ashore, then returning to their own enclosed existence.

But the singular talent – for once I think I may say genius – of the film lies in its translation into visual images of the mysterious and terrible and piteous undertones of even the simplest human life. And when I say visual images I do not mean that Vigo went outside the realistic for illustration; the poetry of this interpretation of life is conveyed without any recourse to extravagant symbolism. The uncouth skipper of the barge shows the girl the treasures of his cabin: an elephant's tusk here, a musical toy there, a jar with human hands monstrously preserved, a mask, a crude picture, the inevitable nude tattooed on his own back – and all at once the audience becomes aware of a life acquisitive, romantic, touching, shut in with its own dream. The husband takes his wife to a rough dancing dive on the canal bank, and a hawker pursues her with the conjuring tricks of his trade, with cajoling, flattery, with waving of silk kerchiefs and chatter of the great city; and behind the odd fantasy of the scene there looms the vast fantasy of temptation and the glittering mirage of desire. The wife, truant, finds her purse snatched by a pickpocket, and there is the terror of cruelty and loss; the husband, deserted, runs madly towards the emptiness of the sands at low tide, and there is the inhumanity of nature in face of human misery. And everywhere the sad poetry of the river, the canal, the anchorage, the port, with the smoke of railway sidings, the tracery of bridges and cranes, the coldness and strangeness of unknown faces. There has come no artist in the cinema to fill the blank left when Vigo died.

February 1943

It is not without interest that Hollywood, whenever it wants to show a young couple having a romantic outing, sends them into a European restaurant in a basement in the foreign quarter. 'I know,' one of them says, 'a little place where they cook spaghetti with meat balls that's out of this world'; or 'Remember Papa Funiculi's onion soup?' 'And the old guy playing the violin?' rejoins the other; and in no time at all there they are sitting at a check tablecloth with two orders of meat balls and 'Together' on an itinerant fiddle.

Possibly this indicates a suspicion that the American way of life hasn't got everything. Or possibly it indicates a desire to avoid yet another of the home cookery sequences which are the curse of the American cinema. I once vowed that I would never again sit through another film in which the little woman puts on a sprigged apron and does the washing up. Since then professional necessity has overtaken me, and I must in the past twelve years have witnessed some hundreds of ghastly domestic scenes: the old rooster cooked to a cinder, the hired help, the midnight raid on the refrigerator, the manly visitor in a frilled bib taking the woman's place at the sink. Not until last week had I seen a film about the domestic relations of two young married people which I wanted to see again.

But now along comes Jacques Becker's *Edward and Caroline* and alters everything. Becker is one of the most gifted directors to work in France since the war; I remember that when at the end of 1944 a Quinzaine du Cinéma Français was organized in a Paris only just liberated, I came away thinking there were at any rate two remarkable new talents to be watched: Robert Bresson was one, Becker was the other. Not a single film by Bresson has been publicly shown in this country, though his latest work, a version of *Journal d'un Curé de Campagne*, is nothing less than a masterpiece. Becker has been better served; at any rate London has seen *Goupi Mains Rouges* and *Antoine et Antoinette*, though I do not think either had the success here it merited. Sometimes the very fact that he is so gifted has caused disappointment. *Rendez-Vous de Juillet*, for instance, a study of the intellectually adventurous young in the Paris of today, had an extraordinary feeling of vitality and high spirits; but because it was Becker's film one expected more, one expected dramatic shape and concentration.

Edward and Caroline has everything that a film by Becker ought to have; and yet it is about one of the domestic uproars which the American cinema makes so nauseating.

In *Edward and Caroline* the trouble begins with a white waistcoat. Edward is a young pianist who is to play for influential guests at a snob soirée; Caroline, his wife and niece of the host, is a born waistcoat-mislayer. She is also a last-minute dress-remodeller; the cloud over the waistcoat is followed by a storm over a shortened skirt; as always on such occasions, calamity calls to calamity, private quarrels become public, everybody feels an irredeemable fool.

Nothing happens which has not in some degree happened to everybody who has ever been young and married. But while the Hollywood film about the advertising man and his wife who ask the important client to dinner merely makes you feel you might as well have stayed at home and quarrelled with your own nearest, *Edward and Caroline* lifts its weighty trivialities into a world of enchantment.

Becker, who collaborated on the script with Annette Wademant, has given individual life to every figure in the comedy, from the waiter who arrives by the wrong door to the speechless soldier on leave who comes at an awkward moment to hear the musician. He has directed his players with delicate understanding; but then of course he has players worth directing: Daniel Gélin, probably the most interesting young French film actor since the war; Anne Vernon, all pretty caprice; and I must single out from a heart-warming cast Jean Galland as the uncle – an illuminating, flawlessly observed portrait of the career host, a creature of tiny nervous gestures, self-conscious composure and well-ordered gaiety.

September 1957

Four months ago I saw in Paris a film called **Casque d'Or**. I saw it almost by chance, for nobody had mentioned its title in my hearing. As a matter of fact I had been trying to see quite another piece, but, the hours of showing proving inconvenient, I walked across the street and, drawn by the name of the director, Jacques Becker, into *Casque d'Or*.

The film was partway through and I tried to avert my eyes until the beginning should come round again. But the old fascination of the lighted rectangle at the end of the darkened hall was too strong. I looked, and, once I had looked, to turn away was like turning from a room full of canvases by Degas, Renoir and Lautrec. I watched to the finish, waited through the short oddments which in a French cinema mercifully replace our second feature, and saw the film from romantic, dangerous beginning to tragic end – in astonished delight, for here is the cinema making a double challenge: by the composition of its story to literature, by the composition of its images to painting.

Casque d'Or has made its way to London with unusual speed; it is now to be seen, under the title **Golden Marie**, at the Academy. The censor has made one barely perceptible cut and given an X certificate, so that we can congratulate ourselves on seeing it not only soon but almost untouched. After looking at it once more I find no reason to change what I wrote in these columns in May: that it is among the best films I have seen in ten years. Its story, by Jacques Companeez and Becker himself, who has scripted and edited as well as directing, is simple: a young carpenter in the nineties falls in with a gang of Paris toughs, is spellbound by one of their girls, kills her bully and finds brief idyllic happiness with her before he is trapped into confessing his crime by the leader of the gang and takes and expiates his revenge. But it is related with a command and a tragic irony which recall Maupassant; every situation tells, and when you think afterwards of the architecture of the tale you feel that it could have been shaped no other way.

Rightly, style and story seem inseparable. But though passages of narrative recur to me, though when I remember the film I at once remember the fight behind the café, the escape from the prison van and the terrible guillotining, the general impression I retain is of a screen alive with sensuousness and luminous figures: two girls in their petticoats laughing in a bedroom, a woman with her hair down leaning out of a window, a pair of prostitutes, all feather boas and flounces, sailing insolently into a room full of dancers. Perhaps the contrast between this confident flesh and the overtaking tragedy it is which gives the tale its especial mood of grief. The brutality of underworld society is allowed to speak for itself. But the brutality and the coarseness are irradiated by tenderness. Casque d'Or herself, the girl with the helmet of golden hair, softens after her first casual summons to the stranger, and at the core of the film is her transformation as she realizes that she has destroyed the man with whom she is in love.

Robert Le Febvre's camerawork and D'Eaubonne's sets play a notable part in the creation of the background of life. But Becker never loses the balance between background and foreground or the proper focus of his picture. His principal actors hold the screen with perfect judgment: Serge Reggiani's laconic, watchful workman, Claude Dauphin's cold, pitiless, treacherous gang-leader, above all Simone Signoret's radiant peony of a girl. Simone Signoret, unlike some of our popular blood-heaters, does not find it necessary to simulate epilepsy in order to appear desirable. *Casque d'Or* recreates for us the sense and image of passion. It seems to me to have the qualities which make a classic.

September 1952

At Cannes last April, after a showing of **Le Salaire de la Peur**, enthusiasm reached a pitch unknown to the cinema outside film festivals, and in the foyer Cocteau with princely abandon embraced the director, H. G. Clouzot. Under the title **The Wages of Fear** the film has now come to London, where it is the first to be shown at the redecorated Academy Cinema; and after seeing it for the second time I am better able to sympathize with the excitement of French audiences.

Not that I was ever in any doubt of the quality of its direction; anyone with the faintest feeling for the cinema must recognize how magnificently Clouzot has used players and backgrounds to create the sense of danger. For that is what the main body of the story is about: living with fear. Based on Georges Arnaud's novel, the film describes a purgatorial drive on behalf of an American oil firm, three hundred miles over primitive Central American roads with lorries loaded with nitro-glycerine, which if jolted is almost certain to blow lorries and drivers to dust.

Put baldly like that, the theme, apart from its anti-American implications, might be the stuff of an American risk-film, all hairbreadth escapes and heroism. And indeed the hairbreadth escapes are here: the stretch of rutted road where the only way to avoid vibration is to drive at high speed, the fallen boulder which must be blasted away and the shower of rocks which may strike the cans of explosive, the fraying wooden staging on to which the lorries must back at the hairpin bend. But the American risk-film is also a success-film – a little sacrifice, a lot of triumph, with weakness redeemed and moral values winning the day. In *The Wages of Fear* there is no sacrifice, unless driving over a screaming man in a morass of oil to avoid bogging the wheels can be called sacrifice. In the long run there is no triumph either.

What I had failed to appreciate at Cannes was the part the interplay of character had in the film. The new arrival, experienced, brutal, among the down-and-outs at the squalid settlement; the callous younger tough who, impressed, brushes off former friends to follow him – the characters are not subtle, and to establish them the preliminaries – a little shortened, I believe, since the first showing last spring, but still long – before the suicidal drive begins are excessive (though the detail of stagnation in these early scenes is ferociously efficient). But Clouzot, who has written his own screenplay, by filling in the sketchy figures of Georges Arnaud's book, has given fear something to work on. When the co-driver of the first lorry panics, it is the crumbling of an arrogant man that we see, and the effect on his companions adds solidity to the plot. I think it is fair to say that the weaknesses of the film can be found in passages where the director has kept to his original, and that where he has elaborated (except in the handling of the last ironic tragedy) he has made, from the cinema's point of view, improvements.

In particular his elaboration of the nightmare drive is brilliantly successful. *The Wages of Fear* is indeed about men in danger. But one thinks of the danger more than of the men. Clouzot, who in his three earlier films, *Le Corbeau*, *Quai des Orfèvres* and *Manon*, showed a savagely pessimistic view of human nature, has gone further now. Men, he is saying, are contemptible, or if they are not altogether contemptible ill-luck laughs at them; the fanatical courage of three out of the four central figures is for nothing. His most telling touches – the blast of wind, for instance, which when a distant cargo explodes blows the tobacco from the hand of a driver rolling a cigarette – go into event, not character.

I have sometimes asked myself whether it was right to attack post-war French 'black' films, a group to which Clouzot's work belongs, when superficially at any rate their despair is in the tradition of France's great nineteenth-century novelists. The answer, I think, is clear in *The Wages of Fear*; the characters, unlike the people of Zola's world, have no size, and at the end one is left without pity for them and without terror of the forces which have overwhelmed them. One respects and admires the strength of Clouzot's style and the vigour of his imagination – an imagination, I may say, which by its creation of cruelties and horrors left a mark on critics usually impassive enough. And after that one simply doesn't care, and not all the fine acting of Yves Montand, Folco Lulli, Peter van Eyck and Charles Vanel, especially Charles Vanel, can make one care.

February 1954

In England, where a timorous male population finds it necessary to take shelter in clubs from its women, the idea of a love affair between a boy of sixteen and a girl of fifteen is naturally disturbing, and a story in which the boy gains his first sexual experience with a much older woman brings a blush to the manly cheek. All the same the film version of **Le Blé en Herbe** (now, after an appearance at the Edinburgh Festival, shown at the Rialto under the atrocious title of **Ripening Seed**) seems to me to have excited disproportionate embarrassment. Colette's novel, after all, was not written as a moral text-book.

Seven years ago Claude Autant-Lara as director and Jean Aurenche and Pierre Bost as script-writers made a brilliant version of Raymond Radiguet's novel, *Le Diable au Corps*. The same talents are responsible for the translation to the cinema of Colette's story. Once more the awkward interim of youth is miraculously described: the full-grown reveries and the half-grown horse-play, the desire to act as an adult while being still treated as a child, the sense of isolation between two ages.

There are passages of searching human observation: the change in the boy's bearing, at first tongue-tied and suppliant before the woman, then confident and demanding; the contrast, after the realization of love, between the girl's triumphant gaiety and the boy's glumness. But the story of fugitive days: the summer holiday by the sea, the young creatures growing up, the woman who recognizes when it is time to make an end of romance – all this is told with an elegance which smooths over the roughnesses of physical passion.

That physical passion is still conveyed is due chiefly to the playing of Edwige Feuillère; her face speaking as clearly as her beautiful voice, the actress in a few short scenes tells us all we need to be told about the woman who has commanded love and suddenly takes flight from the pain of being commanded by it. Pierre-Michel Beck, first seen in *Wild Boy*, gives a rather passive performance; the embarrassments of adolescence are inadequately communicated by pursing the lips. But the direction, the script and the camera carry him through; and Nicole Berger brings to the part of the young girl the sharpness of expression which he lacks. The film leaves behind it an extraordinarily touching sense of feelings altering, life growing. Only the French cinema, I think, has been completely successful in handling themes of this kind; *Le Blé en Herbe* can take its place beside *Le Diable au Corps* and *Partie de Campagne*.

September 1954

No messages, says René Clair, speaking of his own work; no violence and no messages; and looking back one understands perfectly what he means. This is not the cool artist standing aside from what goes on in the world. It is the fastidious artist-dissociating himself from the catch-penny stuff which passes for significant. The promise may not be the first reason why one's heart lifts at the prospect of a film by René Clair, and in particular **Porte des Lilas**. But it certainly helps.

Of course to remark that a film has no message does not mean that it is empty, that it has nothing to say. *Porte des Lilas* has plenty to say. What it says is about people: about their friendship, their loyalty or their ingratitude – or rather it speaks especially about one man, for already in using the word 'people' I imply a portentousness quite alien from the humane and intimate quality of this beautiful film. *Porte des Lilas* carries us back to a world which belongs peculiarly to René Clair: the humble district of Paris, the bistro on the corner, the shoppers and the vagrants, the poor artist, the undercurrent of lawlessness, and the police, a vaguely mistrusted but not vicious element. We believe in it. There are real people in it, people observed with an eye at once affectionate and satirical; there are real streets. But the whole complex of figures and background has been touched by fantasy. It is the creation of a man who takes pleasure in creation.

In this René Clair quarter has been set the story of a shiftless drunk, an amiable, idle drifter on the verges of a working society. Juju is useless: everybody tells him so and he knows it. He thinks only of himself: in his fuddled way he recognizes his own egoism by comparison with the modest generosities of his friend the artist. Suddenly opportunity, adventure and danger explode all together into his life. An armed murderer on the run takes refuge in the shanty of the artist, and frightens the two men into hiding him from the police. Now Juju has something to do. The poor shambling good-for-nothing takes command, insists, is cunning, resourceful, devoted. Sheltering the criminal becomes a purpose. And within the framework of a plot which at a careless glance might appear artificially conjured up, characters betray themselves, interact, develop: the artist injured by his friend's infatuation, Juju all the time more engrossed in serving his savage guest; and the murderer himself, like a caged animal but more treacherous, taking his hosts contemptuously for granted, growing reckless, planning to use some silly bewitched girl as a means to escape.

As one watches, and even more as one remembers, the subtlety of the construction of *Porte des Lilas* comes home. A comic theft, a nocturnal foray, a misunderstood caress – character emerges through the most skilful detail of incident, the most logical sequence; in the background, an ironic chorus, there is the persistent shrill crowd of street urchins, performing, as they mimic murder and escape and pursuit, a kind of ballet. Meanwhile the central figures move towards the crisis of their own affairs: the self-contained artist – a sympathetic performance by Georges Brassens (who wrote the music as well as singing the songs); the arrogant criminal of Henri Vidal; the romantic little dupe at the bistro (Dany Carrel); and Juju, played by Pierre Brasseur with a delicacy, a humorous warmth and a self-neglecting pathos which is the very heart of the story. His performance is one to laugh at, to feel for, to linger over long after the film is ended.

At the last, you may say, *Porte des Lilas* breaks René Clair's own rule; for all its comedy this is a film which admits violence. So it does; but it is a violence which results naturally from the conflict of motives, the reluctant violence of a man who has not seen where his own good nature was leading; it is not foreign to the spirit of René Clair. *Sous les Toits de Paris* also, you may remember, had its moment of violence. I find in *Porte des Lilas* the qualities of irony, tenderness and romantic melancholy which were present in the early film; this is a return to a manner which the artist had lately forsaken. But now the qualities go deeper. The picture the artist draws is more serious, more mature. But it is a picture of the same world.

November 1957

There comes, I imagine, in the experience of every cinema critic a moment when he says to himself: this film may not be made with much technical polish; it is not progressive; it won't be a landmark in the history of the cinema; but it gives me more pleasure than any film for the last five years. That is what I feel about **Jour de Fête**.

I made some reference to Jacques Tati's bucolic French comedy when it was shown at the Edinburgh Festival, but that was eight months ago, and I hope I shall be forgiven for repeating that the piece has the slightest of themes: the visit of a travelling fair to a sleepy village and the local postman's attempt to catch up with the new age of speed. I have searched the story in vain for what a revered pen has called a meaningful relation to the world. I can find in it no comment on social disintegration; it is not about democracy; it doesn't, as somebody at the Press show remarked dejectedly, make you think. It does something in my opinion far more difficult. Any fool can make you think; it takes talent to make you laugh.

I have now seen *Jour de Fête* three times, and each time I laughed afresh. The fact is that the jokes have been worked out to the last fraction of a second; the gags double back on themselves; at a second look you see some quirk which escaped you the first time. The slapstick has the precision which one recalls in the best work of Chaplin and the other great comics of the silent cinema. And

M. Tati, who plays the postman as well as directing, is funny from the word go: funny demonstrating how to erect a flagpole, funny chasing a wasp, funny doing no more than ride a bicycle.

This brilliant comedian has restored something almost lost from the screen: the joke made to your eyes; you don't need a French vocabulary to enjoy *Jour de Fête*. And indeed the whole film with its village setting, its village characters and its village laughter (and, let me add, Jean Yatove's entrancing music) takes us back to the cinema's age of innocence. Whether or not people in this country will like the piece it is not my business to say. But if they don't, I give up.

May 1950

You will observe that these are not the movements of the professional funny man. The disjointed walk, the hesitations, darts, retreats, sudden lunges, the umbrella brandished with a peremptoriness which seems to acknowledge its own defeat – the tall figure with the mackintosh, the pipe and the defiantly squashed hat is not simply a laugh. Jacques Tati, who in *Jour de Fête* ten years ago showed that he was the best comic since Chaplin, has delicately fined down his performance. The Monsieur Hulot of **My Uncle** is in essence the same enthusiastic butterfingers as the hero of *Monsieur Hulot's Holiday*. But the mood is less outrageous. You might almost say this Monsieur Hulot is played straight. He is not a clown, he is a character; an eccentric.

Jacques Tati's new film – new at any rate to this country, though it has been around in France for over a year and has been winning awards both there and in the United States – is about a little boy, his parents and his uncle. The parents have surrounded themselves with chairs made of string, electrically operated doors, lightning cookers, every modern discomfort; in their garden with its idiotic fish-fountain and geometric shrubs even the way you put your feet down is regulated. And the little boy is growing up in an atmosphere of chilly hygiene from which he escapes only when his uncle Monsieur Hulot calls to take him out.

Monsieur Hulot on the other hand is by nature and choice the tenant of Ramshackle Hall. His rooms are reached via a series of stairs and passages which by comparison make the home of the Minotaur seem accessible. The quarter in which he lives is haunted by the undisciplined, the casual, the amiably quarrelsome, the people whose work is never done simply because they never bother to finish it. Even the dogs live a free, scampering, scrounging, buccaneering life. And when Monsieur Hulot, shying like a nervous giraffe but pulling himself together to essay the approaches, awkwardly intrudes into the spotless, stainless, heartless house of his sister and brother-in-law, he can touch nothing without breaking it. He wishes everybody and everything well. But he becomes an engine of pure destruction.

He becomes in fact a living protest. *Jour de Fête* was a protest against hurry; *Monsieur Hulot's Holiday* was a protest against taking pleasure sadly; and *My Uncle* is a protest against regimenting. A good deal of modern art and décor bullies, and Tati reacts against being bullied. He reacts against gadgetry. He reacts against conformity. In a sense he reacts against the assembly line; there is a hilarious episode in a factory, an episode which reminds one of *Modern Times* and *A Nous la Liberté* without really owing much to either of them.

Or perhaps I am giving a false impression by saying that Tati protests *against* anything. To begin with, his latest film, like the other two, is positive, not negative. It it protests, it protests rather for than against; for leisure, gaiety, liberty. Tati is not setting up as a social critic; his argument is personal and humane. And though in his picture of the father and mother smug and snob in their formal house he satirizes the pompous and the pretentious, the satire is not without malice, it is without anger. The couple are in danger of losing their little boy's affection, and he wants them to keep it; ridiculous as they are, he feels for them.

But most of all he feels for Monsieur Hulot, that guileless, inarticulate, indeed silent figure whom he first created in black and white and here perpetuates in clear, lively colour (and usually in long shot). Devastatingly clumsy, born to be the comic scapegoat, Monsieur Hulot cherishes an unconquerable and altogether admirable optimism.

And beneath his gawky exterior, behind the pantomime of bewilderment or reprimand there is a singular sweetness; he is the one who manages to train the reflected ray of sunlight on the caged bird. My liking for him is such that I find difficulty in detaching myself from his tale, in summoning the resolution to say that this time one does not, perhaps, laugh quite so often with quite as much abandon as in the two earlier films.

I think this is because Tati is concerned not only with making jokes but with making observations. The society and the milieu of his story (written in collaboration with Jacques Legrange) are described in a detail which is not by any means always dramatic; incidents are left after editing without the kind of clear-cut point to which the conventions of the screen have accustomed us. As a result the film sometimes appears to ramble, to need a tighter control. And yet one remembers its ramifications, recalls its amused and affectionate and mischievous observations with a clarity and a delight denied to more ferociously professional cinema. And one wants more. Especially more Hulot. Entertaining though the other characters, appreciated though the playing of Jean-Pierre Zola, Adrienne Servantie, Lucien Frégis and young Alain Bécourt may be, I can't help feeling that this time Tati has been a bit too modest with his own appearances. It is a parsonimy which deserves respect. But I can never have too much Hulot. I hope we shall not have to wait long for the next instalment of his adventures.

June 1959

It becomes more and more obvious that many of the new French films, and come to that many of the new Italian films, are part of a general movement in the arts. No use judging them by the standards of narrative and characterization which have served for so long; you wouldn't, after all, reading a novel by Iris Murdoch, expect it to turn out like George Eliot.

The name of Iris Murdoch, as it happens, is not irrelevant to the matter of **Lola** (writer and director Jacques Demy), something in the setting-to-partners of the film reminds me of the brilliant weaving of plot in *A Severed Head*. Not that the new films are literary. On the contrary, they are fanatically cinematic; they move in time and space with the absolute freedom of the cinema. But they have certain analogies with the processes of literature. In *A Bout de Souffle*, for instance, the spiv-hero admires Humphrey Bogart, poses in front of a Bogart poster, models himself on Bogart. In *Lola* the travel-struck hero dreams of a Pacific island where Gary Cooper spent one of the Cooper films; and when at the end a long-lost character reappears his absence is explained by an enforced sojourn on that very island.

The new films, in fact, make references. References to the

American screen punctuate the work of the young French directors, just as passages of classical music italicize it. Not only the American screen. On its title page, as it were, *Lola* refers to Max Ophul's *Lola Montez*. Lola the cabaret-girl of Jacques Demy's film, rehearsing her song-and-dance in a top-hat, is for a moment, as one of the gifted young *Oxford Opinion* critics pointed out to me, the Lola of *The Blue Angel*.

The references are part of a complex interweaving of character-relationships, an interweaving the significance of which it is easy to miss first go. The complexities disclose themselves little by little; *Lola* is a much better film on a second look – and why not? Why should the cinema, almost alone among the arts, be expected always to make its full impact at first sight?

There are three women in the story; each stands for a certain period in the life of one and the same woman. The cabaret-girl – in Anouk Aimée's exquisite performance a breathless, electric, vulnerable, supremely sensuous being – has waited seven years for the lover who left her with a child. A supposed widow (Elina Labourdette), living in ostentatious respectability with her school-girl daughter, represents a later stage; the daughter (Annie Duperoux), a confident, watchful little creature, is at the beginning of the career sketched by the other two.

All three are linked by the young romantic (Marc Michel) who, while befriending the mother and daughter, falls suddenly in love with the cabaret-girl, but who, like her lost lover, will set off for unknown seas – and will do it at the moment when the lost one (Jacques Harden) returns. An American sailor (Alan Scott) offers Lola a transient love – and meanwhile stirs innocently in the schoolgirl the dangerous first passion which has altered the lives of the two older women. The six characters join hands or relinquish; their paths cross or by an infinitesimal moment in time miss one another; every movement, every encounter is plotted with a devoted precision in which irony, affection and an artist's delight all have a share.

Only occasionally does contrivance show above the surface; indeed the delicacy of the manoeuvres is shown by the fact that long after coming out of the cinema you are recognizing other strands in the web, adding other characters – the wanderer's mother, for instance – to the repeating pattern of behaviour. And recalling other intricacies in the repeating pattern of action. Jacques Demy uses his wide screen for beautiful effects of perspective, for huge swinging shots which somehow never disturb one's concentration. And he uses it for gaiety: *Lola*, especially in the entrancing cabaret scenes, is full of high spirits. I hope he goes on to make the trilogy of which, he says, this is intended as Part One.

December 1961

Somehow there is always a murder. Claude Chabrol, whose **La Rupture** (**The Break**) opens today at the Paris Pullman, needs the physical violence in order to translate into narrative terms, the violence he recognizes in human relationships. The murder is not deliberate. It may be, as in *La Femme Infidèle*, the outlet for a sudden rage; or the despairing, psychotic expression of a general disgust, as in *Le Boucher*; at the start of the new film it is a murder not achieved but attempted in a madness induced by drugs.

Why the drugs? For Chabrol doesn't, I think, not at any rate in his later work, rely on mere chance. The young husband who begins the day and the film by banging his little boy against the wall and trying to strangle his wife is an unsuccessful writer. Once a strip dancer, the wife now works in a bar; she supports the family. In a low-temperature film that might be enough to create the tension. Not with Chabrol. One has to look farther away, to the husband's parents, to the rich industrialist father who disapproves of his son's marriage and wants to break it up and gain control of the grandchild. The grandparents are the essential destroyers.

In *Le Boucher*, Hélène, the schoolmistress who won't risk falling in love with the murderer, is treated as the one at fault – though one can hardly blame her for shrinking a bit when, armed with a knife, he bursts into the house in the middle of the night; any more than one can censure the young wife of *The Break* (she, too, is called Hélène) when at the breakfast table she defends herself and her little boy by beating the husband over the head with, I think, a frying-pan.

Is one meant, though, to think her guilty because she then demands a divorce and leaves the young man, a nervous and physical wreck, in the care of his horrible parents? True that in the later Chabrol films the woman is usually blamed; a little, perhaps, even here. But not much; we are on her side. Significant that in the hospital where her child lies half-dead the police, questioning her about the injuries to her husband, should be suspicious; presumably the son of a rich industrialist is more important than an ex-strip dancer. And all through the film her isolation in society is stressed. We are back with the old indictment of the bourgeoisie.

I have not read the novel by Charlotte Armstrong from which Chabrol has drawn *The Break*. Possibly the construction of the book explains the accretion on the screen of odd stock characters, eccentric residents in the boarding house where Hélène takes refuge. The three old ladies playing with tarot cards (the Fates, they seem to denote, but what is Fate-like about them?); the puritanical proprietness and her alcoholic husband and her idiot daughter, all ready to be cast as puppets in a plot to trap the newcomer; the declamatory unemployed actor who conveniently delivers a warning – Chabrol does not as a rule need so intricate an array of figures and incidents to present his view of the human condition.

His view – I had almost said his Morality, for he is concerned not merely with passion but with vice and virtue. The industrialist is the fabricator of evil, the rich man driven by a desire to possess other people's lives; he hires a creature to spy on Hélène and, when spying proves useless, to invent evidence against her. On the one side, then, wealth, power, malice. On the other, innocence; the young wife has only truth and honour to protect her – and, if you look more closely, the imbecility of her enemies; never have I watched a diabolical plot more likely to come unstuck.

Imbecility, that is, if you take the story at any rate partly on a realistic level and not wholly as a struggle between good and evil, the preserving and the destructive principles; and in spite of those Fates and what-not the director has presented a generally realistic scene. Especially admirable is the high-bourgeois background of the grandparents, the deadly smooth social setting of the polite party into which the daughter-in-law erupts. Like all the confrontations between the principals, that is done with superb confidence; in such simplified though not simple renderings of emotional conflict Chabrol never fails.

But perhaps one should have been warned by that air of a Morality. For the characters boldly drawn in the performances of Stephane Audran as the wife, Jean-Pierre Cassel as the spy and Michel Bouquet, as the industrialist there is no easy way out. There has to be violence; Chabrol has a death at the last. But simple death is not enough. So deeply involved a director has to go farther – but where? And with acute disappointment one sees him taking off into symbolism, into the kind of fantasy which today bedevils so much cinema. Three-quarters of *The Break* is clear, hard, sharp. The end is a pricked balloon.

November 1972

With a film one likes so much, where to begin – with the story? the acting? the dialogue? the re-creation of life going on under cool observant eyes? Very little to hold on to in the plot. Nothing much happens. In the end nothing happens – but that displays one of the extraordinary qualities of Eric Rohmer's **Love in the Afternoon** – no connection, by the way, with Billy Wilder's 1957 *Love in the Afternoon*. To make a spell-binding film about a love affair which finally is refused – that, especially in today's sweaty hothouse climate, is itself an achievement. Begin, then, with what doesn't happen.

Nobody bounds into bed. The young husband (Bernard Verley) loves his wife and leads a quiet, happy home life. He may smile, a bit flirtily, at the secretaries in his office; he feels now and then that everything is a shade too sedate, too settled; sometimes he fancies himself accosting a pretty girl in the street. But his imagination never takes him beyond the first audacious words of address; he has only the vaguest feelings of unrest – until a girl whom he used to know but never much liked turns up in his office, unexpected and at first far from welcome.

That brings me to the playing. Bernard Verley presents a middle-class young man, conventional without being dull, who gradually, very gradually, breaks the rhythm of his life, takes time off from the office, makes excuses to his wife, enjoys another woman's conversation; it is the most natural thing in the world, but for an actor, even with a script as delicate as Rohmer's, to make it seem natural is rare. As in most Rohmer films, however, it is the women who carry the plot; and in the handsome girl appearing under the bizarre pseudonym of Zouzou the director has found an actress of powerfully seductive gifts.

Chloé, as she is called on the screen, has lived a wayward, uninhibited life. She is at a loose end; the spectacle of the young husband, attractive but standoffish, always talking about his wife, stirs her. She begins to pursue, occasionally withdrawing to excite the curiosity (and soon the jealousy) of her quarry, but inexorably returning, persisting. And again the gradual shifts of attitude, this time from casual interest to impudent determination. She says she wants a child by him. Perhaps she does, though I think she is portrayed as essentially a predator. And here is another of the qualities of *Love in the Afternoon*; one is so much enveloped by the characters that one begins to ask questions about them. Does the wife, so touchingly tearful at the end, suspect what has been happening? Will the husband falter again in fidelity? Rohmer includes the film in what he calls his six moral tales; but though it does in fact have a 'moral' close it is, like the others, not a model but a study of behaviour and of the influences, sometimes no more than a tiny incident, which affect conduct (the husband's view of his face in the mirror, reminding him of a family joke, frightening him back to himself, is a telling visual illustration).

The director shows life going on realistically enough. But the elegance with which he presents it, the wit – and the film doesn't merely sound witty, it looks witty – remove it from the tedium of the realistic French critics – who seem surprised that 'even foreign audiences' appreciate Rohmer – call him a classical director. Since the business of the classical is to translate into calm and order the movements of the heart, I think the French are right.

November 1972

Let's face it, the cinema this last year or so hasn't been what one could call a regular pleasure. There are splendid films, films I should hate to miss; the cinema extends its range. But it hardly ever relaxes; one comes away feeling disturbed, or depressed, or just plain flummoxed. And perhaps it is understandable that in the present state of society the cinema should be disturbing and enigmatic. All the same one would welcome a minute or two of good temper.

François Truffaut's **Day for Night** is a good-tempered film.

I don't mean that it ignores the painful elements of life. There is grief in it; there is even death (off-screen; and for a moment, recalling excesses of violence, I felt that the classical French critics of Shakespeare had a point). And goodness knows there is worry; for this is a film about the making of a film – and once and for all it dispels the myth that cinema about life on the set doesn't work. *Day for Night* works beautifully.

I think there are two reasons. The first is that it is made out of love. The director in Truffaut's piece (he is played by Truffaut himself) may be harried by trifling decisions about the size of a gun or the colour of a decorative vase. He may be beset by the disasters which a player's temperament can bring. At night his sleep may be tormented by echoes of the struggles of the day. But the whole film reflects devotion to the medium; it is the passion for the cinema which is Truffaut's own passion. The nightmares themselves are interrupted by visions of a little boy with designs on the *Citizen Kane* stills displayed outside a cinema. The passion, one may assume, began early, and not for the first time there is an element of autobiography in a Truffaut film.

The second reason for the success of *Day for Night* is that Truffaut has devised his story not, in the manner so often adopted in films about film-making, as a way of presenting the problems and the absurdities of simulating reality but as a way of looking at people at work. The comedy of technical trickery is there – the view from an upstairs room which is no more than a single wall perched on a platform up a ladder; the fake snow pumped over streets and trees from a gigantic hose. But it is only a background to the comedy or the drama of behaviour. The foreground is held by the film cast and their director. There is the temperamental young star, self-consciousness and amorous jealousy (a sparkling mock-Byronic performance by Jean-Pierre Léaud). There is the gentle, charming English actress (Jacqueline Bisset) who, imported to play a film-wife, manages to complicate her own private life as the wife of the middle-aged doctor who has saved her from a breakdown. There is Jean-Pierre Aumont as an older star, initially apprehensive about playing opposite the actress with whom he had a stormy Hollywood affair; there is Truffaut, playing himself and all the other anxious directors of egoistic, hard-working, unreliable, conscientious and unpunctual artists.

Especially, for one brilliant passage, the scene is held by Valentina Cortese as a star, famous and even notorious in the past, fading now but still displaying a flamboyant personality. The passage is self-mocking: the confident beauty of years gone by pulls out the stops for a rehearsal in which she proceeds to miss her cues, forget her lines and repeatedly open the wrong door. It is funny. But it is not farce. Truffaut is never unkind to his players, and you in the audience are made to share the sympathetic nervousness of the crew as they watch the actress's collapse. Another thing: Truffaut in telling his story of the making of a film does not tell it as if only the stars mattered in the making; the film is an undertaking and this is a story in which everybody is seen to share. The sexy apprentice script-girl, bedfellow of the young star, has a major effect on the course of events. One of the best jokes comes in a scene in which a member of the technical crew, making a casually amorous proposal to a feminine colleague, is embarrassingly taken at his word. Even a kitten having a fit of temperament contributes to the mishaps of shooting.

And subtly the plot of *Day for Night* (the French title is **La Nuit Americaine**) and the plot of the film inside the film are interwoven. At the start the action on the screen may seem fragmentary, perhaps a shade puzzling. But then a film, any film, is composed of fragments; and by the end the pieces of the jigsaw have slipped easily into place. It has been a pleasure; one is sorry it is over and I at any rate come out feeling positively good-tempered myself.

November 1973

About a third of the way through the new Louis Malle piece **Lacombe Lucien**, I had a shock. Good heavens, I thought, this is a very boring film. That, you might think, must be a frequent experience. You would be mistaken. I am rarely bored at the cinema: exasperated if you like, infuriated, appalled, even revolted, but scarcely ever bored. I can find a perverse pleasure in the most idiotic comedy; I can let my pulse gallop with the most improbable of the ghoul-films. *Lacombe Lucien*, it is true, presently picked up a bit, but not much; and it had been boring enough for one to recognize boredom. I have been trying to discover why.

Lacombe Lucien is about collaboration, and collaboration not so much by choice as by a mixture of stupidity and accident. Lucien (Pierre Blaise) is a peasant boy who likes killing – killing rabbits, chickens, anything that moves; it is his only gift. Surely, then – for this is rural France at war – the Resistance is the place for him; and he makes clumsy attempts to join it. But he is rejected; instead he falls in with a party of Frenchmen working for the German police. One could say that in joining the collaborators instead of the Resistance he is tricked. But in fact it is all the same to him.

He has no political views; what matters is that he is given a gun and a hideous little fragment of authority. Now he can kill with impunity.

Important, I think, to note that he acts automatically. He never recognizes, as he satisfies some personal whim, the nature of his behaviour. He can force himself without thinking on the former Paris tailor (a fine performance from Holger Lowenadler), a Jew hiding in the hope of escaping to Spain; he assumes that the man and his daughter (Aurore Clement) will tolerate the crudeness of his manners and welcome the lukewarm champagne which he pours out for them, bottle after bottle. And when, attracted by the girl, he drags her to a party at Gestapo headquarters he is insensible to the humiliations to which he is subjecting her. The circumstances of the times allow him to be callous and overbearing. He has the power; there is nothing in his make-up to stop him using it. He is thus in a way a victim of conditions, acting according not to reason but to instinct, finally reverting, in the company of the two people he has saved – but saved without what could be called conscience – to his first peasant innocence.

The film has been a success in France; the French, it seems, learn with surprise that their countrymen were not all heroic resisters during the war. The discovery might appear belated; but then one has to remember that new generations have grown up since 1945, and like *Le Chagrin et la Pitié* the Malle piece has news for them. Some people have suggested that its theme could be taken as excusing collaboration. Against that one must set the fact that the boy is never presented as typical of collaborators; he works with fanatics and sadists, but having no motives, no convictions, he does not share their guilt; he stands on his own, a solitary wooden-wit. He could be more accurately compared with the Hitler-boys of the early days in Germany, the mindless destroyers, the shop-smashers. But they at least looked as if they enjoyed the job; he scarcely smiles. And his impassivity, I think, is the flaw in the film, the reason why, watching, one experiences positive boredom.

One guesses that the director (he is the producer and co-writer as well) began with the idea of a character involved in events too complex for his understanding and actions for which he is incapable of responsibility. So far so good; and applied to the position of the collaborator the idea has a special force. All the same one needs something to stir interest in the character. The immobile, the blank air of Pierre Blaise is all right for a start. The trouble is that it is allowed to persist. Development is blocked by the very tenacity of the basic idea; nothing changes, not the look on the face, not the character itself. Gradually the whole film takes on a kind of sterility.

June 1974

5 CRITICISM –
A CERTAIN TONE OF VOICE

If the chief task of a weekly film reviewer is to establish and maintain as dialogue with the reader, then tone of voice must play an important part in sustaining that dialogue over a number of years. And inevitably accents and emphases are likely to change from decade to decade. This is pre-eminently the case with Dilys Powell. Throughout her time at the *Sunday Times* Powell initiated what might be described as a weekly conversation on the cinema with her readers, but she was wise enough to sense that in each decade her listeners changed, and that as a consequence her 'conversation' must follow them and not vice versa. Purists might argue that in her desire to accommodate her column to a changing social and cultural climate Dilys Powell ran the risk of becoming all things to all filmgoers. But this is to confuse 'tone' with 'judgment'. And while the wit and humour of the earlier pieces is very different from that of her late work, the firmness of her judgment from beginning to end is consistent. It is the same critic who teases the pretensions of *New Moon*, a creaking vehicle for Nelson Eddy and Jeanette MacDonald, and who thirty years later puts Mike Nichols's *The Graduate* firmly in its place. Powell's enthusiasm for the 'new' is equally consistent; she spots what Raymond Chandler will contribute to the cinema ahead of her fellow critics and is quick to identify the potential displayed in Steven Spielberg's early film *Duel*.

1   A Sense of Humour

'You may recollect, Watson, if I may trouble you to cast your mind back to the autumn of 1889, that strange business known, I believe, to readers of your annals as **The Hound of the Baskervilles**. You will no doubt have observed that an attempt is at this moment being made to reconstruct on the screen the singular chain of events which led up to the discovery, though not the apprehension, of as cunning a criminal as it has ever been my fortune to encounter. (Providence, my dear Watson, though as my biographer you will be reluctant to admit it, is occasionally as tenacious in pursuit of the evildoer as even the criminal investigator.)

'I must confess,' Sherlock Holmes continued, 'that recently my time has been occupied with a number of interesting cases, with, for example, the case of the invisible steel shelters, the adventure of the missing trousers in the Far East, and that little affair of the German in the Polish Corridor, and that, in my anxiety to oblige the Bank for International Settlements in the matter of the Esquimo deposits, I have perhaps neglected to pay sufficient attention to the cinema and its versions of my own trifling achievements. Fortunately, the omission is one which can be easily rectified. I hope with your co-operation to sift the details and detach the framework of fact from the embellishments of scenarists, directors, producers, and actors.'

'Good heavens, Holmes!' I cried as I gazed at the screen, 'Who is that villainous-looking fellow whom we now see, after the mysterious death of Sir Charles Baskerville and the unsatisfactory inquest, entering your rooms in Baker Street? Surely that sinister, burly figure, whom I recognize as Lionel Atwill, with the menacing stare, the resolute set of the shoulders, and the general air of malevolence, cannot be Dr Mortimer, the absent-minded anthropologist, the dingy, amiable practitioner, the "picker-up of shells on the shores of the great unknown ocean".'

'Well done, Watson. It is none other. I think we shall not be far wrong in inferring, from this singular transformation in his appearance and habits, that the poor fellow has fallen into Hollywood hands, and will play a part in the story very different from that intended by his creator. Yes, it is as I feared.

Our unhappy friend is to be used to divert suspicion from the proper quarter. Indeed, the miscreants have gone to the length of presenting his wife, a lady whom, unless my memory betrays me, neither you nor I have previously met, as possessed of mediumistic abilities, a cunning device, again, for darkening the obscurities of this black business. Halloa! Who is this?'

I shook my head. 'I have never seen the man before.'

'You surpass yourself, my dear fellow. Have you forgotten Stapleton, the naturalist, whom in an account of my trifling achievements you once described as "that impassive, colourless man, with his straw hat and his butterfly net – a creature of infinite patience and craft, with a smiling face and a murderous heart"? You know Hollywood's methods. Change the face, the manner and the character. Omit everything which made the man as we knew him a cold-blooded, scheming villain, a foeman worthy of our steel. For what is left of Stapleton the smooth young gentleman now before us will serve as well as any other.'

'Astounding! I presume the softening of the character of his pretended sister, and the happy conclusion of the tender passion between her and Sir Henry are equally designed to satisfy the belief of film manufacturers in the stupidity of the public?'

'I congratulate you. We may further instance the vacuity of the dialogue, the cardboard moor, and the inattention to detail, sufficient in my experience to bring a man to the scaffold, which permits me to appear smoking a pipe other than my black clay. It remains only to exempt from this censure the actor, Nigel Bruce, in whom I readily recognize my old friend Dr Watson. As for the discreet but, in my opinion, excessively benevolent performance of Basil Rathbone as myself –'

Holmes, who up to this moment had observed without asperity the circumstances presented by the film, suddenly leaned forward with an exclamation of horror. A flush rose to his pale cheeks. 'The brutes!' he cried. 'Trapped in an empty grave! They dare to suggest that I could be caught by so childish a trick! I'll have them, Watson, I'll have them!'

I looked about me to see the effect of my companion's outburst on our neighbours. But most of them, persuaded no doubt that a tear-gas bomb had burst in the cinema, had already fled from the vicinity of the strong shag tobacco he habitually smoked. 'Indeed, my dear Watson,' he continued in a calmer tone, 'to explain the motives which provoke the makers of films to exchange a plot and characters inherently fitted to the cinema for a farrago such

as this is a formidable task. I can only refer you to my little
monograph on "Box Office: Seventy-Five Fallacies".'

1939

In the twelve months during which I have been writing about the
cinema in these columns it has been my business to see about 250
films. Of these, perhaps twenty had an individual life, existing
in their own right. The rest may be divided roughly into seven
types, viz.:

(1) Westerns, or the Spread of Culture.

(2) Crime films. These are played by James Cagney, George
Raft, and Humphrey Bogart.

(3) Flying and Spying films or films about Wings.

(4) Films about clothes. In the case of contemporary pictures
the clothes are hung on Norma Shearer, in historical pictures on
Bette Davis.

(5) Stage films, or The Show Must Go On.

(6) Films about Youth at the Prow. Played by Shirley Temple,
Deanna Durbin, Mickey Rooney, and the Dead End Kids.

(7) Films about the Fuzzy-Wuzzies. These are acted by Ronald
Colman and Gary Cooper, who do not, however, enact the
Fuzzy-Wuzzies, but merely the sahibs who know how to handle
'em.

In fact, the film critic in a year spends most of the time seeing
seven films over and over again – generally between thirty and
forty times each.

Now my suggestion is that instead of seven films there should
be one film; that, in fact, someone should contribute to the drive
for economy by producing a kind of grand *Gone With the Wind*
embodying all the incidents and characters of the pictures with
which we are familiar. With a little ingenuity it should be
possible to find a part for every star in such a film, so that
the distressing wave of unemployment which is apt to follow
on any retrenchment would be avoided. Let me give just the
faintest hint of the kind of thing I mean.

At the opening of the film the Iron Horse is seen forging
westward. The track is still being laid: hammer-hammer, plonk-
plonk, crash go the rails; upside down, mebbe, but the boys

are sure laying them. As they work bevies of lovely girls in crinolines and pantaloons cluster round, skipping like Disney lambs and throwing bunches of orchids; but none throws a more accurate orchid than Shirley Temple, the daughter of the Wing-Commander. The overseer cracks his stockwhip: flick! As a joke he has neatly decapitated a peace-loving Fuzzie-Wuzzy, who was standing by reciting the Declaration of Independence.

It is just what they are waiting for, back in Europe; see how they sit round their board-room tables in whiskers, see how they take snuff in the ante-chambers of Versailles, plotting to supply the Fuzzy-Wuzzies with rifles! But at Dead Catfish they know nothing of this. The Hardys have come West again, and Mickey Rooney is in love with the dance-girl in the saloon, who is going to give him such a lesson by-and-by. The Dead End Kids have joined the North-West Mounted Police. And in the little camp they are planning a gala evening to celebrate the laying of the first million miles of track. There is to be a performance of *Othello*, with Mr Rooney as the Moor, and the struggling troupe of ice-skaters are to try out their new ice ballet on the homely little rink. Hammer-hammer! All night they are at work on the railway; the embankment crumbles, the bridge over the rapids collapses, but no matter, they have strung it up again, sacrificing ties, braces, anything for the Iron Horse to go through.

And now everything is on the point of completion; the women are at the mannequin parade choosing their gowns for the ball at Government House, the newspaper boss is taking out the blonde secretary (his rival's wife incognito) to a little intimate caviare, when, hush! What is that looking over the distant ridge of hills? It is a camel; it is the Fuzzy-Wuzzies, ten million of them, all with Lewis guns. The walls of the ice-rink are manned; but how few the defenders! The Dead End Kids, accused of complicity in the sale of arms, are in the Big House; the principal skater is wounded in the hams by an assegai; only Wallace Beery as the old drunken scene-shifter fights on. Nearer come the Fuzzy-Wuzzies; we look at them from the front, then, just to show what can be done from the sides. Still the show must go on. But horror! There is an explosion, all the skates are destroyed. In a desperate venture Miss Temple crawls out through the lines to where the Wing Commander's plane is waiting. She is in it, she is off! But can she make it? Somewhere in the fuselage a time-bomb is ticking, and from the north a blizzard is blowing. The Fuzzy-Wuzzies are still thundering up; front, right, left. Miss Temple has not seen the time-bomb yet, and in the Big House the Dead End Kids, who have mutinied, are being attacked with tear-gas. The ice in the rink is melting, and still there are no skates.

But what is that speck in the heavens? It is Miss Temple's mercy plane, returning loaded with skates; as she passes over the Fuzzy-Wuzzies (still riding hard) she drops the time-bomb. And now the tables are turned. The camels bolt, the ballet put on their skates; the Dead End Kids, making an appeal to the humanity of the judge ('We never had a break, mister') are released. With tears pouring down his face the crippled skater watches his kid brother give a stupendous performance in his place, and Mr Beery, though wounded, has strength enough to shift the scenes throughout *Othello* before he crawls, dying, to lay a bunch of orchids at the foot of the statue of Abraham Lincoln.

You get the idea?

March 1940

After a year of war the London and surburban cinemas, always a barometer of the gravity of the times, are once again reduced to closing early. On 15 September last year it was recorded in these columns that, after being completely closed at the beginning of the month, they had re-opened. That week there were two new films in the West End. During the past week only one new film has been seen: *I Was an Adventuress*, with Vera Zorina, Richard Greene and the remarkable Erich von Stroheim, which goes into the Odeon programme tomorrow. Delayed action, now wholly my own, has up to now prevented me from seeing this piece. In the absence, then, of fresh material, let us look at the effects on Hollywood and its stars of a year of European war. (Or, as the Marx Brothers would say, you look at the effects, and we'll take a look at that blonde who just went round the corner.)

One of the saddest results in Hollywood of the war has been the shortage of beards. The film industry formerly obtained most of its human hair from Central Europe, a source now denied. The 'first serious beard shortage' was met by Mr Westmore, head of Warner Brothers' make-up department, during preparation for *Virginia City* (you remember the beards in *Virginia City*?). 'With the European human hair market destroyed, we must use the next best thing,' said Mr Westmore bravely. 'That happens to be the hair of the Tibetan yak and the Angora goat and the manes of horses.' If in the months ahead any deterioration is visible in Warner Brothers' beards we must remember under what difficulties they are working. No less grave has been the shortage of flying uniforms. Only last week I learned that, owing to the United States Government demand for gabardine cloth for its air service recruits, a major film company is unable to gets its rush order of 500 yards, and that in consequence the filming of 'the Ray Milland-William Holden-Wayne Morris starring feature' *I Wanted Wings* has been held up. 'Dyeing any cloth a blue colour won't work,' said the wardrobe head. 'What we need is the blue and white thread weave material which the Army uses. Plain blue material goes "dead" on film.'

The apathy of Central European hair-growers, the supine inattention, as Gibbon might have put it, of Government supply departments to the needs of the film industry – what other obstacles must Hollywood surmount? The vagaries of public taste, of course, add to the difficulties with which directors and producers have to contend. A year ago, apparently, sophisticated comedy was fashionable. But Herr Goering has changed all that; at any rate, one of Columbia's directors claims to have treated a new comedy 'in keeping with the times by making every detail so broad that you can't possibly miss the point.' Also in keeping with the times, presumably, is the new type of glamour girl. Today, I am assured 'she is a brawling belle with a chip on her exquisite shoulder and a haymaker in each manicured hand.' That takes one back to the age of Clara Bow, described, even in those laconic days, I remember, as a 'Titian-topped teaser'.

But a year of war has brought worse havoc than this to the innocent homes of California. Seized by who knows what instinct of violence and destruction, Dorothy Lamour herself has added, not indeed to the beard but to the human hair problem; the sultry songbird, as some poet has called her, has bobbed her hair. The sacrilegious act was carried out by agreement with her studio; the studio, to which her head, complete with 40-in. tresses, was under contract, gave her permission to bob, Miss Lamour consented for the sake of her art to wear a sarong ('the bewitching South Seas scanties') whenever a film required it. Those who cling to the belief that even in these wild days the human heart remains unchanged will find comfort in the story that the Jungle Princess 'wept a little at the first snip'.

And so it goes on: old traditions destroyed, the old luxurious ways of production lost. But ravaged by the European war and its psychological excesses as Hollywood is, the habits of thoroughness and artistic precision persist. For instance, in a film not yet shown in this country, a singular musical effect is, apparently, provided by a miniature orchestra of clay figures with heads and instruments formed from fruits and vegetables. Six men, working under the table, operate the figures; the orchestra was designed by an assistant professor at a Massachusetts college; and its construction took nineteen men a month to achieve. In addition, three weeks of rehearsal were lavished on this *chef d'oeuvre*. Toscanini himself could not have asked for more. And now who says that the cinema has no place for art?

September 1940

London, says the commentary of James A. Fitzpatrick's latest once-over, with approval, was the home of Chaucer, Shakespeare, Cromwell and Henry VIII, figures, it adds knowledgeably, famous all over the world. The piece in question is one of seven Technicolor Traveltalks (I think I have the name right) about Great Britain; it is called **Looking at London**; and its reasons for recommending our modest capital, the features it singles out for patronage are so fascinating to a Londoner that I cannot refrain, while reflecting on the information it provides, from recalling other examples of informative cinema.

According to Mr Fitzpatrick, London has (in addition to the international distinction conferred on it by the marital experiments of Henry VIII) the Royal Exchange, St Paul's, Piccadilly Circus, the Tower, Trafalgar Square, the Marble Arch corner of Hyde Park, the Houses of Parliament, Buckingham Palace (famous as the residence of Queen Victoria) and one café where customers may sit out of doors. It also has the blitz; but that need not overtire the foreign tourist (for whom, presumably, the Traveltalk is intended) since the landmarks, warmarks and other attractions designated can easily be viewed, in the Fitzpatrick manner, in an hour's taxi ride.

A tactful thought, or perhaps a technical necessity, has shown us our city, all nine or ten monuments of it, bathed in sunshine. Well, nobody in this country, I am sure, would wish to reject this kindly suggestion. All I venture to point out is that the cinema as a rule has taken a different view. Indeed, I think I should be justified in saying that the regular attendant at the movies learns

two things about London: that every street corner has its group
of costermongers in pearlies, executing a pearly song and dance,
and that among the constant features of the climate is a ground
mist, pretty opaque to the height of a man's knee.

London, England, the entry in the film encyclopaedia would
run: marshy spot with low incidence of daylight and high
incidence of murders of Ripper type. Inhabitants, Sherlock
Holmes and Boris Karloff. History confined mainly to fifteenth
and sixteenth centuries, and consisting almost entirely of high-
class executions. Police force composed of comic types with
walrus moustaches. Entertainment for masses provided by
can-can dancers in public houses. Unwanted corpses may be
readily disposed of during Guy Fawkes celebrations, when
vast municipal bonfires offer convenient dumping-ground.
Democracy unknown.

The geography lesson which we all learn in the cinema
extends, of course, to other capitals and other countries. For
instance:

Brussels: Continental fun-fair with Grotto of Love, used by
Monsieur Héger to snatch kiss from Charlotte Brontë.

Balaclava: known for Charge of Light Brigade, point-to-point
won by Errol Flynn.

Paris, France: honeymoon resort, noted for Eiffel Tower and
commodious sewers under Opera House. History consists of
French Revolution, minor outburst of democracy inspired by
America.

Naturally the great medium of instruction which the films have
become embraces a variety of subjects: to geography we must add
music, science, sociology, philosophy, or practically everything.
Under music in the encyclopaedia which, now I come to think of
it, I am planning, we should find:

Symphony: background music composed by hero during
attack of insomnia.

Concerto: race between orchestra, conducted by male star,
and piano, played by female star, who occasionally falls out to
embrace visitor in the wings, without, however, making any
difference to sound-track.

England, there'll always be an: British national anthem, sung,
standing to attention, by members of peerage during air-raids.

Philosophy rather than geography should, I fancy, be the
heading for:

Himalayas: hilly district noted for wisdom of East frequented by eligible bachelors tired of tuxedos and anxious to find out about Things.

And possibly sociology is the place for:

Glasses, horn-rimmed: protective device worn by female star during early part of story to delay recognition by male star of fact, obvious to audience, that she is the little lady for him.

I conclude with an item or two so far unclassified:

Literature: reading matter resulting from unrequited love.

Love: either it's love or it isn't, there's no in-between.

May 1947

Exhibitors in the United States, when accused of not giving a fair show to the British cinema, sometimes reply that it is difficult for an American audience to understand the dialogue in English films. We in this country, they tell us, ought to study the American market. And indeed why not? I am convinced that there is a basic American dialogue which can be adapted to meet the needs of the British cinema too. I will try to illustrate.

Let us imagine the scene to be a log cabin in Old Somerset. Two men in green woollen nightshirts and badly-tied puttees limp out of the woods. 'You know something, Egwulf,' says the older man, 'I'm hungry.' Egwulf knocks on the cabin door. 'Hi, Buster,' he cries. Buster, apparently, is away, and it is his wife Ethelwigga who lets the pair in and gives them their stew. 'There's plenty more where that came from,' she remarks hospitably. But the lodgers are in some sort of political trouble, and when Ethelwigga has gone out, 'We're all washed up!' Egwulf groans as he sits over his mead. His companion rebukes him. 'What kind of talk is that?' he asks.

At this moment Egfrida, daughter of the cabin, comes in wearing a new dress with a zip fastener. 'Pretty fancy, huh?' says the elder lodger admiringly. Egfrida is invited to sing. 'Eggie, nice and easy, huh?' she says to Egwulf, who is to accompany her on his harp. But when the two are left alone together the young man, who is still worrying about the political situation, rejects her proposal of marriage. 'I got to do this my own way,' he says. Egfrida flounces out of the cabin. 'You don't need anyone, you never have and you never will!' she screams (she is an artistic type, and given to longer speeches than most).

Her mother hears of the quarrel and complains to the elder

lodger. 'They don't come any better than my Egfrida,' she sobs. 'That no-good Egwulf! The man reassures her. 'I'll try to straighten him out,' he promises. But though he hides his feelings he too is worrying about the political situation. 'Right now I got some thinking to do,' he excuses himself. And he settles down by the fire, fiddling with his bow and arrows. Ethelwigga indicates that lodgers ought to make themselves useful with the housework, and he raises no objection. 'Better grab yourself some sleep,' he says absent-mindedly.

Unfortunately he is the one who drops off; the bow and arrows slip from his hand, and as he sleeps we watch his dream: a battle which, since it is in dance-form, needs no dialogue (however, it has a theme-song with the refrain 'You're yellow!'). There he is, fighting in the middle of the battle, but before we can be sure whether or not he is winning he wakes up, struggling and shouting; and no wonder, for the cabin is full of smoke, from the cakes which he has allowed to burn to a cinder. 'You lazy good-for-nothing slob!' Ethelwigga cries, rushing in. He picks up his bow and prepares to leave. 'It's been nice knowing you,' he says politely. 'Don't give me that!' yells Ethelwigga, throwing the arrows after him. But just as he is opening the door Egwulf bursts in, accompanied by Buster. 'We won!' he shouts, kneeling. 'You can wear that crown now!' 'Very funny,' growls Ethelwigga. 'Ma,' says Buster, 'meet Alfred the Great!' 'On the level?' says Ethelwigga. 'Well, for crying out loud!'

But Egwulf is no longer listening. 'Baby,' he murmurs to Egfrida; and she replies: 'That's the sweetest darned speech I ever heard.' And as the curtain closes Alfred comments: 'So they finally came to their senses!'

I think it will be found that this set of phrases, with slight adaptations, can be used for all the basic English situations. Henry V before Agincourt: 'What kind of talk is that?' Newton under his apple-tree: 'I got some thinking to do.' Victoria learning of her accession: 'On the level?' And pretty well any of his wives to Henry VIII: 'It's been nice knowing you.' Anyhow I make a New Year's present of the idea to the British film industry.

January 1956

In the hope, presumably, of lessening the tedium of the credits, the cinema has lately taken to giving us a chunk of action before weighing in with details about boom operators and sound engineers. Once first noticed the practice a few years ago when David Lean began *The Sound Barrier* not with the names of the technicians but with the famous sequence of the diving plane. The idea soon caught on. By now we are accustomed to seeing the bank robbers holding up the cashier before the film has formally started, to watching the fugitive in the Western incontinently picking off his pursuers from behind the studio boulders instead of waiting for the associate producer and the Technicolor consultant to open the ball.

As a matter of fact I can't see why we shouldn't take things a stage further and make the whole affair not a flash-back but a flash-forward. Let me sketch a specimen with a familiar nursery story.

My film (a musical with an X certificate) rushes straight in with a menace. An oriental gentleman in a turban is advancing on the audience and, to paraphrase the sacred words of Groucho Marx, pointing a coloured beard at them. He is coming out of a shop over which you can read the words Funeral Parlour; the camera swings to follow him as he crosses the street and goes into another shop labelled Wedding Caterers. This simple scene is performed again and again, with nothing to mark the passage of time except a change of turban. The first of the credit titles now swings forward –

COSTUMES BY. . . .

We next take a look at a wedding breakfast. As a matter of fact the bride is taking a look herself. She picks up a spoon; engraved on the handle she reads a girl's name. She looks at a napkin-ring, and spells out a second name; opening a drawer, she finds a sweater embroidered with a third. As she stands reflecting a girl joins her and contributes the first speech. 'O my fairest sister,' says the newcomer, 'I always told thee he was a no-good nick.' The comment invites the second credit.

DIALOGUE COACH. . . .

But it is too late to waste time on words, and we are rushed through half-a-dozen views of the bride breakfasting with Turban; playing mah-jong with Turban; out hawking with Turban; interspersed with shots of the denigratory sister, who has apparently come to stay. At any rate we see her joining in the flower-gathering and sampler-work which plays so large a part in the duties of oriental wives on the screen.

MONTAGE BY. . . .

The domestic scenes are interrupted when two hands fill the screen, a dark hairy one passing a bunch of keys to a smooth white one; and Turban's voice is heard saying: 'Everything else is thine, sugar, but set not that dainty foot within the Blue Room!'

ADDITIONAL DIALOGUE BY. . . .

There is a crane shot of Turban who, watched from the battlements by bride and sister, is setting off with a crowd of semi-nude bowmen and horses in striped skirts for a day's boar-hunting.

MUSIC ADAPTED FROM THEMES BY RIMSKY-KORSAKOFF.

We cut straight to the door of the Blue Room and a notice: 'Keep out! This means you!' A smooth white hand is turning a key in the keyhole, and with a loud creak the door swings slowly open.

SPECIAL EFFECTS BY. . . .

Horror! The Blue Room is full of decapitated bodies; the heads are mounted on pedestals each with a woman's name.

HAIR STYLES BY. . . .

There is a scream, followed by a close-up of a key falling into a pool of blood on the floor. The hand retrieves it and rubs it with a handkerchief, but the stain won't come off.

COLOUR BY. . . .

At this moment a dark hairy hand is laid over the smooth white one. Turban, back from the boars, gives his wife a backhander; sobbing, she collapses in a corner by the bathing-pool. Meanwhile Sister Ann, who has sent a message home to her brothers, is waiting on the battlements and singing a snatch from *Sadko*. A series of superimposed shots divides our attention between the bride, the sister and Turban, who by now is waving a scimitar; while the brothers are to be seen riding to the rescue in all directions.

CONTINUITY BY. . . .

Finally everything coalesces into a battle involving the bowmen, the horsemen, Turban and the female spectators, which in turn dissolves into the title:

'BLUEBEARD.'

You will admit that by my method the audience can until the very end be kept in suspense about what it is seeing.

May 1957

Genius, said the old insupportable, is the infinite capacity for taking pains. In the world of science, for instance, you will not have forgotten that when Sir Isaac Newton's cat was blessed with a kitten, her owner decided that the augmented family must be provided with means of ingress and egress; he therefore had two holes cut in the door, a large one for the cat, a small one for the kitten. In the world of the cinema, when Samuel Goldwyn was supervising the production of a new film in which Jascha Heifetz appears, he was pleased by the performance of a mongrel dog; he therefore had an additional sequence written in for the dog. It was then discovered that the dog was unsuitable for the part; his face was too dark. The make-up department was called in to groom the new star, who, docile as any Lamour, Lamarr or whatsit, had his face hairs bleached, his eyebrow line remodelled and his whiskers reorientated. I'm telling you.

The transfiguration of the mongrel is just a tiny incident in a life spent in taking pains. Through the weeks, while the outside world is triflingly occupied with guns or butter, as the case may be, in Hollywood they are building a 600-foot lagoon containing 1,500,000 gallons of water, creating a £30,000 jungle, and pasting 3,000 yards of adhesive tape on the soles of the extras who have to run about barefoot in it. A Philippine village has to be constructed, with suitable setting and plausible inhabitants. But real palm trees do not photograph well. So eighty-two old telegraph poles are procured and wrapped in layers of newspaper, a plaster composition is added to simulate bumps and scars, the whole is painted and coated with varnish, and real leaves, also coated with varnish to make them shine, are nailed on. The Filipino women extras have been inconsiderate enough to bob their hair or have it permanently waved. Relax! There are 150 pounds of certified Chinese hair, passed under Government inspection, in the United States; Mr Goldwyn corners the lot for wigs.

Ceaselessly the stars, the stand-ins, the bit players, the stunt men, toil and moil after realism (realism in Hollywood means hiring £2,800-worth of orchids which I probably shan't be able to tell from nasturtiums). In the Philippines film, a number of black oak saplings are embedded in cement and four stunt men are catapulted forty-five feet over a twenty-foot wall. The hero of *The Man in the Iron Mask* is locked into a contraption weighing ten pounds; a locksmith stands by in case of accidents. Leslie Howard uses the Kreisler Guarnerius, which is valued at £13,000, in a musical film. On the other hand, Mr Goldwyn has thirty fiddles made at £10 each for use in another musical picture; they are 'breakaway', i.e., made to smash, and smashed they are in a single scene.

Palm-trees can be faked, but not penguins; penguins have to be hired at a minimum wage of £8 a day. Trained lions, elephants, chimpanzees and tigers make about £20 a day; a party of six trained seals get a living wage of £60 a week. Macaws can be hired, and so can goats, parrots, donkeys, love-birds and sacred Indian cows. Seagulls have to fly on location; it is illegal in California to capture them. But seagulls apart, in Hollywood anything can be hired, anything can be reproduced, from the tears on the face of a blonde to the pitching and rolling of an ocean liner.

In such a world, to boggle over the choice of names for fictitious villains would seem out of character. Yet boggle they do, searching through directories and telephone books to guard against hitting on the name of a living man. Not always can they count on such altruism as that of the business manager who asked only for a slight change in spelling before permitting the use of his name. The name was Eugene Hornbostel. Yes, it's a wonderful Hollywood.

1946

One gets to know the old faithfuls: the drunken lawyer, the defeated boxer, the dope-addict, the son who has never learned the truth about his Pa; they are doled out, one to a film. But **Let No Man Write My Epigraph** (X) is different. This is bonus day.

Let me sort out a few of the themes.

1. *Christmas Eve in the workhouse*. Mother has got the sack, but all the recipients of little Nick's home-produced Christmas cards come to the rescue.

2. *We are the People*. Various hearts of gold appoint themselves the boy's guardians, among them a legless dwarf, a Negro boxer (failed) and a Negress who sings in a saloon about reaching for tomorrow.

3. *Your father was a good man*. Mother croons little Nick to sleep with stories of the family past, omitting to mention that his father went to the electric chair, not the altar.

4. *She did it for her baby*. Keeping up her spirits with gin, mother holds the home together by putting on a tight black frilly dress and giving the old come-hither to the boys in the honky-tonk.

5. *He never told her*. Ex-lawyer on Skid Row is hopelessly in love with Nick's mother, but just hangs about with his tie adrift, drinking.

6. *Take care of your hands, son*. Nick's education as a pianist is interrupted by fisticuffs in defence of his mother's reputation.

7. *Then he bought her*. City slicker wins mother by paying courtroom fine and saving Nick from gaol.

8. *The wrong side of the tracks*. Nick falls in love with the daughter of his deceased father's defence counsel, who seems to have done well out of losing a client and now lives in a penthouse with a piano.

9. *He made me a junkie*. City slicker turns mother into a drug addict. He has plans for Nick, too.

A gun in his hand; the locked door; no-legs to the rescue – I could go on. I could dwell on the impudence, with which the incidents are flung together: a visit from the penthouse pair, Nick to play at the Conservatoire, and bless my soul, there goes Mum again, nipping into the bathroom for a shot in the arm. One might almost feel sentimental about the bearded old themes, the stuff of the screen since the first world war, did not exasperation break in.

Exasperation first of all at the waste of talent. *Let No Man Write My Epitaph* was made in America by Philip Leacock, an English director whose work in *The Kidnappers*, for instance, showed a gift at once delicate and sturdy; even here his handling of the cast succeeds now and then in getting the better of the clichés. Only now and then; and the best of the players – Burl Ives as the lawyer, Shelley Winter as the mother, Ella Fitzgerald as the singer, Jeanne Cooper as a Skid Row girl – survive in spite of their material. But most of all one is exasperated by the obstinacy.

Now is the time, if ever there was one, when the cinema needs to break out of routine. And here we are persisting with the oldest bosh.

August 1960

2   Eyes & Ears for the Absurd

New Moon, mes enfants, and the paquebot is on its way from la belle France of, roughly, June, 1793, to New Orleans; and aboard her Mademoiselle Jeanette de MacDonald, all bimsy in wig and hoops, trilling her way out to the old plantation. Mille tonnerres, who is this in the hold, shirt-sleeved, parbleu, and hair in a chignon? Why, 'tis Nelson, due de Eddy, pretending to be a bondsman. Sapristi, he is discovered by an agent 'straight from Paree'; he waits only to bawl a duet with Mademoiselle before marching his fellow-bondsmen off to fraternité and piracy; and now Mademoiselle it is who, together with 100 brides bound for Martinique, is led to the hold ('Spare your minions! I know my way'). And now the storm, unabated by the choral rendering by the hundred brides of Handel's 'Largo'; and the desert island, sacrebleu; and colonization, and courtship, and marriage, and – tiens, the French Fleet! But what is that they are singing? 'Tis the Marseillaise, harmonized with 'Lover, Come Back To Me'; 'tis the Revolution, 'tis democracy, 'tis the duc de Eddy for President. And what signifies bimsy? Bunk and whimsy, mes gosses.

October 1940

At last, **Gone with the Wind**, (director: Victor Fleming) the film of Margaret Mitchell's thousand-page book, the film which takes three hours forty minutes and three theatres! News of the exploration party sent to see it last week is beginning to trickle in. The members of the expedition were carefully picked for their hardihood, tenacity, and powers of resistance as well as for their previous experience in contests of endurance, and included a number of Channel swimmers, dancing Marathon winners, and pole-squatters. The gallant little band seemed in good heart as they set off, and the spirit which animated them was exemplified in the parting remark of a junior member, who cried, waving cheerily, 'Okay, tutz, see you at Whitsun.'

Large forces of distinguished film players were encountered from the start, among them Clark Gable, bringing to the part of the sardonic ex-gentleman Rhett Butler the nonchalance of a touring vaudeville artist; Leslie Howard as Ashley Wilkes, the well-bred Southern relic whom Scarlett O'Hara so mistakenly adores; Olivia de Haviland and his wife, Melanie; and Vivien Leigh as Scarlett herself. Miss Leigh gave a performance compact of vivacity, coquettishness and rigid egoism, extremely clever and well-trained and almost entirely without interest. The rest of the astronomical cast (except Hatty McDaniell, excellent as the negress Mammy) appeared to be overwhelmed by the catastrophe of the American Civil War in which they were engaged. This was curious, since the military scenes which were the best part of Miss Mitchell's industrious circulating library novel have been omitted or hurried over, with the exception of the view of the wounded lying in the sun at Atlanta, which a member of the exploration party, misled by the Technicolor, pardonably mistook for Bank Holiday on Bournemouth beach. Such interest as the book supplied by giving the point of view of the Southern States was almost completely obscured by the concentration of the attention on the tedious central characters.

A survivor of the *Gone with the Wind* expedition, who has been brought home completely worn out, is stated to have commented on two phenomena encountered on the journey to the interior: the colour of the sky, which, it seems, in Georgia is practically always red, and a curious swishing sound described as incidental music, which accompanies every speech made by the natives. The report is confirmed by a message just received by carrier pigeon, which adds: 'Sinking into a coma. This is tougher than pole-squatting.'

April 1940

It cannot have escaped the attention of my sagacious readers that, just as at the opera Brünnhilde's horse is often a more popular performer than Brünnhilde, just as in the theatre a cat strolling across the stage will steal the show from Olivier and Gielgud rolled into one, so in the cinema the appearance of a dog will set the house in a cluck. The creature lays his paw on the table, and there is a murmur of admiration; puts his head on one side, and sympathy floods through the stalls; droops his tongue and pants, and strong women are in tears. I was reminded of the fact with particular force during the past week when a film – it was the only new one – called **Deep Valley** (director: Jean Negulsco) designed to concentrate attention on the destiny of an escaped convict, in practice utterly failed to distract our thoughts from a dog, of hearth-rug-coat breed and answering to the name of Come On Boy.

This is the more curious since Come On Boy is not called on to perform any of the prodigies of intelligence sometimes required of the quadruped on the screen. He does not, like Rin-Tin-Tin, turn on the baby's bath, or, like Lassie, win the battle of the Aleutians; all he is expected to do is to look amiable, bark occasionally, and know when to get off the set. But then many bipeds have with no more equipment won the adoration of two continents; and I have been wondering whether it might not be possible to turn to better account the doggy sentiments of the general public.

Producers sometimes, greatly daring, allow some idolized beauty of the screen to extend her range; she is promoted, let us say, from the sarong to what is known as the hostess gown (for in the cinema an extension of range is often achieved by a curtailment of leg-view); the swimmer, perhaps, risks a few simple sentences in the vernacular, or the dancer tries over a song, making the lip-and-hip motions while, unknown to the audience, a professional voice obliges with the noise. Surely it is not too much to ask that the dog-star should now and again be permitted to pop outside his usual orbit. What, in fact, I am suggesting – and the suggestion, taking into account the current dog-love, ought not to be regarded as revolutionary – is that Come On Boy and his peers should from time to time exchange roles with those players, less hirsute, whose names are household words. Give us, in a word, some deathless dog-romance.

Let us see how the proposal would work if applied to the present film, a story of a hasty type (Dane Clark) in stir for manslaughter, who escapes from a tool shed during a landslide and is loved by a female hillbilly (Ida Lupino). Boy-dog, in my canine version, has been put on the lead for biting a stranger in a bus; while under restraint he bites somebody else and is chained in his kennel, but manages to gnaw through his collar and take to the mountains. Girl-dog, meanwhile, has run away from home because father-dog has clipped her on the ear, and the two rebels fall in love. But girl-dog is against all this biting; she tries to prevail on her dog-mate to bark first and bite afterwards. What is more, under the influence of love she is reconciled to dog-society; she even begins, in a burst of feminine vanity, to wear her collar low, off one shoulder in fact.

Unfortunately during her absence on a foraging expedition

boy-dog tries to bite a whole pack of police-dogs; he forgets about barking first and nearly bites girl-dog's head right off one day when she comes into the kennel unexpectedly; and he gives a really nasty nip to a suitor-dog who has been hanging round her with a view to matrimony. Clearly he is a misfit in dog society. He must atone; the police-dogs must get their dog, and get him they do. But girl-dog is faithful; she seeks him out where he is hiding in the mountains; and he lies in her paws, dreaming of the pure joys of rabbit-hunting. His biting was a symptom of modern dog-unrest; he meant no harm by it; and all he needed from life was a girl-dog to understand him. The dogs in the audience, particularly the girl-dogs, will not blame him, redeemed by dog-love as he has been; and he dies happy, leaving behind him nothing but the memory of a few bites.

Close students of the screen will, I feel sure, agree with me that much current cinema, far from being injured by treatment of this kind, would be actually improved; the drift of narrative would become clearer, and we should be able to judge with unprejudiced eyes the nature of the moral we are being asked to accept. And the complexity of character to which the modern film about love and the murderer has accustomed us would be not beyond the histrionic powers of any dog-star. There are, as a matter of fact, moments when I feel that the whole cinema is going to the dogs anyway.

June 1940

Dress reformers will, I am sure, be encouraged by the glimpse of interplanetary gentlemen's suitings afforded by **The Day the Earth Stood Still**, a new piece of science-fiction. This is about the arrival in Washington of a flying saucer which for five months has been bearing through space two representatives from an unnamed planet. One of them, an intellectual type, wears his going-away dress, a simple diving suit with what I understand are three-quarter-length sleeves and rolled-rope cuffs. The other, a large but handy robot, is in everyday clothes, a one-piece get-up in pliable metal with sliding-door headgear; this costume has the merit of being impenetrable by blow-torches.

The emissaries, though their sartorial equipment has been well thought out, are in certain other respects inadequately prepared for their visit. It is true that the leader has taken the trouble to learn English (by monitoring the radio); but he has not reflected on the consequences of alighting from a flying saucer and pointing at the flower of the American Army a cross between a thunderbolt and a hatpin-holder. Too late he protests that it was a gift for the President; and the robot, resentful of the bullet in his master's arm, opens his head-doors and melts machine-guns and revolvers with a couple of dirty looks from his patent double million magnifying gas microscopes.

I could have done with more demonstrations of other-planetary science. And I must confess that those we saw in *The Day the Earth Stood Still* showed now and then a lack of originality; for instance, when one of the visitors neutralized, as he puts it, electricity all over the world, I could not help remembering that René Clair's scientist in *Paris Qui Dort* had immobilized humanity nearly thirty years ago with more entertaining results. But then, the cinema has grown solemn since then; the new film interrupts its wonders to lecture us on the dangers of international aggression and the duties of the interplanetary police; and gaiety is restored only by the idiocies of dialogue. Patricia Neal and Michael Rennie accept their situation with gravity, and Robert Wise has directed the story for far more than it is worth.

December 1957

One day last week I woke up with a start. It was the middle of the afternoon and I was in the cinema.

That I should have been in the cinema is no matter for comment. That I should have fallen asleep, even in a small hot theatre, even for no more (as with some disappointment I found when I looked at my watch) than a moment or two is indeed exceptional, for my concentration on the most banal of films is, I assure you, normally complete. But it was more than the moment of inattention which shook me. It was the feeling, not merely that I had been sitting in the cinema for ever (a situation which my addiction to the medium could almost tolerate) but that my colleagues and I had been sitting there for ever repeatedly seeing the same film.

Let me try to give you an idea of what I mean. Last week we had Lesbianism; anal rape; brothels; and high jinks (well, rape to start with) in a convent. The week before we had a cat's cradle of heterosexual legs and a tribute to masturbation. The week before that we had demonstrations of the twelve basic positions – theme, you might say, with variations. The week before that – but I mustn't let the catalogue run away with me, and anyway I ought to be a little more detailed about what is current. All right then, *Myra Breckinridge* (director: Michael Sarne).

Gore Vidal's smart, initially funny but finally nauseating little novel, a satire on the battle of the sexes, the dominant female and the Hollywood myth, has been turned into a film which can't manage the smartness but dilligently preserves the nausea. For the benefit of those who haven't yet heard, it deals with a sex-change, man becomes woman, Myron becomes Myra, a fact which the novel does not at first reveal but which the film with a flourish of carving knives and hatchets makes very clear indeed. The result on the screen is Raquel Welch who, posing as widow of the defunct Myron, turns up at the Hollywood drama school of his uncle Buck Loner, ex-horse-opera star, and claims a half-share in that bogus but going concern. Myra plans the humiliation of the male species; has a trial of legal strength with Buck Loner; and at last with the aid of blackmail and her advantage as a teacher (of Empathy and Posture) manages to strap an unsuspecting student down on a table and assault him with, presumably, a dildo.

If on the screen any vestige of fun is extracted from this lamentable material we owe it to John Huston, whose Buck Loner offers at any rate a recognizable burlesque of the Gene Autry-type cowboy star. Mae West, playing the sexy Hollywood agent who conspires with Myra, can still command the insolently-cadenced come-hither voice; sad, though, that after her long absence from the cinema she should be invited to reappear in a form so dwarfed, so dehydrated. As for that laboratory-made star Miss Welch, her flouncing grinning non-performance makes balderdash of the references to the Hollywood cinema of the thirties and forties – references which in the novel form a relevant critical background but which in the cinema resolve themselves into meaninglessly interpolated clips of Shirley Temple, say, or Carmen Miranda, or Laurel and Hardy.

I emerged from *Myra Breckinridge* pining for a long evening with Norma Shearer.

February 1971

It is many years since I read **Ivanhoe**, a Technicolor version of which, made in this country by an American company, is now to be seen at the Empire, and though my respect for Scott's classic is unbounded, I fear I am unlikely to read it again unless cast away on a desert island with no chattier companion. So, while I remember fragments of the book, I am in no position to argue with the adapter, Aeneas MacKenzie, the script-writer, Noel Langley, and the director, Richard Thorpe, about fidelity to Sir Walter. Was there in the original quite so much banging about in iron head-buckets and chain-mail fascinators? I admit that what recollections I have are chiefly of the gymkhana element. And yet in memory the story seems quieter. Perhaps it will be best to forget Sir Walter and take the film as just another piece of Robin Hoodery.

Here we are, then, back in the greenwood days. Letters are carried by bow-and-arrow, and in the banqueting hall the aristocracy are still gnawing the traditional drumstick, while the retainers sit with understandably modest appetites over large quantities of some substance uncommonly like decaying tree-trunk. On the tournament-ground smart horses are wearing striped night-shirts – though one chic little charger turns out in black with white accessories.

Over at Torquilstone Castle there is never a dull moment. In the basement they are making up the fire for torture. On the walls the scaling-ladders are out, and the besiegers are dropping off in showers. Under an extravagant cover of arrows the invaders have run a landing-stage over the moat; while Ivanhoe is threatening to throw his gaoler off the roof, Rebecca is threatening to throw herself off the battlements and, to show willingness, Lady Rowena herself is hammering on the doors of her turret with (I fancy) a fragment of an early sewing-machine.

To some observers it may seem that, once they have seen the tournament at Ashby-de-la-Zouche, where Ivanhoe's opponents are not so much unhorsed as catapulted from the saddle, single combat can hold no surprises. I beg them to wait for the final struggle between the hero and Sir Brian de Bois-Guilbert, in which the contestants, mounted and armed, one with an axe and the other with a spiked ball on the end of a chain, bash each other about to the sound of dustbin-lids. For the production of this happy tale of fire and slaughter a number of eminent figures – Robert Taylor (Ivanhoe), Elizabeth Taylor (Rebecca), Joan Fontaine (Rowena) and George Sanders (Brian de Bois-Guilbert)

were imported from America. Talents normally domiciled in this
country were prominent too: Felix Aylmer as Isaac, Finlay Currie
as Cedric, and, as Wamba, Emlyn Williams, who to my regret
half-way through the story vanished with howls of exasperation
into a patch of burning Norman castle.

June 1952

The appearance of three-dimensional cinema has started everybody talking about the advantage to a film of a good story.
Technical progress, experts announce with an air of solemn
discovery, is no use by itself; you must have a good story. I
am happy to say that **Niagara** (director: Henry Hathaway) has
a story of a goodness we haven't seen since Blanche Sweet (I
think) saved her lover from execution by shinning up the belfry
and swinging on the clapper of the curfew bell.

And it has Marilyn Monroe. Miss Monroe, whose outline has
apparently done more to set the great heart of America racing than
anything since the Boston Tea-Party, is first disclosed horizontal
in a honeymoon cabin at Niagara. It is dawn, and she is wearing
a sheet and some eyelashes. Her jealous husband George (Joseph
Cotten) has slipped out to look at the Falls; he wishes he could be
like them, big and independent. Presently Miss Monroe, who is
planning to have him pushed over them by a more rugged type,
undulates to the door in a fragment of white tulle and marabout.
Her husband, she tells inquirers, is acting strangely these days.
Having thus prepared them for his end, she reappears in a saxe-
blue suit of adhesive cut and waggles off to do, as she puts it, the
shopping.

By evening she has eeled herself into what I can describe only as
a red satin skin with airholes, and everybody is acting strangely.
'You kinda like that song, don't you?' says an acquaintance who
has observed her paroxysms during the playing of a record called
'Kisses'. Miss Monroe has by now established the character she is
playing, and it is hardly necessary for her to do any more acting,
but trouper that she is she goes right on trying: 'There isn't any
other song,' she murmurs, billowing. Nobody is surprised when
poor George bounces out of the cabin and breaks the record in his
bare hands. 'Your husband doesn't seem to like music,' says the
acquaintance. But then George has unusual criteria. Describing
his first encounter with his wife in a beer-hall, 'She was the most

popular waitress they had,' he says; then, after a pause, 'I guess it was the way she put the beer on the tables.'

Against the splendid spectacle of the Falls, *Niagara* moves from hilarity to hilarious melodrama. Bodies are flung into the rapids, murderers, kitchen-knife in hand, creep into bedrooms in dead men's moccasins, women faint in the morgue or dangle from broken railings over cliffs, there is a strangling in the bell-tower, a rescue by helicopter on the cataract's edge. Miss Monroe, suiting the costume to the action, plays decoy in sky-blue swing-back, exhibits anxiety in scarlet hug-me-tight, and visits the morgue in a black suit whose neckline towards the end of the film is not so much plunging as diving. I approached this richly idiotic film with caution but, as time went on, abandoned myself to an enjoyment which I hope was shared by the rest of the audience. At any rate I thought I noticed the hint of a cheer at Marilyn Monroe's later appearances. But that, of course, may have been for the story.

April 1953

Looking the other day at the latest of the film biographies, a bit of hullo-there about Wagner called **Magic Fire** (director: William Dieterle). I was struck by the similarity which the cinema discloses in the lives of the musicians. One after another the composers on the screen are snubbed in youth, get entangled in revolution, have trouble with the little woman and are acutely sensitive to climatic influences. 'Nature,' as Mathilde Wesendonk remarks to Wagner here, 'can be so inspiring.' I remember a film about Berlioz in which the hero had only to look out of his window during a storm to be able to dash off a 'Fantastic' Symphony.

Wagner, I am happy to learn, was able to pick up a few notes in much the same way, and a passage from *Tristan and Isolde* seems to have reached him on the breeze from the garden during a stay with the Wesendonks. The hostility of Court officials, the debtors' prison – these we have learned to expect. And, naturally, the love stories. Minna, Mathilde, Cosima – in an hour and a half *Magic Fire* gets through its share of romances; and since it embraces also the 1848 revolution and Wagner's friendship with Ludwig of Bavaria there can scarcely be time for much more than a splendid snatch or two (including the fragments borne on the breeze) of most of the operas.

Time is, however, found for encounters with one or two other contemporary figures, with Meyerbeer and, of course, Liszt, an old friend in the cinema. Liszt has always been a keen duet-player; you may recall his performance with Chopin, one hand each, in 'A Song to Remember'; he even played a duet of sorts with the poor mad gentleman living in the drains in *The Phantom of the Opera*; and here he is again, struggling to get his hands on the keyboard while Wagner is banging out a motif from *Parsifal*.

The screenplay is the work of Bertita Harding (author of the book which it follows), David Chantler and E. A. Dupont. It is set against authentic backgrounds, but that does not save it from being richly silly. The cast do what they can, Yvonne de Carlo, Rita Gam and Valentina Cortese moping around, and Wagner himself being played with set teeth by Alan Badel, who for the purposes of the film has joined the glaring school.

April 1956

They have a choice, the figures in *The Towering Inferno* (A). They can be roasted or they can be drowned.

There are variants. Characters can fry while jumping from the 81st floor. They can roast after opening a harmless-looking door which discloses a furnace and an explosion. They can be incinerated while trying a roof-top rescue by helicopter. Or they can be drowned by water released, in a well-meaning attempt at extinguishing the fire, from tanks on a higher floor – an attempt which sweeps some familiar faces out of the shattered glass wall of the restaurant storey. I won't bother you with swaying life-lines, failing elevators or frantic scrambles down burning stairways; you can take it from me that the film isn't short on deaths. Anyway the supply is thought adequate to satisfy audiences in five cinemas.

The result of a partnership between two studios, Fox and Warner, and two directors, Irwin Allen (the producer) for action sequences and John Guillermin for what is left, *The Towering Inferno* is the latest entry in the cinema's Great Disaster stakes; after earthquake, air collision and catastrophe at sea we have conflagration in a San Francisco hotel, the world's tallest building. Fires are nicely dispersed about the loftier of the 135 storeys and the guests at the gala openings are caught a number of floors above the main blaze; there is a scatter of trapped residents as well – a family with a drowsy cat, an adulterous couple ('Do you smell something burning?' the girl says as the smoke creeps under the door).

Who, one asks oneself, will survive? Paul Newman (the architect)? William Holden (the builder)? Steve McQueen (the fire chief)? Faye Dunaway, perhaps? Jennifer Jones or Robert Vaughan? Richard Chamberlain or Robert Wagner? It is distracting, but not as distracting as it would be if members of the cast had a chance, in the intervals of acrobatic shinning up and down broken stairways and lift-shafts, to do a bit of acting. But nobody can find the time – except Fred Astaire who, cast as that stand-by of Great Disasters, the bad hat turned hero, with his customary elegance presents something uncommonly like a human being.

The rest are confined to looking harassed, a feat which after two hours and three-quarters of flaming skyscraper could, I am sure, have been emulated by most of the critics at the Press show. For if you must have a conflagration-film this is the hell of a good conflagration, the stunts superbly executed, the illusion of a desperate situation brilliantly achieved. Once or twice I caught myself wondering what D. W. Griffith would have done if such technical resources had been available to him (not that he did badly in the Babylonian sequences of *Intolerance*). Thinking back now I fancy he would have drawn a stronger moral conclusion from disaster. *The Towering Inferno* merely remarks, not very forcibly, that high-rise buildings ought to have better electric wiring and better fire proofing. In the huge spectacle pity is lost; and I am left reflecting that addiction to Great Disaster cinema is lowering to the sensibilities.

To save animal-lovers from fretting I should add that despite the paucity of human survivors, somebody saves the cat.

February 1975

3 A Sense of Proportion

When a film comes over from Hollywood labelled class you can be pretty sure that the piece will be of impeccable craftsmanship. The direction will be assured, the cutting unerring; nobody will question the solidity of the background the acting will be fluent; everything, in short, will go off with the proper bang.

All the King's Men is a film of this order. It has the right parent (a Pulitzer Prize novel, by Robert Penn Warren) and the right education (screenplay, direction and production by the accomplished Robert Rossen). It arrives flourishing the right prizes: Oscar for the best film of the year, Oscar for the best actor (Broderick Crawford), Oscar for the best supporting actress (Mercedes McCambridge). All America, I understand, is crazy about it. Surely the Old Country, too, should cry Hot Dog!

To the technique, at once massive and glittering, of *All the King's Men* anyone can pay tribute. The piece tells a long, complicated story about the emergence in an American backwoods state of a dictator; the kind of story in which, we are assured, 'any similarity to the name, character or history of any person is entirely accidental and unintentional.' The history of Willie Stark in the film bears obvious resemblances to the history of Huey Long, Governor of Louisiana, who survived an attempt at impeachment in 1929 and was assassinated in 1935; but then the cinema is full of accidents and coincidences. At any rate, the tale of corruption and violence is credible enough: fantastic but not in essentials fake. And it is told against a background dashingly composed.

Indeed, I am inclined to think that the background is the most exciting element in the piece; and by background I do not mean simply the settings so skilfully graded from shack to Governor's house by the art director Sturges Carne; I mean first of all the masses of human beings which shift and change behind the principal characters. Rossen manages crowds with mastery; a concourse of voters from the back country waiting in the square till nightfall for news of their idol, militia battling to hold back an enthusiastic mob. Still more remarkable is the handling of small groups of extras and minor players. One of the excellences of the American screen is its ability to create a kind of texture of background figures. The director, with his patterns of hangers-on in the ante-rooms, his knots of reporters, strong-arm men and platform sharks has given us what I am prepared to believe is the very feel of the shady side of American politics.

Yet I question whether these virtues are responsible for the praise which has greeted the film in its own country. No doubt the acting of Broderick Crawford as Stark, moving from bull-headedness through gratified conceit to egomania, has been appreciated. But one remembers that America is always ready to receive with extravagant respect the treatment on the screen of what is described as a social problem. A third-rate film such as *Gentleman's Agreement* was hailed as a masterpiece simply because it was about anti-Semitism; and when Dieterle's *The Searching Wind* attacked the timidity of the diplomats everybody looked as if the Plymouth Rock had landed on the Pilgrim Fathers.

All the King's Men, in spite of its qualities, is still not superior in craftsmanship to a dozen other American films with humbler material. But it exposes political graft; it has a social conscience; it is not about boy-meets-girl; and that, apparently, is enough for some people. I cannot help feeling that it is not enough to present a character without working it out. Mr Crawford's playing gives the central figure the semblance of life; but Stark remains a superficial portrait, the stuff of pretentious half-educated fiction. And all round him characters are left hanging in air, going nowhere for nothing.

That, you may say, is the inevitable result of compressing a novel into a film. But compression, after all, is the adapter's problem; Rossen, though he has skilfully preserved the flow of narrative, has left his human figures incomplete. And I am reminded that in *Citizen Kane* (a film which has, I fancy, influenced *All the King's Men*) Welles showed that the cinema is capable of implying a character: of leaving the past dark and the future obscure, and yet persuading us that we know all we need to know.

April 1950

Every so often the cinema feels it must insist on its manhood. Its favourite method of doing this is to produce a number of what are called problem films; these may be about prisons, the Jews, the Negroes or the pastime colloquially described as juvenile delinquency. We are going through one of these problem periods at the moment. We have had the social responsibility cycle; now, with the appearance of *The Men* I am afraid we may be in for the physical disablement cycle.

The Men is an American film about the treatment of paraplegia. Its hero has been wounded in the war, and is permanently paralysed from the waist down; he has lost the wish to live, he rejects the help of doctors and nurses and refuses to see the girl to whom he was formerly engaged. The film tells, mainly against a hospital background, the story of his return to life and the part played in it by the love and courage of the girl. It is a bold film, since in a medium not given to plain speaking it describes with some frankness the symptoms and effects of injury to the spinal cord; and it is a hopeful film, since it says that a man's life need not be ruined by even the cruellest bodily injury.

It is also a skilful and at times a touching film. Its theme is illuminated by excellent acting; Teresa Wright brings her singular tenderness to the part of the young fiancée and, later, wife; there is a beautifully fluent performance from Everett Sloane as the doctor; and as the paralysed soldier a newcomer from the stage, Marlon Brando, gives a strong and penetrating account of an isolated, bitter and savage man gradually reconciled to his own tragedy. *The Men* is the work of a talented director, Fred Zinnemann, and of a producer (Stanley Kramer) and a writer (Carl Foreman) whose collaboration has already given us in *The Champion* and *Home of the Brave* two films above contempt. The dialogue is often very much to the point: I have, for instance, a sharp sympathy with the character who declares that he doesn't want to be rehabilitated, regenerated or re-anything else, and he doesn't want to take his proper place in society either. Yet the film leaves me dissatisfied; and my dissatisfaction is not due to reluctance to look disagreeable facts in the face (though I have never been able to understand why looking facts in the face should be so generally revered as an occupation).

Once or twice the facts are, I think, unfairly stated. It is not the practice in civilized society to pause with the restaurant fork half-way to the mouth in order to stare lengthily at the wheel-chair which has just come in; and I doubt whether on her wedding night a young woman who had up to that moment shown nothing but understanding of the sick man's nervous miseries would have made such a fuss about the champagne spilt on the carpet. Indeed the girl's character and feelings are all through only superficially explored. But my lukewarmness has other causes.

The film seems to me to be a result of the half-baked theory that an art which is adult has to deal with problems. *The Men* is all problem; the problem quite overshadows the people. But walk a hundred yards or so eastward to the Rialto, and you will find a comedy called *City Lights* which has no problem, yet makes the new piece look like a cradle-decoration. The cinema is often at least as grown-up as its whiskered brothers-in-art. But that has nothing to do with the contemporary subject, the realistic approach, the wider issues and all the rest of the jargon-ideas.

November 1950

Years ago, when I still noticed what people said about film critics, an acquaintance reproached me sourly with devoting most of my space one week to a French film and relegating some American piece to second or even third place. The French film was no rarefied intellectual exercise (crikey, no: it was Raymond Bernard's story about the first war and a group of unwilling heroes, *Hostages*); all the same what my acquaintance was grumbling about was the general critical emphasis on what he felt was highbrow cinema. I am beginning to think he had something there – or rather would have if he were grumbling now.

For decades – since long before his reproaches to me – a good many film critics have been battling on behalf of the serious screen, of films about ideas (even when there isn't an idea in sight some earnest writer will sometimes manage to discover a symbol, an obsession, a Freudian thesis): adult cinema, perhaps, is the repulsively appropriate phrase. Well, adult cinema has not merely caught up with us; speaking for myself I should say that it is rolling over us and flattening us out. And the most flattening of all is the American adult cinema. A prize example this week: **Mickey One** (director: Arthur Penn). It opens, in one of the fashionable pre-credits runarounds, with a young man, fully dressed and sporting a bowler hat, being laughed at by three jelly-bosomed middle-aged men wearing nothing but towels below the waist and nothing at all above it. Somehow one suspects that this is not going to be funny, and one is damn well right; this is going to be a psychological enigma, a bit of post-Kafka. And like the *echt*-Kafka it begins (begins, I mean, once you have got past the credits) with an air of desperate fact;

you would think that, like the attributes of the stripper in the song in *Oklahoma!* everything it had was absolutely real. It begins, in fact, as if it were going to be a gangster film – and how I wish it were.

The central character, a nightclub entertainer in whose slightly parted lips, slightly ruffled hair and slightly stunned expression one can recognize the lineaments of Warren Beatty, seems to have got in wrong with a gambling mob. He is told by a seated figure (Franchot Tone) who appears first as a kind of stage door-keeper and later as a kind of accountant in a meat-depot (symbolic, no doubt), that he owes an enormous and unspecified sum of money; and since in the background there is a suggestion that somebody else, presumably another defaulter, is having his brains beaten out Mickey One bolts. He burns his identity papers, works as a garbage-can emptier, refuses the offer of a handsome job from a smart club-owner (Hurd Hatfield), shrinks from everybody except an unexpected roommate (the talented Alexandra Stewart) – and yet finds himself cornered on a stage with a spotlight which follows him but no voice which answers his questions.

Kafkaesque heroes are usually searching for some figure, perhaps some authority which eludes them. This hero runs from a pursuer who never shows himself. Mickey One is on the lam from his own sense of guilt and failure; and much as one may admire the way in which nameless fears are translated into the grotesque shapes of night-life or into such concrete objects as the steel grabs of a car-dump, there is no avoiding the feeling that the psychology shows too much – especially in passages involving a Protean, perpetually optimistic, resourceful figure whom I take to represent the generic, unquenchable artist. Arthur Penn (he was the director of *The Miracle Worker*) has talents which won't let you quite get away; and the editing of Aram Avakian and the camerawork of Ghislain Cloquet are dazzling. I recall now that a young American critic told me in Venice last year, when it first appeared, that he found *Mickey One* deeply moving. Perhaps some ancient European disbelief stands between me and such surrender. I can say only that I have seen the film twice; and increasingly I find it empty, boring, pretentious and toshy.

November 1966

Adult: the word is an accolade; bestow it on a film and we all run to congratulate. The latest recipient is an American comedy which to his seeming surprise Joseph E. Levine, who presents it, discovers to be a smasher. 'It's absolutely incredible. . . . I haven't seen anything like it in all the years I've been in the business.' Its title, *The Graduate*, its director, Mike Nichols; its origin, a novel by Charles Webb adapted for the screen by Calder Willingham and Buck Henry.

An Oscar-winner, a critics' delight, included in I don't know how many Best Ten lists; 'clearly the biggest success in the history of the movies,' says a New Yorker article which I happened to see a week or two ago. I did not immediately do more than glance at the opening paragraphs of the article; to begin with I was alarmed by its twenty-six pages of severe sociological and psychological examination, to go on with I thought I should like to form my own impressions first. Still, one can't help having expectations raised by such preliminaries.

It was in cheerful mood, then, that I set off for the Press show the other day. I was ready for anything; especially, since nobody had told me to expect comedy, I was ready for the scenes at the start in which the young hero, back from college loaded with academic and athletic honours, rather than attend a home-coming party and accept the congratulations of his parents' obtuse friends prefers to sit glumly apart staring at a fishtank. Here, I thought, is one of the great American dilemmas about which people are always writing the great American novel: the lack of communication between the generations, the young idealist full of inchoate longings to break away from a materialist society.

But no. Suddenly, with the married woman's onslaught on the cornered frightened boy (for somebody with all those college honours he is pretty slow in the uptake) we were out of the great American novel and into a modern variant on a Buster Keaton or perhaps a Harry Langdon situation; and I must say it was no end of a relief to me. The awkward inexperienced male in the clutches of an experienced predatory female: it is a theme frequent in the cinema, but its development here is attended by discreet audacity: the suggestion but not the illustration of nudity. Hilarious detail: the boy planning an affair who can't even get a waiter to bring a drink, the apprehensive exchanges with the room clerk; and playing which gives the whole business a kind of desperate comic reality – Anne Bancroft's cold practical determination, the nervous idiocies of Dustin Hoffman, who with Mike Nichols's direction really looks like a discovery.

And with experience the new toughness of the boy: that, though it scarcely accords with his earlier bumbling manner, is comic in a deliberately uncomfortable way. In a car? What kind of car? he asks his bedfellow when he learns of her first sexual experience; asks out of amused curiosity, totally without feeling (he always addresses her as Mrs Robinson). The negation of sentiment in the relationship is clear – and necessary to Mr Nichols's theme so far.

But what is Mr Nichols's theme? For next the film makes off in another direction: miserly sexual rage when the married woman suspects a relationship, which this time is indeed sentimental, between the boy and her daughter (Katharine Ross, rather nice, but give me Miss Bancroft). Now, in fact, we are an another kind of novel: not the great American novel but the hot American novel. It is illuminated, to be fair, by some smart Lubitsch-style irony; but imagine, if you can, a Joan Crawford playing the Anne Bancroft part and I think you will recognize the Queen Bee or even the Peyton Place bracket.

Finally, an excursion into romantic fantasy, into Capra country: the boy's interruption of the daughter's wedding, the purloined bride. It is exciting, it is funny, but it has little to do with what has gone before, with the worried youth in a cocktails-and-swimming-pool society, with the farcical acquisition of experience and the jealous paramour. Why, anyway, does the daughter let herself be hustled into marriage with the wrong boy? One needs a bit more explanation, especially since despite the shifts in mood up to this point the action has generally proceeded from character.

Mr Nichols is reported as saying (at last I have read that article) that 'as the movie ends, the real problems are just beginning'; and perhaps on the faces of the breathless runaway pair there is already a shade of something which is not all certainty of bliss. Nevertheless (and at this point I am entirely with the analysis – an attacking analysis – of the *New Yorker* writer) the question put in the opening scenes – what future has the boy in such a milieu? – has not been answered; on the contrary it has been ignored. Yet the mere asking seems to have driven American opinion into a delirium of admiration and self-denigration.

But why? The reaction of a young audience to the hero's final revolt against established authority I can understand; a decade ago young audiences were responding with, I fancy, something of the same delight to the anti-authoritarian personality of James Dean.

The attitude of their elders is perhaps the result of a social and political situation peculiar to the United States. Even so, a critical reaction which has expressed itself in cries of 'adult', 'coming of age' and 'a milestone in American film history' strikes me as absurdly solemn and over-heated. It also seems to me by a distortion of the intentions of comedy to do an injustice to a brilliantly entertaining (though erratic) work. I suggest that you see *The Graduate* for fun, and the hell with the American cinema coming of age.

Anyhow, is it a more adult film than, say, *All Quiet on the Western Front*?

August 1968

What can be done by an able-bodied couple in ten seconds? Plenty, I agree; nevertheless I can't feel that anything overwhelming could be got into the ten seconds excised by the censor from Bernardo Bertolucci's **Last Tango in Paris**. One doesn't, I hasten to say, notice the cut. Marlon Brando, in what has become a notorious scene, orders his girl to fetch the butter; the act of sodomy follows immediately. Imagination ought to be able to fill in the blank; imagination might even do better than the forbidden original. That journey to Paris contemplated before one knew that the film would be shown here, and so little abbreviated, is unnecessary. So what is all the fuss about?

Of course there is more – more action, horizontal or semi-vertical, and a great deal of pretty rough talk; some audiences may find the dialogue harder to take than the action. But let me fill in, not indeed those ten seconds, but the general setting of Bertolucci's film.

A girl (Maria Schneider), looking at a Paris flat, finds the room, dishevelled, hollow except for a pile of anonymous furniture under a dust-sheet, already occupied by the huddled figure of a stranger (yes, Marlon Brando). You know nothing about either of them except that the man appeared distraught when you saw him a minute ago in the street; they know nothing about one another. All the same after a few insignificant exchanges, grumbled on Mr Brando's part, the pair are violently glued together in an erotic embrace. Do I believe in it? Not for a moment; and the scene would lend itself to parody were it not that Brando can present so powerful though not necessarily seductive a sexual image – and that Maria Schneider draws here and throughout the film an extraordinary portrait of a girl not so much innocent (is she meant to be innocent? It isn't my idea of innocence) as amazed, bewitched by her own behaviour and presently imprisoned in it.

The relationship continues: the big hollow room, the two hollow people. One begins to ferret out something about the exterior of their lives. The man has been married; the wife he loved has for no traceable reason committed suicide; look, there is the bloodstained wall; there is her lover (Massimo Girotti) in the desreputable hotel where she lived with her husband. The girl comes from an Army family; you will need to remember that such a household always owns a revolver. In the intervals of her tiring exercises with the man she is engaged in a ghastly piece of cinema-vérité being directed by her boy friend (Jean-Pierre Léaud). All right, so you find out something about the man and the girl, but they don't find out anything about one another. The man insists on no background, no names; you must forgive me if I sound like the text of an early D. W. Griffith – the Boy, the Dear One and all that.

The pair speak sometimes in French (a few sub-titles), but more often in English (he plays an expatriate American); the spectator without any foreign languages will know exactly what is being said. But will he know anything – anything, that is, in depth – about the two characters who are talking? Bertolucci has been reported as making the usual glib pronouncements about the impossibility people 'in our society' find in communicating with one another. His idea, then, was to show two figures in isolation who communicate solely through sex.

True that by force of personality Brando compels one to watch him with deep curiosity. Even in the improbable turnabout of the last minutes with the savagery transmuted into romantic pursuit ('I love you') he still persuades. But if the couple remain unknown not merely to one another but to you and me, if the script, if the whole film declines to involve us, we are thrown back not on interest in human beings but on inquisitiveness about sexual practices. And again I find myself asking what the fuss is about. After all, the cinema has before now offered a variety of vicarious experiences. A more stirring display of sodomy was seen in Bergman's *The Silence*, and a more ferocious one in John Boorman's *Deliverance*. *Flesh* and *Trash* are more explicit about sex than *Last Tango in Paris*. And I am driven to conclude that the fuss is about manufactured characters, about a false situation, about a piece of fake brilliantly executed, indeed, but still a piece of fake.

Ah well, praise the Lord and pass the butter; and now, please let me out of that room.

March 1973

4 *Noting the New*

When last we saw a film made from a novel by James M. Cain it was directed in France by a Frenchman, Pierre Chénal; *The Postman Always Rings Twice* thus became a film with French characters, French in background and feeling. Personally I thought none the worse of it for that; but I still welcome an American treatment of an American subject, and now that a film of a second Cain book comes along, something more than the interest of comparing American and French handling of similar themes makes me glad the piece comes from Hollywood.

Double Indemnity was made by Billy Wilder, one of the many screen writers who have lately taken to direction. Naturally Wilder himself worked on the script; it was another name among the credits which caught my eye. In the last year or so three stories by Raymond Chandler, a new writer in the tough American detective genre, have reached this country: *Farewell, My Lovely*, *The High Window*, and *The Big Sleep*: new, at any rate, to me, and so far scarcely recognized here. Of the three one at least, *The Big Sleep*, achieves something like mastery in its own line; the depiction of a society raffish, corrupt, vicious behind its chromium plating, the mongrel society of the waterfront, the rye parlour, the one-night hotel, and the mansion with swimming pool, the society of blackmailers, gunmen, Bourbon breakfasts and colloquies in fusty bedrooms shuttered all day, fraying away at its fringes into roadhouses, petrol stations, shacks on half-made roads. More superficial, flashier no doubt than the much-admired Simenon with his studies of catarrhal criminals, Raymond Chandler still seems to me to communicate in his slick hard style an American, Pacific coast atmosphere quite as curious as the underworld of the melancholy Continental.

The name of Raymond Chandler, then, as collaborator with Billy Wilder on the script of *Double Indemnity*, it was which struck me; pleasantly, for Chandler's writing is at its best sharply visual, getting its effects by observed detail, the small shocking thing seen. I was glad to learn the other day that a film was to be made of one of his books (though the least expert); in the meantime his work on a story of crime in the James M. Cain manner was likely to be interesting. *Double Indemnity*, indeed, turned out to be a pretty good job. Good first of all because the story is told with much sureness and control: no lingering over the expensive and unnecessary set, no sentimental expansiveness, no description of trivial actions without significance in the plot.

In this film when a character tries to start a car, well, that means something, because if the car doesn't start (and it nearly doesn't) the murder planned to look like an accident is going to look like a murder. Most of the high points in the story of a woman who plots with an insurance agent to get rid of her husband are visually presented: the killing in the car, the faking of evidence, the encounter with the only dangerous witness. Here and there an imaginative precision in detail bears witness to a good eye; the cigarette the wounded man takes from his pocket carries the moist stain of blood. Against this must be set occasional over-reliance on spoken narrative. The tale is told into a dictaphone by the murderer; a series of flashbacks takes us through the crime and its consequences. The device of the dictaphone is economically used. But the visual basis of the cinema must be jealously guarded; and at a time when film after film talks when it should act one is disinclined to forgive even the mild faults of narrative in *Double Indemnity*. It remains to be said that the piece is skilfully played by Fred MacMurray, Edward G. Robinson, and Barbara Stanwyck.

September 1944

Lately the name of Raymond Chandler (music in my ears, my pretty dicks) has crept once or twice into the film credits: as part-writer, for instance, of the script of *Double Indemnity* and again of *And Now To-morrow*. Now a film has been made of **Farewell, My Lovely**, not the very best of his streamlined thug novels, but good enough to be going on with.

It may surprise some Chandler readers to know that this is not the first film to be founded on the book. The first, called *The Falcon Takes Over*, appeared two or three years ago with George Sanders as the Falcon; I am assured, however, by those who saw it (I didn't) that it bore no resemblance, except in a name or two and a scrap of plot, to the present piece, and the fact that it appeared in the Falcon series would seem to clinch that anyway.

Farewell, My Lovely, then, may be taken as the first serious attempt at putting on the screen Chandler's peculiar mixture of harshness, sensuality, high polish and back-street poetry. Some of the poetry (for poetry, I persist, is there) has been lost in the passage from one medium to another. The story has a different finish. But whatever has been subtracted, a brilliantly hard, fast film comes out at the end.

A great deal of the work, of course, was ready done for the makers of this piece; Chandler, with his precise eye and his feeling for the atmosphere of a bar-room, a shack, a deserted office, a phoney intellectual parlour, is a cinematic writer if ever there was one. Yet Hollywood is temperamentally opposed to the make-do-and-mend principle, and credit must go to the scriptwriter, John Paxton, and the director, Edward Dmytryk, for accepting so much of the author's original plan and decoration.

They have certainly not been afraid of his complexity of plot; the first half of *Farewell, My Lovely*, must be bewildering to anyone who frets about a logical sequence of events in a murder film. But the quality of the film is not in the plot (though that clicks into place at the last). The quality is in the sense of movement, the subtly handled lighting, the multiplication of the tiny narrative touches and revelations of character in action. Dick Powell sitting in his office at night, high above the restless neon lights, and the stiffening of his face as he sees, intermittently reflected in the window, the gigantic moron standing silent behind him; the eye's passage along a shaft of light to the twining hands of the dancer, crudely haloed in the vulgar darkness of the road-house; the shabby ferocity of the bar-room behind the half-extinguished electric sign, and the meaningless spaces of the millionaire's house with its mausoleum echoes – these are the moments, these the shots which give the film an imaginative excitement not met with in this genre since *The Maltese Falcon*.

Not that *Farewell, My Lovely* is a patchwork of dislocated pleasures. The story, from its opening under the arc lamp at police headquarters, moves in a connected, racing rhythm; the resources of the camera are used to indicate both the unbelieving eye of the detective and the distorted vision of a man under drugs, but without breaking the narrative flow.

And as the private cop Dick Powell, not until now one of my favourite players, gives us the gradations from contained watchfulness to blonde trouble with an economy of facial expression which is a delight to follow. Mr Powell must now join Humphrey Bogart in the minute class of film actors who, looking at a woman, display something more than the enthusiasm of a clubman choosing a boiled shirt.

April 1945

Two years ago the name of the director Michael Ritchie slid into one's consciousness (it still hasn't got into the Motion Picture Almanac); with his first film, *Downhill Racer*, Mr Ritchie won a reputation which made one look anxiously for a second. When **The Candidate** appeared at the Venice Festival I for one wasn't disappointed; and at a second view the film looks even better.

Apparently metropolitan audiences were not thought quite equal to *Downhill Racer* at the time of its appearance; at any rate it was tried on the provinces first and only after critical applause brought to swinging London. I am reminded of this by seeing another film, **Duel** (director: Steven Spielberg). . . . *Duel* is worth your time.

It is about rage on the roads. At any rate after long cogitation I can't find any higher significance, though I admit that the end leaves one in the air – well, on the edge of a precipice. A middle-aged man sets off to cross California for a business appointment; he drives at a moderate steady pace. In front of him a huge lorry emits opaque and suffocating smoke; he passes. To his surprise it gathers speed and, smoking, passes him. When later a hand waves him on he gratefully pulls out – and swerves back just in time; the signal was unmistakably malevolent. And little by little it is borne in on the driver of the car and on the audience that the lorry means deadly business. The duel is on, the monster, fast, armoured, against the fragile car.

You would hardly think that so slight, indeed so seemingly motiveless a plot (the script is by Richard Matheson) would be enough for a film of ninety minutes. It is plenty. It is plenty because the increase in tension is so subtly maintained, because the rhythm and the pace of movement is so subtly varied, because the action, the anonymous enemy attacking or lying in wait, is shot with such feeling for dramatic effect. The director hasn't, as Mr Ritchie has in both his films, the advantage of an established star. But he is served well by Dennis Weaver, an actor modestly known in the cinema, as his central figure and indeed by all the cast. Mr Spielberg comes from television (*Duel* was made for television); he is only twenty-five. No prophecies; but somehow I fancy this is another name to look out for.

And *The Candidate*. I don't regard this appallingly funny view of American political behaviour (screenplay by Jeremy Larner) as a political film. It isn't about the politics of an American liberal, though Robert Redford looks so much like a Kennedy as to make one take the piece for an inquiry into the principles of the Democrats. It is about an election campaign and the way a decent young man with decent opinions is taken in hand by the party campaign managers. He agrees to stand for the Senate on condition that he fights in his own way. By the end he has been coached into the shape of what his father the ex-Governor (a genial portrait of corruptness by Melvyn Douglas) calls a politician; he has shaken hands, admired babies, made jokes at ladies' parties, tailored his speeches, changed his natural honest approach to win over the electorate.

Possibly those who are looking for an aggressive satire on United States politics would prefer to see the central character in disintegration. But he is never entirely a puppet; he insults the union boss (though he accepts union support), he can't quite go through with some prepared piece of publicity; and while at the last he is looking helplessly for guidance from his manager (Peter Boyle, flawless), while he may have been trapped into renouncing his own honesty of appeal he doesn't appear to have renounced his liberal aims. *The Candidate* isn't so much an exposure of American politics as a sour-funny picture of advertising applied to politics. And Robert Redford as the candidate – nobody's fool but cornered into accepting shifty and vulgar ways of campaigning – gives a beautiful, a developing performance; for once a character who really changes in changing circumstances.

I have said he looks like a Kennedy. How far, in this splendidly constructed work, so superior to the solemn, attacking political films of the past, the resemblance goes I leave you to judge.

October 1972

If you don't share my conviction that the difficult films of today are not the intellectual foreigners, not the Antonionis and the middle-period Pasolinis but the thriller and the crime story I urge you (I urge you anyway, for it is a remarkable piece of work) to see **The Conversation** – if, that is, you accept it as a thriller or a crime story. It thrills all right. But is there a crime? Even of that one is not always sure.

Written and directed by Francis Ford Coppola and with engaging music by David Shire, *The Conversation* opens with an extraordinary shot of a festive square (the scene is San Francisco): music, pop players, a chalk-faced mime jostling passers-by. From the crowd, a confluence of people walking, listening, talking, the camera picks out a figure, a face, perambulating pair, while from a high window a man with a precision weapon looks down; looking with him, seeing a head framed as if in the sights of a rifle, you think of Oswald and the assassination of President Kennedy.

But the unknown observer merely observes; presently there are other watchers. A man in a raincoat, middle-aged, the chin beginning to sag, the back of the neck beginning to fold over the collar (heroes, at any rate central figures in films don't have to be handsome any longer) detaches himself, pursued by the mime, from the crowd and climbs into a van. What on earth is going on? It is dark inside the van, the space crammed with mysterious equipment manipulated by a second man; a third comes and goes. Buttons, wheels, tapes – yes, tapes is the word; for however much the situation may remind you of one President of the United States, now you find yourself reflecting on another. The man in the raincoat (it is Gene Hackman, playing with a miraculous psychological grasp) is what in polite terms is called a surveillance agent. He is the telephone-tapper, the private ear, destroyer of privacy; he is the listener beneath your skin.

Do I spoil your enjoyment by giving these details? I fancy not, for the richness of detail on the screen and the mesmerizing flow of enigmatic action far exceed anything I am saying. Mr Coppola, who began the screenplay long before the word Watergate got into all our vocabularies, says he planned to make a film about privacy but found he had been dealing with the theme of responsibility. True in a way. Harry Caul, the agent, is a Catholic and a man troubled by conscience. At a convention (surveillance agents, it seems, hold conventions at which the latest bugging devices are exhibited) it emerges, almost casually, that after one of his professional triumphs (on a political job, too) three people were murdered. Nothing to do with him, he says. But he is disturbed about the use to which the tapes he is at present producing may be put. That perambulating pair observed in the opening scene are lovers; their looks, glances, their fragmentary talk as they circle in the crowd to avoid, as they think, surveillance, everything has been recorded. Harry Caul plays and replays the tapes, balancing, pulling the individual voice out of the crowd noises. At last he produces a clear, comprehensible conversation – and then is reluctant to hand over the results to the 'director', as his employer is always called.

And it is at this point that obscurity darkens.

By interludes which at the time might have seemed irrelevant had they not in themselves been too engrossing to let one think, the brilliant screenplay has warned us of the kind of man Harry Caul has become. Secretive, suspicious, he walks out on his girl because she asks a harmless question or two, he quarrels with his assistant (John Cazale in a flawless sketch) because the man would like to know something about the job they are engaged on. The spy is gradually being poisoned by his own professional poison. And his obsessions show themselves in fantasy: bloody handprints on curtains, blood flooding a hotel bathroom. By the end of the film, when he finds or thinks he finds his own jealously guarded privacy invaded, his disintegration is complete.

But before that Mr Coppola has driven the spectator into a parallel state of doubt and uncertainty. When Harry Caul takes a long look at the car of the 'director' and the girl whom he is having watched, I begin to wonder if the surveillant has seen the shadow of a crime. But then perhaps there is no crime, merely an accident. If a crime, who is the victim, who are the criminals?

Recalling Harry Caul's desperate attempts to defeat the listener under his own skin, I reflected on the possibility that for the last half-hour of the story everything had been fantasy: for *The Conversation* is a film in which all seems unfinished, every scene cut off before its explanation. But then Mr Coppola wraps it all up, moral concepts, menace, the lot. True that his story is about the responsibility of the civil spy; true, again, that it is about the contemporary annihilation of privacy. But it is also about physical murder; and detecting a tiny change of emphasis, as the tapes are repeatedly played, repeatedly balanced and clarified, you realize that you have been tricked into looking in the wrong direction. There has been a double twist in the plot; and the seemingly innocent it is who are guilty.

July 1974

It begins with contrast. **Days of Heaven** shows you at the start days of purgatory. Black-and-white portraits and groups in the style of a street photographer: a girl at some melancholy task, a party standing in the attitude of resignation characteristic of family photographs, everybody staring bemused at the camera; everywhere the sins of deprivation, poverty, hunger. Then colour, a steel-works, the flaring furnaces, and hot words between a worker and a foreman – and flight, the workman, little more than a boy, bolting with his girl and his younger sister in a bid for air and freedom.

Then indeed there are days of heaven. The journey first, away from Chicago with a party of migrant workers; the wild creatures of the plains stand watching as the train, its human cargo crowded on its back, steams westward; you have the feeling of solitude and excited hope. And the arrival: the party on the train-roof splitting, some riding on, some jumping off to be hired by the foreman of the tall, naked, isolated farmhouse. It is harvest time, they are needed; and in the mild golden light the boy (Richard Gere), his girl (Brooke Adams) and the younger sister (Linda Manz) settle to work in the fields.

Once or twice the pacific homeward procession at the end of the working days reminded me of another film about migrant workers, Lewis Milestone's *Of Mice and Men* made four decades ago. But the film which Terence Malick has now made is more spacious. In its way it is a social picture, a recreation of a passage of history – the flight from the cities and the nomadic sequel. But its images have a sense of repose in freedom which I find unique. Repose does not last; there are passages both of human violence and of the ferocities of nature. All the same it is the sunlit days, the days of heaven which I remember.

To say the film is visually beautiful is not enough. The point is that in Terence Malick's work the images are strictly linked to the nature of the subject and the development of its action. Obviously the opening black-and-white portraits and groups are necessary to the narrative. But the harvesting scenes – the movement of the figures, the plumes of dark smoke from the harvesting machine, the billowing plain – have a different significance. Their lovely calm intensifies the feeling of an interlude in paradise. They are beautiful in themselves. But their composition is a creative element in the story.

Extremes of happiness are apt to be short-lived. The boy and his girl, trying to avoid gossip, have called themselves brother and sister; they have not reckoned with the young farmer (Sam Shepard) who watches the girl, slim, desirable, somehow elegant in her long workaday skirts with her hair blowing in the wind of the plains. They have laid a trap for themselves; it is bound to snap shut. But something more than mistakes and false moves governs the direction of their lives. A few years ago Terence Malick wrote and directed a film called *Badlands*. It made his reputation. It was a story of two rebels, younger than Bonnie and Clyde, acting not in the social context of those two notorious outlaws but in a vacuum of their own making.

The central pair of *Days of Heaven* live for a time inside a group, inside society; they follow certain moral codes. But at heart they too are outlaws, and Terence Malick has created another pair heedless of the consequences of their actions. Like the young creatures of *Badlands* they run; they fancy that flight will solve all problems.

Days of Heaven is superbly directed and acted; see it for a second time and its hold is still more relentless. Nevertheless it is a disquieting film. It may deal with a period over half a century ago; as it ends the First World War is with us. But it is evidence of the sentiments of today. It presents the restlessness, the anchorless mood of a world which has lost its book of rules.

Punch, June 1979

6 ACTING AND STARRING

Stars were not always to Dilys Powell's critical taste. She prefers acting; it is Davis rather than Crawford whom she respects. Yet in a long piece written for the *Sunday Times Magazine* in 1970, Powell almost relents, '. . . after years of railing at the Star System I begin to wonder if whether we weren't better off when the screen was dominated by the fidelity of those unchanging, unquenchable lights.' But it was the 'unchanging' nature of the star from film to film which gave Powell pause for critical thought. Ask not what the star can do for the part, but what the role can do for the star was a dictum that seemed at odds with cinema as a means of expression that ought to aspire to an exploration of a shared humanity between audience and film. Powell's essentially humanistic vision of the cinema did not really have a place for a pantheon of movie deities, unchanging and unquenchable.

It is with ceaseless surprise that I watch the creation of the stars. Star, says the dictionary: 'an actor, singer, etc., of exceptional celebrity, or one whose name is prominently advertised as a special attraction to the public, 1824.' There is, you see, no mention of talent, or indeed of any kind of gift except that of netting an audience. I hurry to agree in advance that it is a gift not to be sneezed at; I merely point out with the greatest diffidence that for once I have the dictionary on my side.

My surprise is owed not to the stars themselves but to those who recognize them; recognize them, I mean, both before and after their light has reached the two-and-threepennies. I can understand a producer who knows a dancer when he sees one; confronted with Gene Kelly or Eleanor Powell, the most timid of backers might well feel that he had something in those feet. I can even imagine the possibility of putting one's shirt on Bing Crosby or Doris Day. But with the general run of straight players I am lost. I shall never stop admiring the perspicacity which detaches Miss X from the flock of, to my eyes, identical woodenpusses. The Piddingtons are not more astonishing than the man who knows at a glance that Mr Y, who looks to you and me just like any other turnip, will send all the girls.

A hideous thought here crosses my mind. Is it conceivable that there really is a difference, not merely in starriness, but in ability, between the chosen and the left? Can it be that the rejected have still less aptitude for learning by heart a short sentence and repeating it with approximately the required inflections? No, I won't believe it; the difference is in nothing except that 'special attraction to the public', the source of which is so elusive and indefinable. Dear Miss Blank, whose only gesture is a slight displacement of the bust; darling Mr Dash, who may be distinguished from a plaster cast by the fact that he moves; gallant What's-his-name, whose partner in the love-clinch is left peering over his shoulder at the audience with a look of understandable incredulity – these and their like draw the crowds by something other than their acting.

My trouble is that even when the star has been chosen,

polished, ballyhooed and put to shine I am so often indifferent to the beauty of the light. Colleagues more sensitive than I am hail the newcomer's eyes, nose, mouth, legs and other assets; they find qualities to adore in a performance which to me seems non-existent or plain terrible. And they are, from the starry point of view, right; the public adores, too, and I am left with admiration on my hands for the players who don't quite reach the heights of the firmament, for the Lloyd Nolans and the Jack Carsons and the Anne Baxters, who, whatever their talents, and their success, never win the hysterical devotion accorded to a Gable or a Grable.

February 1950

Less than two years ago the visit to this country of Mr and Mrs Spencer Tracy was the signal for an extraordinary outburst of fan-mania. The scene, as their train drew in to the London station, was as boisterous as the arrival of Napaloni in *The Great Dictator*; in the stampede unoffending passengers had their luggage torn to pieces, porters were mauled, the streets were thick with bicyclists pedalling hotly towards a hotel suspected of housing the star, and somebody had to buy Mrs Tracy a new bunch of orchids. Manifestations of culture such as this, of course, are possible only in times of peace; but peace or war the idea which prompts them, the idea that the star and not the film is the thing, holds firm. (Who ever heard of a film director being mobbed?)

Of the twenty-three million people who go, or used to go, to the cinema once a week in this country, by far the greater number look forward to seeing not a particular film but a particular player. The annual polls, then, to decide on the most popular stars are valuable to the observer as well as to the man in the box office; they show him the state of public taste, they tell him something about its changes and development. For the past year, now, Mickey Rooney has been the first in the list of stars, both in Great Britain and in America. This in itself is an interesting fact: two great nations unite in plumping for a boy of electric personality and exceptional talent, indeed, but still a bouncing, good-at-heart, in-and-out-of-scrapes, every-mother's-son boy; as much the essence of Boy as in her day Theda Bara was the essence of Vamp. It seems that in America his appearance in a new Hardy Family film is received with something of the emotion, which a fresh instalment of Dickens once aroused in this country;

the public insist that Andy Hardy shall behave according to their notion of a regular little guy, they insist that he shall never tell a lie, that he shall not be too familiar with his father. In many ways the cinema of to-day is as improving as the childhood of George Washington.

Three other players are common to both the American and the British list of last year's ten most popular stars – Spencer Tracy, James Cagney and Bing Crosby; two of them, Tracy and Cagney, far from being the romantic type of hero, and Bing Crosby himself inclined nowadays to desert from the cradle-watchers and join the ranks of the toughs. The popularity of James Cagney is, perhaps, partly a hangover from the gangster period through which films passed a few years ago; the taste for blood has now somewhat abated, blood being commoner in urban life than it was, but swiftness, violence, self-confidence, so neatly personified in the stocky figure of Cagney, still speak powerfully to the people. (All the same Cagney's scenario-writers will have to think up some better films than his latest ones if he is to hold his position.) The case of Spencer Tracy is different. Tracy has been steadily building up a character on the screen as the sincere, honest, tenacious dependable chap: the indefatigable philanthropist of *Boys' Town*, the persistent explorer of *Stanley and Livingstone*, the unsparing leader of men of *North-West Passage*, the pertinacious inventor of *Edison the Man*. He has come to stand for the man who never says die, the man who never lets you down, the family man, the man who likes his old clothes and hates his dress suit – a steady if there ever was one; in his way, again, as much the essence of Man as Mickey Rooney is the essence of Boy. The hold of these two players on the public imagination shows a swing away from romanticism. But the swing has not carried us very far yet; the taste for handsome flummery is still strong. And no player has yet appeared to typify the ordinary girl and the reliable, much-enduring woman. For a moment Deanna Durbin, second last year in the British list, looked as if she might turn into the cinema's average girl. But her screen milieu, unlike Andy Hardy's, has nearly always been well-to-do; butlers and marble staircases have been opposed to the family cookery and the back porch of the Hardy home. Now, of course, Miss Durbin is growing up into a film actress with Viennese tendencies.

Errol Flynn, ousted last year, together with Shirley Temple, Sonja Henie and Alice Faye, from America's favourites, is

in the British list; so are Jeannette Macdonald and Nelson
Eddy, Gary Cooper and (the only British blue to get into
the British international team) George Formby. A certain
proportion of romantic flummery, you see; a proportion
of romantic adventure; comedy fairly represented; but the
advantage is still with the toughs and the realists. It may
be objected that I have not taken into account the quality of
the acting, as if Rooney, Tracy and Cagney were not liked as
much for their performances as for their personalities. That is
of course true to a considerable extent; it does not invalidate
the argument that film actors owe their popularity to their
performances in certain types of part, and that the tendency
at the moment is to prefer the honest John type to the Young
Lochinvar type. This move in the direction of realism in turn
benefits the standard of the cinema by making it more possible
for producers and directors to concentrate on the film rather than
the star; it makes possible films such as *The Grapes of Wrath* and
Of Mice and Men. The public is not yet quite ready to rise to the
occasion; the failure, as far as the box office was concerned, of the
Lewis Milestone film was probably due less to the tragic theme
of the piece than to the absence of popular stars from the cast.
But fanmania notwithstanding, we may perhaps find reason to
look in the future for a shade more interest in the film, a shade
less in the favourite. The crowds who stood in queues to see
Gone with the Wind were sustained more by the idea of seeing
four hours of fiction in Technicolor and the spectacular manner
than by a prevision of the agreeable forms of Vivien Leigh, Leslie
Howard, Clark Gable and Olivia de Havilland. Whether or not
the Australians who, beginning the assault on Bardia, sang 'We're
off to see the Wizard of Oz' were enthusiasts for the film I have
no idea; but audiences in this country were, I am sure, lured to it
more by reports of its trick photography, its fantastic adventure
and its lively tunes than by love of Judy Garland (who has just
made the grade for America's first ten, but not yet for Britain's).

The signs, then, are of a move, however slight, towards the
themes of credible and knowable life. One thing is certain: that
for the time being what used to be called glamour is a cold egg.
Marlene Dietrich had to roll on the floor, kick, scratch and
throw whisky bottles before, in *Destry Rides Again*, she made
a come-back as a star; and I gather that even Hedy Lamarr in
her next film gets mixed up with oil-wells. Even where we
have costume and history (by which, in American films, the

American Civil War is usually meant) the tendency is to go slow on the glamour. *Gone with the Wind* itself, in spite of all the box-office names, the period clothes, the Technicolor and the old Southern gentility, did little to varnish the miseries of war; the scene in the hospital for the wounded, the solitary moment of horrifying realism when Scarlett fires into the Yankee deserter's face, are relevant here. Indeed Hollywood, while turning its attention once more to the fight for independence, the period of expansion, and the struggle for unity of the American nation, period of so many famous silent films, is also realizing by fits and starts that American history gains as a theme for the screen by being treated realistically; Vidor's *North-West Passage* was little more than a recital of hardship, endurance and massacre, and Ford's *Drums Along the Mohawk*, in spite of its share of banal characterization and romantic fiction, conveys a sharp sense of life lived in daily battle against murder and starvation.

In British films the movement towards a kind of realism takes a different form: concentration on known subjects and characters. In the last year or so there has been an increase in the number of films from British studios dealing with aspects of national life: the unemployed miners of the North, the mining valleys of South Wales, the workings of the convoy system; even in such an unpretentious piece of entertainment as *Saloon Bar* the décor and atmosphere of an English pub were pleasantly and honestly reproduced, and the characters were men and women living within the limits of their milieu and class; and there was genuine English character in the court-room scenes of *The Girl in the News*. American films have long had a tradition of small-part *American* character-playing; it is pleasant to see British films getting on with small-part British character-playing, and doing it without caricature.

Sight and Sound
Winter 1940

Audiences at the Empire this week will see, in ***Escape***, an actress almost as celebrated in the days of the silent film as Greta Garbo is today. Some among them, no doubt, will remember her: Nazimova, the star of *Out of the Fog*, *War Brides*, and *Salome*. In *Escape* she makes her first appearance in talking pictures. She plays a minor part; but with a little shock of pleasure we realize that this is not merely a resurrected star, but an actress. (In America, no doubt, her presence on the stage has kept the fact in mind.) She retains something of the breadth of silent film playing and something of the emphasis of stage playing; but within its tiny limits the part is given authority, the command of the trained actress; above all it is given a personality.

This brings us to the question of one of the chief differences between acting on the stage and acting on the screen. The stage player, if he is an artist of any seriousness, will assume many personalities in his professional career; the same actor will appear as betraying Iago and Othello betrayed; Mr Gielgud has played Hamlet, Lear, Romeo, Vershinin, John Worthing, and Valentine in *Love for Love*. The film actor is in a very different case. A young and personable player may alternate between romantic and light comedy parts, he may even venture into costume, so long as it is becoming; but no further. If Hollywood wants a middle-aged character, with all its resources it can afford to go on searching till it finds a middle-aged player who looks and speaks exactly as the character should look and speak. In the unlikely event of Hollywood's deciding to film *King Lear*, it would certainly (indeed, luckily) not offer the part of the old King to Robert Taylor, James Stewart, Tyrone Power, or Errol Flynn. No, the probabilities are that talent scouts sent to scour Britain would return in triumph with some formidable old grey-beard who had never set foot inside theatre or film studio; while the Dukes, Earls, Courtiers and the rest of the Shakespearean train, commonly played on the English stage by ambitious learners from the OUDS, would be assigned to such trusty old Whiskerandoses as Donald Crisp and Henry Stephenson. More likely still, the whole play would be recast, and Lear would become a young American husky stood up by a couple of Society dames, thus making the part a sitter for Fred Macmurray.

The technique of the cinema, with its use of the close-up, has made casting for a film very largely a matter of choosing a player with the right kind of looks; much more so, at any rate, than on the stage. The spread of talking films, with their new emphasis on sound and speech, did something to distract audiences from their concentration on appearances; something, but not much; the visual impact of a film remains, rightly, decisive, and it would not be possible on the screen, as it is possible on the stage, for a middle-aged woman to play Juliet. On the contrary, Juliet must be played by the beautiful and dispassionate Miss Shearer. In so far as film-acting is not merely dependent on the player's looks, it is becoming more and more a matter of exploiting the player's personality. (There are, of course, honourable exceptions, such as Robinson's performance in *Magic Bullet*.) When the silent films disappeared a certain style of acting went with them; broad gesture, caricatured comic miming. It has been replaced by a far subtler style; a style so subdued to realism that a player coming from stage to screen is apt to seem artificial and affected; a style, however, which invites actors and actresses to rely more than they should on their personality. Let me put it like this: in the film industry of today a player will achieve a considerable degree of success by virtue of a personality which is readily communicated through the medium of the film; once he has done that he is never, or very rarely, required to do more than express a variety of emotions via that personality. If he is a Spencer Tracy, he remains reliable, solid, endearing Spencer Tracy, whether he is triumphant or disappointed, a man making love or a man organizing a massacre; he is not expected, as a stage actor is expected, to be a disappointed Jacques, a romantic Orlando, and a murderous Richard Crookback. As good an actor as Tracy would, no doubt, be equal to the demand; the point is that the demand is not made. And the question arises whether film acting as we now know it is acting at all as the stage knows it; whether, in fact, the cinema ought to be judged as a dramatic art in the sense of an art communicated by the medium of trained actors and actresses. The truth, of course, is that it should be a co-operative art; but, despite the focusing of public attention on the stars, one comes to believe more and more in the supreme importance of the director, in whose power it lies to make a star look like a piece of glass and a piece of glass look like a star.

It is remarkable how often the best performances (in the cinema's sense of acting) as well as the most solid personalities are to be found in the supporting players. In *Escape*, for instance, Albert Bassermann and Felix Bressart are memorable, the former in a tiny part; these are both actors in the stage as well as the film sense. So, of course, is Conrad Veidt, whose glittering soft-voiced German General does much to give plausibility to this film. The story, indeed, is an implausible business about an actress condemned to die in a concentration camp, her son (Robert Taylor) who comes from America to find her, and a sympathetic Countess (Norma Shearer) who runs a finishing school with moral standards surely rather advanced even for a finishing school. The tension of the escape, however, is admirably held; and though this does not pretend to be a serious film (*The Mortal Storm*, I take it, was intended as a serious film), but merely an exciting story about a young American who comes bumbling into Germany expecting justice and finding the Gestapo, it struck me as the most convincing picture of Nazi Germany so far: on the surface no murders, no horrors, only polite attentive faces; but beneath, inflexibility, stony indifference, a kind of madness. It is directed by Mervyn LeRoy with untiring smoothness and efficiency, but without much pictorial emphasis; Hitchcock, had he directed this film, would have made it indeed far more unequal, but the camera would, I fancy, have been used to give greater visual impact. As it is the camera follows the story rather than underlining it where underlining is needed. There is, however, one superb pictorial moment when, from the eye of the corpse, marble in its coffin, there steals a single piteous tear.

January 1941

Whether or not Greta Garbo is a good actress I have no idea, but I am sure she is a great actress. Hollywood is crowded with actresses of remarkable talent. The nervous harsh quality of Bette Davis, Ginger Rogers with her tough *gamine* charm, Luise Rainer, all delicate pleading grace – these demand our admiration. Now and then a new player is hailed as a serious actress; the stir over Katherine Hepburn in *Morning Glory* may be recalled. A few years later Miss Hepburn turned out to be an excellent farcical actress, and that was that. But none of these has the quality of size. The good actor has the chameleon's ability of matching his surroundings; his colour changes to suit his part. I am inclined to suspect that the great actor has the reverse of the chameleon's art; he changes the colour of everything round him. Also he is of a size to fill the stage (or the screen) as well as transforming it. Greta Garbo, alone among contemporary film actresses, has this kind of emotional size.

In *Ninotchka* she plays at last in comedy. Three delegates have been sent to Paris from Moscow to sell a Grand Duchess's confiscated jewels. Bearded, spectacled, fur-hatted, they push through the swing doors of the smart hotel and gape, the picture of bourgeois amazement, at its luxury. So much more agreeable than the Hotel Terminus! Shall they move? But what were the words of Lenin? They confer, they are lost; they take the Royal Suite and let the jewel-selling go hang. Moscow, materialist as ever, sends a special delegate to supervise the delegates. The train snorts in the station, the comrades peer at the passengers; can their superior be – yes, it is Garbo, Garbo in a neat Soviet suit and a pudding-basin hat, Garbo ready to correct the authorities on international law, bent on visiting the Paris sewers and the electricity plant, resolute to discover the depth of the Eiffel Tower foundations. The French, says Melvyn Douglas, her self-appointed man-of-the-world guide, the French use the Eiffel Tower only to jump off. 'How long,' says Garbo in her beautiful voice, grave as the echo from a mountain cave, 'does it take a man to land?'

Spring in the North, they say, comes sudden as the swallow; the earth blazes into life. Garbo at the beginning of this film is winter-bound. Love, she says, is a chemical reaction. Then in a flash the ice breaks and dissolves in the swift river; the martinet, the ex-sergeant in the Russian Army, becomes a young girl, laughing at a remembered joke during the austere conference, edging shyly into her lover's room in a new hat, dancing, drinking too much champagne. This release of tenderness and warmth and gaiety is among the most moving pieces of acting I have ever seen in a film. It is, indeed, so affecting that it almost blinds one to the virtues of the rest of the picture – to its occasional wit and its mild but usually palatable satire on Russian character and methods of government, to the general charm and lightness of Lubitsch's direction. It would, however, be unjust to ignore the very good performance of Melvyn Douglas as the enraptured aristocrat. Ina Claire is admirable as his Grand Duchess, and Sig Rumann, Felix Bressart and Alexander Granach make an excellent trio of backsliders from Bolshevism. But Garbo it is who lifts the whole film out of triviality. I know the public today likes its favourites to be under the age of consent. Here is a last chance for audiences to show that after all they prefer a grown woman and a great actress.

February 1940

Anna Magnani is an actress, possibly a great actress, who can command everything of an audience except its tears. I may be thought to say this on slight evidence: a small part in *Rome, Open City*; a leading part in a comedy, *Angelina*, and now **The Miracle** (director Roberto Rossellini). But though we in this country have seen little of Magnani the latest piece surely gives us what we need for judgment; if *The Miracle* does not have us in fountains, the film itself must insist on reserve; and since the film in this case depends on the actress, then the actress it is who fails to move the deepest springs.

The Miracle, which is already being talked about as if it were a cross between the works of the Marquis de Sade and the First Epistle to the Corinthians, is a simple moral fable, forty minutes long, about an Italian goatherdess, a feeble-minded creature who meets a tramp in the hills, takes him for her patron, St Joseph, drinks with him, innocently conceives, and is driven from her village to bear, in a deserted mountain chapel, the child which she believes divine. Obviously it is possible to read into the story implications offensive to religious susceptibilities (it has been refused a certificate by the British Board of Film Censors, and though the LCC allows it to be shown in London, several local authorities have already rejected it). I dare say some will see it as an ironic attack on the miraculous element in Christian faith. On the other hand some, and I am among them, will see it as a film far less dangerous to religion than many of the pseudo-religious fairy-tales concocted, quite cynically to my mind, by Hollywood.

For the attack is turned not on faith but on those who profess faith and practise cruelty; on the villagers who take part in the ritual of the Church, then lead the bewildered lumpish woman in mock procession, torment her and, laughing, drive her into the wilderness. Rossellini and the author of the story, Federico Fellini, have refused to admit any sentimental elements. The victim is introduced to us as a foolish chattering creature; dislodged from her nesting-place near the church, she bundles off with a squalid collection of rags and tins; as she lies in labour she sees nothing but the insolent gaze of the stray goat who has led her up the rocky track to the chapel. Yet it should be possible to discard sentimentality without rejecting pity. Only for a moment, as the woman looks down at her new-born baby, is there a touch of human warmth; all through her agonizing flight anger and horror it is, not pity, which director and actress communicate.

I am not suggesting that Anna Magnani should have given us

a sugar-icing portrait on the lines of Bergman's St Joan. The portrait she does give us is incomparable in its realism; this is acting on a plane scarcely known to the cinema. But I still feel that it should have been within her compass to move us, even within the limits of this angry fable, to an emotion less sterile than anger: to love. *The Miracle* castigates the want of compassion; and itself offers us only bitterness.

January 1950

Bette Davis is not in the World's Sweethearts class of film actresses. That, perhaps, is because she has been always an actress, never merely a face. Most of the films in which she has played – *The Petrified Forest*, *Jezebel*, *Marked Woman*, *Dangerous*, even *The Sisters* – have not been sweetheart-makers. But quite apart from that she has up to now been more of a critic's actress than a public favourite.

As a performer in her own individual style she has been advancing steadily. The hard, clear little voice flawing, splintering, dissolving in emotion; the mouth pulled down at the corners, the quick hands, the unwinking eyes – with tiny touches she makes her effect where another actress would have been riding the whirlwind. She has been rewarded with heavier and heavier parts, more and more exacting emotional situations. In *Jezebel* she was the wilful beauty jolting away on the plague-cart with her dying lover. In *The Sisters* the husband for whom she had fought abandoned her to the San Francisco earthquake. **Dark Victory** gives her another film heavyweight part. But this time it is not, indeed, a world's sweetheart, but possibly a world's heroine part.

I have heard the film spoken of in terms suggestive of something between *Athalie* and the *Oedipus Tyrannus*. We shall not, I fancy, do any good to a serious picture by overdoing the trumpet and the drum. A serious picture *Dark Victory* certainly is, honest, in a way dreadful, offering no concessions to the All's-well-that-ends-well public. I do not, indeed, remember another film with a theme as simple, inexorable, and undramatic as the growth of a glioma. That is the essential skeleton of the story, the surgeon's-eye view. The story we are told, the story which humanity builds on the case-book entry, is of morality's reply to the facts of disease and death. It is to the credit of the picture that the reply is made without over-emphasis, without hysteria.

Bette Davis plays Judith Trehearne, the heiress who at the age of twenty-three undergoes an operation on the brain. Furious in the first place at the idea that illness can touch her, refusing to admit the symptoms of disease, she thinks when it is over that now she is well again for ever. Her doctor, whom she loves, and her friend know that she has only a few months to live. A play might have been written, a film might have been made, with this as the central, ironic situation. It has been rejected, and a simpler but more naturally human problem has been tackled. The girl finds out that the malignancy of Nature has set a limit to her life. The rest of the picture is concerned with her response to this knowledge: her rage with the friends who have not told her the truth, her frantic efforts to fill the days, her final arrival at interior peace and a courageous acceptance of the fact of death.

As the doctor who becomes her husband for the last months of her life, George Brent plays with quiet assurance; Humphrey Bogart is effective as the stable-hand in love with her; and Geraldine Fitzgerald has some moving moments as the friend. But naturally the weight of the emotional problem falls on Bette Davis.

A situation as tremendous in its implications as the central situation of this film requires tremendous presentation; it is not a case for a few tears, a little miniature pathos. And that the makers of the picture intend emotion on the grand scale is clear. 'This is our victory,' says Judith Trehearne to the husband who has taught her not to be afraid, 'our victory over the dark.' In criticizing the imaginative *size* of the film I shall not, therefore, be criticizing it for failure in something it never attempted.

Myself, I feel that Bette Davis is an actress of the wrong scale for this story. Her early scenes are brilliant: the head-strong girl sure of herself, sure of life, the hands madly fidgeting, the face blazing defiance. I have seen the film twice, and each time I found her performance at the climax heartrending. But the subject demands something more, something that Miss Davis, with all her rare talent, was not born to give us. It demands acting on the grand scale. Her performance is not, and could never be, on the grand scale.

She is not particularly well served by the dialogue. 'May I take back every rotten thing I ever said to you?' she implores when, after her wild bid for distraction, she returns to her lover and the search for the inward peace. It is true that at the climax the language is severely simple, never distasteful. But it lacks the flashes of poetry which make *Wuthering Heights* so exciting a film (there it is notable that the most profoundly moving passages are those with the most literary, the most Brontësque phrasing). And it seems to me that Edmund Goulding's direction, with all its feeling for the pathos of human life, the heroism of human death, is wanting in the visual imagination which might have made this picture grand as well as touching. For surely it is the essence of the cinema that it should make its points not only with words but also, indeed primarily, with pictures.

May 1939

Far away in the foothills of California, a girl shouted for five hours a day. That's how long she shouted; five hours a day. Before that she sold programmes in a New York theatre. Between times, she sat drinking coffee in a Broadway drug store. Then she sat for two weeks in a Hollywood hotel. There was no reception committee. At last somebody got wise to her. Somebody took her out into the foothills of California and made her shout for five hours a day. That gave her the voice. That gave her the drainpipe bass. That made Lauren Bacall.

Well, brother voters, there we have her: the new star. The long, pitiless years of training, the sleepless devotion to detail, the sacrifice of self to art, and at the end of it, the new exponent of non-acting, the new stand-still virtuoso, the new get-the-eye-angle-right – and – the-camera-angle-will-do-the-rest expert, Lauren It-Rhymes-With-McCall Bacall. There is, I heartily agree, something to be said for seeing, beneath the tamed jungle which is Miss Bacall's crowning glory, a new face. There is something to be said for hearing a new Dietrich-type voice. But these are novelties which so far hold out little promise of self-renewal. Miss Bacall in **To Have and Have Not** is a bit of a change. But the impression of change is largely owed to contrast with the determination of the film itself to give us the same old stuff.

Not that every effort hasn't been made to give us a good film. The story is from Hemingway (if you like that technician of the laconic overstatement). A more natural born writer, in my opinion, than Hemingway, William Faulkner, is part-writer of the screen-play. The director is Howard Hawks, who has made some good films in his time. One of the best, perhaps the best, of American tough players, Humphrey Bogart, and one of the best of American character actors, Walter Brennan, have been clapped into the cast; while Hoagy Carmichael provides a beautifully sharp little sketch of a jazz pianist. But there you are: even the jazz pianist is an echo from that overrated film, model for the Hollywood cycle on the Free French amongst tropical foliage, *Casablanca*. *Casablanca* had a fat intriguer; *Passage to Marseille* had a fat collaborationist; so has *To Have and Have Not*. *Casablanca* was about an attempt to convey a patriot and his wife from somewhere to somewhere; so is *To Have and Have Not*. *Casablanca* had as hero an American who at first refuses, then consents to help the Free French; so has *To Have and Have Not*. On these familiar paths Bogart moves with his old nonchalant ease, and a pause now and then to take in Miss Bacall: still waters running so deep as to be indistinguishable from stagnation, sulky fires burning so hot as to be indistinguishable from a frost. I won't say the film hasn't, in the absence of anything better, its enjoyable moments. But I could use something better.

June 1945

Even those who have not reached Nicholas Monsarrat's novel (and you can count me in) probably have picked up a bit of information about **The Story of Esther Costello** (director: David Miller), and it is probably unnecessary for me to remark that the film is about a girl who is blind, deaf and dumb, the woman who adopts her, and the woman's unreliable husband. A regular little Titus Andronicus, it abounds in fraud, embezzlement, suicide, murder and rape; all it wants is somebody baked in a pie. However, everything is taken as part of the day's work. After all, this is merely another instalment of Life with Joan Crawford.

When the definitive biography of Miss Crawford comes to be written it will surely disclose a career without rival in suffering on the screen. Blameless or culpable, the actress goes through agonies. She is tormented by amnesia, schizophrenia, failing sight; with scarcely a blink at the reference books I can recall the heroine in a series of tight corners which would have wrecked nerves less steely. The Gestapo, the lynching mob, the gangster's bullet and the execution shed – not since Pearl

White has there been a woman so imperilled. Not that she is passive. She reacts; driven to it, she strikes back. There are times when Miss Crawford plays the cobra queen.

The basic Crawford character suffers especially with husbands or near-husbands. They marry her for her money; they plan to murder her; they chase her screaming all night up and down the streets of San Francisco. Some of them are gangsters; some are just ghastly musicians, and no wonder the poor girl decides to end it all by wading out into the ocean. Occasionally some old fidelity may be seen hanging around, shaggy, large, the bob-tailed sheep-dog type; but what Miss Crawford has to go through, what shooting-matches, what psychopathic frenzies she must endure, before he can fold her in his faithful furry paws is nobody's business.

Of course a good deal of the suffering is not physical but psychological. Poor Miss Crawford is always being jilted. For a while the men are snared by the handsome level eyes, the CinemaScope mouth, the rectangular, cut-glass bone structure; then, oh my fur and whiskers! they are off to fling themselves at the feet of some round-faced teenager – a desertion doubly irritating when the teenager happens to be a member of the family. Miss Crawford, who began as the dancing daughter, has now grown into the injured mother. And in *The Story of Esther Costello* she is injured all over again.

Not that the blind deaf mute whom she adopts is anything but an innocent victim. Nevertheless, Miss Crawford still moves in an ambiance of suffering. Suave in her American women's luncheon club suits and boulder-size jewellery, she commands; she is confident, the lovely matriarch whom Hollywood offers as the image of American high society; but inevitably she moves towards the well-known moment when the hand feels for the revolver in the dressing-table drawer. The difference is that this time, since *The Story of Esther Costello*, in spite of its American director, is a British film, the climax is reached in the London Airport tunnel.

There is another difference: the playing of the blind girl herself. Miss Crawford – giving, I must say, one of her best portraits of well-dressed misery – as her foil has an English actress quite free from the co-ed assurance which often overlays the playing of young American girls. Heather Sears has, so far as I can discover, acted in only one film before this, and then in a small part; she is new and fresh to the cinema, a face with the sharp

contours of unfamiliarity. Whether the gift she shows can be
extended is difficult to judge. But here at any rate she plays
with sensibility and delicate restraint; her performance almost
persuades one that this story of an unfortunate whose handicap
is exploited in a swindling charity campaign is something more
than a bag of old chestnuts.

I must not forget Rossano Brazzi; for this smoothly made,
Americanized piece depends on three characters (there is a fourth,
played by Lee Patterson, but the script won't let him do anything
except look manly and reassuring). Mr Brazzi is called on for
charm: charm with the touch of the sinister which Miss Crawford
is always discovering in her screenmates. Perhaps it is because we
have so often seen him exercising his Mediterranean appeal that
the sinister touch makes so shallow an impression. Watching Mr
Brazzi's expression as he meditates rape, I found myself reflecting
that it would do just as well for a man buying his white-haired
grandmother a Shetland bed-jacket.

August 1957

In France, one hears, **Maigret Sets a Trap** (**Maigret Tend un
Piège**; director Jean Delannoy) has had a great success. Why?

Not that it is anything but efficient. The adaptation of
Simenon's story has what is needed. The mysterious killer
(one of the Jack the Ripper types popular in the cinema); the
policewomen walking the streets as bait; the meagre clues of
button and missing key; the hints of sexual aberration and
the psychological solution – it is puzzling, it is intermittently
exciting, it is not offensive to a modest intelligence, not at any
rate a modest intelligence used to crime stories. Attention may
find during the two hours occasion to wander but not to break
loose altogether. There is a good outburst of hysteria by Jean
Desailly and some cool chic from Annie Girardot. One can enjoy
the film, in fact, without finding in it anything much above the
average. Except, of course, Gabin.

Perhaps one should ask not why this film is popular but why
Jean Gabin still holds his place as a major star. One remembers
him from before the war: as the deserter of *Quai des Brumes*, an
outcast and friend of outcasts, of sad girls in berets and little
mongrel dogs; as the escaping prisoner-of-war of *La Grande
Illusion*, a man of the people, stubborn, indestructible, thinking

of getting back to the simple life of the heart and the senses. That was in 1937; but before that he was famous, had already made a reputation on the music-hall stage; by 1939 he had appeared in a dozen films and more (among them *Pepé le Moko* and *Les Bas-Fonds*). In the spring of 1939 London was looking at *La Bête Humaine* with its extraordinary suggestions of sexual ferocity; during the war we admired what is I think the grandest of all his portraits, the goaded, sullen killer of *Le Jour se Lève*.

There was an unhappy period during the Occupation of France when Gabin worked in Hollywood. But since the liberation he has played in an unceasing flow of French cinema; films about fugitives and detectives, doctors and patients, showmen, townsmen and lusty countrymen. The thick-set figure has grown bulkier, the square, heavy-featured face has fallen into folds and pouches; the lawyer, the family man has replaced the solitary trudger and the bicyclist. The appearance is not romantic. But then it never was romantic. Yet there is no player on the screen today who can excite in the audience a more desperate desire to help; and Gabin does it without moving a wrinkle of that police-dog muzzle.

No use saying he succeeds by being a superb actor. The cinema doesn't want superb actors; half the time it doesn't want actors, it wants something more passive and indeed more malleable. And Gabin has never undergone the actor's disguises, even the disguises normally incident to a career in films. One doesn't see him in a toga or knee-breeches (though I do recall an unbecoming occasion when he played in shorts). One doesn't see him even in a beard. Whatever part he plays Gabin looks like himself – and is like himself, or at any rate the self he displays on the screen.

I believe this stability of appearance and personality is his strong suit, as it has been the strong suit of nearly all the great stars of the cinema – except Nikolay Cherkasov, who is a Russian and doesn't count in this argument – from Chaplin to Spencer Tracy (you don't see Spencer Tracy either in a beard, at least I don't think so, though probably some reader with a crushingly well-stocked memory will be able to correct me).

What Gabin has done is to make us all sorry for him in a special way. He has not set up as the heroic hero, not even in *La Grande Illusion*. He has been the ironic or the mournful runaway, the unlucky killer, the man who trots waving beside the train, misses the boat, gets entangled with a slut; all this, and yet always worth respecting and worth desiring (the stocky figure has never lost its off-hand physical charm). Time may slacken the contours of face and torso, but the audience still agonizes with Maigret as he is balked; still longs to tweak his sleeve and point to a clue; and still thinks Madame Maigret a pretty lucky woman.

August 1959

Talking the other day about Marlon Brando, whose appearance in *Guys and Dolls* has set us all speculating again about his talents, I said that he had not yet shown the range for the great classical roles. But almost as soon as I had said it I found myself reflecting doubtfully on the future of classical acting in an age in which cinema technique is steadily gaining ground.

Cinema acting has achieved a colloquial style quite different from the colloquial style of the theatre. Of course there is still plenty of dead, drawing-room playing to be seen in films; stage acting in a mutter. But at its best cinema acting is excitingly alive. And within the last few years a group of fresh talents has brought a stir into American films. Marlon Brando, the late James Dean, Paul Newman – the group is the product of the New York Actors' Studio. Its members have learned the theories of Stanislavsky's 'Method'; they must live in a character's past as well as act in its present. Easy inter-playing, the broken rhythms and chopped phrases of life, the communication of internal stresses; adapted to the needs of the cinema the Studio-Stanislavsky style has produced interesting results (though some of them, I daresay, would have surprised Stanislavsky).

No doubt some kind of stage training is an advantage in film acting; few of the important figures of the screen have been entirely without it. But the cinema is repaying its debt to the theatre. It may not be training stage players. But it is affecting stage playing, and it is affecting stage production. The influence of cinema technique is apparent in the work of the contemporary American playwrights. It can certainly be detected in the work of Bertolt Brecht.

Brecht's theory of acting is, I know, the reverse of that taught in the Actors' Studio. On the one hand the rejection of illusion; Brecht, with his alienation-effect, wanted to remind the audience that the actor is just that, an actor. On the other hand, identification of the actor with his role; Brando in *The Wild One* becomes the arrogant, lawless boy on the motor-bicycle. And

yet between the off-hand introverted playing of the American
star and the exquisitely calculated, concealed art of the Berliner
Ensemble there is a link: the cinema. Both styles, both theories
react against the grand manner of acting. And to find both
operating at a moment when the young writers of drama as well
as fiction are in revolt against literary forms makes one wonder
whether we are in for a temporary eclipse of the classical stage.

At present the classical theatre has great classical players – in
this country Gielgud, Olivier, Redgrave – to support it. But if
the growth of a new school of playwriting, cursive, anti-classical,
should call for more and more actors in the cursive, anti-classical
manner, the large talents of the future might then drift away
from the traditions we know. Perhaps the coolness I have
sometimes felt towards Brando's gifts, extraordinary though
I realize them to be, comes from my recognition in his acting
of a threat to the forms I have all my life accepted. But no
doubt one should look forward not with apprehension but with
excitement. Shakespeare, we have seen, can be accommodated
on the screen, and Olivier has shown that the Elizabethan line
can be delivered in the confidential tones of the cinema. In *Julius
Caesar* Brando failed with Mark Antony because he was trying
to adapt himself to a grand manner for which he was not trained.
But is the manner necessary? At the outset of the battle between
theatrical and cinematic acting, I begin to wonder. At any rate, I
should like to see Brando tackling a Shakespearian role not under
traditional theatrical tuition but in his own way.

September 1956

For his new film, I read in *Sight and Sound*, Robert Bresson has
used an entirely non-professional cast. Last Sunday I was writing
about the relation between stage and film acting. I am now led by
natural stages and some querulous correspondents to think about
the nature of film acting itself.

The case of the non-professional against the professional actor
is old enough; Pudovkin was arguing it thirty years ago. The
other day it cropped up again with *On the Bowery* in which
astonishing performances were given by a collection of drunks
and down-and-outs playing themselves. In this country the
documentary school has been the champion of the actor-
from-life. But usually the English are too frosty a race to give

themselves away. Perhaps they are too wary as well. We have to remember that Pudovkin got effects from players who did not know they were being photographed; and the Hogarthian figures of *On the Bowery*, even when they did know, in the blur of drink and wrangling often forgot the watching eye.

The employment of the non-professional, of course, puts the responsibility of interpretation on the director. No doubt this can be an advantage. But as a general rule to reject the professional in favour of the player-from-life is surely to limit the range of expression. Those who have seen the beautiful Indian film *Pather Panchali* will remember the grandmother: the bent, furrowed body stumping about in its tatters, the cunning old eyes begging for food, the gestures of resignation and furtive pleasure. Some starving carcass, one thinks, whom the director has found still moving. But no: this is the only professional in the cast. The realism might have been achieved by a non-professional; the terrible pathos needed an actress.

But what kind of an actress? The cinema has developed its own kind of playing. Now and then an artist may succeed with theatrical methods: a Bette Davis can roll her great eyes, flounce, enunciate in the manner of a phonetics instructor, and still triumph. But not often. Long before dialogue, even, the screen had forgotten the grimace and the large gesture. The modern style is muted, flowing, full of changes in tempo and rhythm. True cinema acting: you saw it, if I may recall at random, with Sinatra in *From Here to Eternity*, with Eddie Albert in *Roman Holiday*, Kenneth More in *Genevieve*, James Whitmore in *Them!*, Kathleen Harrison in *Scrooge*, Laurence Olivier in *Sister Carrie*. It may be found in the most trivial film; the emigrant from cabaret may achieve it as well as the great stage actor.

On the other hand there are fine players who never quite reach it; Richard Burton strikes me as a star who gives excellent performances but has never yet become, as, say, Alberto Sordi or Henry Fonda become, a fragment of the life taking shape on the screen. And that cinema acting is not simply a matter of personality and presence is proved by the unevenness of some players. Katharine Hepburn brings it off in *Pat and Mike* but not in *The Iron Petticoat*. Marlon Brando fails completely in *Desirée*.

The stage actor cannot ignore his spectators. At its best cinema acting seems unaware of its audience in the single eye of the camera. The player appears to have regard not, as with even so gifted a peformer as Rod Steiger, for the effect he is making, but only for what he is being and doing; he goes on, as it were, with is life. The technique which enables him to create this illusion of living in private I believe to be partly concerned with motion. The movements of good screen-players are different from the movement of players in the theatre: not only on a smaller scale, but faster, more fluid, and more detailed. This peculiar quality of movement is unattainable by even the least self-conscious of the untrained; and only the elect among the professionals have it in perfection. 'People so exceptionally talented,' said Pudovkin, 'that they can live, and not act, are very seldom met with.' After all one cannot expect to find a Jean Gabin or a Spencer Tracy every day of the week.

October 1956

Though Coleridge can hardly have been familiar with the detective cinema his dictum about the willing suspension of disbelief seems peculiarly apt to the genre.

Probably the observation has been made before; if it has it bears repeating, especially now. One surrenders, one should surrender, to any good film; enjoy now, analyse later. But with today's cinema of crime something new has arrived; casualness. Plot-links are left out. Motives are obscure. None of that final gathering, cosy in the study, which in the British novel of detection used to provide recapitulation and a chance for the killer to chuck himself out of the window. While you are in the cinema, bewitched by the rectangle of colour and movement which is the screen, you accept. You accept Roman Polanski's new film *Chinatown*. But acceptance doesn't last. You come away from, say, The Conversation hauling down your disbelief, arguing with yourself about who killed whom and how (surely not, as some people seem to think, by stuffing the victim down the lavatory pan?).

In print it was Raymond Chandler who pioneered this indifference to precise, logical narrative. Dashiell Hammett gave us the cool, wisecracking, insolent detective; Chandler contributed richness of style, ironical, dense with description; the writing it was which made one forget the narrative gaps.

In the cinema it is something else. Speed, to begin with. In *Chinatown* you don't have time to enquire why the florid lady in the matron's hat calls on the divorce-case detective (Jack

Nicholson) with her cock-and-bull story or why there should be such a change of heart about sueing him on the part of the Los Angeles city official's wife when she becomes a widow (Faye Dunaway, beautiful and beautifully nineteen-thirtyish with her fine arched brows, her hollowed cheeks and the pursed crimson mouth; no wonder Polanski used so many close-ups). Take your eyes off the screen for a few seconds and you miss – well, not a clue; there is only one clue in the film – but some telling shot, some indispensable moment in the drive of the smart, tight, intentionally enigmatic script (It is by Robert Towne, who wrote *The Last Detail*). Keep your eyes on it and you are swept along as helpless as any of the corpses so unaccountably drowned in empty lake-beds.

Speed allied, of course, to characters. I say characters; you don't often find character, developing character, in the cinema of crime. What you find is personality. And that is where *Chinatown* justifies Polanski's claim that it is 'a traditional detective story with a new, modern shape.' I don't mean that it is about not the missing body but the missing water-supply of Los Angeles in 1937. I don't mean even that it ends in a kind of defeat; the Chandler novels and films have a bitter flavour. And this is a very Chandlerish film; why, it even has some of the Chandler favourite figures, a little sister and a rich father. I mean that the nature of the detective has changed.

When one thinks of the detective cinema one thinks of Humphrey Bogart. Not that he played many detectives; more often he was on the other side of the law. But there was *The Maltese Falcon* (interesting to find John Huston, who directed that, playing an important and sinister role in the Polanski film). And talking of Chandler (though other stars appeared as Marlowe: Dick Powell in *Farewell My Lovely*, Robert Montgomery in *The Lady in the Lake*, James Garner in *Marlowe*, as *The Little Sister* was re-titled, Eliott Gould in *The Long Goodbye*) there was *The Big Sleep* and Bogart: the saturnine look, the guttural tone, the lisp, the whole of the personality, tiny in range but powerful in impact. And Bogart was not the only one to play on personality. Just as in reviewing a good thriller, a good detective film (and *Chinatown* is a beauty), one finds that if one is to avoid giving away the plot there is very little one can say, the actor finds that in playing the investigator there is very little to do except let personality rip; look at Walter Matthau in *An Investigation of Murder*.

That is where Jack Nicholson has done something startling with personality. He has effaced it.

This extraordinary player has never relied on personality. From the cheerful drunk of *Easy Rider* to the anxious TV monologuist of *The King of Marvin Gardens*, from the cold womaniser of *Carnal Knowledge* to the tough pitying Marine of *The Last Detail* he has been the chameleon; behind the changing masks of the actor one simply doesn't know him. The voice slightly metallic; the face like a hundred other faces, not handsome; the nose jutting sharply in profile but not remarkable – he might be anybody. And he plays the detective as if he were anybody. Half the time he plays with that rectangular nose, injured in one of the ferocious encounters essential to the cinema of detection, unbecomingly roofed with plaster and Scotch tape.

Impossible to imagine Bogart playing with his nose under plaster. But at least the stuff enables one to identify Mr Nicholson. He has one scene in bed with the beautiful widow; all detective films have a bedroom scene; but here it is a matter of a momentary physical reaction; never, even in the Russian cinema, have I seen a bed less infested with sex. Not good-looking, not seductive, merely nosey (in more senses than one); Nicholson breaks all the rules. But he is alive, he is real; one may not recognize but one remembers him. The film takes life from him. And one looks forward to a detective cinema which, relying not on personalities but on actors, doesn't have to apologize for itself to the high-minded.

Play it again, Jack.

August 1974

Time separates us from the stars of the night, and their light may reach us from long ago. Sometimes the screen stars, too, shine across years, sometimes their brightness belongs to the past. The Gish sisters, the tremulous Mae Marsh, tragic Robert Harron on the Griffith scaffold, baby-face Harry Langdon, Douglas Fairbanks, essence of all-American breezy confidence, and that noble deadpan profile Buster Keaton – they throw their sharpest light from half a century ago.

The fusion of elements which produces a star is always an enigma. Especially one asks what it was, when the cinema firmament was in process of creation, which excited the watchers. Of course the public liked to worship. Valentino or Bobby Moore, Clara Bow or Mick Jagger, the public always likes to worship. I don't think many of the cinema idols were false idols. Occasionally a star was deliberately assembled out of catch-phrases and fairground tinsel – Theda Bara, for instance, a harmless girl elevated to the position of First Vamp and even now remembered for the invitation to one of her victims, 'Kiss Me, My Fool!' Not often, though. The great stars have talent, will work. But there is something else. There is charisma. There is magic.

One can't pin down magic. One can only guess, only hint at inexplicable gifts. Sometimes the gift is physical, a sexual radiation. 'Dear Mr Gable' – the song wasn't written for girls who revered the spiritual endowments of the player nicknamed the King. But a fierce control of the physical, even a rejection of its heat, that too can make the quality of a star. The heroines of the silent cinema, such oddities as Theda Bara apart, usually portrayed virgin innocence – sometimes the roguish, ringleted innocence of a Mary Pickford in, say, *Daddy Long Legs*, sometimes the resourceful innocence of the actress – I fancy it was Blanche Sweet – whom in my childhood I applauded for saving her betrothed from execution by swinging on the clapper of the curfew bell.

Feminine innocence was the fashion then. It was perhaps the result of a persistently Victorian recipe for mass entertainment;

after all, the cinema for years was thought pretty low-class, and intellectual prejudice prevented even the moderately educated from recognizing the achievements of the new popular medium.

But there was at any rate one player – one durable, unforgettable player, for she has not vanished from either stage or screen performance – who gave innocence an extra dimension. Lillian Gish out of the negation of physical seduction drew the power of a great star. It was not that she lacked beauty. She was beautiful, she still is beautiful. But as one of the Orphans of the Storm, or the mother crossing the ice-floes, or the child in *Broken Blossoms* forcing her mouth into a smile, she had the virginal delicacy of a snowdrop. Whatever in her fragile fictional characters befell, in her quality as a star she remained untouchable, inviolate.

Of course Miss Gish profited by the mood of the times. But she also used her own exquisite attributes. All players make use of their natural attributes; the star is the one who deliberately and without visible effort uses those attributes to communicate an always recognizable personality. All right for the personality to develop, to adapt itself to varying circumstances, but it must not change basically. You might almost say that when a star sheds the recognized personality, he or she stops being a star. Marlene Dietrich done up brown and gypsy-fashion in *Golden Earrings* became for the moment just another ham actress. And some trace of truth is needed if the audience is to be persuaded. I don't think the façade can be entirely assumed; the player too must be ready to believe in it. The difficulty is to arrive at the right façade. The triumph of Chaplin himself might have been delayed if he hadn't happened on his tramp's costume, 'everything a contradiction, the pants baggy, the coat tight, the hat small and the shoes large.'

And Chaplin it was who emphasized the essential element beneath the physical externals. 'In all comedy business,' he wrote, 'an attitude is most important, but it is not always easy to find an attitude.' Somehow the clothes and the make-up of the tramp – almost an accident, if there is such a thing as an accident in the development of extraordinary gifts – made him 'feel the person he was'. And as that person, the shabby, truculent, show-off tramp, the public knew him for a quarter of a century. The truculence weakened, pathos crept in, but basically he was the same. Only when he changed his 'attitude' did he begin to lose his hold on his audience. Politics in the United States certainly harmed the reception of *Monsieur Verdoux*. The film is as good as anything he ever did, for he is a great comedian as well as a great star. All the same I suspect that politics did less harm to the success of *Monsieur Verdoux* than the change of the façade of personality. The public wanted their Charlie.

Perhaps most of us really want the star. When the beautiful melancholy of the ageing Buster Keaton was employed in a dismal Samuel Beckett fragment (*Film*, it was called) I felt deeply aggrieved. Like the audiences who wanted Charlie, not Mr Chaplin, I wanted Buster, not Mr Keaton and certainly not Mr Beckett. And Keaton, like Chaplin and the immortal pair Laurel and Hardy trained in the ferocities of vaudeville, was a star who soon found his perfect façade. He learned never to smile, and for a decade the Great Stone Face grappled impassively with mutinous trains, ocean liners or an avalanche of boulders.

Players, I said just now, use their attributes. Keaton had the attributes of a cannon-ball. When he was a child on the stage his father would throw him into the scenery or even the audience; he could fall like nobody's business. Especially he could run. Jacques Tati, one of today's true comic stars, said to me once that physical comedy resided in the legs. Leaning extravagantly, Tati uses his height and his legs. Keaton, face immutable except for his speaking eyes, used his legs. Simply to see him running, torso compactly upright, knees like pistons, was a delirious pleasure. The voice wasn't so good, and when the talkies came the star faded. But the pale eagle-faced, lined but heroic, was still there, and presently in fragments – the bus-driver of *San Diego I Love You*, the pensioner in *Sunset Boulevard*, the pianist in *Limelight* – the gravity, the miraculous timing served once more.

Gish, Chaplin, Laurel and Hardy, Keaton – trained, dedicated performers, all of them. Rudolph Valentino is a different case. Slower in finding his façade – he was a professional dancer, he played heavies before his romantic quality was recognized – he was dedicated not so much to his work as to his own image. And once again the mood of the times helped. The fragile, virginal, fugitive heroine needed a counter-balance. And there was Valentino, dark smooth hair, dark Mediterranean features; set against the charm of Alice Terry or Vilma Banky he was the Sheik, he was the Great Lover, he was It. You could identify with him, or at any rate lonely women could identify with the willing quarry of his amorous demands. His clothes, his manner, invited imitation; audiences were gripped by a kind of sexual hysteria. Absurd – and yet if you look today at his films, especially *The Four*

Horsemen of the Apocalypse, some trace of the physical magnetism persists. He had assumed a role. He began to believe in it. The sincerity which is a necessary quality in the star came to his help.

In the distant black-and-white of the old three-by-four screen, Valentino was the Great Available. Greta Garbo, arriving later in an age growing more sophisticated, was the Great Unattainable. Pola Negri and, especially, Gloria Swanson, famous figures of the silent days who have survived to the present, were illustrious without mystery. But around the name of Garbo there hung veils of secrecy.

On the screen she was the woman of experience, she was Marie Walewska and Mata Hari, she was Anna Karenina, she was the *grande cocotte* of *Camille*; she knew love, she embraced it. John Gilbert, Charles Boyer, Robert Taylor, Ramon Novarro – the brightest stars among her partners paled beside her astonishing invitation. And yet the lovely creature, generous, desirable, was remote. That was, that *is*, her magic; as it has been the magic of Dietrich with her fine elegant bone-structure, her air of an insolence which had something of the patrician in it.

Dietrich is cool, Garbo is warm. Both are out of reach.

The assumption of an attitude – Harold Lloyd putting on the aspect of the small-town youth or the simpleton who somehow gets suspended from the hands of a skyscraper clock; Richard Barthelmess, the transparent Oriental innocent of *Broken Blossoms* who finally settles for the naïve farmboy of *Tol'able David* – this may be the behaviour of an actor, it is certainly the shape of a star. The notable, the pure performers live and work outside such limits. That, I suppose, is the difference between the star and the actor. The performer may refuse the confinement of talent and personality which is the requisite of acceptance as a star.

The Russian Nikolai Cherkassov plays Don Quixote and Ivan the Terrible and Alexander Nevsky; he is a great actor. The Pole Zbigniew Cybulski, immutable but bizarrely seductive behind his dark glasses, was a star. Gielgud is a noble actor; he has never been a star. Laurence Olivier could have been a star ten times over, romantic, intimidating, heroic; he would never submit to the limitations of being only a Heathcliff or only a Darcy. Ralph Richardson and Alec Guinness, Rex Harrison and Trevor Howard and Edith Evans – unlike the famous Barrymore trio in America, who finally devoted themselves to the cinema, the most distinguished of the British have elected for the freedom of the stage as well as the screen. They have chosen to be players, not stars; and one might say the same of the long catalogue of those who, through their gifts have been mainly devoted to the cinema, have reserved their right to be actors, facets of an infinitely variable world: Dirk Bogarde, for instance, David Niven, Richard Attenborough, James Mason.

And yet one can't always draw a line; where, I mean, do you place Peter Ustinov? The star may be the extraordinary player who finds freedom in the limitations of the camera-angle; think of Spencer Tracy, a great actor by any standards. Early in his career Tracy established his character on the screen. He was to be the solid one. Fisherman or delinquents' priest, explorer, inventor, airman, judge, father of a family, he was the man you could depend on, what in pre-racialism days used to be called a white man. There was a time when I thought he was monotonously white. But one had only to see him step right outside the role – for instance in *Dr Jekyll and Mr Hyde*, where his Hyde was greatly inferior to that of another star, Fredric March – to realize that his usual character was the right one. He could play endless variations on integrity. He even played jokes with integrity, suggesting the buccaneering politician of *The Last Hurrah* or the slightly disreputable sportsman of *Pat and Mike*; but behind everything that was best in his work one recognized the shape of Old Dependable.

His instinct for character was backed by flawless timing, an infallible technique; it was easy to take him for granted. But then in the Thirties and Forties and on into the Fifties when he still flourished, it was easy to take great names for granted.

Some of that incomparable vintage are still around – the endearing frog-face of Edward G. Robinson; James Stewart with his amused diction and his rural air, as if he proceeded from indomitable generations of wise-cracking honesty; Henry Fonda, flat voice, straight face, the tall figure intent and controlled in spite of its relaxed movement; and Cary Grant, mesmerizing exponent of comic or dramatic detachment, whether he is diving from the attack of a crop-spraying plane or standing nonchalantly under a shower with all his clothes on. And that giant maverick Orson Welles still exercises his powerful spell. But James Cagney, gangster idol with his muted machine-gun speech, has not acted on the screen for nearly a decade. Humphrey Bogart, outlaw or dick but always with some dark muffled sexual magnetism, has gone; so has Gary Cooper, lean Western horseman and master of the throwaway line.

We simply didn't know our luck in those days, with Katharine Hepburn (mercifully still a lode-star) complementing Spencer Tracy, with other heroes brilliantly partnered by such names – some of them retired now – as Jean Arthur and Claudette Colbert, Irene Dunne and Mary Astor. And always in the background, strengthening and enlivening, were the character players, Walter Connolly and Eugene Pallette, Porter Hall, Edward Arnold, Harry Davenport, Donald Meek, Thomas Mitchell, all the unsurpassed secondary figures of Hollywood's supremacy.

Sometimes a partnership fused into a double-powered star. William Powell and Myrna Loy were two polished players of comedy; together in the *Thin Man* series they dazzled. Or there were the group stars, the Keystone Cops in the early days, or the Marx Brothers, or the Dead End Kids. I suppose the Beatles, anarchic and by now centrifugal, are today's nearest equivalent. But their first appeal was in their music; and again some of the stars of yesterday were stars first by virtue of some special talent: the Nelson Eddy-Jeanette MacDonald partnership, Deanna Durbin and, for a brief and to me painful moment, Mario Lanza among the singers; among the dancers three performers whose talents were certainly not confined to their feet, Fred Astaire and Ginger Rogers and the dancer-choreographer-director Gene Kelly. Worth noting, perhaps, that Eleanor Powell, one of the most brilliant tap-dancers to be seen on the screen, never managed to find the image which would have made her a star.

It is tempting to suggest that a star might be the creation of the role he plays. One thinks of Johnny Weissmuller as Tarzan, one thinks of Sean Connery as James Bond, one thinks of a dozen Western stars. Tempting but probably misleading. There have been other Tarzans, but except for the first of them, Elmo Lincoln, one has difficulty in remembering their names; and an effective successor to Connery's 007 has still to be found. As for the Westerns, scores of solitary sheriffs have walked up the frontier-town square and beat the killer to a quick draw, scores of daring centaurs have cantered over the prairie. But they vanish, they are forgotten; to recall their names stirs no heartbeat. Only the true stars, the Gary Coopers and the John Waynes, survive.

For the cinema is pitiless. It will turn away from its favourites. Lillian Harvey, English heroine of the German screen in the early days of sound, is a faint name now. Nobody talks about Will

Rogers. A world war made Betty Grable a pin-up; more scantily dressed bodies decorate the walls today. Sometimes the cinema will even destroy its darlings or help them to destroy themselves; Jean Harlow and the desperate, heartbreaking Judy Garland and that exquisite waif Marilyn Monroe are among those who, like some ritual sacrifice in *The Golden Bough*, have been crowned and fêted only to become victims of their own triumph.

Marilyn Monroe was vulnerable in life as well as in her films. The face she turned to the world, yielding, soft, apprehensive, was not all pretence. But it was the face of a star; it compelled – this was her magic – a surge of pity and affection. We all wanted to look after Marilyn; obscurely we felt she could not look after herself.

We were right; stars need the strength of steel. Sometimes they have it. Lillian Gish has it. On a different level Joan Crawford has it; so has Bette Davis, who after a long eminence as queen of melodrama has delightedly appeared in films which allow her to parody her own style, her savagely clear enunciation, her flouncing walk, the ferocity of the gaze she turns on her opponents. The newcomer Barbra Streisand looks as if she might have it. And Elizabeth Taylor has it. She possesses an extraordinary gift for nervous tension. The perfect exponent of Tennessee Williams's foreboding dramas, she generates anxiety, she raises pulses. There is a kind of rage in her playing; and sometimes when I consider that intensity I am inclined to think she may be among the last of the true, the indomitable stars.

For though she is an actress too, and a good one, it is first as a star that one accepts her. Today's tendency is towards a range in portrayal which would have been foreign to the famous names of twenty and thirty years ago. Burt Lancaster and Kirk Douglas and Paul Newman drop the insignia of the star and compete with the actors; and once or twice Sinatra has joined them. Rod Steiger offers us the most fabulous of chameleons. Marlon Brando is a star variable, sometimes, to the point of extinction. Only the dead don't move with the times. Fifteen years after his life closed, James Dean is remembered as the sad image of a generation in the first stages of rebellion.

And after years of railing at the star system I begin to wonder whether we weren't better off when the screen was dominated by the fidelity of those unchanging, unquenchable lights.

September 1970

Monroe, Marilyn (1926–62), film actress; brought up in Los Angeles, USA, by series of foster-parents; became photographer's model and attained some notoriety, in the lax society which produced her, by posing nude for a popular calendar; entered film industry, playing small part in *The Asphalt Jungle*, a story of crime reflecting the anti-social tendencies of American surburban life; in same year *All About Eve*; subsequently in *Love Nest*, *We're Not Married*, *Gentlemen Prefer Blondes*, *How to Marry a Millionaire*, *The Seven Year Itch*, *The Prince and the Showgirl*, *Let's Make Love* and other films typical of Western sexual obsessions. Married first James Dougherty, policeman; second Joe DiMaggio, baseball player; third Arthur Miller, dramatist; however, gradual abandonment of proletarian relationships may be ascribed less to bourgeois ambition than to the capitalist forces which circumscribed this unfortunate woman. . . . (Extract from *People's Biographical Dictionary*, 1980.)

Even the heart behind the Iron Curtain must melt over Marilyn Monroe. Certainly a feature of the obituaries which have appeared during the past week has been the note of liking which has mingled with the routine regret. One might almost call it affection (affection at long range; at close range the actress seems to have been something of a nerve-irritant). I don't think I am mistaken in detecting in the general reaction to the news of her death a shade of feeling not often expressed for even the most celebrated names.

The story itself is curiously touching. The orphaned child and the callous foster-parents (from her own account she might have been the Cosette of *Les Misérables*); the success as a model and the admirable truculence over that famous calendar; the desperate pursuit of stability in marriage; the tiny part in Huston's *The Asphalt Jungle* and the instant success; the long list of films, good or ghastly; the visit to London to act with Olivier; the public's insistence, whatever the critics might say, that this was one of the true stars; and then, just as the downy little bird is growing into something else, the nervous collapse and the disaster – it all belongs to the febrile realm of a cinema which is disapearing. Or perhaps it belongs to fantasy, to a romantic idea of what the cinema should be like; perhaps Marilyn Monroe herself, to the general eye, was what the eternal feminine ought to be like.

Instant success: not, it must be owned, instant with the critics. After nearly twelve years I still faintly recall the appearance in *The Asphalt Jungle*, but at the time I failed to single it out; no doubt I am biologically ill-suited to the immediate recognition of a female sex-symbol, but in self-defence I have to say that one or two respected male colleagues failed too. Failed, I believe, because what Marilyn Monroe had to offer the cinema had nothing to do with acting: acting, that is, in the sense of creating a character or a series of characters completely outside the personality of the performer.

The cinema, even more than the modern stage, has shown us another kind of acting: the projection of a personality mutable within a limited range of situations – which was the contribution of, to give an illustrious example, Gary Cooper. I don't believe even that was within the compass of Marilyn Monroe – though in *The Misfits* at the end of her life, when a kind of despair may well have been working in her, she was beginning to stretch out towards new possibilities. I think that at the start of her career a combination of intelligence, physique and a superb instinct for working with the camera guided her to rough out a public image which, come hell or high water, she was not going to change. In severely adverse circumstances, in some healthy breath of the outdoors such, for instance, as *River of No Return*, the public image could not clearly register; but for the rest whether she was eeling around (amidst the richly merited wolf-whistles of the audience) as the lethal seductress of *Niagara* or playing the generous-hearted sweetie of *Some Like It Hot*, what appeared on the screen was the same: a haze of harmless sexual invitation.

Of course the physical charm was exceptional: but then the cinema swarms with actresses of exceptional physical attraction. Marilyn Monroe, peering with her strange air of myopia at the world, whispering to it in her flock-paper voice, offered something more: the trick of uncertainty, of defencelessness. It was something which the cinema had lacked for decades, probably ever since the days when Lillian Gish got knocked about in *Broken Blossoms*. With Marilyn Monroe it could be a witty defencelessness; but it was still, after all the Queen Bees, heroines of the Resistance, and resourceful trigger-girls, what the public subconsciously yearned for. Valentino was adored as the all-conquering male, Marilyn Monroe as the all-yielding female; but somehow the exquisite creature on the screen was not only desirable; she was an innocent into the bargain. A girl who can persuade people of that doesn't need to be able to act: she has it made. Perhaps we shall not see many more stars of such luminosity. Even Marilyn Monroe couldn't keep it up; even she began – to the rage of the public – threatening to act. But in her time she had done enough to justify her position as one of the great idols.

August 1962

7 GENRE

I *The Western*

In a notable column in the *Sunday Times* in the late 1960s, Dilys Powell contrasted the struggle between a duty that had taken her to a screening of Eric Rohmer's *My Night with Maud* and the self-indulgence she had permitted herself at Henry Hathaway's late Western *True Grit*. From her earliest reviews, which included a notice for John Ford's *Stagecoach*, the Western exercised a special hold on Powell's imagination: half myth, half history, a well defined moral framework, and character in landscape were the appeal of the genre. And her tastes were remarkably catholic. Dilys Powell admired Peckinpah just as much as Ford. As she wrote in October 1964, 'There are no bad Westerns. There are superb Westerns; there are good Westerns. And there are Westerns.'

The pictorial quality of a film approximates to the literary quality of a book. Occasionally a book written by a man apparently insensitive to the sound of words may make an impression by its truth or its humanity; occasionally a film put together without apparent regard for its visual effects is memorable for its acting, its wit, or its integrity. But then it succeeds less as a picture in its own right than as a translation from some other medium – from the stage, from the written word. Often, unfortunately, the makers of films fail to make use of their advantages, often they overlook the value in narrative of the background or the relation between men and landscape.

The director, John Ford, has made no such mistake with **Stagecoach**. This is a picture exciting from the start; exciting not simply because it tells a story of a wild journey across the Apache country, but because every point in the story is emphasized by brilliant pictorial effects. There is an attempt, too, rare in a picture of this kind, to differentiate the performers, not by the simple application of whitewash or pitch, but by making them behave according to the separate codes of the society in which they live. The character-drawing may be obvious, but in its way it admirably serves the purposes of the film.

The stage-coach sets out on its journey with an uncomfortable group of passengers: the Army officer's wife and the blonde exported by the Law and Order League, the gambler and the embezzling banker, the drunken actor and the nervous whisky salesman, and lastly the escaped prisoner, the Ringo Kid, who has a date with a murderer at the terminus. They know the dangers, they know that the Indians have risen and the stage must pass through Geronimo's country, but for their several reasons they must go on. The horses plunge and toss their black manes, the cavalry escort canters behind; the coach, tiny in the immense landscape of Arizona, scurries away into the empty valley.

Everybody knows that silence can be much more frightening than noise, and the extraordinary excitement of the film is partly due to the absence, for perhaps the first two-thirds, of violent incident. At the relay station the escort has orders to leave; there is no second escort. The cavalrymen ride away at the fork in the road, the stage drives on into the desert. The plain is silent, the great mesas of Monument Valley watch the coach rattling through the dust. Nothing happens. At the second station there is still no escort; the officer's wife, hearing that her husband has been wounded, collapses. The doctor sobers, the blonde forgets that she is a pariah and helps him; but the Apache signal-fires are lit on the hills, and the party, the mother with her new-born baby, must hurry on. Nothing happens. The ferry has been burned, the ruins smoulder in deathly quiet, the coach struggles over. Nothing happens. When at last the vigilant rocks stir with men and horses it is almost a relief.

The characters react to the tension in their various and not over-subtle ways: the gambler and the drunkard turn heroic; the outlaws of society, the girl and the prisoner, move towards one another; the timid little whisky-drummer, huddling in his deerstalker against the Arizona dust, betrays a faint humanity. But there is another, unnamed character in the adventure – the landscape. Throughout the picture one is always conscious of its presence: of the deserted plain, the huge fortress-rocks, the dust, the waterless valley. Wonderful effects have been obtained by imaginative use of this scene under sunshine and cloud. When the Indians ride out to attack the coach it is as if the desert itself had sprung to life.

Spectacular riding is taken for granted in the cinema. But the riding in this film is dazzling. The cast has no stars, and the acting is uniformly effective in a broad way; John Wayne and Claire Trevor as the anti-social pair add a kind of natural toughness and sincerity. But the pictorial quality is in the employment of background as a partner in the action, which makes the film one of the most exciting Westerns I have seen for years.

1939

As I came out of the Western at the Rialto, **The Proud Ones** (director: Robert D. Webb), 'Not bad,' I thought; though I would not have gone so far as to add, in the current cinema phrase, 'Not bad at all.' Every year I see, and willingly, a few dozen Westerns; routine films, films run up to keep the horses healthy. For the addict any stuff will do, and I never dislike them. *The Proud Ones* is better than routine. The bang-bang is much as usual: the saloon scenes, the target practice, the stalking of hero or villain at night in the dark street of the upstart town. But with Robert Ryan as the Marshal incommoded by attacks of blindness, Arthur O'Connell as a deputy, Jeffrey Hunter as the traditional glowerer and Walter Brennan as a quirky gaoler, the acting is well above the average.

All the same one has only to look at a first-rate Western to recognize the makeshift quality of *The Proud Ones*.

A day or two after seeing the film I had the chance of looking at John Ford's ***The Searchers***. For reasons too trifling to explain I arrived after the beginning and had to drag myself away before the end; the development of the plot when I left was still doubtful in my mind, the relations of the characters were obscure, I struggled to make out who was who. And yet before I had watched for five minutes I knew that I was in the presence of a Western of the first rank. I could not rest until I had seen it again, and all through.

Let me get out of the way the unimportant facts of the plot. The searchers of the title are a boy of part-Indian descent (Jeffrey Hunter again) and an embittered veteran of the defeated Southern Army in the Civil War who hates all Indians beyond reason and humanity (a handsome performance by John Wayne). The search, which lasts five years, is for a band of Indians, Comanches, who have carried off a little white girl, only survivor of the family which reared the boy. There are related themes – the love affair, for instance, between the boy and the girl who impatiently waits for him. There is a range of Western types – the humble, half-witted old vagabond, the belligerent preacher, the nervous settler and his staunch wife – some of them acted by performers familiar from earlier Ford films: John Qualen, for example, Ward Bond, young Harry Carey. Some episodes are only half-explained and some characters play a part in the tale which remains sketchy. But the core of the plot, the search, is never forgotten for long.

I call the facts of the plot unimportant; they might belong to a hundred films, and they certainly do not account for the grandeur of *The Searchers*. The faults of the film are not as easy to dismiss. It may seem puzzling that Ford, whose feeling in the Western can be so warmly sentimental, should allow himself passages of vulgar and brutal horseplay. I suspect that for him the extremes are both necessary, that in the simple masculine world inhabited by the Western heroes the two qualities meet; and that it is precisely because Ford can laugh at the kick in the rump that he is so loving a director of the pioneering story.

However that may be, there are scenes in *The Searchers* which are as good as anything he has ever done; I am inclined to think they are even better than his best. The first shots – the window opening on the glowing plain, the woman looking out to see the soldier riding slowly back from the wars, the muted, deeply felt family reunion – these seem to me quite as good as the famous home-coming in *The Birth of a Nation*. Again and again Ford brings us back to the homestead and the defenceless knot of parents and children; again and again a family waits on the porch, shading its eyes from the sun to watch for the rider returning. The contrast between the oases of human affection and the bloodstained world outside is exquisitely made.

Looking back on *The Searchers*, I fancy that here is a film which can give the answer to those who inquire: What is it that you see in a Western? What do you look for? In some banal story of settlers and Indians there is often beauty of composition, a beauty imposed by the shape and colour of a plain among hills or the natural grace of man and horse; it does not, I know, take a John Ford to give us that. A devoted director, however, can strengthen the composition, and *The Searchers* is full of landscapes so framed as to make one start with pleasure. But John Ford goes further. He establishes a relationship between man and landscape which is emotional as well as spatial.

The VistaVision screen is used here to show us the marigold-coloured mesas, the canyons of Monument Valley where (like *Stagecoach*) *The Searchers* was shot. Riders are tiny against cliffs; a figure, anonymous in the blurring light, waves from the immense shoulder of a rock; fugitives sheltering in a crack of the hills look down on a plain infested with mites who are their Indian pursuers. But going far beyond these splendid studies in landscape-with-figures, Ford communicates the emotional situation of the figures. A man looks out of his cabin at sunset; a streaked, indifferent red sky leans over a plain where suddenly, far off, birds fly up and dust swirls; the man takes down a gun, his wife without a word bars the window; the lamp is hastily blown out, a girl begins to scream. There is the hostile country; and engulfed in it the doggedly surviving homesteads of the pioneers.

Nobody like Ford for suggesting the feeling of the settlement in the wilderness: the moments of gaiety, the terrible transience of mourning in a country where before the first soil falls on the grave men are already buckling on their guns to hunt the killers. Above all, nobody like Ford for suggesting the idea of what we call home. The Western – I have said it a dozen times – is not a literary genre. Its dialogue can be as commonplace as you like, its incidents as familiar. The essence is not in them, but in the creation of an immortal myth in which the characters are the woman in the sunbonnet; the man taking down the gun from the rack by the cabin door; and the rider, monumental against the clear skyline.

July 1956

It is inexhaustible. After all the years of stagecoach and frontier post, the solitary homestead, the Indian massacre, the gunman and the cattle war, the Western survives, perhaps the one completely achieved form of the cinema. Indigenous too, I was going to say – but one has to remember the literary roots, from Fenimore Cooper to Zane Grey and, today, Jack Schaefer. All the same nothing on the printed page has ever had for me the living quality of a good Western on the screen. The quality, for instance, of *The Big Country*.

The Big Country, based on a novel by Donald Hamilton, is the first film in the genre to be made by William Wyler since in 1940 he directed Gary Cooper and Walter Brennan in *The Westerner* (now, by the way, reissued). In the interval a good many things have happened to the Western. The redskin has been admitted to the fraternity. Elvis Presley has joined in the shooting. Occasionally psychology has joined in, too. But in spite of a smarter intellectual level the mood has grown more brutal.

Protesting their hatred of force, the reformed gunmen mow the opposition down in swathes; and revenge becomes a kind of cold-blooded injustice (I am thinking in particular of *The Bravados*). The prairie and the frontier were indeed brutal; perhaps the picture has moved nearer to the truth. But though the depiction of violence may often be necessary, to exalt savagery under cover of a hypocritical morality I find sickening. In any case truth, that kind of truth, is not what I am looking for in the Western. Among my reasons for enjoying the covered wagon cycle is that it offers one of the few remaining refuges from that dreadful old bore contemporary realism.

Possibly *The Big Country*, together with the more modest *Man Hunt*, begins a movement away from the sadism of the last few years. Its hero, coming green to the cattle-country, does nothing that is expected of him: he publicly refuses to resent the drunken baiting, to ride the intractable horse, to fight the man who calls him a liar. Not that violence is excluded from the film. There it is in the gun-duel of the clan-leaders, or in the finely directed scene in which three ranch-hands from the rival camp are rounded up, roped and dragged out of our sight to be beaten.

But Wyler presents it as pointless or odious: in the end as self-destructive. The film loses nothing in excitement. It gains now and then a touch of irony – the fist-fight to a standstill; and now and then a passage of a comedy less raw than is common in the Western – for instance the private struggle with the bronco (the best entertainer in the horse-world I can remember since Tom Mix's Tony).

The Big Country has, in fact, most of the elements one asks for in the Western. Especially it has a feeling of size and space which has nothing to do with its length (two hours and three-quarters). The horsemen, those superb centaurs, trace their arabesques against a background – dusty plain, canyon, cruel mesa – magnificently shot in Technirama. Yet something, I think, is missing: the romantic heart. Wyler, brilliant film-maker though he is, never completely gives himself over to the myth of the West; and in consequence the young figures of the tale – Gregory Peck as the visitor from Baltimore, Jean Simmons as the schoolmistress, Charlton Heston as the foreman, even Carroll Baker as the hard little heiress – never quite come to life, never look quite equal to their setting. It is left to the actors of the older characters to supply the tough-sentimental core of emotion which holds the story together. Charles Bickford, famous veteran, as the rich, implacable ranch-owner; Burl Ives as the enemy, small vindictive eyes rheumy in the thicket of the terrible old face – these are the true, the necessary romantics of *The Big Country*.

January 1959

Asked to select the film which has given me the greatest number of enjoyable moments during the past week I should not hesitate: John Ford's *The Horse Soldiers* wins. My difficulty is in tracing the individual quality of the piece. To get the facts clear first: the screenplay is based by John Lee Mahin and Martin Rackin on a novel by Harold Sinclair, and its subject is a simple, bloody, military exploit in the American Civil War, interrupted by romantic passages in a rather blue-eyed style.

In a bid to take Vicksburg, General Grant plans to cut the supply lines, and a cavalry party is sent hundreds of miles into Southern territory to destroy a railhead and get back as best it can. The cavalry commander (John Wayne in his tough aspect) is accompanied, or in his view burdened, by a surgeon (William Holden); and he has been compelled to take along two women as well. One of them is coloured; Althea Gibson (yes, the tennis champion) gives her an easy and pleasing dignity. The spitfire heroine is played by Constance Towers with little more than routine vivacity; one's sympathies are all the more strongly focused on the purely military plot.

But already I am moving from facts to feelings; and I am back with my difficulty: why should this story of bloodshed, destruction and fratricide be so stirring? I see by the score American Civil War films and tales of raids and forced marches. Many are well constructed and directed; not one has the quality – I will call it devoutness – with which Ford invests his excursions into American myth and history.

The Horse Soldiers is blemished as many of his films are blemished: patches of horseplay, too much manly chest-beating. But the blemishes proceed from the quality which gives his work its frequent splendours. The horseplay and the over-emphasized masculinity belong to his romantic vision, just as, here, the opening camp scene with its vitality and its beautifully disciplined movement belongs; just as the drill-ground march into battle of the schoolboy cadets belongs, or the Southern charge with the Confederate flag snatched from one dying hand after another. Ford really sees the ferocious past as romantic. He is not, as most directors are doing, merely telling a story, he is giving life to what for him is a truth.

When John Huston made *The Red Badge of Courage* he succeeded in catching the outward appearance of contemporary photographs of the American Civil War. I fancy that the special gift of John Ford lies in catching something else as well: the emotion which resides in a contemporary painting, however artless, of a great event.

December 1959

Mean, moody, magnificent – the luxuriant Jane Russell, wasn't it, on whom publicity bestowed the phrase. The true heir to the title is with us now: in his own film, *One-Eyed Jacks*. In the coloured frame of the Western he brings the description to life. He looks dangerous; in the heavy, handsome face the eyes with their brilliant whites and triangular pupils – they are like the inlaid eyes of a classical bronze – blaze fixedly; muffled in his dark crimson poncho he has the air of a revenger's tragedy.

But I must try to think of Marlon Brando's film apart, for the moment, from Marlon Brando.

A Western with a screenplay based by Guy Trosper and Calder Willingham on a novel by Charles Neider; a story of two friends, a betrayal and a long, savage feud; bank hold-ups, gunfights and a girl who softens a ferocious heart – the elements do not differ much from the material one has seen a hundred times. 'I want,' says director Brando (one can't, you see, get away from him for long), 'to make a frontal assault on the temple of clichés'; and he goes on to describe the character played by actor Brando: 'a touch of the vain and a childish and disproportionate sense of virtue and manly ethics.' But this isn't the first Western to imply that manly ethics can be over-rated or that the pioneer heroes were, as he puts it, not brave 100 per cent of the time.

I shouldn't say myself that the clichés have been demolished; plenty of them are still around in the narrative and indeed the characters of *One-Eyed Jacks*. And yet this is not the ordinary Western; not the ordinary good Western; not even the ordinary extraordinary Western. I used to be against Westerns with Mexican hats and Westerns with psychology. I have lately conquered my prejudice against the hats; *One-Eyed Jacks* brings me round to the psychology too. It is not simply that the hero isn't all heroic (frankly I think Mr Brando is getting above himself in his comments on his film). It is that one feels him to be a genuine outlaw: a young man with experiences and motives which exclude him morally as well as physically from the settled world.

The sense of character would not, of course, be much use without the true stuff of the Western. That is present: that, and a bonus. Fine colour one often finds in the American film of the outdoors. In *One-Eyed Jacks* the figures and the background, the colour and the movement repeatedly unite in compositions of mesmerizing beauty. In the morning light a girl in a pink lace shawl and a crumpled white dress runs along the golden shore from her seducer; she sits in a darkly luminous room with the snowy-fringed sea framed in the window behind her; from a high distance one sees the blank sand by the fishermen's jetty furrowed as four horsemen ride past with tiny, elegant, furious movements.

Does one thank the director of photography, Charles Lang, Jr.? Or the second unit photographer, Wallace Kelley? One can at any rate be grateful to Mr Brando himself for going, in a Western, to the farthest West: to the Pacific, whose shot-silk waves, foaming and hissing on the rocks, do indeed, as he intends, deepen the sense of a romantic, subterranean restlessness.

June 1961

There are no bad Westerns. There are superb Westerns (*Shane, Lonely Are the Brave, Red River*); there are good Westerns (*The Big Country*). And there are Westerns: a category in which I include a bunch of titles beginning 'In Old' and 'West of' (with an exception to which I will come in a moment). But none of them are really bad. They are sustained by the great myth of the North American continent, a myth in which religion, basis of the classical and Nordic myths, has been supplanted by history. There is the bloodstained fact of the white drive towards the Pacific – white conquest, white settlement, white self-policing. The Western is the romantic, sometimes the poetic version of the fact. It is a version in which war is translated into the patterns and rhythms of an equestrian ballet, and the landscape is flooded with light. The Western belongs to an optimistic mythology: 'O Pioneers!'

Like any other myth, it has a range of unalterable ingredients. Homesteader, cattle baron, cowhand, sheriff, saloon girl, stage-coach, railroad, covered wagon, Indian, badman, scout, old-timer, insubordinate cavalry officer, family feud, bar-room riot, mission to Washington, gunfight in a deserted street, three horsemen cantering across a powdering plain – you can choose from the list and shift your choice about, but you can't alter the material. When a few years ago there was a move to introduce psychological refinements the very screen seemed to protest: the genre of itself rejects change.

This conservatism may be one of the reasons for the present cult, intellectual as well as romantic, of the Western. Conservatism, since scholarship is more practicable with an art not given to basic change, encourages the scholarly approach: names of directors and writers at the finger-tips, and names far from well known. Again, a conservative genre is a challenge to the director: interesting to see how he turns old stuff into new. But I believe that most enthusiasts enjoy a Western simply because it perpetuates a legend in which pleasure in the romantic virtues is still permissible. Plenty of anti-bombers who would scuttle nervously away from the portrayal of courage in a war film will accept it in a Western; heroism is all right in a myth. And, of course, there are the aesthetic pleasures – the setting of figures in landscape, the arabesques of movement. The Western offers a wealth of the delights which are associated particularly with the cinema, which to those of us who care about the cinema seem to belong peculiarly to the cinema. It offers a kind of joy.

There is often this quality of joy in the work of John Ford. Sometimes inexplicably: why should the heart lift at the moment in **Cheyenne Autumn** when on the huge Panavision screen a dispirited cavalry troop rides under green and golden trees into a stockaded fort? Nothing in the narrative to cheer about; no moral element either; anyhow in the Western one shouldn't expect more than the barest copybook morality. Nor is it much good looking for the director's opinions; a medium so strictly governed by conventions is scarcely the place to air them. For instance: a few years ago Mr Ford in *The Searchers* was telling the story of a white girl whom her uncle plans to kill because she has been defiled by living (under compulsion, too) with the Comanches. But *Cheyenne Autumn* (the script is based by James R. Webb on a book by Mari Sandoz) is about a band of North American Indians who, transplanted to an arid reservation, break away and, chased by what appears to be the greater part of the American Army, attempt a fifteen-hundred-mile trek back to their original hunting-grounds; and here the Indians (played by such distinguished redskins as Gilbert Roland, Ricardo Montalban and Sal Mineo, with Dolores del Rio in attendance), are honourable, dignified and generally worthy of respect.

As a matter of fact Ford doesn't seem quite at home in the pro-Indian passages; their compassion is formal. It is in a bar-room in Dodge City that the film comes to life, with James Stewart weighing his words (and a deck of cards) as an imperturbable Wyatt Earp; and in a panic over non-existent Indian attackers it roars delightedly away, posse in pursuit of nobody and Mr

Stewart at the reins of spirited horses almost outdistanced by a saloon girl in her underwear. This is the kind of scene which Ford enjoys and which, when his tendency to overdo manly riot is kept, as it is here, within bounds, he handles magnificently. And in the cavalry charges against a background of mesa and canyon, in battle scenes from which in the Western fashion the horrors of mutilation and death have been smoothed away, there, too, he is at his masterly old best.

Perhaps it is the absence from *Cheyenne Autumn* of a sympathetic central figure which I find vaguely discomforting: neither Richard Widmark as the officer who pleads for the Indians nor Carroll Baker as the Quaker who befriends them has the authentic heroic warmth (and though as the politician Edward G. Robinson can't do wrong his appearances are too brief to compensate). And perhaps that is why, if I had the choice between seeing again either the long, starry, splendidly mounted and often stirring *Cheyenne Autumn* or the modest piece **West of Montana**, I should choose the latter – and not only for its grace in colour and composition.

Burt Kennedy, who made *West of Montana*, is not a complete newcomer to direction; you would have found his name on *The Canadians* two years ago. But he has been chiefly a writer, and a writer of Westerns; and his script here (it is based on a story by Van Cort) shows how deeply he has assimilated the Western conventions. The opening of the story: the monosyllabic grizzlehead (Buddy Ebsen) camping by the stream, the brash boy (Keir Dullea) who won't take advice, the comic discomfiture, the laconic goodbye – in a flash you are in the world of the slow conversation and the quick draw. It is a world of sentimental fantasies and crude moral notions; grizzlehead thinks it his duty to make a man of the boy by finding him a wife – by mail order.

And a violent world. But to attack this kind of violence seems to me as pointless as to deplore the sexual errancies of Greece's ancient gods. In both cases the story-material is, as I say, settled; you can't make Zeus out to be an Arnold of Rugby, you can't turn a Western into an *All Quiet*. And when, after the goodmen's measured pacing through flying bullets (yes, all the conventions are here) the badman is left a huddled corpse, it isn't death which you have watched; nothing is real, everything is myth; and in myth there is no guilt.

October 1964

Not often do I find myself rushing back to see the beginning of a film, but I had to do that with **The Wild Bunch** (director: Sam Peckinpah). An unforeseen delay had made me miss the first quarter of an hour. With a film running nearly two hours and twenty minutes that might have been a bit of luck – though I had heard that Peckinpah's latest work was really something; still, one never knows. But the minute I sat down and began connecting with the narrative I knew I was hooked. *The Wild Bunch* is a magnificent Western.

Not a romantic Western in the John Ford manner; ferocious, rather, in the manner of Elizabethan drama; it is a tale of men who destroy themselves. The period, unexpectedly, is 1914. Bandits still ride horseback. The internal combustion engine, however, is on its way. Once a majestic motor-car makes an appearance; somebody insists that there are machines which fly; a machine-gun falls into hands which don't yet know how to use it. But the characters of the story persist in the ways of an earlier age. They are gunfighters no longer young, they are the old, professional killers. They can never settle down; they will have no successors. They are an anachronism.

In a way this is a film less about individuals than about groups and forces. There are the bandits who still live on robbery; by 1914 they have been beaten back, desperate and dwindling, to the Mexican border. They are doomed and know it; there is stoicism in their acceptance of the inevitable. Against them, more relics of the past, bounty-hunters who, hired by the advancing railroad, also kill to save their own skins and live. But in the border country where the action is fought there are groups with other aims. There are the power-seekers, a Mexican 'general' and his crew of thugs. There are the peasants who want arms to fight the marauders. And together these groups, ambushing, pursuing, betraying, massacring – occasionally one is reminded of Kurosawa's *Seven Samurai* – present a picture of appalling ruthlessness, Even the children, usually depicted as defenceless innocents, are shown as heartless, laughing little torturers.

The narrative is superbly handled – the opening raid (I was right to go back for that beginning), the attack on the train, the final battle; and when events before the start of the story have to be explained, when, for instance, the relationship between the leader of the raiders (Willian Holden) and the leader of the hunters (Robert Ryan) has to be made clear, it is done with admirable economy in the briefest possible evocation of memory. The picture on the screen is always composed with dramatic effect, the figures tellingly related to landscape or village interior. A moment of fierce action may be cut to scarcely more than a flash, but death, the crumbling of the human creature, is often drawn out in slow motion; the timing conveys both the speed and suddenness of violence and the horror of its consequences.

And the playing – for I must not give the impression that the individual is without importance in this struggle of dying forces or that Sam Peckinpah, so masterly in control of action, neglects character – this is a Western in which playing counts. It is especially pleasing to see such stars as William Holden and Robert Ryan, good actors whom we have long known, growing still better with the years; and there are notable performances from Ernest Borgnine and Warren Oates among the raiders and from Edmond O'Brien, unrecognizable as a whiskery old ex-gunfighter. Portraits of pitiless murderers, though Peckinpah now and then allows a hint of decent feelings long overlaid; but no matter how often and with what insistence the film emphasizes their criminal progress one can't help sympathizing with them. Detach yourself from the heroic myth of the West and you have to recognize that morally there is nothing to be said in their favour. Nevertheless, in their end there is a kind of grandeur. It may contradict the central theme of a film ostensibly concerned to portray the squalors of violence. But the contradiction creates what is finally the tragic mood of *The Wild Bunch*.

August 1969

It often looks magnificent. But what on earth is going on? ***Pat Garrett and Billy the Kid*** was written by Rudy Wurlitzer, co-author of the script of *Two-Lane Blacktop*, so one can expect the conversations to be a bit fragmentary. It was directed by Sam Peckinpah of *The Wild Bunch* (and of *Straw Dogs*, but let's forget that), so the chances are that there will be violence. Why not? This is a Western, and the West was violent; even those of us most addicted to the romantic view would agree to that. And from the title one might guess that the film is about the latter days of Billy the Kid, for Pat Garrett (we all have to do our homework on the West these days) was the man who shot him.

So much for a start. By the end one recognizes that *Pat Garrett and Billy the Kid*, like *The Wild Bunch*, is a study of

decline. It does not aim at the beautiful elegiac quality of
another Peckinpah work, *The Ballad of Cable Hogue*. The note
of regret for the passing of the old West isn't as clear as in *The
Wild Bunch*, where one watched the defeat of the reckless and
the adventurous, men whose way of life was doomed by the
beginnings of a new, a mechanised world (Peckinpah respects
people who are tough, even if they are killers, and somehow
makes one share his respect). Nevertheless, regret lingers. The
man who shoots Billy is a former partner of the Kid; he has
himself been an outlaw, now he is a sheriff; the old friendships
and freedoms are receding. The end of the film is itself a kind of
requiem for romance. Garrett, played with a dry, lean, relentless
authority by James Coburn, guns the Kid down and lets the body
lie. Daylight finds him still sitting in the swing-seat on the porch
where he has slept; he wakes, stands up, mounts his horse and,
indifferent, rides away. It is the break with the romantic past.

   Not that Kris Kristofferson as Billy the Kid presents much of
a figure of romance. Or does he? I may be prejudiced by the
target-shooting at nesting hens which opens the story; but that
is nothing to the target-shooting at men, sometimes unarmed,
sometimes with their backs turned, which goes on throughout
the film, and the actor does little that I can see to make the
character less dislikeable. Nothing, I repeat, that I can see; for
now I must get back to my initial question. The outline of the
plot one can vaguely trace. And, as I say, visually the film is often
fine – not fine in the loving fashion of a John Ford Western but
dramatically composed, the single figure tellingly set against the
landscape or the township, the groups arranged to make their
own narrative effect. And believe me, they had better make it;
for often there is precious little else to go by.

   The cinema has never been a wholly visual art; it has rarely
dispensed with words, whether spoken aloud or presented in
the form of sub-titles. And if they are spoken aloud one likes
to know what is being said. Nowadays it is not uncommon at
the start of a film presenting an unfamiliar or a remote society
to find difficulty in following the dialogue; but one's ear quickly
accustoms itself. Not in *Pat Garrett and Billy the Kid*; not at any
rate my ear and not, I believe, the ear of some of my colleagues.
The volume of sound bellowed round one's head – at the Press
show I sometimes thought I heard an echo from the back of the
cinema; but again and again the words were blurred and lost.

   Who, I began to ask myself, were all these people so busily

shooting or being shot, and why? Had the film been brutally cut? Was nothing missing except the sense? Now and then some favourite old-timer of the screen or some character player from an earlier Peckinpah film – Jack Elam, perhaps, or Slim Pickens, or R. G. Armstrong – would be decently audible. James Coburn would make himself understood. Bob Dylan – a promising appearance in an acting role (he was responsible for the music as well) – was clear enough; so was John Poe as Garrett's deputy, the man there at the kill. But most of the time one spent straining to catch a phrase, a helpful word. And one can't blame that on the editing or the censorship.

September 1973

All the advantages: a distinguished director, famous stars, notable supporting players, a girl, a new face, of astonishing spontaneity – **The Missouri Breaks** (director: Arthur Penn) certainly has gifts. It even has a comprehensible story, and that is something these days. All the good fairies attended the cradle. All, that is, but one.

Arthur Penn began his career in the cinema with a Western, *The Left-Handed Gun* in 1967. Since then he has once or twice returned to the territory, for instance with the ironic *Little Big Man*. Now with *The Missouri Breaks* he is back with straight violence, a developing violence. You might say the film was the tale of a thief, leader of a gang, who is opposed by brutality and corrupted by it; he begins by stealing horses and ends by slitting throats. In mid-course he steals money. He robs a train. Conditioned as we are by the cinema we are disinclined to pass any moral judgment, at any rate as long as the action isn't savage, and in fact it is a comic reaction. Mr Penn is good at investing tension with absurdity.

One notices, as in other Penn works, the way in which the narrative is fragmented. The train hold-up; the establishment of a depot for stolen horses; the meeting with the ranch-owner who is suffering from the thefts; the casual, off-hand beginning of the affair between the gang-leader and the rancher's daughter – scenes are presented, then abruptly broken off without any pretence at linking them with what comes next. But when you look back at Thomas McGuane's script you see that what comes next proceeds logically. With Arthur Penn's direction one is spared the tedium of long expositions – and the fragments do coalesce.

The character of the girl, wayward, oncoming, accepting with only a shade of curiosity the mysterious antecedents of her lover, seems a natural part of the township, the ranch and the empty landscape; just enough is revealed to give her behaviour a reason. . . . And she is played by Kathleen Lloyd as if she had just thought of every word she says. One must remember Miss Lloyd.

I think with pleasure of two figures in the horse-thief's gang. One is Harry Dean Stanton as the laconic rustler who says he took off from home because his dog was shot for 'putting his tongue to the butter.' The other is Randy Quaid, heartbreaking as the frightened prisoner in *The Last Detail*; here he is transformed into the amiable, guileless victim of the Regulator. And that brings me to the stars, the two celebrated players whose names, standing above the title, are intended to bring in the public.

A Regulator, in case like me you didn't know, is a gunman hired by rich landowners to regulate criminals, in other words shoot the lot down; this one is played by Marlon Brando. His chief target is the gang-leader, played by Jack Nicholson; and Mr Nicholson is an actor who, to judge by what I have so far seen, can do no wrong. Grinning mischievously, white teeth blazing behind black whiskery beard, he is unrecognizable except by his voice; one sees only a lawbreaker making a dollar in a lawless society. Marlon Brando, transforming his accent (he is good at accents) into the Irish remembered from *The Nightcomers*, is a fine actor who can certainly do no wrong. I won't blame him for *A Countess from Hong Kong*, but elsewhere in comedy he has failed by nobody's fault but his own. On the whole I prefer him as the victim rather than as in *The Missouri Breaks*, the oppressor; nevertheless his Regulator, chuckling, baiting, the face pale and flabby beneath the stork's nest of fading hair, is on the mark, a scruffy Caligula.

But something is wrong. The confrontation is wrong. So far as the narrative is concerned the two actors are in opposition. All the same they should play as it were together, each drawing strength from the other. What happens is the opposite. Singly each is memorable; together, each is dimmed. It doesn't happen in conjunction with other players. In his scenes with Randy Quaid, for instance, Brando is all smiling, subterranean threat.

For the past few weeks the London critics have been faced with a series of films ranging from the insignificant to the plain ghastly. It may seem ungrateful, when at last one is offered cinema of decent stature, to receive it with discontent. I am grateful all right, but I am not uncritically grateful. For I feel that the Western is losing something, is forgetting something. It grows more violent: that, though I shall always detest the savage handling of the horses, one has to accept. My complaint is that the violence has gone cold. And now I reflect on that missing attendant at the cradle of Mr Penn's film, and it seems to me that the gift denied is the gift of warmth, that what has been lost is the generosity of passion. Respectfully one watches the camerawork, the composition; one follows the players. But one simply cannot feel for them.

July 1976

8   GENRE

II   *Musicals; Bibles, Swords and Sandals; the Biopic; and the Horror Movie*

1 *Musicals*

When I say that **On the Town** (directors, Gene Kelly and Stanley Donen) is the best musical since *Forty-Second Street*, I say it in the knowledge that to many people who enjoyed the song-and-dance in the 1930s the new piece will seem restless, charmless and strident. I am not deaf either, and there were moments when, ravished though I was by the design and movement of the film, I began to fear for my eardrums. I am aware also that *On the Town* is short of tunes to whistle. Let me warn delicate sensibilities that the Empire Cinema this week is not the place to go for an old air on the spinet. And that said, let me repeat: the best musical since *Forty-Second Street*.

The last few years have seen a change in the character of the American musical. Technicolor has had something to do with it; the use of bright, simple colours, reds, greens and yellows, in contrast with blacks and white, has given *On the Town* a chance to emphasize the patterns of the dance in a way impossible to monochrome.

I fancy that currents in the theatre have something to do with it, too. The stage, in creating the fresh type of American musical comedy to which *Oklahoma!* belongs, may well have borrowed ideas from the screen. It gave ideas in return: the modern screen musical, with its delight in the group rather than in the single figure with chorus, proceeds from a general creative excitement which has affected both theatre and cinema.

On the Town is based on a stage piece, but the handling of its theme – twenty-four hours' leave in New York for three exuberant sailors – is wholly cinematic. Everything is imagined in terms of movement; the background, with the camera swinging breathlessly after the players, cutting and dissolving from street to street, rooftop to rooftop, joins in the fun; while in the graceful Fred Astaire-Ginger Rogers pieces of the 1930s the dance was part of the film, here the whole film is dance. The dance is sometimes comic, sometimes acrobatic, sometimes narrative, but whether the audience watches Vera-Ellen demonstrating the versatility of Miss Turnstiles the pin-up or Ann Miller taking a look at anthropology, the picture is composed to display not so much the individual performer as the group in its setting.

And the setting never distracts, as by fussiness and irrelevance it has so often in the past distracted, from the rhythms of the dance; consider the stylized skyscrapers of Gene Kelly's dream-dance, and the simplicity of the design in crimson, black and white of the duet at the practice-bar. To the directors, to their cameraman, Harold Rosson, and to the author of the ballet, Leonard Bernstein, credit must go for a musical in the new style which has all the gaiety, the vitality and the animal spirits proper to a contemporary popular art.

March 1950

A word of warning must be written. **Call Me Madam** (director: Walter Lang) is not a genteel film. It is good-tempered, warm, generous and about as quiet as a massed brass band festival, and anybody who wants a refined afternoon with the finishing school voices to which the English musical comedy stage has accustomed us had better wear ear plugs or stay away. As Mrs Sally Adams, American Ambassadress to the Duchy of Lichtenburg, Ethel Merman bawls the place down. But every note comes out bingo. Miss Merman has superb attack. And as well as technique and authority she has personality of a charm which I can only call commanding. It must be fourteen or fifteen years since, in *Alexander's Ragtime Band*, I first to my knowledge saw her on the screen. Between then and now we in this country have had to content ourselves, her brief appearance in *Stage Door Canteen* apart, with Merman records and with reports of Merman performances on the New York stage. *Call Me Madam* is the English public's first introduction to the actress in her full brilliance. In the circumstances I don't think I am labouring the point in saying that Ethel Merman is terrific.

To survive on the same screen as this controlled tornado is already something and to shine as one or two of the other players shine is an achievement. Perhaps I ought to say that the film is about an unorthodox American Embassy, a threatened State marriage, a proffered American loan and a Ruritanian Foreign Minister who positively doesn't want it. The story admits jokes about Europe and visiting American Senators, fun with long-distance telephone conversations between the Ambassadress and a certain Harry whose daughter Margaret is bothered by critics, and characters including a Princess, a Press Attaché and George Sanders. Mr Sanders is debonair and likeable as the Foreign

Minister; Vera-Ellen and Donald O'Connor as the Princess and the Press Attaché dance with their usual accomplishment. Mr O'Connor gives in other ways, too, a good account of himself. This young actor has come a long way since his early appearances on the screen as a teenager, and his playing in *Call Me Madam* is one of the pleasures of a film which is gay, confident, intelligent, witty and full of the best tunes heard in the cinema since *Top Hat*.

July 1953

For years I have been wishing that Fred Astaire would renounce tapping up and down flights of steps or kicking drums to music, and simply dance for us. He is still the most elegant of film dancers, with a sense of line which makes the magnificent precision of even Gene Kelly, in his own style incomparable also, look a trifle athletic. But it is rare to get the chance of watching undistracted by gadgets and gimmicks. All the happier the interlude in **The Band Wagon** when Astaire and Cyd Charisse, loitering through some vague park, move easily into a dance exquisitely dependent on nothing but the dancing. The film is worth seeing for this alone.

I call it an interlude because its moonlit romantic mood affords a rest amidst the general high spirits and bustle. *The Band Wagon* is a good, lively musical, not quite as good as travellers' tales had led me to imagine, certainly not as good as the one and only *On the Town*, but good enough to enjoy all through. It has an exciting feeling for movement and rhythm, as indeed we should expect from its director, Vincente Minnelli, who has made some of the best musicals to come out of Hollywood in the last ten years. It has even an intelligent and amusing script (by Betty Comden and Adolph Green).

The plot concerns a musical comedy in which a Hollywood song-and-dance star is to appear and which is to be produced by one of Broadway's actor-idols. The producer, however, a man addicted to playing Oedipus by cellar-light, sees the show as a chance to present a modern version of Faust, engages a ballet-dancer as a partner for the Hollywood star and dots the stage with trap-doors and bursts of hell-fire. I could have done with more edge to the satire on the groaner school of theatre, but Jack Buchanan so agreeably mixes the *dégagé* man of the world and a knockabout parody of the portentous actor-manager that

I was consoled. And talking of parody, I must not forget the ballet-sequence at the end of the film, a joke at the expense of the Micky Spillane type of thriller, wittily written and wittily as well as beautifully danced by Mr Astaire and Miss Charisse.

                                                        January 1954

In moments of moral vacillation it is consoling to reflect that the American musical stands solidly for the sanctity of the family; you can be sure that back-stage, behind the sequinned chorus-girls, the ice-ballet and the bits of Dali, the Momma-cult is safe. You can be doubly sure after *There's No Business Like Show Business*, the long, loud, expensive and starry musical in CinemaScope and De Luxe Colour, directed by Walter Lang, with music by Irving Berlin.

There's No Business Like Show Business belongs to the stage-family group of family musicals. I do not pretend to be a mathematician, but I cannot help thinking that the ratio of children to parents is changing. True, in *Mother Wore Tights* Miss Grable was twice a mother; but surely the vaudeville performers of the cinema are usually limited to one child? Cinemascope, however, can be trusted to put an end to the three-by-four-screen system of birth control. To fill the wide screen you need more family; and here they are, counting the parents, five dancing and singing Donahues – six if, as I understand most people would like to do, you take in their prospective partner Marilyn Monroe.

At this point I ask myself if I am not deceived; in some black recess of memory there lurks a suspicion that somewhere, sometime, I once saw a musical about a vaudeville family five strong. But no matter; the point about the new film is that it enlarges the view of family life in show business. It gives us, for instance, an impression of the parents' dismay when the children fail to join them for supper after the show. The daughter comes home late to be rebuked by her father. The younger son comes home drunk to have his head held in a basin of water by his Momma. But it is the delinquency of the elder son which causes most alarm: the boy who, having expressed a wish to walk home alone ('I got some thinking to do'), announces that he wants to be a priest. In *The Jazz Singer* the stage stole a son from a religious calling. Now the religious vocation gets its own back: though Johnnie Ray, playing the boy, makes it hideously clear that he regards ordination as just another piece of show biz.

The defection leaves only four Donahues. But now there is Miss Monroe to be reckoned with: Miss Monroe wriggling in carefully plotted curves from table to table as she sings in her raspberry mousse voice: 'After you get what you want you don't want it.' The threat looks almost as dangerous to the family as religion; for Miss Monroe not only detaches the two younger members from the Donahue act, she drives the son into a state so maudlin, or should I say so Marilyn, that he misses his opening night. Once more I have the suspicion that I have been here before. But again no matter. The family fights back; a substitute is found; and who should it be but Momma?

Perhaps I should not complain of the familiarity of much of the plot since it allows us to meet Ethel Merman again. All the same, I do complain. I complain because Miss Merman, though she carries off the sentiment with much more success than it deserves, is shamefully wasted. Nearly all her material is unsuited to her splendid brassy gifts. I longed to hear her true trumpeting rhythms: in *Alexander's Ragtime Band* which instead was shared with other stars in an ill-advised parody of Scottish style, French style, and so on; in 'Heat Wave', palely whispered by Miss Monroe (does anyone remember the rendering on the stage years ago in *Blackbirds*?).

Indeed I feel that much of the talent – and there is a great deal of talent in the film – is wasted. Dan Dailey has scarcely a chance. Mitzi Gaynor, a true star, shares one delightful number, 'I'm Lazy'. But for most of the time Miss Gaynor is in the background; and Donald O'Connor, though he is allowed in the elaborate and pleasingly staged 'A Man Chases a Girl' to show what a good dancer he is, still has to keep much of his ability in the shadow. For those who want size and quantity *There's No Business Like Show Business* may be the ticket. I find it one of the saddening films which only occasionally live up to their huge promise.

February 1955

If I were to be asked by a literary friend whether or not he should go to see **A Star is Born** I should probably say, struggling to keep a note of commiseration out of my voice, No. It is, I should say if I had the stamina to go on, not for you: not for people who want only an extension of serious literature or a replica of the serious stage. It is not for those who shrink from clichés and sentimentalities. And I doubt very much whether having seen *A Star is Born* will do for you what a visit to, say, *Carmen Jones* will do: put you in the social swim.

A Star is Born was first seen eighteen years ago, when a screenplay by Dorothy Parker, Alan Campbell and Robert Carson was directed by William A. Wellman and played by Janet Gaynor, Fredric March, Lionel Stander and Adolphe Menjou. The new version (CinemaScope, Technicolor) is directed by George Cukor and played by Judy Garland, James Mason, Jack Carson and Charles Bickford. It is a movie about the movies, a film with music rather than a musical: a story, goodness knows familiar enough, about a rising and a falling star. The famous actor (Mason) discovers a new talent (Garland), encourages her, teaches her, marries her, finds himself eclipsed, drinks, is disgraced. The film, in fact, has every opportunity for the oldest ackamarackus. It takes the opportunities – and uses them to make something fresh, exciting, touching and alive, something impossible in any other medium. *A Star Is Born* is for those who like the cinema not as a copy of something else but as cinema.

First of all it must be said that Moss Hart's screen-play, retaining, I imagine, much of its original (which I never saw), is excellent: full of neat satirical jokes, giving, in spite of the length (two hours and a half), an impression of economy and tautness. *A Star Is Born* is for me by far the best of all the films about life behind the cameras, the lights, the wind-machines, and the cocktail bars of Hollywood. But something more than the script distinguishes it from the usual back-screen and back-stage pieces, even the good ones. Script and playing can make an essay in smart, ironic talk such as, for instance, *All About Eve*. In *A Star Is Born* the total resources of the studio, editing as well as direction, camerawork as well as acting, have combined to create the movement, the glitter, the vitality of popular cinema which is also critic's cinema. And Cukor, a director especially gifted in the handling of his players, has seen to it that the glitter and the movement do not blur the human action.

There has been a great deal of talk about Judy Garland's comeback. This prompts me to say that as far as I am concerned Miss Garland never went away; and after *A Star Is Born* I hope she never will go away. The other day we had the chance of seeing her again in an early piece, *Meet Me In St Louis*; ravishing there, in the new film she displays an extraordinary maturing of her talents. It is not only that her singing has a new strength and edge; nobody can do better with a song such as here, 'The Man That Got Away'; and in a satire, admirably staged by Richard Barstow, on what is known as a big production number she shows a gift for parody which is brilliant. As an actress she has come a long way. Pathos she always had; but today the pathos has deepened, and her acting has a nervous tension which, when I saw the film, held the house silent and tear-stained. And her playing is beautifully contrasted with that of Mr Mason, who as the declining star gives a performance of great charm and authority.

A Star Is Born is a rocket: going off with a bang and a scream, slowing for a moment at the height of its trajectory while we wonder if it will fail to explode, then bursting in the dark into tearful sparkles. It strikes me as a film which in ten years' time will still be talked of.

March 1955

'And do you,' the critic is sometimes asked, 'ever go to the cinema for fun?' The answer is: Not often enough. In a sense, of course, I always go to the cinema for fun. As I set off to a morning Press show, leaving behind me the unanswered letters, the unread newspapers and the ringing telephone, I always have a sense of pleasant expectation. Though it varies in intensity – the piece about the incidence of scabies in the Aleutians is less enticing than, shall I say, *Richard III* – I am an optimistic type, and there is always hope. All the same the necessary trip to the Press show is, I agree, not the same thing as the voluntary expedition.

The trouble is that one does not always have the time or, after a day already devoted to the screen, the freshness of mind to enjoy a busman's holiday, a second look at a film. Nevertheless now and then the chance is offered – and taken. It was strictly for fun that, a fortnight after seeing *The King and I* (director: Walter Lang) in Edinburgh, I went off to the Carlton in London to look at it again.

This CinemaScope version makes a long film: two hours and a quarter. Should I go off as happily to sit for a second time through the other Rodgers and Hammerstein piece now to be seen in a London cinema, *Oklahoma!*? I doubt it. So far as familiarity with the music and the lyrics is concerned I have no preference; I know both pieces to exhaustion; and as a matter of fact I like the *Oklahoma!* songs better than the songs in *The King and I*. But the musical at the Carlton is much better composed visually than the one at the Odeon, Leicester Square. And it has Yul Brynner.

I have already said, in commenting on *The King and I* after its Edinburgh showing, that I find Mr Brynner's performance outstanding. Lest there should be anybody left who still has not heard the subject of the film, I must explain that the story is about an English governess who in the 1860s goes to Siam to teach the royal children, and about the influence she is able to exert over a king who is struggling to Westernise his country. This bit of romantic beading on the skirts of history suggests something more; it suggests that the king and the governess are falling in love. The cinema, for all its protestations, is usually perfunctory with the theme of love. Its long, squashed embraces are quite mechanical; its lovers are desexed. Suddenly in *The King and I* we find a moment of real feeling. It is not to decry the pretty and touching performance of Deborah Kerr as the governess if I say that Yul Brynner dominates the screen not only at this moment but through the film. The king is the one to be cajoled, inveigled, smilingly condescended to; and yet, I am glad to say – for the whole story with its air of Western patronage strikes me as a bit of cheek – he is the one we look at, like, respect.

I hope next week, when *Guys and Dolls* will have been added to the films running in the West End of London, to say something about the problems of translating the stage musical to the screen. In the meantime I will content myself with remarking that the dress-and-décor boys have had a beano with *The King and I*. The ballet in Siamese style of *Uncle Tom's Cabin* is glitteringly designed; and in spite of a good deal of Surbiton-Oriental in the palace backgrounds there is an effect of brilliance, splendour and size not all attributable to the new 55mm CinemaScope.

September 1956

Astaire for elegance, Kelly for command: the orbits of the two dancing stars are clearly defined and sharply separated. The grace in Gene Kelly's movements always speaks of strength; the splendidly disciplined figure, an acrobat's body without an acrobat's deformations, even in its most casual inclinations hints at the coiled, powerful spring. Put Kelly in *Funny Face* and his masculine arrogance would burst the seams of this satirical fantasy. But when Fred Astaire dances everything is delicate; the large arabesques of action are made up of innumerable tiny gestures as lightning and as precise as the beat of an insect's wings. Astaire makes *Funny Face* plausible.

I never saw the stage production and have no idea what relation, if any, the film bears to its original. I can say only that Stanley Donen has directed a story, engagingly punctuated by Gershwin songs, about a Greenwich Village bookshop assistant who is noticed by a photographer's experienced eye, snatched from literature and philosophy away to Paris, and smoothed into a fashion model. The cinema specializes in the encounter of worldliness with high-falutin' naïveness, and the conflict between the popular and the intellectual is a favourite subject – so long, that is, as the popular wins. *Funny Face* makes its heroine (Audrey Hepburn) a disciple of Flostre, the sage of 'empathicalism'; and her devotion gives the excuse for plenty of jokes about existentialist cellar-cafés, beards, horse-tail hair, flat heels and frenetic melancholy.

To an educated audience they are not quite the riot which their makers intended, but all the same they are much better informed than most film jokes of the kind. And visually they sometimes go off with a bang – as when Miss Hepburn, looking in her black tight pants and pullover like an amiable, miniature version of Conrad Veidt in *Caligari*, brilliantly executes an empathicalist's dance. Elsewhere her dancing – perhaps intentionally, since she is the innocent among worldlings – does not match in dash the performance, for instance, of such a partner as Kay Thompson, splendidly confident and insolent as the editress of a smart fashion magazine. Yet Miss Hepburn is engaging in the duet with the photographer in the darkroom – a simple, quizzical, non-setpiece of a kind which Astaire does not perform often enough. For the great popular dancers have their obvious failings. Gene Kelly struggles to force his vital talent into self-conscious ballet; Fred Astaire is apt to clutter up his pure line with tricks, creating for himself vertiginous juggler's difficulties. But not here. His electric song-and-caper with Kay Thompson makes its satirical effects by talent, not gimmicks; and his solo with rolled umbrella is inventive without encumbrances.

Existentialism, however, is not the only butt of *Funny Face*; and the second theme provides the best fun. For some time now, as students of the suaver magazines will recognize, high fashion has removed its mannequins from the domestic setting and driven them out sightseeing. The lovely greyhound-limbs glide up the steps at Angkor Vat; the great doe-eyes are rapturously bent on a Picasso or one of Henry Moore's monster crumpets.

Funny Face has seized on the idea of the intellectual model. It is with the background of the heroic, antique sculpture that Audrey Hepburn displays the drapery of the evening dress; with a head full, beneath its up-to-date Little Miss Muffet hat, of Tolstoy that she pauses on the railway platform. The clothes are dazzling, and she wears them, as she wears her rôle, with a charm and a wistful composure which add greatly to the pleasures of this gay and lively musical. And yet they leave me in a difficulty I often find where caterpillar-into-butterfly films are concerned.

Again and again I think the dancer dances better, tapping neglected in the back-yard, before fame puts her in sequins and neon lights. Again and again I find the career woman better dressed in her austere suit before love prevails on her to let her hair down and take to tulle. And to me Miss Hepburn, fetching as she is in her modish wardrobe, looks still more fetching when she first appears in her Greenwich Village outfit of sack-tunic over black sweater and skirt, black woollen stockings and clumping shoes. But then perhaps I am prejudiced by my vague longing to see, once in a while, a film in which the model girl throws up evening dresses, mushroom hats and all in order to become, not for love but for literature, an assistant in a bookshop.

April 1957

Unprecedented step: begin, when writing about a musical, with the music. **Gigi** (director: Vincente Minnelli) is the first film to be shown at the smart new Columbia; the Columbia, on the site of the old Shaftesbury Avenue Pavilion, is the first cinema to be built in London's West End since the war. The double first gives the occasion a celebratory feeling. And with *Gigi* the case, I admit, is unusual; for once the songs do not arrive secondhand, borrowed from some stage success. Colette's story about the innocent girl carefully trained for the rôle of *grande cocotte* has had its earlier metamorphoses: France made a film of it, America made a play. Now the talents behind *My Fair Lady* have moved in: screenplay and lyrics by Alan Jay Lerner, music by Frederick

Loewe. Nine songs, sentimental and sardonic and high-spirited, illustrate, decorate, amplify and develop the plot. Nobody would claim that they have the musicianly interest of Bernstein's work in *West Side Story*. But they have the trick of singing in one's head without driving one off it which marks the good popular tune. I find them captivating.

And they draw life from the film as well as giving life to it. Gigi's puzzled schoolgirl complaint that the Parisians spend all their time making love is much funnier if the singer is scurrying through a city where even the public statues are athletically engaged in amorous exercises; just as the fashionable young man's 'She Is Not Thinking Of Me' is much more pointed when part of it comes over as unspoken thought, delivered with lips sealed and eyes irritably following the suspect hilarity of a mistress.

Like *My Fair Lady*, *Gigi* is about the transformation of a natural human being into a living work of art – and about the war of the sexes.

The two ageing sisters, their raffish past buried but its lessons in etiquette remembered, teaching the girl how to choose a cigar or recognize a precious stone, look on a man as a shy but powerful animal, valuable when semi-domesticated, well worth the pains it takes to trap him. The two men, the blasé prospective lover and his uncle, regard their mistresses as tricky opponents in a modish game with rules which must be publicly observed. Enough of Colette's diamond-sharp exchanges are preserved to give the story a core of character.

And round the ironic centre a sparkling, sophisticated web has been spun: Paris at the turn of the century, the Paris of the sybarites; carriages in the Bois de Boulogne, the wink over the feather boa, champagne and jewels and plump shoulders at Maxim's. Cecil Beaton's designs for the production, both costumes and settings, are at once elegant and exhilarating. The flamboyant public dresses of the young *cocottes*, the well-bred private get-up of the old courtesan who has retired on her spoils – everything delights, everything persuades within this witty dream-world.

There is wit in the incident as well as the dialogue: in the baroque absurdities of the parties which the man about town gives to demonstrate that an unfaithful mistress hasn't broken his heart, in the contrast between Gigi's tearing schoolgirl tennis and the performance of a fashionable lady apparently clamped to the court. And both feeling and wit in the playing: in Louis Jourdan's out-fought, entangled, entrapped young profligate; in the two elderly educationists of Hermione Gingold and Isabel Jeans, the first weakening into affection, the second superbly unwavering in her attachment to the principles of good taste and good money; especially in Leslie Caron's flawless Gigi, an eager, laughing little hoyden with the promise of heartbreak in her face.

Somewhere about two-thirds of the way through the pace slackens, and one has time to recollect and look about. But there is always Maurice Chevalier, at his incomparable best as the uncle, to brisk things up, to sing (it is one of the gayest of the songs) 'I'm So Glad I'm Not Young Any More'; to recall, with corrections from Miss Gingold, an obviously forgotten affair; or simply to share with us a general beaming conviction that love is the only occupation for a sensible man. It is, I hope, implicit in everything I have said that I find Vincente Minelli's direction masterly; but in case it isn't let me say that *Gigi* strikes me as one of the half-dozen best screen musicals ever made.

February 1959

Though in the good days of *Guys and Dolls* and *Wonderful Town*, *Bye Bye Birdie* and *Pal Joey* I used to scurry to stage musicals, something has always warned me off **The Sound of Music**. Probably that something was a highly sugared film called *The Trapp Family* which dealt – it must have been about four years ago – with the same story. The Austrian widower father; the postulant at the convent released to be a governess; the children brought up on nothing but discipline; the singing lessons; the Nazi take-over – it is a story based on fact: but that doesn't necessarily help, not at any rate by the time the cinema gets to work.

But now with the arrival at the Dominion of the film version of the Rodgers and Hammerstein musical (director: Robert Wise) I am caught. Perhaps I had better declare the rest of my relevant prejudices before I go on. I shrink, then, from films portraying some convent full of romantic-looking nuns standing about in elegant compositions and presided over by a wise, tolerant old Mother Superior (here it is an Abbess) who is always prompt with the apothegm; and in this case they are singing nuns into the bargain. When the great W. C. Fields (or was it Ned Sparks?) was asked how he liked children, he replied; 'Toasted.' I feel the same about child-choirs, at any rate unless they are invisible; and here the spectator is suffocated by assorted child-singers.

The Sound of Music, in fact, belongs to the sentimental class of musicals; it offers decent feelings, misty tunes and a refuge from the electric guitar. I find it all a bit smothering. But that is a matter of taste, not judgment; the question is whether in its class the film is well done, and I think the answer is yes. The word cosy insinuates itself. But cosy is hardly right for a setting which takes in the Alps. The director of photography, Ted McCord, has successfully used the Todd-AO screen (and the De Luxe colour) to give a sense of pre-Nazi wealth and splendour – and a sense of size: for instance in the scene at the folk-song festival, with the Trapps spotlit against a huge wall of darkness.

And the playing– Christopher Plummer, giving the unlikely character of Captain von Trapp a velvety charm, does what can be done to reconcile the martinet of the early passages – an Austrian Mr Barrett, summoning his seven children by boatswain's whistle – with the tender lover and family sing-song leader of the second half. Eleanor Parker appears as the rich widow who, scheming to marry the Captain, tries to frighten away a humbler contestant. Her role is a variant on a standard cinema fairy-tale figure; I am glad to say that Miss Parker is allowed to play it with more seductiveness and therefore with more plausibility than is the rule. But the emphasis of the story is on the governess who in this fairy-tale performs the miracle of transforming the whole family. And here is Julie Andrews with her candid look and her bright clear English voice; and Miss Andrews, singing with great dash, is just the ticket for this particular bundle of wholesome girlish enthusiasm.

Whenever I have been rash enough to suggest that a film would be a popular success my prediction has instantly been proved wrong. But it is in no spirit of malevolence that I say *The Sound of Music* is the kind of pretty three-hour trifle which ought to please a great many people. I am not trying to cast the evil eye on it; indeed I wish it well. As long, that is, as I don't have to see it again.

March 1965

2   Bibles, Swords and Sandals

'You see it without the use of glasses' – for once advertisement relies on understatement. You can almost see **The Robe** (director: Henry Koster) with your eyes shut. Professor Henri Chrétien's invention Cinemascope was privately deomonstrated in London some months ago. But *The Robe* is the first complete film to be made in the process, and perhaps I ought to remind you that an anamorphic lens is used, and that the compressed image so recorded is expanded and rectified when projected. By this means it is possible with a single camera and a single projector to produce a wide picture, not so wide as that of Cinerama (which we still have not seen in England) with its three cameras and three projectors, but goodness knows wide enough.

The Robe is shown on a screen roughly two-and-a-half times as wide as it is high. The screen is slightly concave; the curve and the width together may give a tiny feeling of depth in the picture, but this three-dimensional quality is no more noticeable than in many four-by-three flat films, for instance in the extract from *Moulin Rouge* which, together with other snippets, is shown at the Odeon before the main piece. *The Robe* is not stereoscopic, and it is remarkable for its acreage, not its knife-throwing. It is, however, stereophonic, voices coming not from a fixed point but from the appropriate side of the screen – an effect which I find distracting or merely earsplitting.

Reluctantly I have to say that it is remarkable for little else. Based on Lloyd C. Douglas's novel, it is about a Roman who superintends the Crucifixion, who casts lots for Christ's Robe, wins and is tormented by remorse until he becomes a Christian. It is thus able to use a good deal of the material with which recent Biblical films have made us only too familiar: market-scene, palace-scene, torture, Imperial dementia, suggestions of orgy. Few of us will want to defend Caligula, the villain of the piece. All the same I am sorry to see yet another film fostering the popular notion that great Rome was just a collection of Nazis in short skirts.

The scene of the Crucifixion, mercifully, is handled with a restraint broken only by a bit of atrocious acting from Victor Mature, who as a Christian slave is called on to display emotions outside his usual manly range. And the introduction of the figure of Christ, seen first in the distance riding into Jerusalem and later obscured by the burden of the Cross, though I personally found it distasteful, seemed to cause no offence to an audience presumably containing a fair proportion of Christians. *The Robe*, I suppose, might be a good deal worse, and probably would be were it not for the playing of the Roman convert by Richard Burton, who brings to the most debased passages an air of morose good breeding. I will except the final shot, in which, accompanied by Jean Simmons in, apparently, Court dress, he goes to martyrdom – a scene which, had I not undergone the rest of the film, I should have taken for the last entrance of Prince and Princess Charming in the pantomime.

The film, then, is the usual vulgarizing stuff; and to judge Cinemascope on this evidence would be unfair. The weaknesses of the system are obvious. The difficulties of composition in ribbon-space; the tendency of figures in close shot to look squat – at first sight the film would seem to have thrown away such advantages as it has won over the stage. A cinema which can take in so much at a time may well neglect to build its scenes with shots from varying angles and distances, and in any case on the new-shaped screen the old use of detail in close-up is almost impossible. Yet there are occasions in *The Robe* when Cinemascope serves the composition: in the grouping at the Crucifixion, in a seascape, in a chase with four harnessed white horses galloping abreast and the pursuers strung out across a dark wood.

What I cannot understand is why the proportions of the frame should always remain rigid. Years ago Griffith in *Intolerance* created splendid effects of height or width by masking the screen vertically or horizontally. Why not mask it today? For I believe that there are possibilities in the wide frame; but to insist that it must serve for every scene may mean the death of the cinema as an art.

November 1953

No doubt we have brought it on ourselves, and **The Ten Commandments** is a judgment on the critics for taking too lightly the name of Cecil B. DeMille. In the past, there is no denying, even while we shrank from the bloodbath of his films a shade of levity was apt to creep into our comments on

the whippings and the antique orgies. As a matter of fact Mr
DeMille spoke rather severely to some of us about the matter
when he was in London a few weeks ago.

This time he is having no nonsense from any of us. This time
everything is documented. Could Egyptian dancers really have
worn long black pigtails with pierrot pompoms on the end?
There is a mural which says so. Was that the hat the Pharaoh
wore in battle? Judge for yourselves from the carved reliefs on
the spot. Did Mount Sinai really look like that? But it *is* Mount
Sinai, you great turnip-top!

Hurriedly I add that these pronouncements come not from
my own knowledge but are borrowed from the results of
the DeMille researches into '950 books, 984 periodicals, 1,286
clippings and 2,964 photographs.' For while Mike Todd was
sending us ballyhoo calendars to hang on the wall, Mr DeMille
and his collaborators were preparing, ready for despatch to the
benighted critics, lists of references to Philo, Josephus, Eusebius,
Breasted, Wallis Budge, Flinders Petrie, the Koran and Baedeker.
As the result of their endeavours I now have to add to my
archaeological library a stout little volume of over 200 pages
from the University of Southern California Press, Los Angeles,
called *Moses and Egypt.* Before we even got to the film we were
suffocated with scholarship.

Even then Mr DeMille was leaving nothing to chance; he
appeared on the screen to introduce the film himself. A tall,
benevolent but slightly minatory figure in spectacles, he parted
the curtains advanced to a microphone and explained that the
piece we were about to see was a biography of Moses, that the
Bible had carelessly omitted thirty years of the life, but that the
gap had now been filled by a study of Philo, Josephus, etc., and
that anyway *The Ten Commandments* was the story of the fight
for freedom. We had better, his tone implied, pay attention or
it might be the worse for us.

In the circumstances it would be effrontery for me to question
any detail, or indeed any incident in a film which (with a
cast including Charlton Heston as Moses, Yul Brynner as
Pharaoh, Yvonne de Carlo, Anne Baxter, John Derek, Edward
G. Robinson and Cedric Hardwicke) begins with the cradle in the
flags; shows a Moses who, grown up to be a military conqueror
and a possible heir to the throne, suddenly discovers the secret
of his birth, rejects the love of the Pharaoh's daughter and joins
his own people as a labourer; takes in a few plagues and covers in

interminable detail the exodus; and ends with the arrival in sight of the River Jordan.

I must not, for instance, permit myself to wonder whether on the appearance of Moses at the well in Midian six of Jethro's seven daughters really carried on like Merry Pecksniff; probably Mr DeMille would confound me with a quotation from the rabbinical writings of the Midrashim. All I can do is remark that he still manages, in the story of the fight for freedom, to get in the usual bath, with water-throwing and girlish squeals; the usual whipping (poor Joshua, bounding to the rescue of an unfortunate virgin, is nearly cut to bits); and the usual orgy, with a dense mass of extras flailing round the Golden Calf and the more athletic swinging the girls about by any limb which offers.

Of course, one is compelled to respect the organization of the scenes of spectacle: the raising of the obelisk, the river of Israelites straggling off into the distance of the desert. And though the optical trick by which the fugitives appear to cross the seabed between two harmless Niagaras seems to me clumsy in execution, the passage is exciting to watch; Mr DeMille shows here that he has not lost the drive which, for nearly half a century, has kept him among the best-sellers.

With more private scenes he has greater trouble. After all if you want a crowd of 25,000 people you can, funds permitting, hire them. The angel of the Lord is less complaisant. 'At midnight the Lord smote all the firstborn in the land of Egypt'; the director shows a greenish patch of ground-mist bowling through the streets, and brings the story down to the level of an X film about the Thing from Outer Space. The Commandments, Exodus tells us, were 'written with the finger of God' on tables of stone; Mr DeMille presents the divine graving-tool in the shape of a small but irascible rocket. It might be something out of Disneyland.

Beneath the weight of so much narrative the acting is flat; I cannot recall one single trace of observation of character, and the only figure who looks anything like alive is Anne Baxter. With the exception of a few spectacular crowd-scenes the film is visually dull. The details of action are excruciatingly obvious; if a child is seen toddling alone amidst the exodus, one knows with certainty that somebody, Moses probably, is about to carry it. And the whole experience (with an interval) lasts roughly four hours. I am afraid that long before the time was up I was silently imploring Mr DeMille (for a critic, too, can misquote Scripture for his purpose) to let his people go.

December 1957

It is the best chariot race in the world, and no mistake. By now everybody has said so, and it seems repetitive for me to add my Sunday mite on **Ben-Hur** (director: William Wyler). The only hope is that admiration may have special force when it is extorted from somebody who dislikes chariot races, shrinks from Biblical fiction and detests films (with the exception of *Intolerance* and *Green Pastures*) which include the Crucifixion.

I enjoy nearly everything in the cinema. I like tragedies, comedies, thrillers, Westerns and musicals; I like films about baseball, mother-love, the Foreign Legion, schizophrenia, Madison Avenue, the colour-bar, the French Revolution, missionaries, crippled brothers, gangsters, mountaineering, Donald Duck, the American Civil War, trains, the Deep South, vampires, Stalin, Lucrezia Borgia and the Wolfenden Report. Yet when I approach a piece with characters from the Bible my heart sinks. It is inexplicable, it is inexcusable – and it is inconvenient, since as a result I find difficulty in being fair to this class of cinema. Lucky for me that most Biblical films are in themselves so atrocious as to make no claims on serious criticism.

Ben-Hur is another matter. William Wyler has not undervalued the services of the literary writer, and Christopher Fry, S. N. Behrman, Maxwell Anderson and Gore Vidal make contributions to the screenplay of the Hollywood scriptwriter, Karl Tunberg; the film invites none of the guffaws which punctuate the dialogue of, say, *Solomon and Sheba*. Nor is it sadistic.

This story of a Jewish aristocrat who, condemned to the galleys, saves a Roman life and returns rich and honoured to Jerusalem during the Governorship of Pontius Pilate, manages without the squalid tortures of a DeMille film: the death of the injured Roman after the chariot-race is horrifying but not revolting, the sequence in the galleys is brutal but not nauseating. The scenes involving the figure of Christ are handled with reserve. All the playing is directed with the understanding one expects from Wyler. Stephen Boyd may look too much the boy-hero as Messala, but Jack Hawkins, the witty Hugh Griffith, and a grave newcomer from Israel, Haya Harareet, do everything that is asked of them; and as Ben-Hur himself Charlton Heston gets a commendable rage into the role.

So far it looks as if I had nothing to grumble about, and indeed of the parts of this long, opulent film with its colour, its bright, sharp images, its stunning spectacle and its size (it is shot in a wide-screen process called Camera 65) I cannot complain. I still find that the whole is alien from me: alien, come to that, from the best work of William Wyler.

Some of my feeling could be put down to historical prejudice (not racial: I am pro-Semite). The new *Ben-Hur*, like the 1926 *Ben-Hur*, is an attack on Rome: Israel is spiritual resistance, Rome is the oppressor, the Fascist State. Yet the film never succeeds in shaking my belief that the world was lucky to have the Romans around. The Greeks would have been better still, but failing them the Romans were a Power no more cruel and a sight more civilizing than any other people likely at the time to have got a grip on affairs. And I hope my Jewish friends will forgive me if I point out something which nobody would gather from the screen: that according to the available authorities it wasn't the Romans who cried 'Crucify Him!'

But my real quarrel with *Ben-Hur* is that its material bears the stamp of the second-rate. A decent level of writing and a distinguished level of directing have done what can be done with the best-selling mixture of adventure story and New Testament borrowings. They can't give it an imaginative size to match its physical size. One can tolerate the second-rate if it escapes comparison with the first-rate; not when, as here, it constantly recalls the tremendous Christian myth. Beside the august simplicity of the Gospels on which it draws *Ben-Hur* dwindles to an oleograph.

Nevertheless if we must have films of this kind, this is the one to have. After all, the spectacular scenes remain: the sea-fight, the Triumph, a magnificent storm and, of course, the chariot-race – a scene superbly shot, superbly edited, superb in every way. I have never seen anything of its sort to touch it for excitement.

December 1959

SCRIPTURE PRIZES, 1932–61

Most Vulgar: THE SIGN OF THE CROSS.
Most Nauseating: QUO VADIS.
Most Exhausting: THE TEN COMMANDMENTS.
Most Nondescript: THE ROBE.
Most Luxurious Blood-Baths: SAMSON AND DELILAH.
Most Idiotic Additional Dialogue: THE BIG FISHERMAN.
Most Genteel Orgy: SOLOMON AND SHEBA.
Special Chariot-Race Award: BEN-HUR.

Few of even the most distinguished directors can resist an invitation to have a go at the Biblical film, or at any rate the film with a near-Biblical theme. William Wyler and *Ben-Hur*, King Vidor and *Solomon and Sheba*; George Stevens has plans for the New Testament; and you might make a note that the Italian producer Dino de Laurentiis has *Barabbas* coming along, not to mention the complete Bible, ten hours of it. Now Nicholas Ray, cult-idol of a new generation of critics in France and England, turns his hand to a life of Christ.

King of Kings, it is a title blessed by the late Cecil B. DeMille, who used it for one of his early moralities. But Cecil B. DeMille in the late twenties hadn't got what Nicholas Ray can command in the early sixties: colour and the brilliant definition of 70mm. Super-Technirama. On the enormous screen Mr Ray has plenty of scope for the talent which, I am told, French critics have discerned in his work: the organization of space 'with the freedom of a Cezanne.' And it is true that towards the end of the film – that is to say about two hours and a half, counting the interval, from the time you sit down – there is a shot of the Deposition which for a second faintly reminded me of some Italian master: the Giovanni Bellini Pietà in the National Gallery, perhaps. But two hours and a half is a long time to wait, isn't it, for a supportable moment.

The potentialities of CinemaScope and its successors have encouraged the Bible-cycle; you can get more Israelites on a wide screen. But even in the old four-by-three days the history of the cinema was punctuated by outbursts of religious fiction. The screen discovered early that spectacle was a gift; in 1902 France was already producing *Quo Vadis* – a twenty-minute version; Italy was to turn out a *Quo Vadis* of her own in 1912, and another in 1923. Indeed the Italians, before the first world war, were the pioneers in religious spectacle, and it was not until D. W. Griffith took a hand, first with *Judith of Bethulia* and then with the New Testament passages of *Intolerance*, that America began to compete. By the 1920s however, with the 1925 *Ben-Hur* and DeMille's *King of Kings* and *The Ten Commandments*, it was America first and the rest nowhere. And in the 1950s, from *The Robe* to De Mille's second version of *The Ten Commandments*, America led again – though Italy mustn't be quite left out: Italy provided the studios for the shooting of the second *Ben-Hur* as well as planning her own endurance tests.

If history is not merely co-incidence, there must be some cause other than the invention of the gigantic screen for the recurrence of commercialized religion in the cinema, and I have been wondering if it is fanciful to connect the two great cashings-in with a certain kind of moral climate. Both occur after a savage war at a time when the screen allows extremes of violence and consistently implies casual sexual behaviour.

There have been plenty of critics to point out how in the twenties DeMille profitably united moral reprimand and a gratifying picture of sin. In the fifties and the early sixties the picture of sin has been overlaid by the image of violence: people can sin – in the Elinor Glyn sense of the word – without much social interference, but violence still fetches in the police; violence therefore becomes the more seductive. And violence is ready in the Biblical film: in the enslavement of the Israelites and the persecution of the Christians, in beatings and tortures and, yes, crucifixions. The Biblical film gives sadism a permit.

Reason enough for shrinking from the *genre*. There are other reasons too. In the cinema the changes have always been toward greater realism, greater visual clarity; and realism and clarity, where the supernatural, where the divine is concerned, are the enemy. Translated to the realistic screen the towering, ferocious characters of the Old Testament drop into absurdity. Worse, the noble, candid figures of the New Testament turn insipid. For educated spectators with religious sensibilities to watch without rage and shame such a dwarfing strikes me as arguing a state of tolerance bordering on the saintly. Difficult to expect the Resurrection of the blue eyes and auburn wig of Jeffrey Hunter.

Not that Mr Hunter in the role of Christ – to come back to *King of Kings* – is anything but modest; there is a kind of glazed seemliness about his performance. Philip Yordan's script – with certain textual modifications of the Authorised Version – has succeeded in rendering the story of the Gospels in a dull drone; the Beatitudes themselves sound as if Mr Selwyn Lloyd had been called on to read a news bulletin embodying some unsatisfactory Test Match scores. Naturally, the modifications are not only textual. Christ calls on John the Baptist (Robert Ryan, doing the best he can in the circumstances) in prison. Barabbas becomes the leader of the Jewish Resistance party. Judas, believing that arrest will force Christ to work a nationalist miracle and overthrow the Roman Occupation, betrays from patriotic motives (a few quislings such as Caiaphas apart, nobody is really to blame except the usual foreigners, the Romans and the Idumeans).

The way is thus open for some interpolated violences: assault on fortress, general litter of corpses. It is open also for something less expected: an intentional blurring of the divinity of Christ.

I don't mean the unavoidable blurring which, if the Christ is to be seen as here fully and in close-up, is inherent in the appearance of an actor, any actor, no matter how good. I don't mean either that the supernatural elements in the Gospel stories are entirely missing; it would be a bit of a problem to make a *King of Kings* without mentioning the miracles or the Resurrection. I mean that here the miraculous elements are at war with the general tone of a film which emphasizes the mortal hesitations and not the divine attributes of its central figure (come to that, the Virgin Mary – Siobhan McKenna, looking like somebody's aunt impersonating the Mona Lisa – seems better endowed than her Son with extra-sensory perception).

Magi, miracles, *noli-me-tangere* and all, this still boils down to a film about the non-divine. Believers and agnostics alike should be warned; and that is why I have decided to confer on *King of Kings* both my 1961 Scripture Prizes: (1) Dullest; (2) Most Undenominational.

Sayings of the Week. Salome, of John the Baptist: 'His heart should be ripped from his buddy.'

Nicholas Ray, of the film critics: 'They are not hip enough with the times of Christ.'

November 1961

Size, and nobody to support its weight: no great figures; no persuasive and commanding players. Wrong: one – Rex Harrison. But then, the Ides of March impend over the first half of **Cleopatra**, and Mr Harrison, of whom I have never felt fonder, is killed off before the interval. However, before reflecting on what, in the three and a half hours of Todd-AO and De Luxe colour now to be seen at the Dominion, we aren't given, let us consider what we have got.

To start with we have both the distinguished amours: Caesar and Cleopatra, and Antony and Cleopatra; the script-writers – Joseph L. Mankiewicz (who directs), Ranald MacDougall and Sidney Buchman – begin a bit earlier than Shaw begins and end at about the moment when Shakespeare ends. We have – with respectful bows in the direction of Plutarch, Suetonius, Appian and a writer with whom I am inadequately acquainted, C. M. Eranzero – the battlefield of Pharsalia; Julius Caesar's arrival at Alexandria with more battle, the burning of the library and the startling of young Ptolemy's hash; the birth of Caesarion; Cleopatra's entry into Rome; the assassination of Caesar; the triumvirate and the battlefield of Philippi; the gradual ascendancy of Octavian; the meeting of Antony and Cleopatra at Tarsus; the marriage with Octavia; and the battle of Actium: in fact a good deal of history – and a good deal of fancy-work.

Beneath all this weight, an enormous cast among whom you may or may not recognize Pamela Brown, George Cole, Michael Hordern, Hume Cronyn, Roddy McDowall, Robert Stephens and Kenneth Haigh. You may note that I use the word cast; the difficulty for the performer of getting out from under the scenery, the sets, the costumes and the colour and making an impression not as a member of the cast but as an actor (or actress) is severe.

At the beginning I thought the challenge was going to be met. The business-like manner of the Roman military gentlemen, the preoccupied entries and exits – Caesar's entourage look as if they had jobs to do and were used to doing them in kilts and breast-plates; indeed all through the film the wearing of classical costume is carried off by the men with a proper confidence. But then the opening scenes are dominated by Caesar; and Rex Harrison is the very portrait of cynical experience. It is a fearful let-down when Elizabeth Taylor is unrolled from the famous carpet.

I must be clear on this: I admire Miss Taylor, and I mean as an actress; the febrile shades of feeling in *Suddenly, Last Summer*, even in that ghastly *Butterfield 8* – I was beginning to believe she could never be uninteresting. But Cleopatra asks for something more than the display of nervous tensions which Miss Taylor with her up-to-the-minute style controls.

It may be unfair to expect a range and power of voice which are not at her disposal. It is not unfair to expect range of feeling. This Egyptian is presented as a woman with world-ambitions, But she has no drive. And Richard Burton as Antony must assume an enslavement for which on the screen no adequate reason appears. Mr Burton, for all his thundery romantic personality, has not except in his earliest roles struck me as an interesting actor on the screen. Here he brings off one or two passages of clumsy bewilderment and Roman despair well enough; their theatrical manner suits him. But it is disconcerting to find that the cause of his transports is nothing more than a pretty girl in a black-and-gold wig.

For when you come to look closely you see that Mr Mankiewicz has made a film about the barge she sat in. The trouble is, that there is nobody, or next to nobody, sitting in it.

The barge itself, I admit, really is something: the barge figuratively speaking, the barge standing for all the beautiful extravagances of this extravagant spectacle. And it is beautiful; let's have no mistake about that. The long, balanced lines of battle array – true, that has been done often before. But the elaboration of the sets, the gilded lions, all the bestiary, griffins, hawks, eagles, bulls, dogs, cats, of Rome and Egypt; the lotus-flowers and the patterned floors, the statuary, the blazing colours of draperies and ornaments right down to the statutory regalia of hooks and tassels with which Miss Taylor painstakingly poses – the detail is not delicate, but in the mass it has a richness which is exciting. And the huge set-pieces: Alexandria and its harbour, the arrival at Tarsus, especially the sweep into Rome, all painted masked Nubians, and dancing-girls with hawk-wings, and Cleopatra's gigantic sphinx-carriage trundled in by a couple of hundred roped swaying slaves – there is a kind of vulgarity which by its own boldness becomes beautiful, and this is it.

Gratefully I must acknowledge that one is spared the customary torture-scenes. And yet, as the hours wear on, another kind of death-wish seeps into the display of vastness. I don't mean merely that the final scenes, denied the impulse of emotion, slow down to a crawl. I mean that the cinema of spectacle seems to be killing itself. It can't, surely, grow any bigger, can't exhibit grander sets, do battle over wider deserts, drown more extras in seas more immense. But perhaps in this very extremity there is hope. What it can do is to hire better script-writers. After all, three-quarters of one's discomfort over *Cleopatra* comes from the fact that all through the first half one longs for Shaw, and all through the second one pines for Shakespeare.

August 1963

3 *The Biopic*

Edith Cavell, when in October 1915, she was court-martialled and shot, was a woman fifty years old. She was tired after a life of duty and effort, most of all after the strain of the last year, spent nursing the wounded and helping them to escape across the frontier; she was, she said, thankful for the ten weeks' rest which her imprisonment had given her. According to a brochure issued by the distributors of this picture, she was taken out of the prison of St Gilles at two in the morning, five hours before she had expected, to a place two miles away, and shot there as she sat on a kitchen stool. I have not heard that at the time of her death she had physical beauty beyond what faith, courage, and an indomitable devotion to the common cause of humanity conferred on her.

In Mr Herbert Wilcox's film the part of Edith Cavell is played by Anna Neagle. Miss Neagle is not without experience in the portrayal of middle-aged or even old women. In this picture, however, the actress has not been invited to simulate any age other than her own. The Nurse Cavell we are asked to believe in is a young and beautiful woman on whose face life has not written. Her bearing is rigid with responsibility and the habit of command; but the responsibility is carried by youth, and she stands to face the firing squad. Miss Neagle gives, indeed, a remarkable performance. The grave face scarcely stirs; only a widening of the eyes, a compression of the mouth, a shadow flickering across the features; but there are anxiety, relief, resolution. Her scene with the young German dying in her hospital is extremely moving; and the final minutes when, her executioners waiting for her, she puts on her cape, takes her gloves and her prayer-book and, with a reassuring, half-secret smile to the gaoler, walks out of her cell, could hardly be better.

Nurse Edith Cavell in general has dignity. The photography is often fine, and the effects of light and shadow are severely beautiful. I am, however, unable to appreciate the casting of Zasu Pitts as one of the conspirators; as well make Eddie Cantor play Hotspur; she turns the catastrophe to farce, and when she tips the refugee in his barrel into the river one expects Oliver Hardy to pop out. Nor have I ever been able to understand why in an English-speaking picture Germans should have a foreign accent, or interlard their English with Jawohls. There are weaknesses in

the film, and, as it seems to me, errors of judgment and sentiment.
But it is a piece worth criticizing and worth praising. My most
serious complaint is of a failure in courage. The life and death
of its central figure are, indeed, touching enough. But truth,
though it may not always be stranger than fiction, is often more
heartrending. This is, after all, a biographical film; why not,
then, show Edith Cavell as she really was? *Professor Mamlock*
would not be improved if its hero, instead of being shown as a
dumpy little Jew, were presented as a figure from the Olympia
pediments. And I ask whether in this case the tragedy would not
be more poignant if Mr Wilcox had had the courage to show us
not a composed young woman, but the tired elderly woman of
history – not beautiful, not appealing, but quite simply heroic,
waiting for the firing squad on a kitchen stool?

                                                              1939

It would be difficult to make a film about Florence Nightingale
which was entirely without interest. Even the shadows of
extraordinary people are not quite ordinary; and Miss Nightingale's
story is so strong in itself that, however weakened by the
sentimentality or the inaccuracy of its narrators, it can never
completely lose its power to move. It would be wrong to say
that *The Lady with a Lamp*, Herbert Wilcox's new film, had not
a moment worth seeing. No matter how you blur it, the tale of
the Crimean enterprise must keep something of its pity; and Anna
Neagle, who plays its heroine is not incapable of pathos. So much
conceded, it must be added that while to disinterest us in Florence
Nightingale is next to impossible, *The Lady with a Lamp* has a good
try.

   The film is based on the play by Reginald Berkeley; the script
is by Warren Chetham-Strode; the cast includes, as well as Miss
Neagle, Michael Wilding, shockingly miscast as Sidney Herbert.
It is a long time since I saw Mr Berkeley's play, and my memory
of it is imprecise, but I fancy I am safe in saying that, wanting
the blessings of cinematographic technique, the piece was able
to restrain itself from doing what the film does – trying to be
everywhere at once and put everything in. As a matter of fact,
Mr Wilcox's chronicle film bears not a great deal of resemblance
to what I remember of Mr Berkeley's play. No doubt other
literary sources as well have been drawn on (though none is

acknowledged). But whatever the researches which have made the film possible, the character presented is still the character not of history but of legend.

I do not mean that the facts of Florence Nightingale's career are not here: they are, too many of them for the space. We are told how Miss Nightingale wanted to nurse at Salisbury, how she refused Richard Monckton Milnes, how she became superintendent of a London Institution for Sick Gentlewomen, how when she arrived at Scutari she refused to let her party do any nursing until invited by the Army authorities; we are reminded of her struggles to get proper supplies and given the names of those who hindered her; we see her illness at Balaclava, Lord Raglan's visit, her return to Scutari on a stretcher. It is true that her great period of work after the Crimean War is only sketched in; on the other hand for the earlier period much minor detail is given: the desire of the British Ambassador to spend funds collected for the sick and wounded on building a church in Constantinople; a gift from soldiers of an owl to take the place of one she had lost; Sidney Herbert's advice to rest: 'Ni lire, ni écrire, ni réfléchir.' The details are accurate; they may all be found in Cecil Woodham-Smith's book, *Florence Nightingale*. Something else is to be found in Mrs Woodham-Smith's superb biography; a portrait of a woman of genius; but the film has not managed to include this.

It seems to me inexcusable nowadays to present Florence Nightingale as a tender heart who was kind to invalids. The reality of the ferocious dynamo who altered the whole situation of the British soldier is in any case a thousand times more exciting than the legend of an angel. Mr Berkeley, I am sure, was aware of this; and there are faint signs that the film is aware of it; Miss Nightingale is shown writing a number of letters, and on one occasion she speaks almost sharply to a nurse. But whatever the references to historical fact, the character we see is the old fiction of a Victorian Lady Bountiful calling with the soup. The opportunity was there for a great and heroic film; and we have been fobbed off with Sixty Glorious Years, a series of disjointed scenes from the life of a sweet gentlewoman.

September 1957

'To say "I love you" would break all my teeth.' The words are spoken by a screen actor impersonating Paul Gauguin; they ring false. They are not in fact counterfeit. Gauguin wrote them himself; you will find them in his Journals. And yet in the cinema one doesn't believe in them. Why? Have they grown stiff with translation? Is it that they are delivered without belief? Or must one look farther for the reason, beyond the particular instance to the general problem of portraying an historical character?

Endless difficulties must have faced those responsible for the film about Vincent van Gogh now at the Curzon, *Lust for Life* (director: Vincente Minnelli; producer: John Houseman). On the one hand, the story must have a dramatic shape acceptable to a popular audience; on the other, there are the demands of biographical truth. Certainly there is plenty of documentary evidence. The painter wrote his own record in letters; and for part of the story, the first madness at Arles and the dreadful business with the severed ear, there is the account of another man who was in a sense to die for painting, Gauguin.

Yet for some reason the makers of the film have based their story on a novelette-biography written over twenty years ago by Irving Stone. It is true that the novelist used the sources freely, incorporating in his text word-for-word passages of description by others. It is true also that the film sometimes goes over his head to his originals, and that a good deal of the narrative is spoken in extracts from the letters to Theo (played by James Donald). And yet the voices of the characters are only too often heard through a suffocating curtain of commonplace and even vulgarity. Much of the sacrificial tale is sentimentalized – and coarsened: Gauguin no doubt was a brutal cynic, but I cannot believe he was the brutish dolt portrayed by Anthony Quinn.

I must make it clear that I am not complaining of the occasional so-called Americanisms; the English hold no special rights of translation from the languages of the Continent. Indeed when original phrasing is used it is, as I say, not necessarily effective. The solution, I feel sure, would have been to entrust the reshaping of the story from the start to some writer who would have felt free to cast the dialogue in forms with neither the rigidity of literal translation nor the banality of colloquial Hollywood. Had this been done *Lust for Life* might have been something like a masterpiece. For now I must end my grumbling and say that even as it stands Vincente Minnelli's film almost triumphs over its own faults. The cinema delights in showing the artist as the extravagant lover who incidentally happens to be a painter or a musician. At last the screen gives us a man who lives and dies, first and last, for his work.

I should never, I confess, have thought that Kirk Douglas could draw such a portrait. He has always been safe as the boxer, the policeman, the corrupt journalist; suddenly he is no longer merely the competent actor but the creature who suffers, the real human face. It is perhaps an accident that Mr Douglas, bearded and bristled, looks so heartbreakingly like the van Gogh of the self-portraits. It is not an accident that he communicates an artist's ferocious urgency – and without letting us forget the goodness which touched even Gauguin. 'When Gauguin says "Vincent" his voice is gentle.'

In Arles before the war a friend and I once tried to discover if anybody still remembered Vincent van Gogh. His house was there all right; outside, the Arlesians playing bowls in the street; everywhere in shutters and doors and walls Vincent's own blues and chromes and sulphur colours. Yet in that savage beautiful city with its Roman echoes and its hot nights sly with stray dogs we could find nobody who stirred at the name. Since then there have been documentary films about the painter; and now at last the cinema sends half-way round the world to tell against the proper backgrounds the life of van Gogh. The colour is splendid, and ill though the shape of the CinemaScope screen fits the canvases of the artist, their brilliance is magnificently reproduced. And I think one can say that intermittently the passion is relived: the exploding sympathy with the fertility of the earth, the abandonment to sun and light which is itself a kind of love.

March 1957

Somehow it always comes out much the same. There are the humble beginnings in small-town society or in the poor Jewish family; there is the conviction, shared by nobody, of potential talent; then the move, if a journey is necessary, to New York; snubs, struggles, disappointments, followed by the lucky break; the star falls downstairs and nobody except the girl third from the left in the back row of the chorus knows the part. Fame! But frailty intervenes, love intervenes. The domestic partner feels out of things; the marriage cracks up, there is the resort to the bottle, the failure of inspiration, life slumped in a garret. But in the biopic, as the biographical picture has come to be called, there is still hope, there is regeneration, there is a general and final reunion at Carnegie Hall – though perhaps I should add that if the subject is a composer he is apt, by the time Carnegie Hall is reached, to be dead.

Do I exaggerate? Not much, not where the showbiz biopic is concerned. This week we have a handy illustration in *Lady Sings the Blues*. True that this version, directed by Sidney J. Furie, of the life of Billie Holiday offers variations of the generic theme. The famous black singer is shown here beginning her career not in an impoverished family but in a brothel; she takes not to drink but to drugs. But there is the usual false start; there is the triumphant tour, names of cities, names of states signalled by hysterical review-headings; hands applaud, reporters shove, grudging early patrons ripen into dear old friends; and again one reflects on the monotonous pattern of the lives of singers, actresses, popular composers, all the darlings of the singing, dancing cinema.

Looking back, I recognize various phases of biography on the screen. Reformers were once favourably received; you may remember Spencer Tracy in *Boys' Town*. Inventors had a run. Don Ameche, playing Alexander Graham Bell, invented the telephone. Mickey Rooney as Young Tom Edison began the career which was to be carried on in *Edison the Man* by guess who? Spencer Tracy. (The great Tracy must have had peculiar affinities with biography, for he was an explorer too; remember Stanley and Livingstone?) And scientists – I miss the scientists; beautiful Greer Garson coming home one night to find that she had discovered radium; and, in a brief period when the cinema gave the impression of caring about the work done as well as the domestic circumstances in which it was carried out, Paul Muni as Pasteur and, as the discoverer of a cure for syphilis, the unforgettable Edward G. Robinson in *The Magic Bullet* – for once a film about a man immovably dedicated to an unspectacular humane profession.

I suppose it is to be expected that in today's violent climate a life spent in the laboratory or the study should be a doubtful draw. The soldier, yes; Patton, yes; and though one of the many honourable qualities of *Young Winston* was its emphasis on the circumstances and the development of character (notable that the most exciting passage in the film dealt not with battle but with the delivery of a political speech) you can't say that Churchill's life was short on action. Painters, then, have not been popular, though one recalls Jose Ferrer stumping about on his knees as Toulouse-Lautrec. True that Ken Russell succeeded in finding stir enough in *Savage Messiah*. True that in thinking of the biographical film one must always remember Kirk Douglas in the splendid *Lust for Life*; but then one can't count on many painters being like Van Gogh and cutting off an ear. Writers have not had much of a look-in either, not, that is, unless they have the special interests of an Oscar Wilde, or the reputation of a Byron (so unsympathetically presented in the current and fanciful *Lady Caroline Lamb*), or can claim the romantic escapades of a pair of Brownings.

Perhaps the predilection in favour of the entertainer or the musician is understandable. After all, the scenarist can always fill in the dull patches with a song or a short extract from an orchestral work. Orchestras provide spectacle and can be eked out with shots of the audience and prefaced by an account of how the work in question came to be written (composer caught in a thunderstorm, subject to hearing nocturnal celestial choirs, etc.). I can see, in fact, why the list of showbiz biopics is the long one, why people make films about Eddie Cantor and Al Jolson, Grace Moore and Gertrude Lawrence, Ziegfeld, George M. Cohan and the Dolly Sisters; and if I add the sainted names of Tchaikovsky, Chopin, Liszt, Berlioz and Wagner it is because on the screen these composers have sometimes been presented in the guise of showbiz personalities.

What, though, I cannot see is why the films have to be not only so dull but so difficult to distinguish one from the other; why the story of Cole Porter (*Night and Day*) should have so many resemblances to the story of Fanny Brice (*Funny Girl*) and the story of Stephen Foster (*Swanee River*). Probably one ought not to grumble. After all, to the non-addict one Western must seem very much like another; but the devotees are still not deterred. The Western, you may say, is a myth. But so, I suppose, is the showbiz biopic. The figures of cabaret and the stage themselves create a kind of myth.

The trouble, I am afraid, is that on the screen few of them are anything like as pleasant to meet as, in a Western, the horses.

April 1973

Horror in the cinema is not easily defined; if it were, censors would be less erratic in the use of the 'H' certificate. Not long ago an essay in irrational fear by W. F. Harvey was translated into a crude American film, *The Beast with Five Fingers*, in which a plump white hand scuttled about the floor, hid on the bookshelf, escaped from the uncomfortable position in which it had been nailed to a board, and, thrown into the fire, emerged, slightly charred, to throttle its jailer. This, apparently, was merely adult; whereas an unassuming little moral tract some nine or ten years ago called *Boy Slaves* received the apotropaic certificate, presumably because it showed an ill-treated and hunted boy terrified by the threatening shapes of a forest at night.

The Anglo-Saxon people have learnt the habit of laughing at horror: or, rather, they have learnt to provide themselves with the kind of fable about the freak and the monstrosity which invites nervous laughter. One recalls the colossal ape of *King Kong*, striding over the skyscrapers of New York; one recalls more than one version of *The Phantom of the Opera*. It is worth noting that as technique acquires a higher polish, as the elaboration of sound and colour becomes accepted, the rendering of the freakish and the horrible grows less effective. Lon Chaney's Phantom, gliding about in the sewers invisible save for his breathing-pipe, was far more alarming than Claude Rains's, sawing away at the chandelier immediately above the diva with, apparently, a small nail-file. And Lionel Atwill in an early essay in colour, *The Mystery of the Wax Museum*, his wax face suddenly cracking to show the burnt features beneath, could have given any number of marks to the painted revelation of corruption at the end of *The Picture of Dorian Gray*. Horror in the American cinema, indeed, has been almost standardized. It has become largely a matter of mad scientists with extensive electrical equipment: a mechanical age has its mechanical horrors. The first of the *Invisible Man* films did much to popularize the concept of the basic insanity of scientific research. But one can look back much farther than that: for instance, to *The Monster* in the twenties, with its serio-farcical story of the lunatic posing as the director of a sanatorium and preparing ingenious experiments (electrical, of course) on the human frame. A long list of Frankenstein films has followed: Frankenstein crossed with Dracula, his Monster inextricably confused, as the years go by, with such accretions as the Wolf-Man. Such machine-made tales can hardly raise a laugh today, much less a shiver.

Let us acknowledge it, the English like to laugh and shiver at once. Ever since *The Bat* (an American play, by the way) in the mid-1920s, the basis of the stage thriller – which generally includes some element of the terrifying and the horrible – has been comedy; and an actor such as Tod Slaughter, who preserves, in his archaistic way, the tradition of melodramatic horror, is received and expects to be received as a creator of farce. Horror which is not consciously a little ridiculous is out of favour with the English public, who herein differ from the French. France, after all, it was which gave us Grand Guignol. But then the French are an intellectual people: and the deliberate pursuit of the horripilant is largely an intellectual pleasure. It certainly is no longer, as it once was, a means to morality. The medieval Church painted pictures of Doom on its walls; hell-gates, fires and torments confronted the congregation, who were certainly not disposed to ridicule this simulacrum of damnation. In the art gallery of today the ingenious horrors of a Hieronymus Bosch have not much more than the fascination of the absurd.

The cinema, with its extraordinary powers for distortion and deception, should excel in this sphere of horror. Certainly it has an interesting tradition of the horrific, beginning with Méliès's adventures in the frightening trickery of the camera: the decapitated body, the figure appearing and disappearing. But the primitives of the cinema explored the possibilities of fantasy mainly with an eye to comedy; it needed a more sophisticated talent to understand the possibilities of dread. Sophisticated and, perhaps, already in a sense decadent; the titillation of the sense of horror does not belong naturally to the cinema's heroic mood. It is essentially an aesthete's fancy: an aesthete's or, sometimes, a neurotic's. Thus it is that many of the best studies in the macabre which the cinema has known came from the German screen in the period between the end of the First World War and the rise of National Socialism. National Socialism, of course, had its own living horrors; understandably it rejected the shadow-horrors of the imagination: the more understandably, perhaps, since these very shadow-horrors had been a symptom of the sickness which became dominant at last in the Hitler régime. In his exhaustive psychological history of the German film, *From Caligari to Hitler*, Siegfried Kracauer has traced, sometimes perhaps over-ingeniously, the strain of fatalism and despair which led the German people after the shock of defeat to resign themselves to authoritarianism. And indeed, as we look at it now, the German cinema of the 1920s betrays a curious surrender to the dark and the brutal: there is a kind of black magic hanging over Robison's *Warning Shadows* and Lang's *Dr Mabuse*; though the element of fantasy and the macabre is less obvious with *The Last Laugh* at the end of the silent period and *M* early in the sound period, the brutality is still there. The quality of horror in the German fantastic film is something much more spontaneous, and belongs much more, in the Lawrentian sense, to the blood than the horror of the French *avant-garde* films, which are basically intellectual, however much their makers may talk about Freud and free association.

Of course the cinema may set about the evocation of horror in a variety of ways. Some of them have by now become conventions; we need not linger over the heavy black shadows, the banal symbols of monstrosity of the mass-produced American film: the smooth faces growing lupine before our eyes, the haggard young gentleman in evening dress flattening himself in his cloak into the figure of a bat, the terrible electrical toys sparkling and hissing. But the truly imagined symbol can never become a convention; and when we think of the genuinely horrific in the cinema we think first of the shocking image. Not the shocking realistic image: the Russians in their war films have made calculated use of the horrible fact – the grinning skull in Dovzhenko's *Battle of the Ukraine*, the clawing hand of the dead Goebbels in *Berlin*; but their films are almost innocent of horror in the sense under discussion. It is the French, with their eye for the anarchistic detail, who have excelled in the choice and presentation of the image aesthetically shocking: the wounded hand swarming with ants, the eye slashed by a razor. Images such as these, which are the material of the surrealist film, might be compared with the cruel and horrible physical imagery in which Edgar Allan Poe clothes his dreams of terror, had they any logic in their employment. But the French surrealist cinematographers have presented the horrible and repulsive image, not in logical waking sequence, but in a series of disconnected shocks. 'They accepted', says Luis Buñuel of himself and Dali, his collaborator in *Un Chien Andalou*, 'only those representations as valid which, although they moved them profoundly, had no possible explanation. Naturally, they dispensed with the restraints of customary morality and of reason. The motivation of the images was, or was meant to be, purely irrational. They are as mysterious and inexplicable to the two collaborators as to the spectator. NOTHING, in the film, SYMBOLIZES ANYTHING. The only method of investigation of the symbols would be, perhaps, psychoanalysis.'

But the image, used, as it was by Dali and Buñuel, simply to excite in the spectator a helpless revulsion, is a kind of shock treatment which can hardly be applied to the average cinema audience; it comes under the heading of pathology rather than aesthetics. The technique of the horrifying direct image, in fact, imposes its own limitations; and the cinema has generally been more successful with the distorted or indirect image. One thinks at once of the curious disquiet aroused in the audience by the lunatic perspective of *The Cabinet of Dr Caligari*; one thinks of the shifting and coalescing shapes in the drunken vision of the old commissionaire in *The Last Laugh*. One thinks, too, of an odd horrifying effect achieved by the distortion not of shape but of scale in *Zéro de Conduite*, where the tiny dwarfed figure of the headmaster arouses a chill of apprehension. An interesting exercise in distortion is to be found in Robert Siodmak's American film, *The Spiral Staircase*: a film on the conventional theme of the schizophrenic killer, lifted out of its class by the imaginative quality of its visual design as well as its playing. The murderer feels impelled to destroy what is imperfect: he sees the heroine, who is dumb, as a creature without a mouth; and the audience too, looking over his shoulder at the girl's image in the mirror, sees her face fading away into a blur.

In *The Spiral Staircase* the essence of the horror is that it is only half-defined. Or perhaps I should say that true horror in the cinema is achieved less by presenting the fact, the object, than by suggesting that the fact is unnatural and the object deformed. The camera forgets only too often the force of the half-said, and with its talent for memorable statement neglects the terrors of the hint. Yet in Paul Leni's *Waxworks* the most horrifying episode is, not the fable of Ivan the Terrible watching in the dungeon the agonies of his victims, but the tiny sketch of Spring-heeled Jack, a figure guessed at in a multitude of shadows. In the same way the most dreadful moment in *Day of Wrath* is, not the second when the witch is pitched face down into the bonfire, but a passage in which the action is hidden from us. It is the scene of the witch's questioning and torture: and Dreyer, who uses camera movement with such sinister meaning, allows us to look, not at the fleshy shapeless body of the old woman, but at the faces of her questioners: the camera pans over the group of figures, over the faces with their expressions of interest, curiosity, cruel patience; and the spectator is torn between his own hateful curiosity and a natural humane disgust at its object.

In *Day of Wrath* there is a shot of the pastor coming home on a stormy night: as he follows the path through the empty luminous darkness, a goat watches him from behind a hedge; and without a word said the spectator has suddenly a sense of the presence of the powers of evil. But fifteen or so years earlier, in *Vampire*, Dreyer had explored far more assiduously the realm of suggestion. In *Vampire* the eye can only guess at the nature of the shapes which move in the half-light of the house or flit across the park. Once the supernatural becomes completely visible and tangible it loses its terror and attains the state of the natural; Dreyer never lets us come face to face with his phantoms. He has, in fact, recreated the horror of dream: in the sequence in which the man fancies himself in his coffin, carried through the streets looking up at the tilted houses, there is that dreadful blending of the objective and the subjective which is nightmare. And one thinks of Henry James and *The Turn of the Screw*, with its quiet devils enveloped in the fantasy of extraordinary evil.

The shocking, the distorted, the suggested – yet there is one realm of horror into which the cinema rarely ventures: the horror of the ordinary. We encounter it in *Dead of Night*, when the architect wakes from his nightmare and finds himself repeating it awake: once more he drives down the country road and draws up at the matter-of-fact country house; there is nothing in the imagery here to frighten, but only in the implication of normal sights and sounds and actions. And hand in hand with the horror of the ordinary goes the horror of light. The convention is that only the dark is terrible: stage horror is acted with the lights turned down, and Grand Guignol flourishes in shadow. But just as Robert Rossellini in *Germany, Year Zero* showed us that ruins in sunlight can be more dreadful than dark ruins, so there is a terror that belongs to the full blaze of noon on the screen. After all, white is as much the colour of fear as black.

'M for horriplant'
From: *Diversion – 22 Authors on the lively arts* (1950)

9 FAITHFUL TO THE BOOK . . .
. . . FAITHFUL TO THE FACTS

'. . . a film of a novel is to be judged on its merits as a film and not on its fidelity to its original' is the first sentence of Dilys Powell's review of Robert Stevenson's version of *Jane Eyre*, released in England in December 1943 with Orson Welles as the most compelling of screen Rochesters to date. But it is less the self-evident truth contained in Powell's remark that matters than what it reveals about her approach to cinema in general. In any number of her weekly columns she tells her readers that she has quite deliberately not read the novel or play on which a particular film is based, as if she were determined to assert the textual independence of the cinema. At the same time does Powell protest too much, and in her protests reveal how often her judgment of a particular film is based on the theory and practice of literary criticism? One should not perhaps expect it to be otherwise with an English film critic, but it does not necessarily follow, as has been remarked in some quarters, that this is a disadvantage. Indeed one could argue that a defining characteristic of the best English school of film criticism has always been an attention to the literary tradition which feeds into cinema. Just as a continuing preoccupation with realism has been the hallmark of certain kinds of English cinema since the 1930s, a point often debated by critics such as Powell. And the second part of this chapter shows clearly where Powell's sympathies lay in that debate.

1 *Faithful to the Book*

The Grapes of Wrath is not just a film, not just a tragedy, not just a social indictment even; it is an experience; it is history unfolding like a terrible fungus; it is America. Not the cinema America: no lovely silk legs, no Civil War; not the vicious-naïve underworld America of the gangster film either. This is the huge, bleak, sunny, terrible America of the land: the Waste Land.

While we in Europe, these twenty evil years, have been too busy at our own iniquities to think much about the major infamies of the New World (the minor ones, of course, are always more spectacular and more amusing from a journalist's point of view) America has not been too busy rapping us over the knuckles to commit one or two gigantic social injustices of her own. Well, here, in this film of John Steinbeck's novel, is one of them: the story of the migration from the Dustbowl States to California. The drought comes, the wind, the dust, the blown soil; the share-croppers, men whose grandfathers died in winning the land, are driven from it by the owners; there must be profits, where twelve families worked a single tractor tears up the soil, the dooryards, the very houses. The families migrate. The Joads pile their belongings on the ramshackle truck, they load themselves on it: the father and mother, the sons and daughters, the young children and the man on parole, the ancient stubborn grandparents, still holding to life with a cunning, pathetic, squalid, animal tenacity. And the truck pulls away, leaving the dust to eddy round the forsaken shack; along the great highway, through the naked new towns and cities, past the ironic State signs – You Are Now Leaving New Mexico; Come Again; Arizona Welcomes You – past the dark watching Mexican faces, through the flocks of sheep huddling on the road, across the dreadful moonlit desert to California. To California, the promised land – which welcomes them not with work but with starvation, which herds them into fly-blown rotting camps and then burns the paper hovels they have set up, which refuses them the last rights of a human being.

Here it is then, the battle of an earthy peasant life against a petrol-pump and hamburger-stand civilization, a conflict in which, amidst the assaults of callousness and rapacity, the poor retain the essence of generosity, resolution, courage. That is the assertion of the film, the single positive set against its indictment. Even that positive the director, John Ford, has presented in no romantic light. Indeed the realism of some of the early scenes is scarifying: the grandfather, superbly played by Charley Grapewin, fumbling and clawing and drooling in the extreme decay of age, the grandmother cackling and gobbling in a frenzy of greediness, the whole group living with the resourcefulness, the self-reliance and the casual messiness of a family of foxes. But Ford has handled the whole story as one never expected to find an American picture handled, using now wonderful pictorial effects of dark and candlelight, now the light of day falling coldly, precisely on the disgraces of starvation and misery.

The film moves in a slow, minatory tempo, and many of its sequences are in a pure documentary technique. The scenes, for instance, in the Okies' camp have such an air of reality that I can hardly believe they were acted. The wretched tents and shanties, the dazed faces, the hopeless figures shambling away as the new truck drives in – can this possibly be reconstruction and not actual truth? It is only towards the end of the picture, where Steinbeck's tale is not followed to its bitter conclusion, that Ford's grasp weakens. Perhaps it was not possible, conditions being what they are, for the film to go quite as far in condemnation as the novel. On the other, the positive, side, too, there is a softening here, due, I think, partly to the fact that Ma Joad (a finely natural performance by Jane Darwell) does not occupy the central position she holds in the book, and her tenacity and heroism do not therefore emerge as forcibly. The passages, too, in the Government camp, where for a time the Joads are received as men, with human respect, are robbed of some of their sharpness by a reshaping of the original story. But the film remains a terrific denunciation, a terrific manifesto. It is faultlessly played by a large cast in which Henry Fonda, as Tom Joad, and John Carradine, as Casy the preacher, are owed great praise.

July 1940

Why in American films about eighteenth or nineteenth century England must all females move as if on castors? Here, now, are the Bennet Sisters, Greer Garson, Maureen O'Sullivan, Ann Rutherford, Marsha Hunt, and Heather Angel, dressed even for the homeliest occasion in a flutter of white furbelows, scurrying down the street at Meryton with the concerted action of a flock of albino starlings. The news has reached them that Mr Bingley has settled at Netherfield; and lest the audience should be in any doubt as to the importance of the event, the Bennets and the Lucases race home in their carriages, passing and repassing one another in the Hertfordshire lanes in a style strongly reminiscent of *Ben Hur*. The manners of Meryton have, indeed, acquired a certain freedom since Jane Austen described them; for here is Mr Bingley leering agreeably over a sick-room screen at Jane, who ogles back as the doctor examines her uvula. Gatecrashing is, apparently, on the up and up; the invitation to the Netherfield party bears the postscript: 'Please bring this invitation with you.' Elizabeth has become an accomplished archer and gives Darcy a lesson in scoring bull's-eyes; Lydia and Kitty have learned to drink and are tipsy at the party; and when Lydia returns with her Wickham she arrives with an equipage by Korda's *Henry VIII* out of *The Sign of the Cross*.

Can this be *Pride and Prejudice*? Well, yes; the story is sufficiently preserved, even enough of the original digaloue is used for the film to be immediately recognizable as Jane Austen; perhaps there is an injustice in singling out the instances in which Hollywood has got the better of Hertfordshire. The best thing in **Pride and Prejudice** (director: Robert Z. Leonard) is the contribution of Greer Garson, who, as Elizabeth Bennet, gives a performance of singular charm and (for this, after all, *is* Jane Austen) good breeding; it is not often that the cinema distinguishes between the surface of the swell kid and the lady. Yet even Miss Garson fails to reproduce the acidness of Jane Austen; this Elizabeth has high spirits, intelligence, wit, but none of the faintly spinsterish edge of her original. This toning down is in keeping with the rest of the characterization in the film. Mr Bennet's sallies, as delivered by Edmund Gwenn, proceed more from the tolerance of an amiable recluse than from the cynicism of the disappointed man; this Mr Bennet, far from declaring Wickham to be his favourite son-in-law, refuses in moral father fashion to shake hands. Melville Cooper is delicious as Mr Collins; but this is a roguish and not a monumental snob. Mary Boland interprets Mrs Bennet's hen-coop silliness in terms of Middle West matriarchy; while feeling no doubt that Edna May Oliver's well-known bonhomie must not be wasted, somebody (not, I fancy, Aldous Huxley, who is part-author of the screen-play) has insisted that her Lady Catherine de Bourgh shall have a heart of gold. Only Darcy, well played by Laurence Olivier, is substantially unchanged. Still, the film is a pleasant enough entertainment, and it remains only to commend the foresight of the character, I forget which, overheard playing a snatch of Mendelssohn.

November 1940

My sagacious readers will not need to be told that a film of a novel is to be judged on its merits as a film and not on fidelity to its original, and when *Jane Eyre* appears, with the beneficent air of a classic for Christmas, they will not immediately begin searching for divergencies from Charlotte Brontë. When they find that the whole of the St John Rivers episode is left out, they will possibly agree that this was a sound idea. The telescoping of incidents, the simplification of events may seem a justifiable concession to the pictorial requirements of the cinema. They may even admit – though this I doubt – that there is something to be said for the final appearance of Rochester, not in his retreat at Ferndean, but tottering in shirt-sleeves amid the débris of Thornfield Hall. All this they may accept, but the question still remains: is this a good film, or has it, in the words of Beachcomber, come out beer again?

To begin with Rochester (Brontë's, not Benny's): the part has been given to Orson Welles: offhand I can think of no film actor, except Laurence Olivier, who could have played it better. At the same time, the performance is wanting in tenderness, at one end of the scale, and bitter humour at the other; Rochester becomes a completely Gothic character. And when we look again we see that the whole film is Gothic. The novel has its sunny moments: hedges full of roses, roads 'white and baked', primroses making 'a strange ground-sunshine', 'a propitious sky, azure, marbled with pearly white'. The film wears a midnight look throughout: coaches rattle away under black skies, characters paddle knee-deep in the ground-mist which Hollywood regards as inseparable from English landscape, and a candle or two fight the minatory dark of the interior scenes.

I suspect that Welles, who is associate producer, is partly responsible for this Stygian decor: the quality of the lighting (or should I say darking?) is often reminiscent of the Welles films, and the use of shadow to suggest an hour of day, a mood of heart, often has the Welles assurance. But the director,

Robert Stevenson, has not succeeded, as Welles succeeds, in giving variety to his treatment of a theme. The alternation of the satirical and the sombre in *Citizen Kane*, of the hysterical family quarrels and the lyrical love passages in *The Magnificent Ambersons*, contributed to a rare authority of structure. *Jane Eyre* is not innocent of monotony, with its unrelieved Gothic settings and types. Even the heroine herself is conceived as an angelic, edgeless character, an Agnes Wickfield; Joan Fontaine, who plays the part, affects the coiffure of Charlotte Brontë but in other respects might be giving a performance as Norma Shearer. Stripped of its variations of character, stripped above all of its sharp, lively writing, the theme of *Jane Eyre* is, to be honest, little superior to the theme of *The Way of an Eagle*. The film, clinging to the cinema's tradition of transparent characterization, has needlessly rejected the bizarre and moody creatures of the novel. It could still have clothed the story in its own kind of writing, the writing of the visual imagination. The possibility has not been ignored, and there is enough pictorial sense in the piece to make it well worth taking seriously. But the visual writing is not sustained, or perhaps it is sustained on too limited a range of tone. As a result, the story continually obtrudes its melodramatic conventions.

December 1943

It is not often that a novel or a story can be turned into a play or a film without suffering a great deal of alteration in the translating. I did not see the play, but this film *Of Mice and Men*, which I am told follows it closely, astonishes by its fidelity to Steinbeck's story. There are, of course, one or two cases where the original intention has been softened (apparently the public, though it can withstand the effect of the printed word, cannot be trusted to rally its moral forces against the impact of the spoken word). But as a whole the story is played as it is written, and, most interesting of all, the greater part of the dialogue is taken almost word for word from the book.

The success of this transference is due to the curious level, clipped quality of Steinbeck's dialogue, which never relaxes its restraint, never, even in emotion, slides into the flowing lines of literary dialogue, always preserves the harrowing brevity of the sentences of the poor and the unlettered. It is capable of implying, rather than expressing, emotional intensity; but in the book *Of Mice and Men* the compression of the story leaves no room for the pause which is so important in the presentation of an emotional situation. The film, finely directed by Lewis Milestone, makes effective use of just this device – for instance, in the scene of the shooting of the old swamper's dog. The farm-hands sit gossiping and playing cards in the casual shadowy shed with the sleeping bunks; as Carlson (Granville Bates) urges the owner to let him shoot the dog the others, pitiful, interpose their talk, unwilling to look at the misery in the old man's eyes. The old man catches at every excuse, droops, at last consents; the dog, stiff, mournful, shabby, half-blind, drags on the rope, halts as he is led past his master, looks up with sad old eyes, shambles out into the dark. There is little in the scene which is not there in the book. But the whole effect, the effect of the wretched nervous interval until the shot is heard outside, is greatly heightened by the slow tempo at which the incident is played. And the acting of Roman Bohmen as Candy, the old man, gives it a depth of pathos which is missing from the objective brevity of Steinbeck's narrative. Mr Bohmen's performance is superb throughout; the picture he gives of helpless and despairing old age, helpless indeed and bewildered and resigned as the old dog itself, is so heartrending as almost to obscure the major tragedy of the film.

This major tragedy is foreseen from the very start of the picture; from the first moments when George (Burgess Meredith) is seen half-angrily watching over the childish giant who kills a bird, a puppy, without understanding what he has done, disaster seems inevitable. But something in the handling of the little community of farm-workers, something in the treatment of the background – the glimpses of pacific fields with the teams moving home at evening, the moments of happiness when George and Lennie and Candy plan to buy a farm and make a private world for themselves, the feeling of men's work, men's suffering going on steadily, passionately amidst the impersonal tranquillity of nature – there is some quality here of beauty and pity as well as dread. The film is excellently acted by everyone: by, as well as those already mentioned, Betty Field as the vain, vulgar, stupid girl who invites her own death, by Lon Chaney, Jnr., as the mindless giant who kills her, by Charles Bickford as the leader of the farm-hands; there are, mercifully, no stars to intrude their tedious flat personalities into this picture of life. It is a picture which, for all its grief, is not depressing; and if it should be said that this is no time for adding to one's own melancholy, let me reply that it is sometimes well not to lose from sight the individual pity of the lives of men.

April 1946

Browbeaten by the cinema as I have been into accepting personal responsibility for the war, the housing situation, famine in the Far East, juvenile delinquency in the Middle West, gang warfare, alcoholism and mutiny on the Bounty, it was without surprise I learned the other day that the tragedy of *Madame Bovary* (director: Vincente Minnelli) was all my fault. My informant was none other than James Mason, who, wearing as Gustave Flaubert a moustache and a look of understandable resignation, introduced the piece in a scene based, very remotely indeed, on the author's trial for offences against religion and morality. Don't blame me, said M. Mason-Flaubert, blame society: *your* society, which produced Emma Bovary; and off he went into a recapitulation of the story.

Madame Bovary thus gets by not only the public prosecutor, but also the conscience of the Johnston Office. There are, of course, changes in the plot, especially where Charles Bovary (played by Van Heflin) is concerned; he knows of his wife's adultery from the end of her affair with Rodolphe, and therefore makes after her death none of the discoveries with which the novelist wrings the man's heart and ours. Modifications such as these one expects in the cinema; but I must confess I was startled to find Flaubert's story of a country doctor's wife – a story framed wholly from human passion, human weakness and the struggle to find drama in a monotonous provincial life – turned into one long round of exciting events.

In Robert Ardrey's screenplay Emma's wedding celebrations become a battle between a pugilist bridegroom and the licentious guests; the little doctor's wife at the Marquis's ball turns everybody's head; the flight with Rodolophe is planned not for midday but midnight, and the runaway stands, becomingly wreathed in scarves, in the shadows outside Lheureux's shop only to see the coach go tearing past without stopping for her. Perhaps one could accept these dramatic inventions – inventions devised, after all, with the idea of translating Flaubert's emotional situations into the terms of action proper to the cinema – if the film had an intensity of feeling equal to its original's. But when all is done the result is cold; handsome, elaborate, and lifeless.

Part of the fault is Jennifer Jones's. Here is a good actress, an actress with intelligence, feeling and technique – but without, at any rate so far, the inexplicable personal command which used to make Garbo a lodestar. But I think the trouble goes deeper. The cinema in its dealings with the classics has rightly understood that there is a question of size. But it has made the mistake of confusing size with richness: of substituting splendid background and wealth of event for the grandeur of the human figure. *Madame Bovary* is an enormous book. It is also a very sober book; and sobriety is what we find lacking in this film and a dozen other versions of literary masterpieces.

October 1949

To anyone who took the trouble to look at the recent exhibition of film designs and drawings in the Victoria and Albert Museum the first two or three minutes of **Oliver Twist** are illuminating. The adapters of Dickens's novel, Stanley Haynes and David Lean, who is also the director, have begun their story a stage farther back than their great original; we meet Oliver Twist's mother, not dying in the workhouse, but struggling across the moors through storm and dark to its distant light. John Bryan's sketches in the exhibition, faithfully interpreting the script which they accompanied, showed every phase of movement: the stormy clouds, the reeds in the wind, the tossing branch, the cart-track and the menacing skyline and the tiny figure wavering over the crest. And here in the film, precisely translated into photography, are those same symbols: clouds, reeds, branch, track, skyline, figure. The designer, in fact, working with the director and the cameraman, has a major part in the architecture of images which is cinema.

Throughout *Oliver Twist* there is evidence of this emphasis on preparation and collaboration; nothing, in the studio-made scenes, has been left to chance or the inspiration of the moment: why should it be? This is an extraordinarily careful film: careful in construction, timing, cutting, movement, lighting, and details of gesture and dress. And careful in its preservation of the skeleton of Dickens's book (since skeleton is all a film has time for). The skeleton has, perhaps, lost a rib or two in the move from page to screen; and does the femur really go that way up? The Maylie family have been left out, I think without great loss; our stomachs have not been thought strong enough for the dreadful picture of Fagin in the condemned cell; Mr Brownlow turns out to be Oliver's grandfather; the Artful Dodger it is, not Noah Claypole, who spies on Nancy, and Dickens's passion for never wasting a character in the wind-up of the plot is thus ignored. But the omissions amount to no more than a justifiable simplification in a two-hour film; and though I regret the change by which Oliver is made to share in Sikes's last scramble over the roof, the boy's presence at the end with Fagin gang certainly makes more comprehensible, for the purposes of the cinema, a narrative which the novelist could afford to let wander.

The story, then, is there, exciting, varied, full of movement and life. What about the characters? *Oliver Twist* is Dickens's second novel; rich though the book is, it is thin compared with, say, *Bleak House* or *Our Mutual Friend*. Irony has not learned its strength; the attacks on the inhumanity of institutions are savage but lack the terrible edge which maturity was to give. The cinema runs less risk of failure with *Oliver Twist* than with the monumental later novels. Even so there is the impossibility of encompassing more than a fraction of the original, and David Lean and his collaborators have rightly concentrated on the translation of character, situation and comment into pictorial terms. The excellent Fagin of Alec Guinness tells us who and what he is by his looks as much as by his speech; we know the delicate and touching Oliver of John Howard Davies as soon as we see him.

Yet I believe the film could have afforded to go further in the direction of pictorial character. Francis Sullivan's portrait of Bumble is not odious enough; it is not simply that his performance is too soft, he does not look odious enough; and Bill Sikes (Robert Newton) is out-caricatured by his dog. It is when the piece most nearly approaches the spirit of Cruikshank that it is most successful: in its sketch of a workhouse deathbed, above all in its picture of the thieves' meeting-place and the squalid streets of a pitiless London. The passages which describe the pursuit and bringing to bay of Sikes are all good; and the figure of Fagin gives point to every scene in which he appears. But only in Guinness's playing does the Dickensian irony of character emerge. And the ferocity of the novelist's assault on cruelty and viciousness has vanished.

Oliver Twist suffers, I suspect, from the very care and prevision with which it has been made: from its very skill. There is no room in it for a mistake, and none for the magnificent outbursts of rage, grief and passion which are the essence of Dickens. Like its predecessor *Great Expectations* it is always admirable, often beautiful, and sometimes a shade cold. Readers of Dickens will understand what I mean when I say that, with such material, one of the highlights of the film ought not to be Sikes's attempt to drown Bull's-eye.

June 1948

In an age which has taken Shakespeare's Renaissance Prince, generous, callous, witty, violent, tormented by metaphysical wonderings and ravaged by sensuality and disgust, and crumpled the giant figure into the image of our own prized adolescent ills, it comes as a shock to see a Hamlet who is a man and errs, rages, melts, suffers as a man. Sir Laurence Olivier's production of **Hamlet** restores something which had long vanished from the play: sympathy with its hero; that awed and loving pity by evoking which the tragedian gives his audience some touch of the divine, making them at once judge as men and understand as gods. For me at any rate sympathy comes for the first time with the realization, none so easy in a reading of the text or even in most productions of the piece, that the Prince is a man unhappy in the ordinary human sense, not interestingly unhappy in the case-book manner, but solitary and full of grief. The whole play is thus brought back within the compass of experience, without losing the grandeur and intensity by which its poetry removes it from *common* experience.

Since we are dealing with a film of two and a-half hours drawn from a play of four and a-half hours, let me forestall the purists who will complain of the shock to their nerves produced by the manipulation of the text. Yes, Rosencrantz and Guildenstern are out; young Fortinbras, whose incursions into the story serve mainly to confuse, is out, and with him the soliloquy 'How all occasions'; Reynaldo is out, the First Player's recitation is out, and the great 'O what a rogue'. The Mousetrap is reduced to dumb-show; and Alan Dent, whose ingenious textual editing has admirably preserved the complex central narrative and the essential shape of character, could not save, to give an example or two of the immortal flowers, Ophelia's 'O what a noble mind' and Hamlet's 'Let the bloat king' and 'Imperial Caesar'; while 'To be or not be be', delivered, like most of the soliloquies, partly as thought, partly as speech, has been put after instead of before the meeting with Ophelia.

Very well, then, so we lose some of the people and some of the poetry; and I shall not be the only one compelled to return to the original. Compelled is the word; I do not remember feeling a sharper desire to enrich one experience by another than the longing which sent me hurrying home from the film last week to read and re-read the play. I wish I could with equal confidence defend those passages where the cinema, far from shortening the text, doubles the word with the pictorial image. The murder of King Hamlet; the death of Ophelia; the sea-fight; and Ophelia's first encounter with the distracted Prince – although this last gives Olivier the opportunity for a touching piece of miming I cannot help thinking that thus to illustrate the spoken narrative is to impoverish, not deepen.

Of course there are other things to criticize; the Ghost's graveyard voice, for example, blurs the rhetoric. But let us set against the faults the film's contributions to the understanding and enjoyment of Shakespeare. First, Olivier's own performance as Hamlet. I need not tell those who have seen him play, say, Richard Crookback with what superb irony he can deliver the sardonic aside; here the witty, the punning, the insolent, yes and the bawdy line become coherent with the poetic character, with the sweetness of Hamlet's bearing towards his friends. This is a performance full also of magnificent physical flourishes: the savage triumph at the end of the Play, the swallow dive from the gallery after the duel. And the interpretation intensifies as well as clarifies. Hamlet in this version overhears Polonius's plot to bait the trap with Ophelia; that is not a new reading, but how, as it is here presented, it sharpens our understanding of the 'To a nunnery' scene! And there is one moment at least which seems to me genius: Hamlet with the Player Queen, pulling a fair wig over the dark head, brushing back the fringe, and staring with stony misery as the boy stares back – the boy with the face, under the flaxen hair, of a blunted Ophelia.

Again and again Olivier's audacity has been justified. In so small yet telling a matter as his own fair-dyed hair: why on earth, one thought to oneself, insist on a blonde Prince? Yet now one sees that, in the black shadows of Elsinore, the fair shining head gives point and balance to the whole picture. In so very great a matter as the choice of *Hamlet* for a film: by the end one no longer thinks of the piece as filmed Shakespeare, but accepts it simply as a splendid production of a masterpiece. Yet looked at as cinema it is full of beauties. By a frugal use of cutting and a bold use of the moving camera in a setting designed to give both space for composition in movement and the sense of a society enclosed, the stream of speech has been preserved; the images, too, have a long, poetic flowing. Extraordinary effects have been produced by deep-focus photography: effects in the observation of character and in the description of emotional subtleties. I should be less than fair if I failed to praise the camerawork of Desmond Dickinson, the designs of Roger Furse and William Walton's fine music.

But for once it is to the acting that one returns and returns. Eileen Herlie plays the Queen with, especially in the Closet scene, a moving passion, though the performance lacks a touch of opulence. Jean Simmons as Ophelia shows exceptional talent; yet the character wants here, I think, the extremes of sensibility which would explain the fall into madness. Basil Sydney's King, Norman Wooland's Horatio are performances in the round; Terence Morgan makes a pleasant enough first appearance on the screen as Laertes; Peter Cushing is an excellent Osric; for Felix Aylmer's Polonius and Stanley Holloway's Gravedigger there can be nothing but gratitude. It is an unusual occasion when in the cinema one can feel that the subject is not character in action but character in conflict with itself: the tragedy of the human heart. The indefinable excitement with which one comes away from the film proceeds from an occasion more than unusual: an occasion, I think I can say, both historic and noble.

May 1948

'There never,' said Whistler, 'was an artistic period. There never was an Art-loving nation.' Whistler must surely have changed his mind had he survived into an age which not only goes to a Picasso exhibition as to a Cup-tie Final, but, apparently, reads Shakespeare as it reads the daily newspaper. A fortnight ago I should have said that the English public, all but a tiny section, was distinguished by its indifference to the literary classics, regarding Shakespeare as a subject for misquotation and the upper forms

of schools. The uproar which has followed the appearance of Sir
Laurence Olivier's film of *Hamlet* has taught me better.

The country, it seems, is shocked to the very drums of what
an eminent contemporary has called its civilized ears by the
'liberties' taken with the text. Young Fortinbras, though one
would never have suspected it, is everybody's darling; not a
home in England but insists on his restitution, together with
the political complications of the most complicated play ever
written. The names of Rosencrantz and Guildenstern are on
every lip; leave them out, and you might as well plan a world
conference and forget Russia. The Freudians, of course, are quite
broken at the thought of a Prince instead of a case.

I am, I admit, disturbed to encounter what Gibbon would have
called a supine inattention to the fate of Reynaldo, who also has
vanished without trace. But I console myself when I find that
the public conscience is exercised, not only by the omission
of characters and the transposition of scenes, not only by the
disappearance of two of the great soliloquies and a variety of
other passages, but by the most minute textual changes. People
like myself who have read Shakespeare for their delight and seen,
generally with a vague disappointment, perhaps half-a-dozen
stage productions of *Hamlet*, might, even after the re-readings
of the play consequent on seeing the film, have tamely endured
a few verbal modernisms. Not so the sensitive public. 'Meagre'
for 'maimed', 'hinder' for 'let', 'creed' for 'rede' – at every word
they leap in their seats with cries of Miscreant!

It is impressive to consider how, in what has been wrongly
thought an era of anti-culture, we are surrounded by those who
'pursue Culture in bands'. Forget Shakespeare? In every audience
at the Odeon there are, we know now, souls 'remembering him
like anything'. One might, of course, put down this epidemic of
scholarship to the Englishman's habit of recalling his traditions
only when some lesser breed without the law, in this case the
cinema, lays hands on them. I prefer, myself, to think that the
current display of sensibility proceeds from a temper which
fails to recognize that a work of art changes with time and
circumstance, speaking to the twentieth century, for instance,
in tones quite different from those heard in the eighteenth or the
nineteenth, and likes its masterpieces all immutable, all sacred,
and all dead.

May 1948

And so the house came to be haunted by the unspoken phrase: *There must be more money! There must be more money!* The children could hear it all the time, though nobody said it aloud. They heard it at Christmas, when the expensive and splendid toys filled the nursery. Behind the shining modern rocking-horse, behind the smart doll's house, a voice would start whispering: 'There *must* be more money! There *must* be more money!' And the children would stop playing to listen for a moment. They would look in each other's eyes, to see if they had all heard. And each one saw in the eyes of the other two that they too had heard.

In these words D. H. Lawrence, on the second page of his short story, *The Rocking-Horse Winner*, tells the reader how the cold, extravagant life of the parents constricts and twists the life of their children; in a single paragraph the emotional situation has been uncovered. How is the cinema to tackle this problem of exposition? **The Rocking-Horse Winner** is the first of Lawrence's stories to be adapted for the screen: the adaptation has been made by Anthony Pelissier, who has also directed. On the face of it the story appears comparatively easy to translate into cinema. The plot looks perfectly straightforward; there is enough incident, enough action, to provide material for the camera; the development does not depend on that sexual mysticism which with Lawrence so often took the place of character-drawing. At a first glance *The Rocking-Horse Winner* is a ferocious little story about a socially ambitious mother and a sensitive boy who, struggling to answer the unspoken demand for money and more money, discovers that he has the gift of foretelling the winners of horse races – and in the end pays for his gift with his life.

That, briefly, is the surface of Lawrence's story. Whether Mr Pelissier looked beneath the surface in making his adaptation I have no means of knowing; all that can be said is that the film as it stands presents no more than a superficial rendering. Or perhaps I should say rather that *The Rocking-Horse Winner* on the screen is an attempt at a literal rendering. Honourably literal it certainly is. There have, of course, been certain amplifications. Where a page of exposition serves Lawrence's purpose, the film needs explanatory scenes and a variety of incidents. And, presumably to satisfy the moral sense of the British public, the film does not end with the boy's death; the mother has to repent before the curtains can close. But for the rest there has been a respectful adherence to Lawrence's text; most of the author's dialogue has been used and his descriptive phrases have sometimes been incorporated; and when the script-writer has felt it necessary to amplify, the interpolated incidents have been written in with sympathy and skill.

The result is a film which certainly disgraces nobody. It has, after all, a serious and unusual subject. The quality of the technique is exceptional; the camerawork, by Desmond Dickinson (the lighting photographer of *Hamlet*) is often beautiful; and the all-round standard of acting is high. I am not among those who have faulted John Howard Davies's performance as the boy; were the film a profound exploration of Lawrence's tragic bitterness his playing would indeed want depth, but for this respectable literal version it serves admirably. As Bassett the gardener, the boy's partner in betting, John Mills (whose production the film is) contributes a beautifully self-effacing portrait; and there is an excellent sketch of the man-of-the-world uncle to whom the child confides his gift of prophecy by Ronald Squire. I do not think Valerie Hobson, who plays the mother, has ever been seen to better advantage. Miss Hobson is an elegant actress who is rarely allowed to display her elegance on the screen; here she successfully conveys a beautiful woman whose heart, not yet quite frozen, is fretted by some unknown quality in her child.

And yet, creditable in many ways though *The Rocking-Horse Winner* is, one cannot help wishing that the tragic intent of the original had been more deeply explored. Lawrence did not simply write a story about a little boy with a supernatural gift. He wrote a story about the anguish which proceeds from a neglect of human emotional needs; and he insisted, as he insists throughout his work, on the mysterious connection between human figure and background. The house, in his story, is as greedy, as tense and distracted as the people who live in it. When the boy manages by some secret arrangement with the lawyers to give his mother his winnings she becomes, not more contented, but colder; and as Lawrence says, 'the voices in the house suddenly went mad, like a chorus of frogs on a spring evening'. The film takes Lawrence's voices quite literally: there they are in the cinema, whispering from the sound-track. The trouble is that this kind of realism is rarely convincing. It was not convincing in the film of *Great Expectations*, where Dickens's fancy of farmyard creatures accusing young Pip as he runs through the morning mists was literally translated in terms of talking cattle; indeed it convinced so little that one critic took a whole passage for an interpolation.

Beneath its laconic phrases, Lawrence's story holds a threat which is never conveyed in the film. And it seems to me that the way to convey it lies, not in a faithful rendering of dialogue and descriptive phrases, but in a translation into imagery proper to the cinema. A film, with all its resources of lighting, movement, pace and composition, has extraordinary powers to suggest; and it is suggestion rather than statement which is needed here: imagination rather than reproduction. By the highest standards, *The Rocking-Horse Winner* fails as an interpretation of D. H. Lawrence. But as a skilful piece of narrative with excellent technical qualities it is well worth a visit.

'Films Based on Books',
Britain Today (March 1950)

'I suppose,' the boy said, talking of his role, 'I am the Angel of Death?' And indeed he is; and suddenly, as Dirk Bogarde described to me the colloquy with the prentice actor, the traditional phrase illuminated the film of **Death in Venice**. Illuminated too, the Thomas Mann story which Luchino Visconti has magisterially translated to the screen; or rather I should say that the film itself clarifies and for me deepens the argument of its original.

After seeing *Death in Venice* twice I am haunted; it is as if in Bogarde's portrait of Gustav von Aschenbach one had been watching a friend dying. I feel a need for exorcism. Perhaps I should begin, then, with fact. The story is about an internationally famous figure who goes to Venice to recuperate. Mann made him a writer but is said to have taken Gustav Mahler as model, and Visconti, restoring the hero to the profession of composer, has with overwhelming emotional effect used passages from Mahler's Third and Fifth Symphonies. Strange, said Bogarde, to be acting a book rather than a script. A script of course there was, devised by Visconti in collaboration with Nicola Badalucco – one, however, which in general has the air of exceptional fidelity.

True, Bogarde spoke of a departure, the introduction of a musical friend (Mark Burns) who argues as in Mann's story the hero argues with himself. And there are other departures. The disturbing view of the stranger at the mortuary chapel in Munich is out and the film begins with the arrival in Venice; rightly, for the symbols of mortality – the ferry trailing its black smoke along the horizontal lines of slatey sea and sky, the coffin-like trunk on the gondola and the boatman like some inexorable Charon – are clear enough.

Perhaps one should say that Visconti does not change *Death in Venice*, he extends it. He gives his hero a past which is not to be found, not all of it, in Mann's novella but which if you look hard enough into the thicket of words you can find in other works where Mann offered up his own self, his own experiences, his own struggle to achieve a 'balance' between art and life. You can find it in *Dr Faustus*, where Adrian Leverkühn recalls some of the events which the figure in Visconti's film recalls. Like Leverkühn, Aschenbach has lost a loved child, like him carries the memory of a visit to a brothel and the 'poison butterfly', the 'Hetaera Esmeralda'. On the screen the black-plumed ferry – Visconti says it is a funeral ship – is named Esmeralda; thus from the start Aschenbach is linked not simply with Mahler but through the figure of Thomas Mann's fiction with Mann himself.

I find the complexities, the flashbacks which somehow place the central figure, an enrichment; they never detract from devotion to an original which is half a tale of a dying man's infatuation with a beautiful boy and half a fable, an allegory perhaps, of an artist's pilgrimage through corruption. And the boy (Bjorn Andresen) is indeed beautiful with his contained, graceful movements and the face of a Botticelli angel; one would not have thought it possible to find so perfect a Tadzio. But then the director never fails in his re-creation of both the mood of *Death in Venice* and the detail of figures and background. From the Polish mother (Silvana Mangano, exquisite and exquisitely aristocratic in Piero Tosi's dresses and Pasquale de Santi's photography) to the most obscure member of the polyglot crowd of families, Russian, American, French, English, in the hotel or on the Lido beach everything is precisely imagined. Five months of shooting and tireless care for exactness: Bogarde talked of the resuscitation of the 1911 Hotel des Bains with décor and staff and visitors, the lovingly chosen views of tiny canals and deserted squares, the insistence, since this is a Venice not simply stricken by cholera but clouded by the sirocco, on working just after dawn when the light was pale and it was even a problem to persuade the sleepy roosting pigeons to play their part in the Piazza.

Visconti says he had to wait till he was old enough to make *Death in Venice*. Dirk Bogarde, offered the part of Aschenbach, wondered at first if he was too young. 'It is the only time I have ever had to begin entirely by technique. I didn't *know* Aschenbach. And he is dying all through the film; I had to move like a dying man, but not always dying in the same degree – when he first sees the boy he recovers a little. And naturally Visconti arranged the sequence of scenes as it suited him (we couldn't, for instance, have the Hotel des Bains for more than a strictly limited time), so the action wasn't chronological and I had always to be remembering what stage of dying I was in . . . No, Visconti and I never speak on the set. We understand one another without speaking.' Nevertheless there was the anxiety of his first scene.

'I had to go up that flight of steps from the terrace outside the Hotel des Bains – I hardly knew what was happening, people were moving around, extras were coming out of doors, I thought I should never get to the top.' Then the word Cut – and for once a touch of encouragement from the director.

Not, as you can see, the approach to acting of a man who does not deeply feel the role he is playing. Without extraordinary sensibility he would not have achieved that stooping hunched figure and the shades of Aschenbach's solitary incuriosity, the first stir of interest, the terror of moral involvement, the helpless surrender to infatuation. Least of all could he have achieved that heartbreaking final movement of hope as the dying man struggles to follow the gesture of the boy pointing seawards to an unknown horizon. It is the surrender, physical and spiritual, of the actor to the character. No wonder that when it was all over he spent days uncontrollably shaking in nervous exhaustion. He still could not escape from Aschenbach.

On the audience, too, *Death in Venice* makes grave demands. And now I have to say that with an elegance which irradiates the Teutonic mass of its extraordinary original the film is for me preferable to the novella. In the past quarter of a century there have been films potentially more influential (not, of course, necessarily for good). I can think of none which has been more truly a work of art.

March 1971

2 *Faithful to the Facts*

Paisa, the second film made since the war by Roberto Rossellini (the first was *Rome, Open City*) has been awaited in London a long time. I say in London, for Edinburgh stole a march on the English last year by showing it at the Documentary Festival. Now it is here one understands the excitement of those who saw it earlier; it brings to the picture of war a pity at once savage and tender which is quite foreign to the studio-made film – or, come to that, the contemporary documentary film. No wonder the documentary workers in this country are beginning to talk (late, but still) about smartening up the old ackamarackus. ('It is a distinct advantage in these days of austerity,' somebody wrote the other day in the admirably provocative *Documentary Film News*, 'to have a dash of entertainment in any message you may want to convey to a message-saturated public.')

Not that Rossellini is trying to convey a message, unless it be one to which – if I may stick to documentary prose style – there would be no sales-resistance: that war is hell. *Paisa* is the story of the Allied advance from Sicily to the valley of the Po: a story not of armies but of individuals. It is made up of six short stories: a Sicilian girl is murdered for warning an American patrol of the presence of a German patrol; a Negro forgives a little boy for stealing his boots when he sees the squalid chaos in which the children of Naples live; in Rome a girl, innocent at the Liberation, becomes a frowsy harlot in six months; a Resistance leader is killed in Florence, in the marshy plains of the north partisans are rounded up and massacred, in a hill-monastery a Franciscan community denies itself the food brought by the first American arrivals and fasts in the hope of bringing to grace two of its visitors, a Protestant and a Jew.

Except for the gentle and ironic Franciscan episode the film is inspired by anger over suffering – and a conviction that humanity is indivisible: the Negro sees in the slums of Naples the mirror of his own ostracism. Or a conviction rather that humanity is indivisible except for the British, who in *Paisa* are set apart by the ingloriousness of their share in the campaign; when they are not sitting around like tourists, discussing (in a brilliant scrap of burlesque) the architecture, they are carelessly allowing their planes to be shot down or giving orders designed not to benefit the partisans but, in the dear old phrase, to save the British Empire.

Perhaps some day Rossellini, who has already admitted the Germans to the human family, will let the British scrape in too. In the meantime we must not be too sensitive, but should take this exceptional talent as we find it. *Paisa* is a half-way house between *Rome, Open City* and *Germany, Year Zero*; it has the dramatic concentration of the first and the pitying, desperate vision of actuality of the second. Vision, not report; Rossellini, who shot his film with the real background of Lombardy, Rome newly-liberated Naples, and used much of the time non-professional players, transmutes fact into the stuff of the imagination. And, since imagination is more powerful than any document, we know, sitting in the cinema, that life in the wake of re-conquest was just like that: the handful of fighters in the marshes, the sniping in the streets, the ecstatic crowds, and the tawdry aftermath.

October 1948

After *Rome, Open City*, *Paisa*, and now a second look at **Germany, Year Zero** one begins to get a clearer idea of what Rossellini is doing. Much as I admired *Rome, Open City* I felt that its impact was partly accidental, the result, not of the director's art and indignation alone, but also of the accident of poor physical material which gave the story the air of fact: the accident also of time: show the film ten years hence when rage has died down, and I doubt whether the flesh will still crawl.

With *Paisa* the stylistic individuality was much more marked; the visual images were flung at the audience with the savage indifference of life itself to aesthetic refinements of composition and lighting; except in the monastery sequence, the merging of fiction into fact, fact into fiction, was barely perceptible. *Germany, Year Zero* takes us a step farther. This story of a Berlin child's wretchedness, corruption and suicide has no borderline; this fiction, one feels, is fact.

When I saw the film at a private showing last year I thought that it had an element of pity. I think now that I was mistaken; the piece, as painful at a second visit as at a first, communicates terror, horror if you like, but strangely no pity. And it seems to me that the absence of pity is the consequence of the very insistence on fact which is the basis of Rossellini's style. Squalor, sickness and death are not pitiful through a telescope or under a microscope; they become pitiful by virtue of imagination.

Rossellini builds up a dreadfully solid picture of the family with the sick complaining father, the son afraid of registering because he has fought to the last as a Nazi soldier, the daughter drinking with the occupying troops for the sake of a cigarette or two; and the sequence in which the little boy wanders alone and rejected through the bleached ruins of the city has no equal for its sense of desolation. The situation in itself is artificial enough. But Rossellini all the time insists that it is fact. He insists by his backgrounds of rubble and lifeless streets; he insists by his camerawork, shooting into the light and leaving his figures in dull shadow with no romantic aureole; he insists by cutting which flicks between close and long shot with the effect of a slap in the face. And he persuades us. Since he will have it so, this is not an interpretation but the fact of post-war Berlin; and in winning our acquiescence he sacrifices our pity.

April 1949

On the steps of the labour exchange a crowd of Italian unemployed gathers. There is work for a billposter; a man sitting on the other side of the square is called; the job is his, but he must have a bicycle. Well, he says, despondently, he has a bicycle and he hasn't. No bicycle, he is told, no job; all right, he says, then he has a bicycle; and off he goes to find his wife as she struggles, with buckets of water from the pump, down the rubbly slope and up the dingy stairs. The bicycle has been pawned; very well then, they must pawn the sheets and redeem the bicycle. They watch the pawnbroker's man climb to toss their bundle on top of a hundred other bundles; as they turn away with the money, behind them an elderly man hopefully lays a pair of field-glasses on the counter.

That is the opening theme of **The Bicycle Thieves**, Vittorio de Sica's tender, heart-rending and magnificently humane tale of poverty – the pitiful margin between life and hunger: in essence it is the whole theme. Antonio must work or his family starves; to work he must have a bicycle; he recovers his bicycle – and on his first day at work the bicycle is stolen, the margin is gone. The man and his little boy spend all next day struggling vainly to recover the bicycle; they search the markets, they find and lose witnesses; at last the father, desperate, turns thief before the boy's eyes; and as the two, the hollow-cheeked man and his son, walk away through the crowds, the weeping child with a gesture of infinite understanding takes his father's hand.

The story, as you can see, is simple: it has variety of incident, it has tension, but the incident is always perfectly natural, the tension is the tension of life, not theatre. When you think of the film afterwards – and, believe me, you will not get it out of your head for days – it is the presence, the inescapable, warm presence of living people which you will remember. There is, I am told, only one professional player in the cast; the workman (Lamberto Maggiorani), the child (Enzo Staiola), the families, the police, the friends, the expressive faces in market, street and church, all are amateurs. I have, perhaps, seen on the screen individual performances more dramatic, but I have never watched so complete, so unquestionable a re-creation of the whole texture of life. It is not only that character is superbly acted; character is superbly observed: a child injured in his pride behaves with just such tearful, angry aloofness, an old man badgered wears just such an obstinate mum look.

And de Sica and his cameraman, Carlo Montuori, have given us an unforgettable setting. This is not the romantic Italy; it is not the dramatic Italy to which the post-Mussolini realistic cinema has introduced us; it is the Italy which works; it is the shabby suburb and the distant line of new white buildings, the tram in the morning light, the market square, the crowd swarming from the football match, the wide motor road, the embankment, the huckster watched by the silent shell of ancient walls. When the camera lingers beyond the needs of direct narrative it is never without reason, but rather to show us the to-and-fro of the city; a child, perhaps, pestering a passer-by for alms. *The Bicycle Thieves*, in short, is doing something which the cinema alone can do: describing for us the actions and the sufferings of the individual against the huge, indifferent movement of life. Its pity is touched with irony, but not with bitterness; and for once I can beg you not to miss a film which observes the human creature with nothing but sympathy, forgiveness and love.

December 1949

Documentary somehow isn't the right category. Documentary conjures up the image of industrial diseases, model factories and a surfeit of herrings; and the fact that the class embraces a hundred other subjects still doesn't change the greyish tinge which its name has acquired. *The Savage Eye* is not a document, it is a muffled explosion. If you want its forerunners you should look not to the record-of-improvement school but to the Mark Sufrin-Lionel Rogosin *On the Bowery*.

The creators are three: Ben Maddow, screenwriter of *The Asphalt Jungle* and *Intruder in the Dust*; Sidney Meyers, who made *The Quiet One*; and Joseph Strick, director of *Muscle Beach*: at least these are the chief names, though a crowd of artists and technicians were their assistants during the four years it took to produce the film. The result of their collaboration is an assault on contemporary society: the story of a lonely young woman's experience of a big city, Los Angeles. The woman has divorced her husband, she is bitter and disgusted; she wants to avoid all human relationships except the impersonal; and she is taught a lesson: that is all. Even for this simple plot players are needed, and Barbara Baxley appears as the woman. But most of the figures in the urban landscape are not players. They are the people of the city, watched as, unconscious of the camera or indifferent to it, they go about their pursuits: ordinary people in ordinary pursuits, extraordinary people in extraordinary pursuits, desperate people in desperate pursuits.

The frieze of Hogarthian faces grinning under the ropes, yelling viciously at the all-in wrestlers: the stripper obscenely writhing and posturing ('Nobody,' says Miss Baxley's voice sardonically, 'ever got pregnant *that* way'); the piteous street accident; the drunken hulk blinking where he huddles on the pavement – the eye is savage all right. Once there is a moment of appalling tragic intimacy: a faith-healing scene with a press of old women tottering forward, half-crying, to declare their ills: 'Lord, fix her up,' gabbles the healer in a mechanical drone, 'let Him bless you now, God bless you, child, go on in and pray some more.' Certain passages – the strip-teaser's dance, and a gathering which might perhaps be described as a perverts' fancy dress ball – must have set problems for the Censor. He is to be congratulated on his forbearance, a year or two ago the film certainly would not have been passed with cuts so minute.

As a visual report on human fantasies and extravagances *The Savage Eye* is masterly. But what after a second visit still exasperates me is the commentary: an interior duologue – brilliantly delivered – between the central figure and her conscience (spoken by Gary Merrill). 'How do you spend your nights?' says conscience to the woman trying to forget her husband: 'Sweating alone in the black embrace of the imaginary man?' – and the chat goes on in a mixture of popular psychology and cinema-poet's prose. 'To break the withering prison of the body' – the phrase is used as we watch a party of harmless middle-aged customers in a beauty-parlour; inoffensively preoccupied shoppers in a bargain basement have eyes 'like dreaming tigers, cruel and sad.'

All right then, let us say that the gaze, so grimly bent on the scabrous or the degenerate, is that of the woman herself, still raw from her personal catastrophe; admit that at last she is . reconciled, her 'no-one-loves-no-one' turning to 'everybody-loves-everybody'. Even so, the end merely exposes the soft pappy heart of the argument; and all that has happened is that the savage eye has learned to condescend. There has been no withdrawal of the suggestion that it is pretty reprehensible to play cards, have a drink in a bar, or try to tighten up the stomach muscles.

What, in fact, I dislike in the film is its Puritanism. But it is a Puritanism detectable only in the gloss put on what we see. The word it is which twists; the camera for once does not lie. And what it shows us is a lot of people suffering, behaving, or acting according to their tastes. The picture is funny, pathetic, cruel, terrible; and it is worth going miles to see.

November 1959

It is not a moralizing film, far from it; nobody is condemned. Nevertheless it raises moral problems.

All the President's Men (director: Alan J. Pakula) deals with Watergate, and Watergate is an American tragedy; one has to live, as we in this country live, a long way off to look at it as a tragi-comedy. Indirectly the film concerns Nixon and the exposure of corruption. Directly it is about two Washington Post reporters, Carl Bernstein, played by Dustin Hoffman, and Bob Woodward, played by Robert Redford; Mr Redford it was who had the idea of making the film. Assigned to what looked like a misguided burglary, Bernstein and Woodward uncovered an appalling political conspiracy. They were the chief instruments in the ignominious collapse of a President and an administration; and the moral problem lies in the question of justification for making a film, an entertainment, concerning the offences of living public figures.

The film has been called a film of detection. Essentially that is what it is, only the detection deals in history. It was an extraordinary chance which placed the disclosures in the hands of two newspapermen – chance and the ineptitude of the Watergate intruders, who in June 1972 set out to raid and bug the Watergate offices, headquarters of the Democratic National Committee. Wearing their natty business suits, loaded with picklocks, cameras, bugging devices and walkie-talkies, they had not even the sense to be quiet about it; no self-respecting burglar could have been so careless.

The revelations which followed their capture and finally involved the President and eminent members of his staff were endlessly complex. Today the names which emerged – Mitchell, Haldeman, Ehrlichman, a dozen others – are familiar but hard to place; one needs a Who's Who of the White House and the departments of American government. William Goldman based his script on the book by Bernstein and Woodward; they too, together with the director, took a hand; the result keeps the lines of the story clear, and wisely the President's men, the implicated and the accused, are kept at a distance; they are names heard only, they are people seen only, as Nixon himself is seen, on the television screen; unlike the witnesses against them, they are never recreated by actors.

And Mr Pakula has kept the action subdued. The two reporters proceed by tiny stages – through rebuffs, through unwilling admissions; a name gives a clue, a clue leads to another name, another fragment of information. Are the ramifications too remote for a British audience? One might have said yes if they had not pursued with such dramatic cunning – and if fate had not come up with a piece of Hitchcockery.

For there, plumb in the middle of the anti-trail inquiry, is a mysterious informer. He has no name, unless Deep Throat, the title by which he is mischievously known, is a name. He can be met only secretly in the darkness of a garage. Appointments have to be made by flying a red flag from a balcony. Is he real? one might have taken him for a fiction, a character invented to brighten a record of endless taking of pains. But Woodward, who is shown in colloquy with him, insists that Deep Throat exists; and already there are rumours linking him with the CIA.

The episode is both a bonus and embarrassment. It gives the film a nub of excitement; but it offends Probability. Nevertheless there it is; anything can happen in Washington. And Mr Pakula says he wouldn't have made the film had he not been persuaded of complete authenticity.

The feeling of authenticity depends on accuracy not only in fact but in performance. *All the President's Men* has two stars, Hoffman and Redford; and these two stars are asked to play the roles of subordinates. The real star of the film is Jason Robards, formidably yet genially commanding as Ben Bradlee, the Washington Post's Executive Editor. It is a magnificent performance, and the two reporters must react to it. They must move and speak as Bradlee's employees. They must be two young men who 'want to eat', as one of their bosses (Jack Warden) says to another (Martin Balsam).

And that is among the first things one notices: they play straight, no showing off, no heroics, no glory-stuff. For Dustin Hoffman the submergence of personality may not have been so difficult; he is, as Mr Pakula says, a character-actor. Robert Redford is not simply a star, he is a star-performer. He is used to shining. But here the physical brilliance is dimmed. The young lion becomes the discreet interviewer, the man on the telephone taking notes; the face is intent, blinkered against everything except investigation. It is a credit to Mr Redford – and, I think, to the director as well.

Mr Pakula is modest about his part in the direction of players. For instance, he gives all the credit for Jane Alexander's fine performance as the Bookkeeper to Miss Alexander who, he says, after what he had accepted as a satisfactory scene, asked to be allowed to do it again – and added the telling breakdown. I think he must accept some of the praise for Mr Redford's remarkable concentration on both the surface and the inner devotion of a good investigating reporter.

One more observation. The investigations, the interviews are conducted, most of them, in darkened rooms; even the exteriors are often shadowed; it is a violent contrast with the newsroom, huge, bleak, not a corner escaping the brutal white light. It is to the newsroom that the two reporters belong. They are the servants of its demand for the pitiless truth. And that, I suppose, is where the justification for the making of *All the President's Men* lies. The film is not about the fall of Nixon, or the disgrace of political aides, or the complicity of great departments. It is a stunningly well-made reconstruction of a hunt for facts. One may have qualms, as I have, and still admire the brilliance of the job done. I don't think anything as close to life – close in time, close in personalities – has been done in the cinema before.

May 1976

10 'CORNERSTONES'

An older version of film history was constructed by selecting a canon of two hundred or so masterpieces and judging all other work against the standards and achievements of the films within that selection. And although such an approach may now be academically unfashionable, there is no doubting its popular appeal. It was only comparatively recently that the National Film Theatre in London ceased its annual programme of 'cornerstone' films, while every January film critics on serious newspapers continue to produce an annual list of what they regard as the best films from the previous twelve months and the magazine *Sight and Sound* has until now invited these same reviewers at periodic intervals to select their ten best films ever made. Given that Dilys Powell has been reviewing the cinema for nearly half of its brief history, it is inevitable that she has encountered a good many of these 'cornerstone' movies at their first British screenings, *Citizen Kane*, *Les Enfants du Paradis*, *Rashomon*, Michelangelo Antonioni's trilogy of films from the 1960s, for example. What follows is a selection of Powell's first responses to some of the key works in the history of the cinema.

'It is like writing history with lightning,' Woodrow Wilson is reported to have said after looking at *The Birth of a Nation*. Indeed, after the rare good fortune of once again seeing this great cinematic monument (at a private showing), one had the sensation of coming out of a thunderstorm: an artistic as well as a historical thunderstorm. Two views of the film, the first when it was originally shown in this country (America first saw it in 1915), the second now, do not make me suppose I can add anything fresh to the mass of critical appreciation produced in thirty years. But it is worth while to recall the astonishing achievement of *The Birth of a Nation*. Even after seeing the piece straight through today, all three hours of it, without musical accompaniment, nobody could say that achievement was of merely antiquarian interest, nobody could say it had been essentially diminished by the perspective of time.

The first, the main achievement is in the use of the screen for historical narrative. Here is a great chunk of history in which one believes as one believes in the *Iliad* or the *Aeneid*. I choose deliberately parallels from heroic or legendary history; for though D. W. Griffith's masterpiece has an amazing background of realistic detail, though Griffith makes a great point of his accurate transcriptions of incidents and scenes from the American Civil War, the film is basically a rendering into broad, simple, human terms of a vastly complicated period; the human figures gather up into themselves the problems of multitudes.

We have had fairly lately another example of the historical complex presented in terms of the human individual; oddly enough it was the same historical complex. I refer, of course, to *Gone With the Wind*. But where *Gone With the Wind* reduced the gigantic panorama of history to a painted backcloth for the cavortings of a group of vulgar little egoists, *The Birth of a Nation* preserves the historical scale: the background is huge, the broadly stylized figures, for the very reason that they are stylized, are not dwarfed.

The size and the magnificence of Griffith's battle scenes are a revelation today, when the wealth and mechanical efficiency of the contemporary cinema so often blind one to its want of poetic imagination. The terrifying precision of Sherman's army on the march; Atlanta burning, and the scurrying confused horde of refugees; the battle of Petersburg, and the fitful movement of men behind the drifting smoke of artillery; and the dreadful relics of war, the tumbled bodies lying and dangling on the ramparts – all this has a grandeur to which the word epic is for once not inapplicable. From a technical point of view I found the use of long shots particularly interesting: not only in the battle sequences, where the juxtaposition of long and close shots lends extraordinary reality to the scene, but in, for example, the narrative of the suicide of the young girl. The flight through the woods as she finds herself pursued by the renegade negro, the appearance of her brother desperately following in search – the distant views of the three tiny fated figures, darting, hiding, running amidst enormous trees and rocks have an excitement which would be lost in close view.

The brings me to the human narrative of *The Birth of a Nation*. It is easy enough to say that, just as the historical narrative is coloured by violent prejudices, so the human narrative is over-simplified and crude. Yet, if one accepts (and why not?) the conventions of early film characterization, these American families are no more crudely drawn than, say, the virtuous characters in a Dickens novel; they are, in fact, handled with much the same kind of large humanity, much the same broad sympathy and love. Indeed, I would go so far as to say that Griffith was, in his prime, a nineteenth-century humanist working in a twentieth-century medium. And, speaking for myself, I should welcome today some infusion of that unashamed humane sentiment into the smart machine-made films I see every week.

July 1945

1   The sense of space is one of the extraordinary qualities in an extraordinary film, *Citizen Kane*; . . . it is not space in landscape but space in architecture, the emptiness of the palace, the space which hems in the solitary human soul. The piece is an attempt to explain a public life, or, rather, a plea that the life is not explicable. Charles Foster Kane dies, the newsreels set out the gigantic facts of his career – his wealth, his audacity as a newspaper proprietor, the scandal which ruined his political

career, the fabulous, battlemented seclusion of his latter days. He died on a word: Rosebud. What, who was Rosebud? The reporter sets off on his inquiry, interviews the blonde, drunken widow, the business associates, he querulous friends, consults the diary in the tomb-like memorial library, wanders round the Kane place – Xanadu, Kane called it – with its staircases and corridors, its jumble of statuary, its crates of antiques never opened. A character emerges, a character possible, one would think, only in a great material civilization, a character beginning with generous impulses and hardening at last into egomania; a man with tender and with berserk moments, a colossus of a man, but always an enigma. For this is no story neatly rounded off with romance or nostalgia. This is an adult film, technically and psychologically adult, recognizing the ultimate obscurity in which every human life moves; one of the few, the very few films to present not an abstraction, but a man.

It is brilliantly played by Orson Welles (also writer, director, and producer) as Kane and by the Mercury Actors, scarcely a name among them familiar to the cinema, as the rest. Gregg Toland's camera-work, ranging from the newsreel technique of the opening to the menacing lighting, the shadowed faces and vast doomed vacancies of the exposition, does much to make *Citizen Kane* one of the most remarkable films of this and many another year.

2   There has been in some quarters a tendency to chide Mr Orson Welles, for the individual technique of his film: to chide him with a great air of urbanity, indulgence, and elder criticism, but still to chide. The man, they say, moves his camera about: much as the greyer beards might have rebuked Victor Hugo for venturing to move the caesura. Nobody, indeed, has suggested that this makes his film a bad film; the implication is that it is a remarkable film in spite of the hardihood of its experiments. I will refrain from tedious and mossy analogies with dramatic and literary experiment and creation; and let nobody suppose that I take the quality of this brilliant piece to be due to its technique. I should like to point out merely that in this, as in any other work of art – for *Citizen Kane* is a work of art, an imaginative creation communicated by cinematography – the technique is inseparable from the theme. Mr Welles is a man

with a rare understanding of the potentialities of the cinema and a still rarer capacity for using them. There is no question here of experiment for experiment's sake; it is a question of a man with a problem of narrative to solve, using lighting, setting, sound, camera angles and movement much as a genuine writer uses words, phrases, cadences, rhythms; using them with the ease and boldness and resource of one who controls and is not controlled by his medium. The virtuosity, the *command* of Mr Welles and his cameraman, Gregg Toland, are sufficiently illustrated by the contrast between the newsreel exposition of Kane's life, with which the film opens, and the psychological inquiry which follows into the motives behind the known events. But it is not virtuosity only. In the first place the harsh lighting, the hurried movements, the lightning cutting give us the superficial, the public man; in the second place the events are repeated in a style which reinterprets them, invests them with sad meaning, a style which hints, emphasizes, and then draws over the strange story the veil of human defeat. The camera moves, voices mingle and echo in caverns of space, with narrative purpose and not from exuberance; a face is shadowed not because it makes a beautiful individual shot, but because the character, the motives of the speaker are shadowed.

I have been interested to hear of an interesting experiment being carried out in Manchester, where the Ministry of Information has placed a projector in the City Art Gallery and is arranging a series of its film shows during alternate weeks between now and Christmas, and where the Manchester Film Institute is co-operating by putting together programmes for the intervening weeks illustrating some aspect of the cinema. I should like to suggest that some day a Film Society should present extracts from *Citizen Kane*, setting side by side sequences from the newsreel narrative and the interpretative style. That would, I think, dispose of any idea that Welles's treatment is arbitrary or extravagant.

October 1941

Though the name of Carl Dreyer is familiar to every student of the cinema, his films have up to now been little seen in this country. *La Passion de Jeanne d'Arc*, made at the end of the silent period, is a familiar memory to some; *Vampire*, from the beginning of the talking cinema, is known probably to a handful only. A Dane who has worked in Sweden and Germany as well as France, but who, unlike so many of his Scandinavian and German and French contemporaries, never emigrated to Hollywood, he now reappears as a director in his own country; and *Day of Wrath* serves both to introduce to England the Danish sound film and to revive a great individual reputation.

Long before the new piece came to London I had heard of it as a concealed comment on the Nazi system of government (it was made during the occupation of Denmark); and though now I have seen it I believe, and am confirmed in the belief by conversation with Dreyer himself, that the comment was at most only half-conscious, certainly to read into this story of seventeenth-century witchcraft and pious beastliness an attack on political terrorism is the easiest thing in the world. However, it is not as a reflection of contemporary events that *Day of Wrath* is most interesting.

The theme is, broadly speaking, that of moral infection. An old woman, guilty probably of no more than temperamental obstinacy, spite and the habit of picking groundsel under the gallows, is denounced as a witch, tortured and burned alive; her persecutors find in their own consciences the fulfilment of her curses, until at last the innocent are contaminated by superstition and turn self-accusers. On the surface Dreyer seems once or twice to have clouded the moral by confusing two kinds of guilt; the girl whose infidelity gives the piece its moral climax is not guilty of the mumbo-jumbo of witchcraft, but she is guilty of adultery; she does not conspire to kill her husband, but she does wish him dead. And here and there some delicate linking of event with the stage properties of witchcraft makes the spectator hesitate; for instance, as the pastor, walking home at night, stumbles and halts in a sudden premonition of death, the traditional goat, horned and bearded, peers at him from the field. But on reflection one sees that the background detail merely serves to create the necessary atmosphere of suspicion; that the apparent confusion of guilt is not really confusion but a deliberate emphasis on the linking in human life of the seemingly irrelevant. Beneath the surface the moral is clear enough: cruelty begets fear, fear begets wrong. The fact that the illustrations are sometimes almost unbearably realistic, that the camera dwells almost tenderly on the evidence of brutality, is no argument against the basic theme.

The subject is unusual and striking enough; but what makes

Day of Wrath an exceptional piece of cinema is the quality of the treatment. Those who have seen *Vampire* will remember the incessant movement of the camera, the swinging view of a room, the tilted walls and trees sliding past the man carried in his coffin. *Day of Wrath* uses camera-movement less freely, but with an extraordinary and sometimes frightening deliberation. Dreyer here (as in *La Passion de Jeanne d'Arc*) forces the eye to linger on the details of watching faces while all the time it longs and dreads to see the victim of their study; again and again he withholds the central figure while the camera wanders slowly over background, over crowd, over the sadistic setting of drama. And the tension is horribly heightened by the handling of sound.

Dreyer, I believe, was one of the serious directors to welcome the arrival of the talking film; certainly one understands from this film how in the silent days he must have missed the scream off-stage, or rather off-screen. He likes, too, to balance and vary the voices of his players; there is something infinitely shocking in the range of the old tortured woman's tones, now screeching or whimpering in pain, now pleading, now threatening in the deep notes of despair. At this point a word should be said about the acting. The playing of the young wife and the pastor is good; but the film is dominated even after her death by the old witch; and though one must ascribe this domination partly, indeed, to the quality of the direction, to the ruthlessness of the scenes of questioning and execution, much of the effect is due to the performance of Anna Svierkier. The tear-mottled face, the old, podgy, naked back – so much more affecting than the smooth lovely features and young elegant ribs of, say, Linda Darnell in a similar fix in *Anna and the King of Siam* – this the camera can do, but not the speaking gestures of terror and fear and defiance. The actress here has lent herself entire to the purpose of the story; and the director has known how to wring out the last drop of pity.

Dreyer, indeed, has had practice enough, as those who remember his handling of Falconetti in *La Passion de Jeanne d'Arc* will agree. *Day of Wrath* has in the first half something of the concentration of the earlier film; yet lacks its stark horrible grandeur. In the fantastic touches of the new piece there are echoes of *Vampire*; but the boldness of that gothic extravagance is absent. The second half of *Day of Wrath* moves slowly, though less slowly in retrospect, when the rhythm can be seen as a whole; what weakness there is lies here, in occasional artificiality and stiffness of action. But the film will, I think, be remembered for its realistic treatment of the incredible; for its vicious tension; for the unrivalled horror of its picture of human callousness.

November 1946

It is three years since Eisenstein's book *The Film Sense* was published in England, but not until last week did that massive and occasionally elephantine piece of critical analysis come to life for me. *The Film Sense* began with a reassessment of what used fashionably to be called montage; the joining of film shots, pieces of film, in order to create by their juxtaposition something beyond the significance of the pieces taken separately. Then it went on to consider the effect of the transition from the silent to the sound-film and to argue that the principles of composition remained unchanged, that the new development meant simply the welding of another element, the sound-track, into a 'polyphonic montage'. The process might have been seen and heard at work seven years ago in *Alexander Nevsky*, a passage from which Eisenstein analyses in his book; but the application of his theories is so much clearer in his new film, ***Ivan the Terrible***, that one may be excused for recognizing only now just what he is getting at.

Ivan the Terrible is a historical character study set against the background of sixteenth-century Moscow: a background half-barbarous, half-Byzantine, so rich and close of texture that one can almost smell the furs and the silks and the oil. It is a nationalist film, imperialist even; its theme is the emergence of the first Tsar, his fight to dominate the boyars, and his struggle to extend Russian borders. The piece was planned as a large-scale work in two parts; what we see now is the first part, which, after showing the defeat of the Mongols, the conspiracy of the boyars and the murder of the Tsarina, and the establishment of a kind of Imperial guard, ends with a pilgrimage of the people to beg Ivan, who has left the capital, to return to Moscow. The part of the Tsar is stupendously played by Nikolai Cherkassov (the Tsarevitch in *Peter the Great*, the professor in *Baltic Deputy*, the hero of *Alexander Nevsky*); this is a performance classical in the best sense, building from within the character of a man ruthless in the pursuit of national unity, tormented by loneliness, a man raging with ambitions and schemes. The notion of violence is conveyed less by action than by inward fire; indeed, the figure of the Tsar is often static in the midst of action; and the contrast between the monumental hero and the eddying movement of crowds creates a kind of visual counterpoint.

This brings me to Eisenstein's theory of composition in the cinema: to the fact that Eisenstein, unlike so many of our artless little daubers, actually composes his shots, composes his sequences, composes his film. How deeply he is interested in sixteenth-century imperialism I have no idea; it is of his interest in the aesthetic problems of cinema narrative that the new film constantly speaks. *Ivan the Terrible* opens with the crowning of the Tsar: close-up of crown, back of the royal head, embroidered vestments, suspicious and jealous and ironic faces of onlookers, candles, figures of priests, the crown lifted, sceptre and orb, a bass voice chanting in ascending quarter-tones, and at last the face of Ivan, rigid beneath a ritual shower of coins. Each shot, each gesture is answered by a musical phrase; the voice of the archbishop is echoed by the tolling and clashing of bells; a man speaks over the voices of the choir. I will not try to examine here Eisenstein's theory of the correspondences between the visual movement traced by the eye and the movement of the music; I will merely point to the extraordinary effect of orchestration, composition for eye and ear at once, produced by the combination of Prokofiev's music and a series of visual shots composed both individually and in association.

All through *Ivan the Terrible* there is this same effect of integration: action, gesture, background, sound, speech, music harmonized: ikons, candelabra, shield, battle-axe, siege-guns, lion-heads, swan-necks, the magnificent complex of decoration woven into a textural whole with the sound-track. That this should appear so striking is, no doubt evidence of the poverty in composition of the films seen every week. The fact is that Eisenstein is still one of the few, the very few directors who look on a film as a complete work of art, not as a talking picture with sound effects. And so when, in this rich, almost stifling texture, he suddenly uses his camera simply and boldly, the result is not a trick-shot but a piece of poetic description; the huge bearded shadow on the wall dominates the screen as the Tsar dominates Russia. And so when *Ivan the Terrible* seems to move slowly and in drawn-out action (just as, to be frank, *Paradise Lost* is boring now and then) it is till the work of a great master.

September 1946

Looking back at **Les Enfants du Paradis** after a first single visit (inadequate for a full judgment of this elaborate and beautiful film) I find myself recalling it as a painting rather than a narrative – though goodness knows it has plot enough. It is not that the piece wants movement and rhythm: occasionally, it is true, the movement is faintly disjointed, now and again the rhythm is slightly broken (the result, perhaps, of a cut); but there is the action proper to the cinema; this is not a film which resolves itself into a series of isolated shots. On the contrary; rather it is a painting which has also the attributes of a film. One remembers from it the solid shadows, the startling contrasts, the figures detaching themselves from the rich background of stage or street; but one remembers too the interplay of character, the architecture of continuing action, the explosion of event.

The setting of *Les Enfants du Paradis* is the Paris of the 1840s: the boulevard of the vaudeville theatres and the mimes, with the raree-shows, the acrobats, the clowns and dancers. Jacques Prévert's script and Marcel Carné's camera acquaint us with this confused undulant life before taking us in Pagliacci fashion behind the scenes to show us the romantic torment of the clown, the amorous vagaries of the naked beauty in the peep-show; and though the emphasis of the film thereafter is always on the individual character, uniquely suffering or injuring, the spectator is never without consciousness of the picturesque jolly savagery of the crowd from which the individual emerges. The story is enormously and deliberately contrived; nothing happens simply or dully, but always with a theatrical flourish; an insult, a duel, the beginning of a liaison, everything belongs to the convention of romantic violence; hearts break and do not mend, and their owners belong to the stage as much by their private as by their public lives.

But instead of diminishing the compulsion of the narrative, this unity of feeling actually increases it. Two at any rate of the principal characters – Deburau the mime, Lemaître the actor – belong to theatrical history; and though the personal adventures in which *Les Enfants du Paradis* involves them are presumably invented, as an imaginative reconstruction of the mood of their time and setting the piece is difficult to resist. It is, in fact, a painting of a period, a painting in which for once in the cinema the very exaggerations become convincing. And a painting of a society still under the spell of the romantic movement. The sad clown, the ironic tragedian, the criminal enthralled by a kind of diabolism – these are the figures of nineteenth century sublime-and-grotesque. And as if to give the unmistakable Hugoesque flavour, Carné and Prévert have added a figure monstrous in outline: the betrayer of the underworld, the ragged filthy peddler to whose appearances the playing of Pierre Renoir gives such sinister stress.

This brings me to the acting: to Jean-Louis Barrault's Deburau, to Pierre Brasseur's Lemaître, to Arletty and Marcel Herrand and Louis Salou. Barrault with the clown's mask-face and the exquisite dancer's gestures; Brasseur's panache tinged with melancholy – in the cinema of no other country is there such acting. Nor can I think of anyone to touch Arletty for a speaking immobility; nor anyone else to make, as Louis Salou makes, a living insolent creature out of an abstraction of dandyism. Yet as I think back now over the film it is none of these faces that I see, but the vicious gratification on the face of Marcel Herrand as the criminal by desire; not, fine as his performance is, by virtue of greater talent, but because his is the figure which most sharply expresses the romantic fatalism of the whole work. And because something in his face with its elegantly odious make-up, the sneer, the carefully arranged curls, reminds one of the portrait on canvas; for when all is said and done *Les Enfants du Paradis* is a painting of a period and a setting indeed, but still more of characters, of people.

December 1946

Sunset Boulevard is the most intelligent film to come out of Hollywood for years; lest the idea of intelligence in the cinema should lack allure, let me say that it is also one of the most exciting.

To what degree it will excite people who don't know what films were like twenty-five years ago is, perhaps, open to question. For the movement here is not the stir of the chase, murder, the police cars shrieking through the streets – though that comes in too. It is the movement of history which leaves the human being behind. *Sunset Boulevard* stands or falls by its success in illuminating the change in manners and taste which came over the cinema with the end of the 1920s and the first mouthings of dialogue on the screen. Its central figure is a woman ageing not simply in years: she is an actress who has aged professionally. Audiences which have never enjoyed silent film acting and learned to accept its conventions can't be expected fully to appreciate the subtleties of its re-creation here.

Never mind, there are plenty of other qualities to enjoy. *Sunset Boulevard* does an audacious thing which must in prospect have sustained Billy Wilder and Charles Brackett, writers and, respectively, director and producer of the piece, through many a dismal bit of studio routine: it takes a darling of the silent cinema, Gloria Swanson, and a great silent director who is also a brilliant actor, Erich von Stroheim, and puts them into a story which might conceivably have been true of some such actress and some such director.

A young script writer of today hides the car he can't pay for in the garage of a neglected Hollywood mansion. The mansion, he finds, is not quite empty. An arrogant ghost in dark glasses summons him in, a severe butler leads him upstairs; the ghost is a forgotten star, the butler is the director who discovered her and who, faithful in her eclipse, still nourishes her dreams of immortal fame by secretly writing letters which she believes to come from the outside world. The writer stays to help with the immense outdated script of *Salome* on which she has been working for years: DeMille, she insists, will direct it, and she will be a great star again. Little by little the young man finds himself trapped. The woman falls in love with him; he is petted and loaded with presents, an orchestra plays for him to dance on a floor once honoured by Valentino; when he makes a bid to escape she tries to commit suicide.

The story, I say, might conceivably have been true of some phantom from the cinema's legendary past. Nothing was too bizarre for the idols of the silent age. That was the era of champagne and leopard-skin, of four divorces per head and going to bed in a thing like a Roman galley; it is one of the virtues of *Sunset Boulevard* that its extravagances are historically possible. And by setting side by side the present and the past, the cynical young writer with his wisecracking friends and the middle-aged, passionate woman with her theatrical poses, the film conveys a criticism of both worlds: of today's flimsy vulgarity and the ostentation of yesterday, when a film star might have an organ large enough for the Albert Hall in her drawing-room and bury her pet chimpanzee in a coffin lined with red satin.

And the acting, with a refinement rare on the screen, emphasizes the gulf between past and present. The young writer, excellently played by William Holden, has the casual gestures and speech accepted in the actor of today. Gloria Swanson makes every movement and tone a little more than life-size. In a truly outstanding performance she shows us a woman to whom playing a part has become second nature, and an actress to whom acting is life; here is the star of the days when a face had to speak without words.

I recall with particular admiration three scenes: one in which she impersonates Chaplin; one in which, with Buster Keaton in the party, she plays a mournful game of cards; and one in which she sits watching her past self on the screen. Readers of Peter Noble's lively biography of Stroheim, *Hollywood Scapegoat*, may recognize that she is looking at a fragment from *Queen Kelly*; the moment has added point if one remembers that Stroheim, who here in his character as ex-director and butler acts as projectionist also, did in fact direct Miss Swanson in the film in 1928, 'I am big,' says the actress in *Sunset Boulevard*, 'it's the pictures that got smaller.' There is something in that; and this film reminds us of the heroic age when the screen had the directness, the spontaneity, the confidence and the emotional simplicity of a young popular art. It reminds us by its own single deficiency: want of pathos. But a certain clinical detachment in the manner of the piece cannot destroy its claim to be regarded as an exceptionally distinguished work.

August 1950

We had heard a great deal about **Rashomon** (director: Akira Kurosawa), which won the International Grand Prix at Venice last autumn against all comers, but nothing I had been told had conveyed to me the peculiar qualities of this Japanese film; and it was in a mood of enjoyable curiosity that I went to see the piece last week. As a rule one knows only too well what to expect.

Rashomon, based on a book by Ryunosuke Akutagawa, is the story of a single violent happening in the remote past told by four narrators, three of them distorting the truth, the fourth observing it but concealing part of it. A man is found dead in the woods ('Rashomon' apparently, means 'In the Forest'). A bandit is captured and confesses to the crime; but his account is quite different from the story of the man's wife; and the dead man's own version, given through a medium, contradicts them both. There was a treacherous attack, everybody agrees to that; there was a rape; there was a death; but whether the death was by murder or suicide or in a fight is not agreed. Each man tells a tale which does him some credit; the bandit's story is all audacity and devil-may-care, the victim portrays himself as too noble to survive disgrace; and the woman presents herself as a helpless innocent broken by the brutality of the one and the scorn of the other. But it is an encounter between three discreditable figures which the onlooker describes.

In praising this savage film I ought to make clear that my especial recommendation is not for the camera-style, which, accomplished though it is, does not deviate far from late-silent European. There are one or two striking tracking shots, the more striking for not being in a Western hurry to get somewhere quickly; and now and then the camera settles on a closeup or circles round a figure in a way which reminds one of the work of Dreyer in his middle period. But the interest and excitement of *Rashomon* are not in Eastern adoption of Western technique and style, but in the nature of the story and the manner of the playing.

The film is a story within a story: witnesses repeat the evidence for a listener, and as each lie betrays itself we are involved in the struggle not only to find out the facts but to discover why they are being falsified. The three main figures are trying to hide weakness or wickedness. But not all the distortion is deliberate: each has an idea of himself as a character, each presents a face to the world and unconsciously shapes his account of events to suit it. To say that *Rashomon* is a film about character is only half the truth. This is character not in the Western sense but in what I will risk saying is the Eastern sense: the levels of human behaviour which lie beneath the singularities of the individual.

The playing, again, recalls at times the silent cinema we used to know: large gestures, facial expressions given their full value by the attentive camera. And the players get no help from the background, which consists of a wood, a bit of featureless courtyard, a tumbledown gateway and a rainstorm. You might say that in some ways the acting is stylized: the bandit (Toshiro Mifune), the murdered man (Masayuki Mori) and the woman (Machiko Kyo), repeatedly use certain movements, certain inclinations of the head to convey emotion. But there is a great deal of carefully observed detail as well: Toshiro Mifune's first look at the woman, for instance. It is possible, of course, that the strangeness of a film coming from Japan affects judgment. But even taking that into account I find in *Rahomon* a mixture of the mysterious, the legendary and the realistic which sets it apart. At any rate I can't forget it.

March 1952

Suddenly a new film. Really new, first-hand: a work which tells a story of its own in a style of its own. One is almost afraid to touch it . . .

Hiroshima Mon Amour is a Franco-Japanese film about memory. It is a story of love and death, but chiefly it is a story about a woman who reluctantly and agonizingly is thrust into remembrance of things past. The encounter with memory is Proustian in that it is set in train by a trifle: the chance gesture of a hand. But the object of memory has a savagery remote from Proust's world. Naturally: for the writer, Marguerite Duras, and the director, Alain Resnais, the past is the last war. And nobody who has seen *Nuit et Brouillard*, Resnais's terrible, reticent documentary about the concentration camps, would expect this director to find it reassuring to look back.

In his first feature film remembrance, that sudden searchlight, is focused on the end of the war. A Frenchwoman acting in a pacifist film is visiting Hiroshima; she has met a Japanese architect, been attracted by him, spent the night with him. There is the physical background: the rebuilt town with its tea-gardens and its hospital, its neon lights and its museum of atomic monstrosities. And there is the emotional background of protest: a protest unspoken and unheard except in a kind of interior duologue which accompanies the opening love-scene, the woman's voice recalling the aftermath of the explosion, the man's voice denying that an outsider can grasp the enormity of the event. No, he repeats as the appalling newsreel shots illustrate her reflections; no, you have seen nothing, you have understood nothing.

This, one thinks, is going to be a film about the Bomb: a good, humane, brave, unshrinking film about the Bomb. It is some little while before one realizes that the destruction of Hiroshima is to be used not as the main argument but as a symbol of inhumanity. One of two correlated symbols. The other is the experience of the Frenchwoman during the last winter of the war, and at the hands not of the enemy but of her own countrymen, even her own family.

The experience in France, like the experience in Japan, is real enough. It comes to the surface at first in a brutal, momentary fragment from the past interpolated without explanation in the present; then as a series of scenes, mutilated, mysterious, disordered, following one another in a quickening rush until the whole story is out. The piecemeal narrative makes the revelation painfully exciting. Alain Resnais and Marguerite Duras have used the flashback precisely as memory uses it: the mind recognizing an association between an image in the present and an incident long ago, then swerving back to now; the past re-offering itself not in chronological order but higgledy piggledy. An obvious way, one might say, with the flashback. But then the best stylistic inventions often seem obvious after somebody else has invented them.

It is not only the past which in the film is shown in fragments. The present, too, from the morning when first we see the man and the woman lying in an embrace to the dawn of the next day when she is due to leave Hiroshima, is a succession of scenes chronological, certainly, but without conventional links. The pair talk, their confidences are exchanged, in snatches, in dramatic bursts, against settings their movement between which is taken for granted. And yet the narrative – in spite of what is perhaps too marked a change of pace after the woman's story is out – presses forward in an extraordinary dramatic unity.

The lovers do indeed talk and talk; and when, a few months ago in Paris, I first saw the film I wondered how it could without loss be transplanted to England. The translation works. The subtitles are explanatory but not overwhelming; in the difficult opening scene the woman's voice has been satisfactorily dubbed by Moira Lister. There is always the delicate music (by Giovanni Fusco and Georges Delerue) with its suggestions of passion, alarm, tragedy. And there is always the astounding contribution of the two leading players: the Japanese Eiji Okada with his stillness, his tenderness and his urgent, protective questioning; and, as the Frenchwoman, Emmanuelle Riva, making her first appearance in a film. The happy face turning haggard as memory strikes; the voice distractedly identifying today's lover with the lover of years ago – it seems not so much a performance as the acceptance of an experience.

As I say, a savage experience; but not a savage film. For all

its reminders of cruelty and callousness, *Hiroshima Mon Amour*
is full of pity; and this complex work sends one away reflecting
that hatred is a kind of murder. To hate, it implies, is always
wrong. One must not hate an enemy: nor even a friend.

January 1960

1961: September. Read reports from Venice Festival of enigmatic
new film, directed by Alain Resnais from script by Alain Robbe-
Grillet, which makes *Hiroshima, Mon Amour* look old-world if
not winsome. Criteria of film-making overthrown, everyone in
an uproar, and it wins the Grand Prix.

October. Embark on preparatory course of Robbe-Grillet. Sit
up nightly over *La Jalousie*. Transfixed; why didn't somebody
tell me?

November. Watch television programme introduced by
Derek Prouse and including flashes from enigmatic new film,
directed by etc. When is the damn thing coming to London?

December. Sudden appearance *passim* of articles about enigmatic new film, etc. Determined to preserve element of surprise
so don't read articles, but am half-demented with expectation.
Shall I nip over to Paris where film is running?

Christmas. Harold Hobson, back from one of his Paris forays,
presents me with Robbe-Grillet's published script of enigmatic
new, etc. After battle with curiosity, stick to decision not to read
before seeing film.

1962: January 1. Everybody still writing articles about
enigmatic, etc. Pallid with frustration.

January 25. Admitted to private preview. Hallelujah, it's
superb. But enigmatic? Perfectly clear to me.

February 6. Attend second preview. This time completely
floored. Rush home and read script, no help at all.

February 18. Derek Prouse in fine interview in the *Sunday
Times* reveals that Resnais and Robbe-Grillet disagree on
interpretation of their own work.

February 19. Attend Press show. What do I care what this
audacious and lovely film means?

So now it is here: **Last Year in Marienbad**, directed, as I keep
on saying, by Alain Resnais from a script (now available in
Richard Howard's translation, published by John Calder) by

Alain Robbe-Grillet. At the start let me point to three exquisite performances – by Delphine Seyrig, Giorgio Albertazzi and Sacha Pitoëff (the odd man out); to the dazzling photography of Sacha Vierny; to the editing of Henri Colpi; and to the brilliant use of the Bavarian backgrounds of Nymphenburg and Schleissheim. That done, probably the most useful way I can begin is by saying how the film itself begins. It begins with a murmur which, if I may allow myself an ambiguity not, I think, inappropriate to the occasion, is also a silence and a speech.

A man's voice, level, grave, is describing a progress through an enormous, impersonal hotel. Now you hear it distinctly, now some effect of confused or fading sound reduces it to a faint, whispering accompaniment to the cold, rich images over which the camera meanwhile glides: empty corridors with cross-corridors, arches with solemn mouldings, halls with candelabra, scrolled ironwork, baroque sculpture. But it repeats itself: that you can distinguish.

And the images are repeated: at first, while the hotel displays a crowd of elegant, expressionless residents, with deliberation; presently, as the tempo quickens, in savage stabs.

But especially the words echo: the urgent, the imploring or the denying sentences which soon, in snatches of overheard talk – or overheard thought – break into the stillness of the interiors. The descriptive introduction leads into a view of a remote, frozen theatrical performance; later, in the final scenes of the film, we shall be reminded of the phrases spoken on the stage. Everything turns in on itself, and time, in this love-story, is a circle. That is why at a first look I thought the film simple to understand; all, I said, is explained if you accept it as a fantasy of after-life, a reunion of the dead.

Of course I was wrong. But love-story: that was right. For soon the voice heard at the start attaches itself to a character, the suppliant who obstinately reminds the beautiful, reluctant girl of an encounter and a promise, last year in Marienbad. At first she refuses to admit recall. Can he induce her to remember, to fulfil the promise, to leave the dark wraith of a man who watches her, who haunts the glacial rooms, who endlessly plays a game with match-sticks? Is there in fact anything to recall, or is last year's encounter an invention, perhaps no more than a shadow in the imagination?

I say: at first she refuses to recall. You may say there is no first and no last in a film where every phrase seems the echo of an earlier phrase, every image the reflection of an original; where there is no past, where everything takes place now, in the present, at the selfsame moment. One is aware, though, of extraordinary tension: the sense of imprisonment and the sense of fear; the visions of violence – a rape, a murder, a suicide; the significant passages of half-release, gay or desperate, in the geometrically-planned garden and the park with its ornamental waters; the vague terrors which invest the idea of deciding on complete escape.

Yet the visions of violence are merely the imaginary terrors we all in anxiety conjure up for ourselves. Even the tiny incidents – a shattered glass, a heel broken by the gravel of a path – seem remote; they are accompanied, more often than not, by dialogue about something quite different: just as during a conversation, any conversation, one's thoughts may wander. For with the freedom of thought the characters are transported instantly back and forth in the field of time in which the film exists: not only with the freedom of thought but actually by thought. Thinking, remembering, they become for a scene or a fraction of a second what they think or remember, wearing the clothes, speaking the words, tracing the gestures which live in their minds. *Last Year in Marienbad* in fact takes a long stage further the experiments with memory, the telescoping or even the annihilation of time, which astonished us in *Hiroshima, Mon Amour*.

Yet to talk of experiments is to imply an artifice and a coldness as alien to the new film as they were to the old. I called *Marienbad* a love-story. It should rather be called a love-film; and to try to tell its story is as misguided as to argue about what happened to the lost girl in *L'Avventura*. Whether love happened, or was remembered, or was imagined is beside the point. What is important is that the labyrinths of love have been explored, and that one accepts the adventure as one accepts an obscure but splendid poem.

February 1962

First, the facts. The director is Luchino Visconti, aristocrat by birth, revolutionary by artistic inclination; celebrated producer of theatre and opera, inspirer and devotee of the great Callas. ('Callas,' he said coldly on my once venturing to remark that when I heard her she was not in good voice, 'is *always* in good voice.') The film is **Rocco and His Brothers**: cause of uproar at last year's Venice Festival, where the jury bizarrely preferred to acclaim Cayatte's *Le Passage du Rhin*; cause of more uproar in the field of censorship, and particularly Italian censorship, which abbreviated two passages; now to be seen in a version trimmed a shade further. Of course one regrets the cuts. But the effect is still thunderous.

The two scenes which have frightened the censors concern the first a rape and the second a murder: both vital to the film both marking a stage in the life and downfall of one of the chief characters. The story is of a peasant family from the impoverished South of Italy who come to the North in search of work and a better life. There are five brothers in the family: one (played by Spiros Focas) already settled in Milan, four who, their eyes turning to catch the miracles of the city, bundle out of the train with their widowed mother at the huge, indifferent railway station.

Let me say here that the scene of their arrival is a little masterpiece; and that Milan comes alive on the screen: a masculine city. It is Visconti's birthplace and family home; he knows the cafés, the tall apartment blocks, the roads under snow or rain, the sightseers at the cathedral and the haunters of the back-street boxing-ring.

Superficially the film is divided into five episodes, each with the name of one of the boys. But the episodes interlock to create an organic whole: the destiny of simple beings in a complex and corrupting society.

It is also a hostile society. The Northerners despise what they regard as the fecklessness and ignorance of the Southerners: the emphasis on the division of Italy is important to Visconti, important in the film. The youngest of the boys – he is still a child – may one day see a better life; Visconti leaves us with a muted phrase of hope for the regeneration of the South, perhaps even the regeneration of the world: the political note does not obtrude, but it is there. The elder boys are absorbed into the city – become boxers or mechanics, marry, have children; adapt themselves to it or suffer from it; one of them, Simone, is destroyed by it. And he it is, not the saintly Rocco – a character so bent on forgiveness that he sacrifices others as well as himself – who emerges as central to the film.

Rocco and his Brothers has some splendid playing; Katina Paxinou (the mother) and Annie Girardot (the prostitute) would stand out in any company; and one might be tempted to say that it is the superb performance or Renato Salvatori which brings the figure of Simone into relief. One may remember the finely modelled, harrowed features of Rocco (Alain Delon); one is pursued by the look of Renato Salvatori, at first naïve, with both the slyness and the mulishness of a young Mediterranean peasant: then in turn bewildered, obstinate, furious; at last debased and terrified.

But there is much more than a performance to consider. The disintegration of a nature not strongly enough based to withstand the brutality of the boxing *milieu* or the moral squalors of a great city – it is a variation on a theme essential to Visconti's view of society. The stories of all the other brothers are attendant on the tragic failure of Simone.

The film is not a sequel to *La Terra Trema*, the first part of Visconti's unfinished trilogy of Sicilian life. Its characters are not Sicilians; they come from a different place and a different life. All the same the later work begins where the earlier left off. The desperation of poverty, in *La Terra Trema*, is driving men northwards, away from the land and the sea; this, says *Rocco and His Brothers*, is what may await them.

But in the twelve years which separate the two films Visconti's work has been deeply affected by his experience in theatre and opera. The remote, austere friezes of figures against the Sicilian landscape are replaced by enormous, dramatically composed, savagely shifting groups. There are fierce effects of chiaroscuro – for instance in the scene in the homosexual's opulent house, and in the terrible, magnificently directed passage (now, as I say, abbreviated, but still terrible) in which Rocco is forced to watch the rape of the former prostitute by his brother. And the leading characters advance towering to fill the foreground, to perform their solos and duets against the complex of background figures in gymnasium or bar-room or factory-yard. Only once does the projection of emotion run out of control – in the murder confession, where the family lamentations, though true enough, I realize, to life, seem to me out of proportion, out of true, in the cinema.

It is here that, for showing in this country, the film has been slightly trimmed, and I can see why – though naturally the man to do any trimming ought to have been Visconti himself. As for the violence which from time to time invades the film, it belongs to the characters, to the South, to the conflict between North and

South; and its explosions here are part of Visconti's protest against humanity's organisation of its own affairs. It is scarifying, but it is never false. And *Rocco* joins the band of films which, these last months, have given one new hope for the cinema.

September 1961

Colour in the cinema, once a source of anguish and a longing for dark glasses, has become a positive pleasure. It gives the landscape of the Western a fresh glow of life. Visconti uses it to enrich interiors already splendid and to bathe in golden light the Sicilian fields of *The Leopard* (I speak of the original colour, not the version shown in this country). In *Une Vie*, Astrue and Claude Renoir can create exquisite designs with girls in long fluttering dresses running towards a peacock sea. And Jacques Demy, planning in collaboration with designer and cameraman the hangings and the wallpapers of *Les Parapluies de Cherbourg*, can cast a spell of cyclamen, olive, rose, purple, coral.

All the same, watching Michelangelo Antonioni's **The Red Desert**, I felt that I had never before seen colour in a film.

At the start, the impression of looking at reality. The wet glistening road running beside the factory, the plumes of smoke, the girders and the pipelines, the stains of rust on concrete – it was as if for the first time in the cinema one saw the colours of steel and stone. Threatening in the cold misty light, the huge industrial structures which envelop the characters of the story begin by seeming uncompromisingly true: beautiful facts, but still facts. Not for long. Soon, just as the inhuman cries of machinery resolve themselves into electronic voices, the colours of the urban images become the colours not of reality but of poetry: an abstract of reality.

Antonioni, in what is his first departure from black and white, attacks the problem in a new way. Colour, he says – as he talks his watchful, withdrawn, rather severe face is illumined by passionate conviction – is not invariable; it can change with weather, light, the time of day, it can change with one's psychological attitude. It follows, then, that this director needs to make his won colour; that he must use his settings as if they were canvases. And so he does. He paints on them; for the scene in which the central character, vaguely attempting escape from her neuroses, plans to open a shop he paints a whole street, houses, ground, everything, in washes of grey and fawn. Ruefully he told me of one location shot in which a wood behind an industrial complex contradicted the urban effect he wanted. Nature must be somehow subdued; he had the trees painted white so as to fade out behind the man-made scene. But when the time came to shoot, the sun stood behind the wood; the perverse branches came out black; and a new location had to be found.

Naturally he is constantly disturbed by inability to control absolutely, as a pinter can control, the shades he employs. For colour to him is not a decoration or an emphasis on reality. Most coloured films one can imagine in black and white. Not *The Red Desert*: here the film is colour, colour is the film. Why 'red'? I asked. The factory yard blotted out by an explosion of smoke, the canal mottled with an oily discharge, the ship silently berthing in the mist to hoist the quarantine flag: this is a desert place, obscure, secret. 'I had thought of it,' said Antonioni, 'as something made by men, made with human blood.' And indeed the contributions of nature, trees, grass, flowers, have been almost erased, and the heroine is immured in a man-made worlds where even in the nursery a clicking electric toy, like some infant Cyclops, watches all night with remorseless eye, and the child's spinning-top is used to demonstrate the principle of the gyroscope.

To Antonioni himself it is not a desert. To him the man-made world is alive and full of promise: more alive, more exciting than the world of nature. But while the film reflects his feeling for the beauty and the vitality of the industrial and scientific complex, it still looks at life through the eyes of the central character; and to her everything is hostile. *The Red Desert* is a study of a woman who cannot adapt herself to the modern world of machines, of scientific progress. She exists in a state of nervous crisis which at its extreme has driven her to attempt suicide. Feeling that she is standing on quicksands, she looks frantically for stability, but is incapable of providing it herself; so that in all her human relationships she wants instead of giving to be given love and support. She imagines a safe solitude, a bay of bright sea, bright sand, everything, as she puts it, singing – and as she describes her dream the colour on the screen turns from steely greys and stony browns to sea-blues and fawn-pinks and the soft purple of the Mediterranean horizon. For a moment the perplexing questions of human endeavour have been excluded from paradise.

Antonioni is far from the cold intellectual creator he has

sometimes been made out; as you talk to him you can feel not only his involvement with his medium but his anxiety for his characters. He works, he says, not intellectually but instinctively: and often incidents in the film, while they reject rational explanation, seem essential to the mood, perhaps to something beneath the surface of narrative. The white-sailed ship seen from the bay – a symbol? a chance detail turned, by that instinctive gift, to account? It doesn't matter; the mysterious visitor strengthens the sense of dream; one accepts the image, just as one accepts Antonioni's way of telling his story: episodes following one another without links, without explanation, without the dissolves, the technical effects which conventionally indicate the passage of time.

I asked him why, as in *L'Avventura* and *La Notte* and *The Eclipse*, the character who carries the emotional burden of the film was again a woman: did he regard women as especially sensitive to today's crises? No, no, he said: he had lived among families of women, he might say he knew a good deal about women, but his next film – and he had five themes in his head – might be about a man. Meanwhile in *The Red Desert* it is on Monica Vitti that the emphasis of the acting once more falls. As the man to whom the woman turns vainly for help Richard Harris makes a negative impression: it is a grave failure in the film. From Carlo Chionetti there is a sympathetic, slight sketch of the husband who is at home in the age of electronics. But Monica Vitti – uncontrolled hysterical gestures, tiny involuntary muted cries, the face, the body suddenly shrinking into despair – touchingly portrays a creature defenceless against the pitiless new worlds; this is the real breakdown, the fragmentation of the human being.

One should not, perhaps, speak of the film as having, in the usual sense of the word, a story. *The Red Desert* is about not so much what happens as what is. And what is – the huge pressure of the new world on the individual – Antonioni observes with solicitude but without sentimentality, without pessimism. He is on the side of progress, the pylons, the great steel towers, the perilous drive towards the unknown. In him the cinema finds the romantic poet of the anti-romantic.

April 1965

11   THE DARKER SIDE

During the 1970s a younger generation of readers came to believe that Dilys Powell's evident distaste for certain aspects of the cinema of that period, in particular a less restrained attitude to violence on the screen was evidence of a hardening of the critical arteries. In retrospect this was far from being the case, since Powell's espousal of liberal humanism had led her to deplore certain kinds of cinema long before the 1970s. And it should not be forgotten that she had been a champion on behalf of the publication of *Lady Chatterley's Lover* by Penguin Books in 1960. We may dissent from her judgement on Michael Powell's *Peeping Tom* and consider that the final sentence in her review of Sam Peckinpah's *Straw Dogs* to be overstating the case ('For the first time in my life I felt concern for the future of the cinema'), but that is not to doubt the sincerity or the consistency of her critical position.

Murder on the contemporary screen comes in a variety of sizes and styles, the biggest and the most gallant being, of course, the American. American murder goes bang bang, with the door flung suddenly open, the figures in fedoras nipping for cover, the hand sliding down the bedpost to dangle, dead. (There is plenty of this kind in *The Killers*.) A frequent variant these days is the killing, preferably paranoiac, with psychoanalytical effects – always good for a bit of class: the trail neatly laid to incriminate some darling innocent, the bland cunning murderer, the dreams and symbols. (See *Spellbound*, or see this week *The Dark Mirror*.) Or, of course, there is murder with a laugh, murder with a song, murder with cabaret even; but all big, all splendid. It is only when Hollywood comes to give us an English murder that we get dingy crime. Homicide in England, apparently, is like the climate, damp and dim. In *The Verdict*, as a tribute, no doubt, to English reserve, we don't even get a glimpse of the corpse – which in any case would be scarcely visible through the prevalent floor-mist.

The Verdict (after Israel Zangwill) pays its tribute also to English justice, shown hanging one innocent man and nearly hanging another; one recalls, of course, a similar mishap with American justice in *Scarlet Street*. But it is rare for the cinema to advertise the possibility of so capital a slip, and *Scarlet Street* was received with some reserve in America; and it now strikes me that the reluctance to draw any attention to the showing in this country of *Strange Incident* may have been partly due to the fact that the film ended with the hanging of three men for a crime they did not commit. But whatever the fate of the innocent, on the screen the guilty at least never escape; the very best a murderer can hope for is to go mad in the snow.

Nothing as romantic as this, however, happens to the admirable performers of *The Verdict*, Sydney Greenstreet, Peter Lorre and Joan Lorring among them. But the film, like the rest of the week's programme, raises the whole question of morality in the cinema. In *The Verdict* the emphasis is on murder. In *The Dark Mirror* the emphasis is on murder and madness. In *The Killers* the emphasis is on murder and cold brutality. Isn't this perhaps overdoing it a little? Are there no other subjects? On the surface, it is quite true, all is neatly tied up in moral convention: killers get killed, in the end justice prevails. But there is something more than surface morality to a film; there is an attitude of mind, there is or should be a sensibility to the undertones of morality.

Take *The Killers*, a story of gangsters, revenge and a double-cross too elaborate to be recounted here, the whole starting from a short story by Ernest Hemingway. The opening sequence, indeed, is almost a reproduction of the story as I remember it: the quiet snackbar, the steely insolence of the killers, the abortive hold-up; and from the story some touch of pity and horror has crept into the sharp, finely times picture of action. But from this point the film rockets away into a superficial narrative of violence. A man without known connections or background is murdered: the agent from the insurance company, investigating, finds out scrap by scrap the story of the dead man's life and the reason for his death. The broken boxer falling into bad company; the flashy conscienceless beauty who enslaves him; the prison sentence, the falling out of thieves, and at the last the piles of dead: bodies in hospitals, bodies in bars, bodies on stairways – never anything beyond the facts of brutality, never any attempt to look beneath for the true pitiful springs of action.

Perhaps the reply of the American cinema to the charge of violence without genuine motive would be the current smattering of psychiatry; as, for example, in *The Dark Mirror*, with Olivia de Havilland playing twin sisters, one guilty of murder, the other providing her with an alibi, and Lew Ayres industriously working away at separating innocence from paranoia with word-association, ink-blobs, and lie-detectors. Miss de Havilland, by the way, gives one of her controlled pretty performances, though in the last reel, when the final unmasking calls for a display of madness, she is perhaps playing out of her own league; the small neat features do their best, but all they can crumple into is a refined girl's look of distaste for an unemptied ashtray. For the rest, the piece has its conventional excitements; but we need not, I fancy, take its psychology very seriously; and all the casebook hints are no more than the excuse for another murder film.

I shall, I hope, not be taken to imply a general condemnation of the thriller, the story of murder or the gangster film. We have these past few years, seen brilliant and beautiful examples of the film of violence: *The Maltese Falcon*, *Farewell, My Lovely*, *The Spiral Staircase*. But *The Maltese Falcon* had curious and bizarre flashes of character as well as an imaginative direction which subtly underlined the emotional references of the story. *Farewell, My Lovely* by lighting, camerawork, the rhythm of visual composition gave a kind of poetry to the tawdry background of crime. And *The Spiral Staircase*, partly through the exquisite playing of Dorothy McGuire, partly through the ornate beauty of the décor, and partly through a daringly subjective form of narrative, imparted pity as well as terror to madness and murder. It may be noticed that Robert Siodmak, who directed this film, made also *The Dark Mirror* and *The Killers*. Hollywood lives on repetition and imitation; a director, having made a good film in a certain mode, is expected to do the same trick again and again. Perhaps the present superfluity of films of violence is no more than another case of repetition. But it is a dangerous repetition, since it affords a handle against the cinema to those mistaken critics who, blind to the rare potentialities of the screen, see on it nothing but the obvious follies and crudities.

I had almost forgotten to say that *The Killers* is competently acted by a cast including a new player, Burt Lancaster, as the central figure, Albert Dekker as the heavy, and Edmond O'Brien as the persistent investigator.

February 1946

It is, I suppose, three or four years since the wave of manliness which now engulfs the cinema began roaring over from America. At the beginning, like landlubbers unused to gale warnings, we did not recognize the signs. In the films of the first twelve months after the war manliness was apt to be confused, sometimes with amnesia, sometimes with what the cultured giants of the screen like to call amour; the new men of the early post-war period demonstrated virility by clipping their sweethearts one over the earhole, or, more simply still, by failing to remember whether or not they had committed a murder.

As time went by, however, amnesia, schizophrenia and the rest of the psychological decorations were discarded. Forgotten were the arts of love and the casebook; Ovid joined Freud (or possible

Krafft-Ebing) in the dustbin; and the cinema, drumming on its chest, came out with 'Brute Force'. Since that day the spread of manliness has been terrific, both on and off the screen; and manliest of all among the spectators have been the intellectuals, who by now can scarcely bear to look at a film unless at least one character in it is beaten to death.

The absence from **Knock On Any Door** of outstanding brutalities may, indeed, prevent the piece from winning the prestige enjoyed by less accomplished work; here we have no more than a scrimmage or two, some violence in the reformatory, a suicide, a murder and a last backward look from the criminal on his way to the electric chair. And here, too, the general manliness of the theme is overlaid by a good deal of democracy and moral sentiment in the handling; if Pretty Boy Romano did in fact murder a policeman, argues his lawyer (excellently played by Humphrey Bogart), that wasn't his fault; it was the fault of society.

One is sometimes tempted to protest that if society is to be held responsible for the goings-on of the gangster, society must be allowed also take the credit for that section of the public, a minority no doubt, which rejects the life of crime. But let that pass; *Knock On Any Door*, whatever the banality of its message, is an accomplished film; its direction, by Nicholas Ray, has both sensibility and force, the acting of John Derek (as the slum boy), and of a number of secondary players is to be admired, and the detail in many scenes – in, for instance, the judge's chambers at the court-room – is memorable. At the same time the piece is not in the same class with the same director's *They Live By Night*, nor with some of the strictly manly films we have seen lately; to give an example, *The Set-Up*, justly praised the other week by my friend and colleague Cyril Ray, is much superior in its character-drawing and its social observation.

The truth, I fear, is that the best talent of the American screen is at present going into the cinema of savagery: a fact which has not escaped the critics in France, where the 'black' films of Hollywood are greatly admired. In Paris a week ago people were urging one another to visit *Champion*, an American boxing piece admired here too, though overshadowed by *The Set-Up*. Always eager to march with the times, however manly, on my return from holiday I went to see these two stories of the ring. Both imply criticism of a system or of a society; both attack the corruption of the boxing ring, and *The Set-Up* draws a magnificent and horrifying picture of a blood-thirsty audience. I still cannot help thinking that films presenting physical brutality in such intimate detail must tend to debase rather than deter.

July 1949

Focus puller: not, as you might suppose, one of the tax-dodging types being got at in the Budget, but a useful and indeed indispensable member of a film studio camera crew. Anyway the hero, or perhaps the villain, of **Peeping Tom** (director: Michael Powell) is a focus puller; and the job is getting him down. Every now and then he pulls a knife (confusing it, no doubt, with the focus). I know I don't usually tell the story, but I will make an exception of this horror.

Focus and pocus pulling, or at any rate photography, runs in the young man's family. When not in the film studio our cameraman (Carl Boehm) is sitting in his private studio, running though the film his father, an authority on nerves and a dab at torture, made of him as a child: little boy climbing fence to spy on Park lovers; little boy woken by bright light deliberately flashed in his eyes; little boy terrified by lizard planted on his bed; little boy forced to inspect death-bed of mother, to observe mother's hasty successor, to turn on her a camera presented by father (a player in whom one discovers, dimly since the focus has intentionally not been pulled, the director Michael Powell himself; the child, I am told, is his own son).

Grown up, the son has no subject for nervous vivisection handy, but one can be made. The idea is to film someone in the process of being murdered. To do that you need to murder someone. More than one person, really. There's many a slip: maddening, after going through all that bother to find later on that the light had failed or something, just as the victim was tripping backwards into the open trunk.

Still, the special equipment works a treat: the camera tripod-leg with the cap which conceals the knife, the distorting mirror in which the victim sees her own panic. And everybody is most obliging. The ambitious stand-in (Moira Shearer), presenting herself in the deserted studio for her secret test, executes a jolly dance to fill in the time before her throat is slit; nobody observes the lights burning on the set. The girl upstairs (talented Anna Massey) never notices the focus puller is as crazy as a peewit: the only character possibly crazier being the visiting psychiatrist.

Perhaps one would not be so disagreeably affected by this exercise in the lower regions of the psychopathic were it handled in a more bluntly debased fashion. One does not, after all, waste much indignation on the Draculas and Mummies and Stranglers of the last few years; the tongue-chopping and blood-sucking, disgusting as they may be, can often be dismissed as risible. *Peeping Tom* is another matter. It is made by a director of skill and sensibility: the director whose daring and inquiring eye gave us the superb *camera obscura* sequence and the entry into the operating room in *A Matter of Life and Death*.

The same stylist's view it is which now and then makes the torturer's stuff of the new film look like the true imaginative thing, the Edgar Allan Poe horror, instead of the vulgar squalor it really is. The dark-room with its mysterious ticking machines, the film set barred in by lights like flaming swords, the murderer silhouetted against the screen on which the voiceless face of his victim yells, the dreadful grey little film of the scared child set in the lurid night colours of the photographer's studio: after paying due tribute to the camerawork of Otto Heller, one still recognizes the director's old delighted intentness on curious detail, the old triumphant capture of the fearful moment.

Then one remembers that even in his best period Michael Powell would suddenly devote his gifts to a story about a maniac who poured glue over girls' hair. He has got beyond glue here. He has got to the trick knife lovingly embedded in the throat, to the voyeur with sound effects, to a nauseating emphasis on the preliminaries and the practice of sadism – and I mean sadism. He did not write *Peeping Tom*; but he cannot wash his hands of responsibility for this essentially vicious film.

April 1960

'Last night I saw the ultimate film . . . it is the essence of all great comedy, combined in a single motion picture!'
(PETER SELLERS)

Dear Peter:
I was both surprised and pleased, before I saw **The Producers**,

to read your commendation in the advertisements. Surprised because it was the most enthusiastic reaction I had encountered to any film since a colleague of mine ecstatically found Betty Grable endowed with (I quote from memory, but I think I have it right) the most huggable and pinchable feminine appendages he had ever dreamed of. Pleased because I was happy that you should have had such a smashing time – and because our old friendship and my admiration for your work encouraged me to hope that I should share in the ecstasy.

Anyhow you were not alone in enthusiasm. The film had won its author and director, Mel Brooks, an Oscar for the best original screenplay (it was his first shot at writing and directing a feature film); and lest anybody should ask who is Mel Brooks anyway I was glad to be reminded that he conceived and narrated what to me is one of the funniest cartoons ever made, Pintoff's *The Critic* (another Oscar-winner). All this and Zero Mostel too – you will understand with what urgency I scurried off to the Prince Charles Theatre.

But now I have to explain why my pleasure in your remarks was short-lived.

The Producers is about the New York theatre. A down-at-heels producer (Zero Mostel) who retains only his ability to charm money out of frolicsome old ladies discovers from a chance remark by an accountant (Gene Wilder) what he believes to be a cast-iron way of making a fortune: raise a large sum, put on a show guaranteed to flop after the first act and pocket what is left of the dough. He is lucky enough to find an imbecile script in praise of Hitler by a lunatic unreformed Nazi who goes about, hissing, in a storm-trooper's helmet. He hires a semi-nude Swedish secretary ('Ve make loff now?'), a hippy called LSD to play Hitler, and a director (male) who wears a decolleté evening dress and has a jealous bearded assistant in tight-fitting black and a long gold necklace. A parody of the theatre, then, a farce, a burlesque, an exercise in the zany.

And an exercise in the playing of farce, parody, burlesque. Now here I meet my first difficulty. I am sure Zero Mostel is a brilliant comedian. Everybody tells me so, and I recognize that what he does is done with unrivalled skill. My trouble is that he doesn't make me laugh. His face assumes expressions which may well roll many spectators in the aisles; not this one. I am sure Gene Wilder and all the other players are a perfect scream to somebody or other; with me after an initial weakness for Mr

Wilder gravity sets in. Can it be that the material is inauspicious? I must tot up the items in the laugh-in. There is the familiar joke about theatrical 'angels', the familiar joke about homosexuals, the familiar joke about hippies, the familiar joke about obliging secretaries, the familiar joke about Swedish sex and the familiar joke about theatrical directors who talk about art and turn out an idiotic musical. They are all, I agree, combined in a single motion picture. I still don't laugh.

But there is one new element, the Hitler-joke. The Hitler-play, designed to show that the Führer was a dear kind fellow, opens with a number ('Spring-time for Hitler and Germany') performed by a chorus in a jack-booted musical-comedy version of Nazi uniform. And now I really don't laugh. The scene turns the stomachs of the audience on the screen, but only until they smell a take-off; it goes on turning mine. I stopped long ago finding jokes about hippies amusing. Jokes about Hitler I have never thought funny.

To laugh or not to laugh – the 'essence of all great comedy' is, I know, a matter of opinion, and I admit that when I saw the film two people in the row behind me were laughing fit to bust. Nevertheless I wonder whether American comedy as exemplified in *The Producers* isn't perhaps setting off in a direction a bit private, a bit inhospitable to British critics. Am I at any rate out of step or out of laugh with the American public, the Oscar-givers, Mel Brooks, Zero Mostel, Gene Wilder and even you?

Yes, I damn well am.

Yours, etc.

October 1969

Reluctantly I begin with **Straw Dogs**. I should prefer to forget it. But the central figure is played by Dustin Hoffman. The director is Sam Peckinpah, who is also co-screenwriter. The very title is chosen (from the Chinese) by Mr Peckinpah; man, it implies, is the equivalent of a sacrificial object, a straw dog, incapable of controlling his destiny or his behaviour. And the film was made in this country.

No, one can't ignore it.

Based on a novel by Gordon M. Williams, *Straw Dogs* is about a married couple living in a farmhouse outside a Cornish village. The husband (Mr Hoffman) is a small pacific American who has chosen this isolated spot in order to write a mathematical treatise. He has a blackboard with calculations in chalk and appears to know the difference between a plus and a minus sign but is otherwise slow on the uptake. The wife (Susan George) is a local girl previously well-known to the local boys. She has an interest also in mechanical mantraps, but for the rest shows the mental equipment of a hamster.

Even on the screen the union of these characters seems demented. But perhaps some kind of warning is intended; perhaps the film is an object lesson for innocent American mathematicians contemplating residence in Cornwall. Just to give an idea, there are adolescent girls who invite his dangerous embraces. There is a village drunk who if crossed will crush a pub glass in his bare hands. The locals never stop sniggering at the American and leering at his wife. There are, in fact, what in the cinema business are called dark forces at work. It is no surprise when one of the four lecherous types hired to rebuild the garage purloins the wife's panties and somebody hangs the cat.

Not that any of this melodramatic bosh greatly matters – and the director, to be honest, manages to give it quite a bit of a frisson. It is when we get to the *Straw Dogs* message that nausea sets in.

Some people found Mr Peckinpah's *The Wild Bunch* painfully violent. It was violent all right, but in the context of a Western and with the director's superb control of composition and movement it never struck me as offensive. *Straw Dogs* is different. After a particularly disgusting rape it arrives at a battle in which five repulsive drunks bent on breaking into the farmhouse and lynching the village idiot meet the American, his mildness now transmuted into an ecstasy of hideous slaughter. Feet are smashed, eyes are soused in flaming spirits, a man is thoughtfully battered to death; blood everywhere, corpses everywhere – and don't forget that mantrap. One might say that Mr Peckinpah was bringing the outside inside, translating the Sioux or the Apache massacre from the Western to an English living-room. But no redskin attack, no paleface revenge I ever saw on the screen was as mindlessly revolting. 'I hated violence,' the American says somewhere, 'long before it was fashionable to hate it.' But hatred of violence isn't fashionable. Films are making violence itself fashionable.

For the first time in my life I felt concern for the future of the cinema.

January 1972

Violence, Anthony Burgess implies in a coda to his novel, is a mark of adolescence; you may grow out of it. Violence, Stanley Kubrick maintains in the film which, with the omission of the coda, he has drawn from the novel, is persistent; governments find it comes in handy. Violence is everybody's topic nowadays.

One must not be conned by one's admiration into soft-soaping Mr Kubrick's film. *A Clockwork Orange* has passages savage to the point of nausea. It is far more savage than *Straw Dogs*. The violence is not Peckinpah's revolting mixture of realism and melodrama; it is cold, sometimes amused, sometimes delighted – amused or delighted by the appalling skill of its own portrayal. The film opens with menace. Nothing on the screen but the huge close-up of a face, illboding, the hair bunching from a wide bowler, the eyes, one of them fringed with false lashes, watching from under the downward tilt of the head. The camera draws back to show Alex (Malcolm McDowell), the teenage horror-hero and his bully-gang drinking themselves high on mild-and-dope in a futuristic café sexed up with tables in the shape of chalk-white rainbow-wigged nudes. Then we are off on an evening of ferocity – an assault on a tramp, a battle with a rival gang, a murderous drive in a stolen car, a horrible rape.

Merciless but not pointless. Without the horrors the counter-horror, the manipulation of the human mind, won't work. Come fresh to it without reading the book first, and *A Clockwork Orange* gives you from start to finish a frightening surprise. All the same it shows a logical development from Kubrick's earlier work. Young Alex kills, is jailed, and to escape from jail volunteers to undergo what turns out to be aversion treatment. Painfully he is turned off violence, turned off sex, turned off – but let's not give everything away. Let's say that the treatment gives a weapon not only to those authorities who plan to use him for political ends but to those individuals who want to revenge themselves on him. Malcolm McDowell's extraordinary performance slides with astonishing conviction from phase to phase; the pitiless delinquent becomes a pitiable automaton. And in the helplessness of the human creature caught in the trap of science one sees also the predicament of the innocents (comic innocents, but still) of *Dr Strangelove* and the riderless journey of the last cosmonaut in *2001: A Space Odyssey*. Kubrick is not an optimist about the human race.

Like the characters in *Dr Strangelove* the boy is a pawn. He is useful first to the Government, then to the Opposition, then, with fresh and cynical manipulation, to the Government again Kubrick has taken what is essentially a fable and strengthened his attack on the duplicity of politics. *A Clockwork Orange* becomes a satire, a kind of spiv's Modest Proposal. And when the satire is recognized as satire it is easy to accept other elements in the film.

Anthony Burgess, writing his novel as the personal narrative of the boy, invented for him a teenagers' slang, James Joyce only much, much easier. Kubrick drops most of the esoteric language. He omits a few though not many of the scenes of violence. Then he sharpens action.

No hanging on to the tail of movement; every scene snaps to an end at the exact moment when its usefulness is exhausted. The density of Mr Burgess' argot is replaced by a density of visual and aural detail; murder is committed with a giant white plastic phallus, a victim getting his own back (Patrick Magee in a masterly and terrifying display of vengefulness) speaks in a sudden shout which makes you start. The violence shows itself as fantasy violence, stylized, played out to the strict accompaniment of music which is sometimes classical and sometimes 1950s popular.

The cast is all you could hope for, and Kubrick handles his medium with a confidence almost insolent. For the rest – the flashes of farce, the variations on distance and distortion and dream-imagery – he has given us the most audacious of horror-films. And the most inhuman.

January 1972

Sometimes one is pursued by a film; I am pursued by Rainer Werner Fassbinder's **The Bitter Tears of Petra von Kant**. The first time I saw it I was obliged by some valid but forgettable reason to leave before the end. Naturally when it turned up during my visit to the Stratford, Ontario, Film Festival I seized the chance of seeing it right through. Now it has come to rest at the Gate Cinema in Notting Hill; I scurry after it again.

Not that I resent the third look. At first one is inclined to think that the deliberate postures, the calculated compositions in the enclosed set have little to do with what one used to call cinema: why not give one's time and space instead to the familiar excitements, say to the current horror story *It's Alive*? (which isn't half bad). But the screen changes and rejects the old rules; it must be allowed to choose its own way; helplessly one is trapped in the stifling room where Petra von Kant (Margit Carstensen) lives insulated against all worlds except her own. A fashionable dress-designer, she is slavishly attended by the silent Marlene (Irm Hermann) who in fact does the designing, runs errands, suffers abuse and watches from behind a screen of distance and darkness the passionate love from which she is now excluded.

For Petra, who has spoken contemptuously about her divorced husband and his physical approaches to her, now finds herself violently attached to Karin, a pretty, rather vulgar young model who presently treats her with equally callous contempt. And Fassbinder, who has several times concerned himself with the nature of masochism, in this lesbian sex-ballet shows the roles reversed; the tyrant becomes the victim, the object of love takes control, the slave of love packs her bags. As in Iris Mudoch's *A Severed Head*, there is no attempt at exterior realism. Petra, her psychological situation reflected in her exotic clothes, changes not only her wig and her dress but her very face from situation to situation; the Petra, physically attracted, offering the scheming Karin a job as model is a very different woman from the Petra agonizingly awaiting a telephone call from the ambitious self-seeking girl who has left her.

Emotion is thus translated into visual images, as its phases are symbolized by the frozen gestures of the huge dressmaker's dummies in the background and as its lesbianism is emphasized by the male figures of the mural which climbs above these quarrelling, accusing live figures. The mural, a friend from Stratford, Ontario, tells me, is Nicolas Poussin's *Midas and Bacchus* from Munich; and perhaps, as he suggests, it does indeed represent one of the contrasts in the film: money (for Petra is surrounded by scroungers) versus passion. Fassbinder's film is compounded of emotional contrasts; enslavement cynically confronts declarations of freedom. But finally there is a solution. For *The Bitter Tears of Petra von Kant* is about liberation. Petra is liberated from her desire to possess; and in liberating herself she liberates the silent Marlene. But masochism has no use for freedom. As Marlene leaves, taking with her the doll which is the image of Karin and thus of bondage, she completes the liberation of Petra; yet one is tempted to see her departure not as a move for freedom but rather as a rejection of the liberty which has been offered.

And by now I am beginning to feel a need for liberation myself.

Fassbinder's film has an extraordinary command. But after more than two hours I am glad to escape from the Poussin, from the dressmaker's dummies, from all the airless hothouse fantasies; for essentially this strange, prehensile piece is not a human study but an exercise, a means of confronting the abstract ideas of emotional tyranny and emotional abasement.

May 1975

12 OFFSCREEN

The inexorable deadline imposed by writing a weekly column rarely permitted Dilys Powell to write at length about the issues surrounding the cinema but away from the film screen. None the less Powell has written regularly about censorship, about the effects of technology on film aesthetics and the act of criticism. On all of these matters Powell's point of view is guided by common sense, and one can only admire the skill with which she weaves a discussion of general issues into a column which has the chief purpose of reviewing a week's new films. On reading a longer essay, say on the pleasures of a film festival, one cannot but regret that Dilys Powell has written so little at this length. On the other hand the final piece in this selection, 'And so to Bed', is a reminder of just what Powell could achieve in around a thousand words, deft and witty, but serious about the pleasures afforded by cinema. Never, however, ever solemn.

1 *Censorship*

Not long ago eight cinemas in the West End were showing films with an X certificate; American and European films were about equally represented in the list, and equally prohibited to anybody under sixteen years old. The cinema is the only form of art in which censorship in this country consistently distinguishes between what is permitted to an adult and what is permitted to his children. Nobody could have prevented you from taking your child to the theatre to see *A Streetcar Named Desire*; but although on its passage to the screen the piece has been slightly disinfected, you may not take him to see the film. It is worth considering what are the special difficulties which force the cinema into a censorship different in kind from that of the theatre.

We have no State censorship of films. The British Board of Film Censors was set up in 1912 at the request of the film industry itself; its purpose was to confer respectability on that vagabond the cinema and, as Rachael Low puts it in the third volume of her excellent *History of the British Film*, 'to protect the trade from harassing local variations in the definition of an "undesirable" film.' Local authorities had and still have the power to license public cinemas and say what may or may not be projected in them. After a long struggle the Board won general acceptance of its certificates. But a local authority can still reject a film passed by the Censor or give consent for the exhibition of one he has rejected. The Board has often been more liberal than the local authorities. But in trying to set a standard for the majority it has in the past neglected the needs of the minority.

The cinema is always open to moral attack: from the Churches, from magistrates, headmasters, parents and diehards of no particular occupation. Anybody who sees a little boy fighting in the street may blame the cinema, as if there had been no young ruffians before 1895.

There were at first two certificates: U films which children might not see unless taken by an adult; A films which children might not see unless taken by an adult; later a category was added from which children were excluded altogether: H for horrific. But children have a way of finding complaisant adults to take them to the cinema. And here comes the difference between screen and stage. Children don't go alone to the theatre; but by tradition they can go by themselves to the cinema; I myself remember, once I had got over an early revulsion from the screen, trotting off with a friend to some pieces which, if not exactly rare, were at any rate curious. As for the printed word, the book 'undesirable' for children is often just that: undesirable. I doubt whether any child would desire to wade through *From Here to Eternity*. The cinema is easier to understand, harder to forget, and far less boring.

Perhaps authority was right in trying to protect the young from certain kinds of cinema; my own experience insists that it was certainly right in trying to protect them from terror excited by cruelty on the screen. All very well to say that parents should decide which films their children are to see: how many parents have a look for themselves before taking the family? But, in protecting the young, authority did injustice to the rest of us. Adult films to which the H certificate was inappropriate could not be shown uncut lest some child should see them.

To remedy this injustice category X was introduced a year ago. The X certificate does, it is true, deny you the privilege of taking your little girl to see a young man in *Quo Vadis* being crucified and then set alight. On the other hand, without the X certificate you yourself would not be able to see *La Ronde*; you can't make this witty and elegant film suitable for infants by hacking bits out of it. And let nobody suppose that the new measure puts us out of step with the Continent. On the contrary: most European countries have their own form of X certificate. Holland, Belgium, Italy, Western Germany, the Scandinavian countries and France all control the films which children may see.

It is significant that people should complain when every film programme in London is not designed for audiences under sixteen years old. We don't (except at Christmas) order the stage for the benefit of children; but until the censorship adopted its present enlightened policy we did so order the screen. And then the high-and-mighties attack the cinema for being childish! It can be little else as long as we refuse to admit to it the adult subject and the adult comment. Now the Censor has made a first step towards allowing it in this country to become adult. The X certificate is, paradoxically, a relaxation of censorship, not a new restriction. I for one am thankful for it.

April 1952

During the Dark Ages from which we emerged just over a week ago some of us were privately shown an American film which has two points of especial interest: it is splendidly made, and it is in trouble with the censorship. The title is **The Wild One**; the director is Laslo Benedek, who made the film of *Death of a Salesman*; the star is Marlon Brando.

The Wild One is about a covey of adolescent hooligans (in this country I suppose they would be described in the repulsive phrase Teddy Boys) who after a motor-cycle rally come raring into a little town and break the place to pieces: fight, drink, wreck cars and shops, bait and manhandle harmless inhabitants and have a shot at rape. The local cop cowers in his office with a bottle of whisky, leaving the rougher of the citizens to organize their own beating-up party; they seize the invaders' leader, who, attracted by a local girl, has just saved her from his own followers; hideous brutality, an escape, a fatal accident, arrival of sheriff with reinforcements, dismissal of everybody with a caution, hint of leader's possible redemption, curtain.

One is left with blood still on the boil and ears still singing from the bellow of motor-cycles, and that in itself is, no doubt, a testimony to the efficiency of *The Wild One*. The film is, as I say, splendidly made: superb handling of the mob of vicious boys, brilliantly contrived tension as, to the accompaniment of the drumming engines, the temper of the gang rises and crowd insolence turns ugly. And Brando as the leader gives another extraordinary performance in the manner of *On the Waterfront*. This time he shows us a boy who, beginning as a dominator among his own kind, instead of winning sureness loses it, an adolescent whose surface of physical conceit is cracking.

Perhaps I should remind those less constantly splashing about in the shallows of the cinema than a newspaper critic that the powers of the screen censor were altered, in my opinion for the better, four years ago when the X certificate was introduced; no film bearing this certificate is supposed to be exhibited to anyone under the age of sixteen. It is a delightful illustration of the workings of British democracy that even so the censor's ruling need bind nobody. The censor is not a Government official. He is appointed in self-protection by the film industry; his opinions can be set aside, his certificates changed, by any local authority. *The Wild One* has been refused even an X certificate; in the view of the censor it should not be shown at all. But through the amiable offices of certain local authorities it is in fact being shown in several provincial cinemas, though not in London, where the LCC also has set its face against the film.

Unlike the Americans, the British have no censorship code, no list of rules to be followed. But when the Board of Film Censors impose an X certificate they usually do so in the belief that the film is likely, sometimes to corrupt or frighten, but just as often to shake a child's faith in authority or in the ability of its parents to protect. *The Wild One*, I assume, was thought likely to corrupt or incite to violence audiences of the very age which with the X certificate can scrape into the cinema. Much though I admire the intellectual fury with which the film is made (and the liberality of the local authorities who permit its exhibition), I am bound to say I think the Board was absolutely right.

Of course it is easy to claim, loftily, that one is opposed to censorship of all kinds. To uphold censorship is to mark oneself down a Podsnap. And yet to abandon it entirely is difficult. Would its opponents admit the public, for instance, to a hanging? Exclusion, after all, is a kind of censorship. And I cannot help feeling that the contemporary cinema, so easily attainable and understandable, so powerful to inform and persuade, is a different matter from, let us say, the work of Boccacio, which recently engaged the attention of censors of another kind. I have always opposed those who see in the screen in general a dangerous influence. But obviously there are films which at a particular time and in a particular setting can be dangerous. *The Wild One* with its exciting rhythm, its adolescent arrogance and the inventiveness of its destruction seems to me to be one of them.

All the same, I am glad to have seen it, and not only because of its skill or the interest of the censor's decision. Eighteen years ago a reforming film called *Dead End* made a stir; it was a story of city streets and neglected boys with no outlet for the violent impulses of youth. The Dead End boys of today are the unpunished mob of *The Wild One*: dangerous boys on motor-bicycles, drumming along the road with the savage intentness, and in something very like the uniform, of Hitler's young thugs. In brutality the American film, I am afraid, has already come of age.

May 1955

Uproars over screen censorship grow scarce. It felt quite like old times the other day when an East German film, *Operation Teutonic Sword* (which makes an attack on General Speidel) was refused a censor's certificate.

The workings of film censorship in this country are puzzling to the outsider. The British Board of Film Censors is not a Government body but an autonomous organization: protection against the inconveniences of conflicting local censorships, protection against the possible errancies of its own members. The Board's decisions are generally accepted. But any local authority may ignore them; and any local authority may issue its own licences.

So when *Operation Teutonic Sword* was refused a certificate by the Board the case was taken to the LCC. The Public Control Committee, in whose hands such matters normally lie, turned the film down; but on a final appeal to the whole Council a licence was granted (by one vote, 59 to 58). The film could then have been exhibited in the London area – and in Essex, where also local permission was won – had not the news that General Speidel was contemplating legal action produced a nervous hush in the proceedings.

The Board when rejecting *Operation Teutonic Sword* gave as reason that the film attacked a living person. The reported debate of the LCC however, showed that many members regarded the issue as political: and the ultimate decision to grant a licence no doubt came of a desire to resist any suspicion of political censorship. A very proper desire; and I hope I am right in thinking that in this country of the three types of film censorship, political, religious and moral, the first is nowadays not often exercised. Nor, I imagine, is the second. At any rate the one which attracts most attention is moral censorship; and in England morals mean sexual morals.

In this sphere the policy of the Board has become much more enlightened since the end of the war (and the introduction of new blood). One remembers, to take an example, how coarsely, eleven years ago, *Le Diable au Corps* was mutilated. But under a later regime such films as *Casque d'Or* and *La Ronde* were left almost, if not completely, untouched. The present Board has sanctioned the passionate and sardonic honesty of *Room at the Top*. And today a cinema can show, with an X certificate, a piece dealing pretty explicitly with homosexuality.

One or two interesting facts about our censorship have lately come my way. On nudism, for instance. Only a few years ago the cinema was forbidden to show the female body naked even above the waist (front elevation, I mean, and a White body; it was O.K. with African or Polynesian skins). Today full-length disclosure is possible with a little discretion, if I may so translate *cashe-sexe*; London screens are bursting with nudes, male and female.

Since the Board, rightly taking such displays of flesh to be anti-erotic, regularly gives them an A certificate, I was for some time at a loss to understand why Robert Dhéry's delightful revue *Femmes de Paris* was turned down altogether (it got its licence from the broadminded LCC). The reason I now discover, is that the nudes in *Femmes de Paris* were theatrical nudes. Documentary nudes, nudist camp nudes, are permitted. Theatrical nudes, except when they are what is called incidental, are out. You couldn't, I am afraid, call M. Dhéry's young ladies incidental. Purposeful is perhaps the word.

In a very different field, discussion is still going on about an American film dealing with capital punishment, *I Want to Live*, which is said to go into excruciating detail over the operation of the gas-chamber. On the other hand *Torero*, a Mexican account of the career of a famous bullfighter, has now, after minor excisions, been licensed. Films which include animals, by the way, are subject to special law: an Act of Parliament forbids the screen to show action involving cruelty to animals. Under this rule cuts, I am told, are frequently made. The result would often seem to be rather to keep cruelty out of sight than to prevent it. But for that the censor is not to blame.

Nowadays, of course, we are all against censorship; at any rate I don't think I know anybody who is prepared to declare himself in favour of it in principle. In practice a good many of us are inclined to make exceptions – though not where we ourselves are concerned. Censorship is always for the other guy; there are times when I hear myself talking most illiberally about raising the age for admittance to X films. And once you accept an age limit you accept the principle of censorship. Sometimes, though far less often than I used, I disagree with the decisions of the British Board of Film Censors. Yet we might be far worse off: throttled for instance, by a State-run organization (and what about political censorship then?). And I am haunted by the thought that if film censorship were abolished and the responsibility left to the exhibitor timidity might triumph. We might see nothing but Anna Neagle musicals.

March 1959

Censorship is an impossible job. Excise from a film passages which you consider harmful or unjustified and you have the critics growling; the adult public, they well say, ought to be allowed to choose for themselves. Leave everything in, and brickbats fly from members of the public worried about the moral effect not on themselves – they naturally are incorruptible – but on the child, or the adolescent, or the feeble-minded, anyway on somebody else.

The problem has been with us ever since, indeed long before, a British censor, faced with a scene in which a young and passionate couple were about to commit the indiscretion of getting into bed together, excised the view of them under the sheets and cut to a shot of a dormant fire suddenly and symbolically blazing up, then dying down, leaving the audience to wonder why somebody had, presumably, poured a can of paraffin on the coals.

Possibly the critics are partly responsible for the current uproar in which local authorities are using their right to reject the decisions of the British Board of Film Censors, a central body set up half a century ago to avoid the awkward differences of judgment between region and region which are now showing themselves. Three titles are especially relevant, *The Devils*, *Straw Dogs* and *A Clockwork Orange*. Nobody could deny that the third was disturbingly violent (though young audiences take it as farce and merely laugh); but the violence was the expression of ferocious satire, and few film critics complained. The other two, though both were made by men of exceptional talent, many of us found nauseating.

But – for now I must speak for myself – one was not asking for a ban on either of them. One was pointing to what seemed a contradiction on the part of a censorship which had not shrunk from the purging and mutilating and burning of *The Devils* or the raping and man-trapping of *Straw Dogs* but had flatly turned down a film, *Trash*, which to some of us (and censorship, after all, is a matter of opinion) seemed not only less objectionable but positively moral. We were, in fact – well some of us were – asking not for less but for more liberalism.

The trouble was, as it always has been, that people are curious about things which they are warned against; one critic who had written a scathing review found it used as an enticement. Of course they are curious also about what is forbidden. At Southend, one reads, the local council looks at all films with an X certificate; and the worthy councillors ban about one in every four of them. I should not be surprised if Southenders were to be seen streaming off to the cinema in some more permissive areas.

Probably most people feel that for children there should be some form of censorship – though if the question comes up I recall the occasion, long ago now, when I had incautiously agreed to talk about films to a group of quite young children. The fidgeting was deafening. Suddenly I thought that Hitchcock's *Blackmail* would serve to illustrate the point I was trying to make. 'They wanted to cut the bread with a knife,' I said clearly, 'with a KNIFE.' The class sprang to attention and I had no more trouble with them. Children may or may not always be as sensitive as is commonly supposed, and I have sometimes wondered whether the beautiful film of *The Railway Children* wasn't a shade too delicate for anybody under the age of fourteen. Meanwhile the X certificate is there to protect the young; and cutting bits out of X films, or banning them altogether, is hardly going to help a section of the public which isn't going to be allowed to see them anyway.

For now we come to the heart of the present controversy. The discontented local authorities and the people who are now demanding a Royal Commission on film censorship aren't protecting children; they long to protect you and me, and the danger is that we may find ourselves a great deal more strictly protected than we like. I confess that there are times when I should be quite glad to be protected against the insufferable tedium of some idiot sex film or the ferocities of Mr Ken Russell and Mr Sam Peckinpah. But then I have to go to see their works; you don't.

What about, for a change, blaming the public for their unbecoming tastes? And of course one should blame the film-makers, especially those most gifted (and both Mr Russell and Mr Peckinpah are superlatively gifted), for their failure to communicate their ideas without what in another medium would be called a literal translation. The cinema at the present time is, I believe, doing itself harm. But I cannot think that the remedy is more legal repression.

During his term of office as censor John Trevelyan, who retired last summer, came in for a good deal of criticism; but as far as I can remember it was nearly always criticism from those critics who felt (as indeed I occasionally felt) that he could afford to be more liberal.

He took it all with massive calm, patiently answered questions and complaints – and worked with a caution which brought results. Problems, I know, were simpler then before a new young generation found itself with the power to demand a new young freedom (freedom which, scorpion-like, runs the risk of stinging itself to death). It was the readiness of educated public opinion to accept more liberalism which was apt to be considered.

The producers of some serious but difficult film – a Genet, for example – might be urged to try it on the GLC; and at that period the GLC's film viewers were a very properly liberal lot indeed. If a GLC certificate for London was granted, some other liberal body would perhaps help; the Academy Cinema was usually ready to show the film; and if reputable critics reviewed it favourably, then after a reasonable interval it would get a certificate from the British Board of Film Censors. The public was being led: gently, but led. I hope that it is not too late, and that local authorities are not by now too much incensed, for a return to peace and reason.

The present Secretary of the Board, Stephen Murphy, came to the job at a particularly dangerous moment. He has had only a few months of it. I think he ought to be left alone to try again. Otherwise, I very much fear, it is back to that blazing grate and that paraffin.

March 1972

2 *Colour*

Colour, it may be said pretty safely by now, has emerged from the period when it was simply a new trick in the cinema: something for the groundlings. Only natural that its early appearances should have been greeted, by those who found the film an exciting new means of communication, with cold looks. Already once in its life the young artform had looked like out-growing its strength: when sound and dialogue came, twenty years ago to threaten the mobility of the camera, to restrict the rhythm and slow down the tempo of a medium which by rights is all rhythm and timing. And just as the purists in the cinema had shrunk from the new potentialities and new responsibilities of the talking film, so the admirers of monochrome shrank from the dangers and opportunities of colour. With justice – on the evidence of nearly every colour film in the period before the outbreak of the war. Loss in definition, loss in solidity, a kind of blurring in narrative values – the only thing colour had to offer at the start, it seemed, was expensive.

In the past seven or eight years things have changed. Changed first of all, technically. Colour is still expensive, but it is no longer necessarily hideous: it no longer substitutes, for the dramatic blacks and whites and greys of the monochrome film the illusion of an animated Neapolitan ice. Colour values have become more readily controllable; defining lines have grown sharper, the frame of the screen holds depth, perspective. In America this new technical command has been put to two chief purposes: the creation of a richer, slicker, noisier school of musical, and the elaboration of the film of action. Today, we have reached the point at which the American musical in black and white comes as a surprise.

If this were all that colour had to offer (though there is no denying that now and then a landscape in a Western, a passage of rhythmic colour in a musical, has its beauties) one might think the purists were right. But now and then in the past few years there has been something to consider beyond this best-seller stuff: there has been a *Henry V*, a *Western Approaches*, a *Blood and Sand*. Two of these examples come from Britain: for this country, handicapped though it has been by shortage of equipment and the general difficulties of war, has shown itself bolder in experiment than Hollywood. Colour has not been for spectacle: nobody can call *This Happy Breed* spectacular. I will admit that, personally, I found the tones in *This Happy Breed* in general too sweet and melting. Yet the fact remains that here was colour being used in a domestic subject, for the depiction of everyday human character; and that the narrative did not suffer in solidity.

I spoke a moment ago of *Western Approaches*: the first of the British semi-documentary films, in the class of *Target for To-night* and *Coastal Command*, to be made in colour. With *Western Approaches* the difficulties were infinitely greater. This time it was not a question of work in the studio (though studio work, of course, was involved); it was a question of catching and holding the endless and terrifying variety of the sea: the long, sullen, steely swell, the veils of spray, the primrose dawn. Faults there were but the feeling was there: Homer's wine-dark seas; a narrative and emotional effect had been created in colour which would not have been possible in black and white.

A narrative and emotional effect: that is the point. Up to now the tendency has been for colour to use the cinema: the moment must come, if the film is to survive as an art, for the cinema to use colour. When *Henry V* astonished the critics, it succeeded because, almost for the first time, colour had become an essential part of the narrative: the story was told, the characters were presented, in terms, not only of movement and dialogue, but of colour; colour gave edge to excitement, pointed contrast, accentuated rhythm. The dark Rembrandtesque tones of Olivier's face, turning his eyes as he thinks, deepened the mood of his great soliloquy in the camp at night. The brilliant blues and yellows and scarlets of the morning French army heightened the sense of relief from vigil, the sense of released action and fulfilled expectation. And all through this brilliant film the colour of the dresses against the soft neutral shades of the architectural background was so handled as to direct the spectator's attention; to guide his eye; in fact to narrate as the cinema should narrate. Some time ago, visiting the technicolour studios at Harmondsworth, I had the interesting experience of looking, in expert company, at a new print of the opening sequences with the scene in the Globe Theatre and the first entry of the player; and all at once a massing of colours which before had seemed to be merely pretty resolved itself into a deliberate dramatic plan in terms of colour.

Films in which colour and lighting in conjunction are beautiful as well as dramatic remain rare. One recalls the lovely El Greco-ish scenes beneath the crucifix in the matador's room in *Blood and Sand*, and the vicious contrast of the crimson blood spilt in the sunlit arena where the crowds roar outside. And one recalls exquisite passages of romantic colour in *Caesar and Cleopatra*: a figure seated in a window, and, beyond, a subtle hint of trees and the sea. A hint: for what is needed if the colour film is to improve on monochrome is not realism: not realistic houses and chairs and tables, not pink cheeks, not postcard seas and mountains. That kind of fact can be left to the newsreels (the Victory Parade, after all, can be filmed in Technicolour). The need is for a poetic use of colour – the kind of handling we sometimes find in Disney: the under-water sequences in *Pinocchio*, the pink elephant sequences in *Dumbo*. Disney, of course, can shape his material. He has no tedious human faces, no inconvenient solid objects to deal with. But the cinema of flesh and blood, too, can create and control and shape its material, as *Henry V* shows, as *Blood and Sand* shows. All that is needed is the poetic imagination in those who create the cinema of human life.

Sight and Sound
Summer 1946

3 *Three-D*

It seems that the public may have to accustom itself to the term 3-D. This is not a regulation about derationing or a pet name for the hydrogen bomb, but a kind of film: Three-Dimensional. For some time reports from American have told of various systems for giving the impression of depth on the screen, and there have been rumours of this producer or that experimenting with three-dimensional films. Last week the news came that one of the big companies was taking a major risk. Twentieth-Century Fox, it appears, has announced that all its important films are now to be what I will venture to call deepies.

I must not call 3-D a new kind of film. Nearly two years ago short stereoscopic pieces were being shown at the Festival of Britain. Faintly exasperated by the enterprise, the cinema trade hastened to remind us that even then stereoscopy was not new; no more it was, and I myself can remember before the war cowering at the Empire in pink spectacles while from the screen missiles appeared to hurtle into the audience. What is new is the importance at present attached to three-dimensional cinema.

There are two schools in the battle of the deepies. One, the true 3-D school, requires the spectator to wear special glasses. To this group belong the British Stereo-Techniques, the system seen at the Festival, and Natural Vision, a method used in America to make, in colour, the first three-dimensional feature film, *Bwana Devil*. The other group employ systems which, though they are said to give the illusion of solidity, are not strictly three-dimensional but panoramic and need no special glasses. Of this kind is Cinerama, which has been exciting New York since the end of September.

Cinerama uses a camera with three lenses, each photographing in colour on a separate section of film, and a wide convex screen: three projectors throw each an image on to the screen, the three pictures side by side forming one panoramic picture. Cinemascope, the system to be tried by Twentieth-Century Fox, also uses the wide screen. But it is claimed to be less complicated, needing one projector only. This system, too, is not new, but derives, according to an expert in the *Kinematograph Weekly*, from a method invented by a Frenchman, Henri Chrétien, in the 1930s.

To try to prophesy about the deepies would be imprudent,

especially on the part of someone who has seen films in only one of the 3-D systems, and in none of the panoramic systems. A friend who has watched Cinerama was ironically reassuring: it can't displace our dear old cinema, he said. And yet the times are propitious for change: television, shrinking audiences, producers desperately looking for a gimmick. He spoke, too, before the adoption by Twentieth-Century Fox of Cinemascope; before the news that nearly every studio in Hollywood, in the usual mad scramble not to be left behind, is going in for some form of three-dimensional cinema.

A change to panoramic or stereoscopic films would mean vast expenditure on equipment, in the case of Cinerama or Cinemascope on huge new screens, and one can understand the exhibitor who isn't longing for 3-D Day. All the same, I can't help remembering how, a quarter of a century ago, Warner Brothers saved their bacon by showing the first feature film with synchronized speech, and frightened all Hollywood into making nothing but talkies.

February 1953

4 *Cinerama*

At last Cinerama. Up to the present, only reports from America:
the huge enveloping screen, the visitors tottering out pale with
awe; but now, almost exactly two years after its first exhibition
in New York, **This Is Cinerama** (producers Merian C. Cooper
and Lowell Thomas) has come to the London Casino.

I ought, I suppose, to remind readers what Cinerama is – or
perhaps it would be better to point out what it is not. To begin
with it is not CinemaScope, the system using the wide, shallowly
curved screen on which you may have seen a dozen films from
The Robe to *The High and the Mighty*. It is not Superscope, which
none of us has seen yet but which will burst on the world any
minute. It is not Vistavision, which so far has been demonstrated
here privately only. It is not 3-D, the stereoscopic system which
askes the spectator to wear glasses and then throws knives at
him. For the spectacle at the London Casino the visitor needs no
glasses, and he sometimes feels that he himself is the projectile.

From this rich confusion let me extract the word Cinerama
and say that the present entertainment is shown on a deeply
concave screen, the largest we have seen yet, seventy-five feet
wide and twenty-six feet high: roughly three-by-one, that is to
say, against CinemaScope's five-by-two. The camera used has
three lenses taking simultaneous photographs; three projectors
throw the images side by side on the screen, and the three pictures
are fused into one panoramic view. Fused, I say, but the word
flatters; there is a blurred line where the lateral pictures join the
central one, and a figure crossing it is sometimes caught as if
in a distorting mirror. One or other of the component films
slips from time to time into a kind of St Vitus's dance, giving
rise to unworthy doubts about the stability of, for example,
the Rocky Mountains. The colour in the three pictures is not
always precisely matched; the left-hand side of Venice looks a
shade cooler than the right. The curved screen produces curved
pictures; every stretch of water dips in the middle, and much
more steeply than with CinemaScope in its early days.

The technical faults are worse than I had expected. But I dare
say they would seem less glaring had we seen Cinerama earlier.
Cinerama was the first of the new systems to be commercially
developed; New York saw Cinerama first. We in this country

began a year ago with CinemaScope, a later development which, instead of combining three films, photographs with a lens which squeezes a wide image into a narrow one and projects with a lens which re-expands. We are thus already accustomed to a wide screen, a wide image without joins, and the extent of Cinerama may not be as surprising to us as it was to New York. All the same it is quite a shock when, after Lowell Thomas's introductory outline of cinema history, drearily delivered in black-and-white on a conventional-sized screen, the curtains slide back and we find ourselves tearing about on a vast, coloured roller-coaster.

The impression of this first scene is astonishing: the sensations of being in fact on a roller-coaster – the speed, the giddiness, the upper stomach carelessly mislaid at the first crest – all are there. And the noise: Cinerama uses stereophonic sound, and efficiently, far better than I have hard it use before. The first half of *This Is Cinerama* consists of unrelated scenes: bull-fight in Madrid, military tattoo in Edinburgh; a good many are chosen to show what sterophony can do, among them I suppose the performance at La Scala in Milan of a scene from *Aida* (the Triumph) – though here I was too much depressed by the banality of the dancing to listen for the direction of the sound. The second half is almost entirely spectacular; and here Cinerama is at its best.

I am not thinking of the scenes in Florida which open the second half; these are indeed spectacular, but they tell me little I do not already know or guess about aquaplaning and the female form. It is in the aerial views that Cinerama shows its quality. We are taken on a flight across the United States: New York, Chicago, the wheat-plains of the Middle West, the Utah copper-mines, the Rockies, the great canyons and the heights. Suddenly there before one's eyes is the size of America, the space conquered. The scene is noble, its composition majestic, its colour splendid; this is something I have never been made to look at before. Does Cinerama in its present stage mean an advance in the cinema? Of course not: *The Great Train Robbery* in 1903 was a much better *film* than *This is Cinerama*. But even in its present stage it can be dazzlingly beautiful.

October 1954

Most of us have done the decent thing by Cinerama. We have granted that it has size. We have remarked that its colour is sometimes beautiful, that its landscapes are often noble, and that if you want to look at the Grand Canal at Venice in triptych form you should see Cinerama, and Bob's your uncle. Nobody would deny that for giving you the sensation of being fired from a gun thee is nothing to touch it.

But since the days, over three years ago now, of the first programme, since that first ringing announcement: Here is Cinerama! a question has been left in the air: where do we go from here? And now that the third programme. **The Seven Wonders of the World**, is on view at the London Casino, one begins to think it is time the question was answered.

The virtues noted in the earlier versions are still present. There, for the roller-coaster-minded, is the stir of danger without the risk: flying under Brooklyn Bridge, rattling out of control down the curves of a mountain railway. There are the occasional beauties: a rainbow hangs in the spray of the Victoria Falls, a rosy cloud on the African plain turns into a swarm of pink dots and dashes which are flamingos. And there are the tremendous landscapes – though it is perhaps a pity that, owing to the enthusiasm and indeed the expertness of the stunt pilot responsible for directing the air photography, so many of them should appear to be slowly turning turtle. Without Cinerama, urges better nature, that fragment of oneself which is bent on making an honest woman of the thing, without Cinerama my chances of seeing the Iguassu Falls in the middle of South America would be slim indeed.

Unfortunately the buildings and the landscapes and the ceremonies which the Cinerama cameras circled the would to record are handicapped in making their effect. They have to rise above an ear-splitting sound-track. And they have to live through Mr Lowell Thomas's commentary.

The lecture imposed on the round-the-world trip ranges from the glibly reverent to the matey. We are looking, a little shaken by distorted perspective, at the interior of the Parthenon; a couple of Euzones, Greek Guardsmen, in their white ballet-skirts, long white woollen stockings and tasselled caps, stroll across the cella. 'Could they,' inquires the voice, sonorously, 'be Plato and Socrates?' After a visit to Japan (a visit distinguished by little except hideous Westernized dances, all parasol and grin) the regulation pair of child-befriending G.I.s boards the Clipper: a group of local beauties looks on. 'So long, Yum Yum!' exclaims the narrator: 'So long, Pitti Sing!' In the extraordinary Orient, in the Saharan waste, in the august city of Saint Peter we are continually being reassured: you are safe, home is round the corner, you are still within reach of the ice-cream soda, the hamburger and the handy digest of history. (The Pharos, the commentary confides, used to be fortified: that's where Caesar made love to Cleopatra.)

The levelling process quickly succeeds. It is not long before even one's better nature grows surfeited and begins to protest that the Iguassu Falls are no better than any other old cataract. Niagara, Victoria, Iguassu: with the appalling cosiness of travel which Cinerama affords they become just a lot of water.

Of course, it is not Cinerama alone which is destroying the sense of astonishment. The extensible screen, the advances in colour cinematography – all conspire to make one blasé. The Watussi dancers of the Belgian Congo? If I've seen that kind of thing once I've seen it a dozen times; I'm up to the ears with that Commonwealth Royal Tour stuff. Mount Sinai? You mean that old thing out of *The Ten Commandments*? Angkor Vat? Not *again*, for goodness' sake. The stupendous cannot long survive the insolent familiarity with which the cinema has infected us, and only two or three times during the two hours of *The Seven Wonders of the World* did I feel excitement; once, as a matter of fact, on seeing one of the few of the monuments I had looked at in the stone: the Gizeh Sphinx.

Size, noise, and a lot of disconnected rushing about: what else can be done with the huge concave screen, the three projectors, the five speaker systems and the feeling of eyestrain? Up to now Echo, I fear, with her customary discourtesy merely raps back: What?

March 1958

5 'Criticism is not an exact science'

Fifteen years ago this month I received my first fan letter. I had been film critic of *The Sunday Times* for a week or two, and my last article had been devoted to Korda's version of *The Four Feathers* and Renoir's version of *La Bête Humaine*. I opened the letter with girlish optimism.

'Your "criticism," ' it began, 'strikes me as being rather cheap and crude. I realize, of course, that being a "critic" and a woman, it is your natural desire to appear to your readers as as "intellectual" a type as possible, and to show yourself as *thoroughly appreciative* of all foreign films, particularly those having the ever-fashionable theme of a good, interested, as-twisted-as-possible sex complex as a basis, so dear to the hearts of the majority of women. Your judgment bears as much crude resemblance to a really fair, decent, and constructive criticism as a lump of butter to a howitzer. Please,' the writer thoughtfully concluded, 'do not bother to reply.'

For sentimental reasons I have treasured the letter, and as I read it today after fifteen years of films morning and afternoon I ask myself whether in the interval things have changed in the cinema. In obvious ways, of course, change is taking place at this moment. The screen is altering its shape, growing wider and concave; a struggle is going on to decide how wide it shall grow and by what method its sound shall be produced. Change of this kind may be dangerous for the time being because it diverts attention from the proper business of the cinema, gives the technicians power over the artists and tempts producers to put their energies into mimicking life instead of making it. But the films have survived enough progress to make me chary of opposing what is new, no matter what form it may take. There are people today enthusiastically making talkies who were quite sure in 1929 that dialogue would ruin the cinema.

The danger in the short run is that changes in the mechanics of the screen may narrow the choice of subject. When the cinema began to talk it was all for films of stage plays; now that the screen is turning panoramic the fear is that it will produce nothing but spectacle. We are in, people say mournfully, for endless repetitions of *The Robe*. But the screen did not need Cinemascope to make spectacle. I look back fifteen years to the first film I reviewed. It was a revival of *The Sign of the Cross*.

The subjects of the cinema don't seem to have altered much in a decade and a half. Films about the threat of war, air defence, gangsters, Indians, crooners, Tarzan, Hollywood, Texas, spies, aggressive foreign Powers – for Nazis read Communists, and you would think you could show the films of 1939 and 1940 without complaint. Some of the directors, some of the stars are the same; Korda still has to be reckoned with, Renoir is still a famous name, and so is Gabin, player of *La Bête Humaine*. De Mille is still at work; lovely Garbo has not made a film for years, but you can still watch, amidst the new faces, Spencer Tracy or Gary Cooper, established stars in the 1930s. Yet the cinema has changed, and the change is not a matter of new screens or the increased use of colour, not a matter either of smooth new faces or lines deepening in old ones. Without such guides one would, I believe, know a contemporary from an old piece.

As you would expect, there is a change in technique; the new films are sharper, brilliantly polished. But I think that the cinema itself is growing sharper. It is not simply that the screen is rejecting some of its old sentimentality, and that in the place of Shirley Temple fifteen years ago you find today Brandon de Wilde, the tough little boy of *Shane*. I mean, too, something more than the substitution of Marlon Brando and the gorilla-hero for the affable mugs of the 1930s. I mean that the cinema shows as a whole – and let me repeat as a whole, for I am aware that there were exceptional, attacking films in the late 1930s – less reluctance to look at the rough edges of life.

The historical experience of the 1940s no doubt is partly the cause. Perhaps the influence of the Continental cinema which my correspondent so heartily disliked has helped. I believe that British films, transformed in the last fifteen years, have helped too. I know that the change admits a great deal of crudeness and violence, and I won't deny that I often regret the cinema's age of innocence. All the same, recalling the films of 1939 – and how dim, how woolly many of them seem – I find myself to my surprise concluding that the cinema is better than it was when I began writing in this column. I shall try to elaborate on this startling theme next Sunday.

                                                              April 1959

Last Sunday I found myself saying that the cinema today was an improvement on the cinema with which I was dealing when, fifteen years ago, I first wrote as a film critic. The discovery of this view alarmed as well as startled me. There is nothing more unpopular nowadays than optimism; optimism is reactionary. But say the cinema is going downhill, say there are no directors in the first rank and the players aren't what they were, and you are heard with respect. The further back you put your golden age, the smaller the audience with the experience to contradict you. There is a reputation to be made by anyone with the nerve to insist that since in the 1880s Edward Muybridge used the Zoopraxiscope to demonstrate the Attitude of Animals in Motion, films have never been the same.

Of course the screen has lost some kind of magic since it learned to talk; something is always lost when an art is past its first youth. I admit that I sometimes miss the superb self-confidence of a cinema which had not recognized the subtleties of human language; I could give examples but, to stifle cries of King Charles's Head, I refrain. I still feel, when I look at today's films, cheerful about the future.

This cheerfulness is due first to the conviction of which I wrote last week, that we are doing better now than in 1939. True that in that year of half-peace and half-war there were splendid and extraordinary works: *Stagecoach*, *La Bête Humaine*. But my list of the year's best films contained pieces which today I should feel bound to apologize for including; and I am appalled to see what bits of routine nonsense made up the weeks and the months. The last years have certainly been richer in outstanding works; think, among the films 1953 brought to this country, of *Les Jeux Interdits*, *Shane* and *Diary of a Country Priest*; and the routine stuff was, I am sure, less shabbily asinine. We have, after all, more sources than in 1939. As well as the French cinema there is the Italian to draw on; the Mexicans and the Japanese have joined in. And some of the old sources have bettered themselves. In 1939 we had in this country no more than two or three directors to be reckoned with. I don't have to stress the difference today.

But my optimism goes further. The end of the 1930s was a time of decline in the cinema; the war saved us from a much steeper fall by forcing new subjects on the combatants, and left behind it ideas which came to life in pity and indignation and laughter in the late 1940s. Experience had made the indignation harsh. I don't believe that films such as *Los Olvidados* and *Nous Sommes*

Tous des Assassins or even *From Here to Eternity* would have been possible before the war; their attack is quite different from the melodrama of, say, *I Am a Fugitive from a Chain Gang*. But even though films were more interesting after the war, anyone at all sensitive to the atmosphere must have recognized an unsettled feeling. The cinema was beginning to think itself a little behind the times, especially with television putting up its goal-posts on half the suburban houses in England.

Change is on us now in all the extravagance which characterises the screen at its moments of technical discovery: 3-D, wide screen, Cinemascope, Cinerama, Superscope, Vistavision, four-track magnetic sound, Perspecta sound – we still have not learned the meaning of the names. Yet I don't in my bones feel that the uproar is to be deplored. I believe that this fury of mechanical invention is a sign of life.

Many of us have dreaded a period, such as we had at the start of the talkies, when the screen momentarily forgets everything it has learned; and I confess I still don't see how, except by masking, the vast new screens are to be reconciled with the architecture in detail which is the cinema's method. One grumbles, of course, about the bad films which are bound to be made when new techniques are tried. But already the techniques are better managed: *Kiss Me Kate* and *Hondo* look positively agreeable in 3-D, *The Command* is full of splendid compositions in the shape which Cinemascope imposes. Even when the films are atrocious there is a feeling of life in the air. In fact I am ready to believe that, far from hindering the creative flow of the cinema, the new inventions are going to stimulate it.

April 1954

Three months ago my colleague Derek Prouse wrote in these columns a perceptive and eloquent review of a film made with small money and smaller names by the young American actor John Cassavetes. The piece had arrived in this country without fanfares; it was in fact being shown exclusively to members of the National Film Theatre. Since then there has been a rush to join the movement in which Mr Prouse was a leader: long interviews with the director, a prize at Venice. And now that **Shadows** is on public view at the Academy Cinema one feels there is little, except possibly a reminder, to add.

Shadows, if I may remind, was made without a hard-and-fast-script. The players were students, coloured and white, at a dramatic school organized by Mr Cassavetes; in the Method manner they were given a theme to develop rather than dialogue to interpret. The result is a fragmentary glimpse of a New York half-world inhabited by Negro cabaret-performers, shiftless violent boys and half-educated arguers at studio parties; the relations between white and coloured people provide the narrative thread. The film is described as an improvisation. Well, premeditation creeps in. But in the restless movements, the hesitations and interruptions and blunders of the talk one can indeed find the reflection of unpremeditated human behaviour.

Moments of truth; extraordinary playing; strange interludes in a family half-Negro, half-crypto-Negro – certainly it is the mesmerizing film which I had been led to expect. And now that I have agreed with everybody in sight perhaps I can try to explain why I am only half-mesmerized.

My reason, I think, is Mr Cassavetes' choice of theme. The subject is the current chic subject. While the popular cinema declines in popularity the smart cinema grows smarter. It is chic to make films about racial prejudice, the beat generation and boys in leather jackets; about young men who, enjoying a vague grudge against the society into which they were born, drift about in shoals, like herrings. The battering-rams of criticism used to be directed against British films with a patronizing, middle-class, all's-well theme. Today it seems to me quite as conventional to celebrate the rootless anti-middle-class. The really revolutionary thing to do would be to make a film in praise of an elderly stockbroker who had retired to Worthing to grow asparagus.

In laying so much emphasis on the subject of *Shadows* I am no doubt running foul of the new generation of critics, who say – very reasonably – that a film, while its theme may need elucidation, should be judged by aesthetic standards, in fact on the qualities which differentiate it from a book, say, or a play. (I had, by the way, been misled last Sunday when I said that the new group had no interest in subject; a reading of some obligingly offered issues of *Oxford Opinion* has shown me where I was wrong.) Their own writing takes us back to the opinion that the director is the true begetter of a film; it rejects the more recent theory that the writer is the responsible creator.

Mr Cassavetes now confronts us with yet another candidate, the actor who develops his own situations as he goes along. It is a third view which, however, does not take into account the visual beauty achieved by cutting and camerawork: *Shadows* is full of elegant glimmering and darkling effects, images which often reflect the doubts and humiliations of the human creatures concerned. And yet I can't help feeling that these elegances themselves, these groups ceaselessly flowing and flitting, these neon-sparkling urban nights, are themselves a shade modish; that the smart contemporary theme finds its match in the smart contemporary décor.

October 1960

'Seldom have I been more angry!' The thunder came not, as you might suppose, from a headmaster addressing the fourth form on the subject of some incident in the dormitory, but from a reader exasperated at having been 'snared and deluded', as he put it, by a recommendation from me into seeing a film (*Le Rideau Cramoisi*) which disappointed him. His rage was the greater since he was (I hope still is) a constant and as a rule, apparently, satisfied reader. 'It was rather,' he wrote later, by then more in sorrow than in anger, 'as if one's favourite dog had suddenly whipped round and bitten one for no apparent reason whatsoever.'

Until recently I had regarded such skirmishes as a private fight between me and my correspondents – though occasionally, it is true, the Editor gets called in. 'Dear Sir' (I quote), '*Can't* a man be found to do the films for *The Sunday Times*?' But now the whole matter of film criticism has become a subject for public discussion.

Two or three months ago I wrote briefly of the new generation of film critics, in particular of *Oxford Opinion* and its contributors' insistence on aesthetic rather than political or moral standards. (I am grateful to *Oxford Opinion*; though I believe the aesthetic to be only part of the judgment required of a critic, one can never be reminded of it too often.) Since then *Granta* has come out, in a number devoted to the cinema, with some smart all-round puncturing; and I have been glad to make the acquaintance, on the committed side of the fence, of a new, attacking, quarterly journal of film criticism, *Definition*.

It is my business to criticize films, not critics, and I do not propose to join in the free-for-all. Since last Sunday, however, no new films have appeared. It seems the moment to ask oneself what exactly this column ought in busier weeks to be doing and being.

Naturally everybody, including me, would like it to be better: but how? More 'analytical criticism'? (Cambridge). More 'willingness to assess in detail the social and moral content of a film'? (*Definition*). Less willingness to assess in detail etc.? (Oxford). And while one notes the general suggestions of the new groups the particular pleas of one's own readers must not be neglected. One must, I mean, tell the story of the film so that the correspondent will know if he is going to like it. One must not tell the story lest it should be ruined for him. One should point to the beauties of individual scenes so that the spectator knows what to look for. One should avoid insulting him by pointing to the beauties of individual scenes; he is perfectly capable of finding them for himself.

It is, one is told, the director who matters. It is the writer ('basically it the story which counts'). It is the producer. And the cameraman ('You *might* have mentioned the photography'). And the editor. And the composer ('Madam, you have no ear for music'). And the players ('Why not give credit to the actors and actresses? D'you expect *them* to alter the story, which you evidently don't like? Neither do I, much. But I shall see it, none the less, just *because* you've slanged it, and to give it a square deal'). And there is one's own performance to consider. The rubbish should be 'slashed . . . It is evident that your conscience has become completely atrophied by association with the people connected with this salacious trade.' On the other hand the writing should be 'more kindly', with 'a happier approach'. It should never go beyond a tone of 'mellow raillery'.

The pitfalls multiply. Space should be given to explaining one's reasons for attacking a film. Space should never be to a film one wishes to attack, only to a film one admires. One's constant 'belittling of Hollywood' is disgraceful (and doubtless Government-sponsored, writes Anon.). In the meantime, one's adverse criticism is 'doing its share to ruin the British film industry.' And while dodging the traps one must find time to discuss short films and films for children; arrange for cast lists to be given at both the beginning and the end of a performance; stamp out Communism; and always use (a) the word British instead of English and (b) the word English instead of British.

The only thing, you see, which gets left out is any suggestion that the critic might positively delight in the cinema.

In the circumstances one sometimes dreams of an all-purpose review: something for everybody. It would tell a story, but the wrong one, thus spoiling nobody's fun. It would be committed, but to what nobody would be able to discover. It would offer stylistic analyses of scenes which nobody could recognize. 'This repulsive/exquisite American/British/English tale of unbridled sex/shy virginity,' it would say, 'owes its political/aesthetic impact/collapse to the devoted/trivial work of the director/script-writer/designer/focus-puller/head grips. The film, one would add, 'is suitable/unfit for school treats/gatherings of the Empire Loyalists'/annual general meeting of the More Chatterley Club.'

Though I would take a bet that even so somebody would feel snared and deluded. All one can hope for is to avoid argument with the fiercer correspondents. For instance, the reader who once wrote: 'Several people have died here as a result of disagreeing with me.'

January 1961

Criticism is not an exact science. It cannot be taught as geometry can be taught; impossible to demonstrate its accuracey as if it were a jet engine or a rocket to the moon. On the contrary, it is a wavering, contradictory affair, periodically changing its theories; even practitioners who are contemporaries find agreement impossible. In the cinema, for example, *Movie* (at present dormant) was always at loggerheads with *Sight and Sound*.

These solemn-faced reflections are the result of a recent letter, or rather an envelope form an anonymous correspondent who enclosed a cutting from this column with all examples of the first person singular accusingly ringed. There have been other missives of the sort; one is used to them. One does not take much notice of one's anonymous correspondents; indeed one learned long ago that, since criticism, as one has just said, is not an exact science ond one's correspondents adopt contradictory views, it is silly of one to be affected by the fury of even the signed letter. This week, however, the scarcity of new films gives one room for a bit of experiment – and for a bit of reference to some new books about the cinema.

There are, of course, various methods of avoiding that first person singular. One can resort to the sexless Continental third person singular. One has just been doing it. But not so long ago one's friend and colleague Patrick Campbell wrote an article brilliantly deriding the practice; that rather shook one. What, one thought, about those handy third-person phrases 'the writer' and 'your correspondent'? Or the flat statement without attribution, the impersonal dogmatic judgment? Or what about the first person plural? For some unfathomable reason that gives less offence than the singular; at any rate nobody complains about its incidence in *The New Yorker*.

Very well then: we have been reading two books of critical analysis of the cinema, both excellently illustrated by stills: *Films and Feelings* by Raymond Durgnat and *Movie Man* by David Thomson. We admired them both; but we were struck by the difference of approach between them. Mr Thomson, writing in a rather dense style, treats the screen as at once a symbol and in implement of a society moving steadily away from the associations of art. For him the camera is 'a scientific recording instrument', and the cinema is at last beginning to realise itself not as a theatrical but as a photographic medium; its job, in fact, is not to 'define' behaviour but to observe it. Of the ending of Godard's *Pierrot le Fou* he writes: 'It is the complete dissolution of the humanist tradition': the phrase, we felt, is not disapproving.

Mr Durgnat, on the other hand, can accept artificial styles of acting; or he can accept Dreyer's methods of manipulating until the player becomes 'part of a visual composition'. Your correspondent would not suggest that *Films and Feelings*, though it is written in a manner a good deal racier, is basically a less intellectual study of the cinema than *Movie Man*. But Mr Durgnat is concerned, as Mr Thomson is not concerned, to examine popular reactions to popular films as well as intellectual reactions to intellectual films. His book – a collection of essays with a coherent view – is essentially a defence of enjoyment; and he takes some pretty long running jumps at 'anti-emotionality' in film criticism.

What your correspondent found especially interesting was the difference of opinion on individual directors and individual films. Mr Durgnat: 'Unless the critic accepts, and keys his sensibility to pictorial values, he will be unable to pay more than lip-service to the real richness of such directors as Eisenstein. . . .' Mr Thomson: 'The nature of Eisenstein's cinema is essentially poetic, and as such is in opposition to film's nature so that, with television's constant prose, his films seem increasingly pretentious.' Mr Thomson writes with some approval of the *Exodus* of Otto Preminger; but Mr Durgnat: 'His *Exodus* does for Israel what George Stevens' *Giant* does for Texas (nothing, in CinemaScope).' Your correspondent is saddened by that view of *Giant*, and more than saddened when Mr Thomson writes of Marilyn Monroe: 'The conclusion dawns that Monroe was so out of date that the silent screen might have been a more proper medium for her.'

But that is not the point. The point is that the writer (which writer? this writer, of course) can now come back to the first paragraph of her article: critics disagree, criticism is not an exact science. An example of the flat statement, the impersonal, dogmatic judgment: maddening, is it not? There are, after all, people who claim that criticism can indeed be a science; and to express a personal opinion under the guise of a fact seems to the writer, to your correspondent, to one – hang it all, to me – an insufferable piece of vanity. It is therefore in a spirit of modesty in more senses than one that, reverting to the first personal singular, I comment on **Yoko Ono No. 4**. Miss Yoko Ono's eighty-minute film consisting of 365 close-ups of naked bottoms, male and female, walking to the accompaniment of conversation (funny now and then) from their unidentified owners. Perhaps Mr Thomson has got to the bottom of it when he writes 'Art will decline as meaning subsides.'

August 1967

6 Underground Cinema

Four figures on the screen, two male, two female (well, more or less). The men lean over the back of a settee, the women sit in the foreground: one, dark, solid, impassive, holds on her lap a white cat, the other, luscious in a golden wig (and played by a female impersonator) lolls against her. Somewhere off-screen male voices are carrying on a conversation – 'marriage of convenience,' one hears before the talk rambles on to such more popular topics as homosexuality.

Presently Goldenhair takes from her handbag a banana, voluptuously peels it, eats it; then another; and another. The last of the bananas, unpeeled, she caresses, rubbing it languorously against her thighs; an even more intimate gesture is hinted. Once she leans to kiss one of the men; once the second man pours a drink over the head of her neighbour, who has looked on affronted at the embrace. The action (yes, that's all) lasts seventy minutes. It is perhaps excusable in the white cat to make repeated attempts to escape.

Andy Warhol's film *Harlot* – it is the director's homage, if you can call it that, to Jean Harlow – was among the works shown in the National Film Theatre's week of American underground cinema; tonight sees the last programme in London, but the whole boiling now moves on to the provinces and university film societies. I use the word 'underground' since it is familiar, it identifies. But I am told that the title is a journalistic invention which gives a false impression, as if the movement were based on obscenities and revolutionary politics; New American Cinema is the term accepted by the creators.

All right: of the films I have seen (they took me a good ten hours) only one or two carry a political protest. Mr Warhol's film (and even that I should call refrigerative rather than inflammatory, sexually speaking) represents stylistically as well as in its theme only a fragment of the movement. The New American Cinema is extremely varied.

There are the films in which for hours (it seems like hours, and sometimes it really is hours) next to nothing happens, if one uses the word 'happens' in the sense applicable to the dear, familiar, commercial cinema of love and death. Love may still be there: for instance in Gregory Markopoulos's hour-long, coloured toyings with an androgynous theme, *Himself as Herself*: the hero dressed as a man is enamoured of himself dressed as a girl. Death may be there: Mr P. Adams Sitney, the engaging enthusiast who is touring Europe with the programmes, described for my benefit a film on which my endurance has not yet been tested, Stan Brakhage's *The Art of Vision*: for four and a half hours, if I understood him rightly, it relates with the solar system and the interior organisation of the human body the progress of a man climbing a mountain and finally falling off it. But in such examples, at any rate in *Himself as Herself*, action is not only deliberate and repetitive, it is almost invisible. Avert your eyes for a second and you miss a crisis: somebody has resorted desperately to opening a door or coming downstairs.

But this, as I say, is only part of the movement. There are films, for instance the work of Bruce Conner, which use as their material clips from old Westerns, say, or newsreel shots (one of Mr Conner's works employs this method in dealing with the assassination of President Kennedy). There are animated collages: Harry Smith creates a grotesque cannibal world from black-and-white cut-outs of human figures, birds, animals, machines. Sometimes, in contrast to the static style of Andy Warhol, who as long as his piece of film holds out simply shoots anything in front of his camera, there is a frenzied speed: abstracts, erotic visions, the gestures of a naked girl dancing, the coloured figures of a circus flash so fast before your eyes that to catch a single image is almost impossible.

Often there is overlapping movement. New York's bridges swim past one another; a train, fields, a station, in the beautiful *Castro Street* of Bruce Baillie, join in a dream-like flow. There is nothing new in the technique of supermposing one photographic image on another – or composing a layer of three or four images. I am not even sure that the New American Cinema itself is all that new. Plenty of experimenters – Man Ray, Germaine Dulac, Len Lye, Bartosch, Alexeieff, not to mention Buñuel – had thought of multiple exposure, dostortion, abstract patterns and the assault on the sub-conscious mind thirty or forty years ago (I don't think though, that any of them were as boring as Andy Warhol). What to me seems new is the extent of the current movement: perhaps I might say its acceptance, at any rate in the United States. It isn't private any longer.

I asked Mr Sitney if it was a movement of protest against Hollywood. Certainly not, he said: some of its exponents enjoyed ordinary Hollywood films, Westerns perhaps – not intellectual films, he added hastily. Rather it is a movement towards individual authorship. Some of the directors want to get away from the deliberate effects of editing, some don't, but all feel the desire to do their own creating by means of a camera. Some of them are painters. And the relation of the avant-garde cinema with painting is surely significant; I am reminded that in France in the 1920s Fernand Léger made a film, *Ballet Mécanique*.

A great deal of modern painting and sculpture is de-humanised. The New American Cinema takes not so much the human as the narrative element out of films: mood, not emotion or feeling related to action, is the substance. Modern painting has affected a public at first reluctant: furniture, fabrics, posters show that influence. Interesting to see whether the latest avant-garde cinema can influence the commercial screen or whether it will remain the pleasure of the specialised audience. Not so specialized, as a matter of fact, in the United States; young audiences, says Mr Sitney (not the intellectuals, who hurry to Bergman and Antonioni) have been conditioned by repeated showings at the universities to take the unconventional styles for granted.

And it is worth noting that here the National Film Theatre has been crowded all the week; that one of the New American film-makers, Steven Dwoskin, has settled to work in England; and that the London Film-Makers Co-operative, a new group which 'questions . . . the traditional assumptions about the nature of the cinema itself' and of which he is a director, has just published a first catalogue of controversial, the-hell-with-it works for hire.

April 1968

Festival Fever

For the critic, one competitive festival a year is plenty.

This has not always been my opinion. Before the war, when it first entered my head that I might go to a Continental film festival, I viewed the prospect with an emotion which it would not be extravagant to call awe. The elegance, I fancied, would be intellectual as well as social. All the women would be dressed by Schiaparelli (for the days of Dior and Givenchy had not yet come); all the men would be Eisensteins; all the films would be masterpieces. In short I pictured the gathering as something between Plat's Academy and Versailles under *le roi soleil*.

Let me give a rapid impression of the actual experience of a journalist at a Mediterranean festival.

You are, perhaps, disinclined for the initial junketings. It is purely for the films that you are going. You will leave your colleagues, then – the metropolitan French, the confident Italians, the Germans, the Swedes, the Belgians, the closely co-ordinated contingent from Eastern Europe and the sparse, retiring English – to settle in before you arrive. You will turn up a couple of days late, thus giving the Battle of Flowers or the regatta on the Canal a miss.

Your train or your aircraft turns you loose in a town where everybody, even the arrival of the day before, miraculously ranges in colour between honey and mahogany. The Festival authorities have obligingly booked accommodation for you. In your bedroom you drag out some crumpled article of holiday dress; then you set off for the festival centre. Suddenly your own skin, which up to that moment has appeared perfectly normal, takes on the shade of cold veal. Your clothes, too, are a mistake: too pale, too formal, and definitely of the wrong vintage. Exposing to the sun as much of yourself as you dare, you hurry along back streets; it is a relief to get into the building, humming though it is with the irritability of journalists, photographers, publicity men and harassed officials. But you, have some difficulty in finding the right office; you intrude on the Director-General's secretary, who is trying on the telephone to pacify the leader of the Russian delegation and who receives you rather tartly, before you reach your goal. Here you are amiably greeted and given a folder full of programmes and your credentials: a book of cinema tickets and a hotel voucher which entitles you to bed, breakfast and two square meals a day with a good swig of wine for a week – or one square meal a day for a fortnight. The book of tickets will probably display on he cover your identifying photograph. It will also have a number corresponding with a number of a pigeon-hole which is to serve as your professional letter-box. Your first action, then, must be to call at this Festival *poste-restante* and announce your number, whereupon you will be handed a bundle of correspondence. Included you will find a copy of the day's Festival newspaper, a card for the day before yesterday's Battle of Flowers, notifications of three films all being shown *hors festival* at the same hour in widely separated districts, the promise of a press conference by the distributor of a Bulgarian documentary, and an invitation to a reception being given by the British delegation. There will be also a leaflet about a local restaurant and an urgent recommendation of the Casino. On the envelopes the spelling of your name will be imaginatively varied, the attribution of your sex uniformly erroneous.

So much for the theoretical arrangements. Now let us see how they operate in practice.

But the time you have secured your credentials you are late for the afternoon performance, but since you have come for the cinema and not for the society you go in just the same. The main film, a North Korean version of *The Government Inspector*, has already begun, and a good many of the spectators are already leaving. To have your work presented at an hour when the elegant world prefers to be sleeping or on the beach is in itself derogatory, and the afternoon performances are not regarded as chic. However, the hard core of the festival audience – the most conscientious of the critics, a few Party members who feel bound to applaud the North Korean neo-realistic movement, and of course the North Korean delegation – is still vociferously present, and the director and the star, who has got herself up for the occasion in national costume, get a patter of hands at the end. As you come out into a foyer still reflecting shafts of sunlight you can hear your colleagues grumbling about the Festival: the quality of the films, the allocation of seats, the arrangement of the programmes, and the absence from some individual pigeonhole of an invitation to the Mexican cocktail party. One of them, a Dutchman whom you met once at Edinburgh, courteously salutes you; have you, he asks, seen *Gobi*? No, you say, you have just arrived: what is *Gobi*? Ah, you must see it, he replies; Italian neo-romanticism, savage, beautiful, it may win the Golden Pigeon; who would have thought the Italians could do it? Any chance, you ask, of its being shown again? Oh, surely, he says; it was put on in the morning, nobody knew anything about it, hardly anybody was there; write your name down on the list. You thank him excitedly and hurry back to the pigeonhole office, where on the notice-board there are several sheets of paper scrawled with the names of journalists who want a repetition of some film or other; you add our name to the list for *Gobi* and, for good measure, to everything else on the board except a Swedish documentary about breast-feeding.

As an afterthought you ask the clerk if there is anything in your pigeonhole. Yes, there is an invitation to the Mexican cocktail party for this very evening. You had not intended to waste time on social fripperies, but this may be a chance to work yourself into the festival; in any case the next film performance is not until nine o'clock. You change into more formal dress (luckily you have been billeted conveniently near, not twenty minutes' walk up the hill) and set off for the second grandest of the hotels, where the party is being held. A dull roar can be heard through open windows, and the approaches to the hotel present the appearance of the Chamber of Deputies during a national crisis. At the entrance to the ballroom a furious queue is massed. A woman trying to get in without an invitation is driven mercilessly back by a waiter; you own card is snatched from your hand as, at last reaching the end of the bottleneck, you are propelled violently forward by the pent-up force behind you. Almost at the same moment a pretty girl in bull-fighter's costume gives you a packet wrapped in cellophane. Unwrapping it, you discover a small plastic model of Mexico City Bull Ring; and holding this in one hand, in the other a glass of champagne, you bore through the guests. There are two thousand of them and seem to be more.

The film that night is a Mexican story about a bull-fighter. During the interval your Dutch colleague passes on to you a rumour that a special showing of *Gobi* has been arranged for the next morning. You manage to collar a Festival official who confirms it; nine o'clock in the small Festival cinema. You learn also that a midnight supper-dance is being offered, as the phrase is, by the Argentine delegation; but you have not been asked and, after standing in the foyer for a few moments to watch the emergence, amidst plaudits, of the Mexican bull-fighter you force your way through the departing audience of exhibitors and critics, social eminences and exquisitely dressed starlets, past the pavement crowds gaping from behind police barriers, and back to your hotel.

You beg to be called early, and next morning you are indeed waiting at the small Festival cinema by nine o'clock. By nine-thirty about twenty people have collected in the auditorium; at ten o'clock they begin a slow clap. At 10.15 the lights to down and you can distinguish on the screen the credits and the opening scenes of a film. It is the North Korean version of *The Government Inspector*.

I will not catalogue the events of the following days, nor will I describe the gradual weakening of your original hopes. You attend, with enthusiasm at first, the press conferences held, with interpreter, by the head of the Yugoslav delegation or the author of the Venezuelan comedy. But little by little the insidious atmosphere of the place and the occasion gets the worse of you. There will be, you find, no films during the daylight on Saturday. You therefore accept the invitation to a regional lunch at the much advertised open-air restaurant in the hills or on the island; several hundred other people have accepted it, too; you find yourself beginning to look out for the clusters of celebrated faces, American, French, Italian, which emerge from the splendid dachshund cars bouncing up the gill-road. Recklessly you give way to enjoyment.

You still miss none of the official entries, you struggle to keep up with the non-competing films shown in local cinemas in the morning, or during the cocktail hours, or at midnight after the evening performance is over. But you cease to regard the festival as an intellectual treat. Once, it is true, you find yourself sitting next, at some jamboree, to the famous script-writer, the much-admired novelist, or the venerated director. But he, too, wants to enjoy himself, not talk about the aesthetics of the screen. Anyhow he is there on business. He hopes to market his work, or at least to keep people talking about it. The distributors, the producers, the exhibitors are there on business, to buy and sell. The stars are there on business, there to be seen. Yet at the end nobody, if you are to believe what you hear, is satisfied. The delegations who must go home without a prize, the stars who have been inadequately fêted, the business men who have failed to bring off the expected deal – they are all complaining; it is doubtful, apparently, if they will ever visit the festival again. You are in half a mind to grumble yourself, though you must, if you are honest, confess that the whole affair has been a tremendous lark. You have been most hospitably treated, you have nothing in the world to grumble about.

Except, of course, the films. You have travelled half-way across Europe to see the films; you have been seeing them at the rate of four a day; and not more than one in twenty was worth a stroll down the road. (You have not, of course, managed to see *Gobi*.)

The buzzing foyers and the parties; the teen-age fans, like dogs after a cat, hunting some irritable star into her hotel; the wine-drinkings, the organized expeditions, the sardonic journalists looking down their noses as if ballyhoo were alien from their normal experience – these are common elements in the film festivals of the western Continent. Of course there are differences. Berlin, making all its speeches in triplicate, German, English, French, has a faintly hortatory air. To the normal, the international uproars – the complaint from the Japanese about their portrayal in some Chinese film, the protest from the Russians, who insist on the withdrawal of a West German entry – Venice sometimes adds religious feuds, the Catholic and the anti-clerical parties dividing angrily on some ecclesiastical theme. Karlovy Vary? It is ten years since I attended a festival in Czechoslovakia; but from my last visit I recall plenty of occasion for political arguments. There remains one festival which is both uncommercial and uncontroversial. For the calm of perfect amity there is always Edinburgh: non-competitive, non-showy, conducting its affairs, so far as the cinema is concerned, modestly in the shadow of the general Festival. Nobody protests at Edinburgh. Nobody, come to that, appears to be present on anything so vulgar as business. The visiting celebrities are not there to do a deal. They are not even there to be seen; you will not encounter crowds following some exotic star the length of Princes Street. The utmost in advertisement you will find is a suggestion that you should take a trip to such of Scotland's gardens as in some charitable cause are open to the public in August and September. The social occasions are controllable. Promises are kept; and if a film is to be shown at 9 a.m. that film is shown. The officers of the festival are unfailingly efficient and obliging. The critic is regarded as a friend, and his desire to see a film he has missed is if possible gratified. There is a club for those interested in the cinema; you can always find someone to argue with. Edinburgh, in short, does what one dreamed of years ago; offers without ballyhoo, without commercialism, a meeting-place, an international confluence of films, film-makers and critics.

And yet you are dissatisfied. It is all a shade too calm, too fraternal. In your heart you find yourself missing uproar and the ballyhoo. After all, you tell yourself, the cinema is a popular, not a cloistered art. The heroic vulgarities of its past have attained in our minds a kind of sanctity; why should we insist that the present should be all prim good taste? But once more it is about the quality of the films that one most bitterly complains. Edinburgh wants to show films from as wide a world as possible. The selection committee can reject; but it is unlikely to discourage by rejecting the first film ever to be submitted by, let us say, Patagonia. Internationalism, like commercialism, demands concessions and there is no tedium to equal the tedium of brotherhood in the cinema.

Good films at the right moment: that is the problem. In 1957 the *Sunday Times*, working in association with the British Film Institute, presented a festival of films chosen from all the other festivals of the year. There was thus a wide range to choose from; and since the aim was to show no more than about a dozen feature films in all, a programme with unusual merits resulted. But even this modest and on the whole happy venture showed me the appalling difficulties which normally face the organizers of a festival. The new film by the admired director will not be ready in time. The interesting experimental piece has not yet been sub-titled: it will be too late. There is nothing suitable from America – and though you have no intention of giving way to commercial pressure, there really ought to be a contribution from the United States. Your programmes are excessively melancholy in tone; the screen, at the end of each film, is piled with corpses.

But especially there are not enough good films: worthy films, perhaps, but major films of festival stature, no. Technicians want, of course, to see their work set beside the production of other people. I have often thought there might be a festival of what I will call student work for the benefit of film-makers. But there simple is not enough exciting, creative cinema to go round the multiplying festivals of the present. As I say, one competitive festival is plenty.

International Film Annual, No. 2, 1958

8   *And so to Bed*

Typical shot – one might almost say signature-shot – in a film of the 1960s: man in bed, bare shoulders, virile fuzz on chest, sheet pulled up to pectoral muscles; leaning on elbow towards him in three-quarter view, a girl, sheet allowing shadowy hint of bosom and a smooth expanse of shoulder-blades.

Bed: it is fascinating to trace the progress of this valuable film property in the history of the cinema. I have been looking through the list of works reviewed in November 1954. A Western; a musical; Stewart Granger as Beau Brummel; Ava Gardner as the Hollywood star of *The Barefoot Contessa*; a story about an adopted child whose real mother reappears; an Arn Sucksdorff animal piece – there may have been beds in sight, but they accommodated no couples. Today's typical shot would have made a stir ten years ago. But in 1959 came *Les Amants*, or as much of it as we in this country were allowed to see. In 1959 came *Hiroshima, Mon Amour*' with its astonishing opening shot of the lovers (and the terrible suggestion of bodies dissolving in a nuclear furnace). Since then, bed every day, even on Sunday.

In the early days of the cinema bed had a severe practical use: it was the thing you died in. Occasionally a moral warning might be introduced: bed could be what the cad tried to throw you on to (for the moment, of course, I address a feminine audience); but as a rule it served as the setting for a well-attended family farewell, edifying to parents and children alike. With the arrival of sound, however, there was a change. Telephones and alarm clocks came in; bed (and now I permit myself to speak for both sexes) was where you woke up. You slept on your stomach, and when the telephone rang, when the alarm clock went off, without taking your face out of the pillow you groped blindly for the source of disturbance. In the thirties and forties I must have sat through scores of these awakenings – always, and this is important, from single beds. That was the era of the twin bed, of segregation. And with the twin bed went a certain innocence. I once (it was in 1952, towards the end of segregation era) saw a film in which a woman, living with a man who posed as Hitler, failed for years to notice that he was really her husband in false eyebrows.

The thirties and forties embraced moments in which bed was

where a girl sat to take her stockings off: happy memories of Arletty and Dietrich. With the fifties, despite the Hitler film, a new spirit was abroad. And I mean abroad; France it was which sent us a piece called, accurately enough, *The Bed*; and it was from France that the first rush of films about prostitution arrived. But it was not until the sixties that we reached the full bed period: bed with everything. Bed with the housemaid (*The Servant*), the air hostess (*La Peau Douce*), the sister-in-law (*Psyche 59*), the murderess (*The Girl Hunters*); the problems of getting the girl to bed (*Marnie*) and the frustrations of failing to get her to bed (*Yesterday, Today and Tomorrow*); bed sophisticated (*Cyrano et d'Artagnan*), primitive (*The Demon*), professional (*Irma la Douce*), interrupted (*The Carpetbaggers*) and all-round (*The Silence*); bed with meals (*Life Upside-Down*), between drinks (*Goldfinger*), in the intervals of burglary (*Topkapi*) and without any intervals to speak of (*To Love*).

Suddenly, as I recall whole days, in particular at film festivals, spent with eyes trained on a Laocoön-complex of heaving pectoral muscles and shoulder-blades, I am struck by the thought that the great sex symbols of the past never went in much for bed on the screen.

Goodness knows I am not complaining of the new freedoms which the 1960s have brought. All the same it is a bit odd that Ramon Novarro, say, or Pola Negri should have been viewed in circumstances generally so chaste. It is a long time since I watched the films of Jean Harlow, but I am pretty sure she was never seen in anything resembling our current signature-shots. If you consider the it- and Oomph- and Seater-Girls the story is much the same. Clark Gable was rarely one for clinches between the sheets (and Valentino, of course, preferred the desert tent). Garbo has always been the grand illusionist: a distant reflection of passion. Or think of Marilyn Monroe – and again it is the suggestion of desire, not the statement, not the gesture.

But the point is that the suggestion is powerful; and that with repetition, scene after scene, semi-nude after semi-nude, the statement begins to grow meaningless, or even deterrent. I can't help feeling it would be a pity if on the screen bed were to become an anti-erotic symbol.

March 1965

Index of Films

Where a film is the main subject of a review, the page reference is given in **bold** type.

Index of Names

OXFORD

MORE OXFORD PAPERBACKS

This book is just one of nearly 1000 Oxford Paperbacks currently in print. If you would like details of other Oxford Paperbacks, including titles in the World's Classics, Oxford Reference, Oxford Books, OPUS, Past Masters, Oxford Authors, and Oxford Shakespeare series, please write to:

UK and Europe: Oxford Paperbacks Publicity Manager, Arts and Reference Publicity Department, Oxford University Press, Walton Street, Oxford OX2 6DP.

Customers in UK and Europe will find Oxford Paperbacks available in all good bookshops. But in case of difficulty please send orders to the Cash-with-Order Department, Oxford University Press Distribution Services, Saxon Way West, Corby, Northants NN18 9ES. Tel: 0536 741519; Fax: 0536 746337. Please send a cheque for the total cost of the books, plus £1.75 postage and packing for orders under £20; £2.75 for orders over £20. Customers outside the UK should add 10% of the cost of the books for postage and packing.

USA: Oxford Paperbacks Marketing Manager, Oxford University Press, Inc., 200 Madison Avenue, New York, N.Y. 10016.

Canada: Trade Department, Oxford University Press, 70 Wynford Drive, Don Mills, Ontario M3C 1J9.

Australia: Trade Marketing Manager, Oxford University Press, G.P.O. Box 2784Y, Melbourne 3001, Victoria.

South Africa: Oxford University Press, P.O. Box 1141, Cape Town 8000.

THE WORLD'S CLASSICS

The World's Classics series makes available annotated editions of the major works of such important women writers as Jane Austen, the Brontë sisters, Fanny Burney, Maria Edgeworth, George Eliot, and Elizabeth Gaskell.

VIRGINIA WOOLF

Edited with notes and introductions by leading scholars, Virginia Woolf's most popular works are now available in ten World's Classics.

Between the Acts   Edited by Frank Kermode
Jacob's Room   Edited by Kate Flint
Mrs Dalloway   Edited by Claire Tomalin
Night and Day   Edited by Suzanne Raitt
Orlando   Edited by Rachel Bowlby
A Room of One's Own, and Three Guineas   Edited by Morag Shiach
To the Lighthouse   Edited by Margaret Drabble
The Voyage Out   Edited by Lorna Sage
The Waves   Edited by Gillian Beer
The Years   Edited by Hermione Lee, with Notes by Sue Asbee

Also available:

Virginia Woolf: A Writer's Life   Lyndall Gordon

OXFORD POETS

Oxford has one of the finest lists of contemporary poetry. It includes work by important women writers from Britain, Europe, and the Commonwealth, including Anne Stevenson, Penelope Shuttle, Carole Satyamurti, and Gwen Harwood.

FLEUR ADCOCK

Time Zones

In this lively new collection, Fleur Adcock's subjects range from domestic matters—recalling the birth of her son some years back; remembering her father, the news of whose death in New Zealand reaches her, the expatriate, in England; working in her own London garden—to matters of contemporary concern, such as the Romanian bid for freedom in 1989, and support for Green causes, including the anti-nuclear stand.

'She is an eminently readable poet, whose quiet accuracy sometimes makes me laugh out loud.' Wendy Cope, *Guardian*

Also available:

Selected Poems   Fleur Adcock
Orient Express   Grete Tartler
Letters from Darkness   Daniela Crasnaru
Broken Moon
Changing the Subject   Carole Satyamurti

MUSIC IN OXFORD PAPERBACKS

Whether your taste is classical or jazz, the Oxford Paperbacks range of music books is in tune with the interests of all music lovers.

ESSAYS ON MUSICAL ANALYSIS

Donald Tovey

Tovey's Essays are the most famous works of musical criticism in the English language. For acuteness, common sense, clarity, and wit they are probably unequalled, and they make ideal reading for anyone interested in the classical music repertory.

CHAMBER MUSIC

Chamber Music contains some of Tovey's most important essays, including those on Bach's 'Goldberg' Variations and *Art of Fugue*, and on key works by Haydn, Mozart, Beethoven, Schumann, Chopin, and Brahms.

CONCERTOS AND CHORAL WORKS

Concertos and Choral Works contains nearly all the concertos in the standard repertory, from Bach's for two violins to Walton's for viola—fifty concertos in all. The choral works include long essays on Bach's B minor Mass and Beethoven's Mass in D, amongst other famous works.

SYMPHONIES AND OTHER ORCHESTRAL WORKS

Symphonies and Other Orchestral Works contains 115 essays: on Beethoven's overtures and symphonies (including Tovey's famous study of the Ninth Symphony), all Brahms's overtures and symphonies, and many other works by composers from Bach to Vaughan Williams.

Also in Oxford Paperbacks:

Singers and the Song   Gene Lees
The Concise Oxford Dictionary of Music 3/e
Michael Kennedy
Opera Anecdotes   Ethan Mordden

LITERARY BIOGRAPHY AND CRITICISM IN OXFORD PAPERBACKS

Oxford Paperbacks's impressive list of literary biography and criticism includes works ranging from specialist studies of the prominent figures of the world literature to D. J. Enright on television soap opera.

BRITISH WRITERS OF THE THIRTIES
Valentine Cunningham

'He has steeped himself in the period . . . *British Writers of the Thirties* is by far the best history of its kind published in recent years . . . and it will become required reading for those who wish to look back at a society and a culture in which writers, for all their faults, were taken seriously.' Peter Ackroyd, *The Times*

'a serious and often brilliant book, provoking one to argument, forcing one back to known texts and forward to unread ones . . . it is simply so packed with information that it will speak as much to readers with an interest in social history as to the students of literature for whom it was first intended.' Claire Tomalin, *Independent*

'this should henceforth be the standard treatment . . . a minor classic of literary history' Frank Kermode, *Guardian*

'brilliant survey and analysis . . . Mr Cunningham's narrative is cleverly constructed, wonderfully detailed, and he deploys his findings to great effect.' Charles Causley, *Times Educational Supplement*

Also in Oxford Paperbacks:

Fields of Vision   D. J. Enright
Modern English Literature   W. W. Robson
The Oxford Illustrated History of English Literature
edited by Pat Rogers
The Pursuit of Happiness   Peter Quennell

THE OXFORD AUTHORS

General Editor: Frank Kermode

The Oxford Authors is a series of authoritative editions of the major English writers for the student and the general reader. Drawing on the best texts available, each volume contains a generous selection from the writings—poetry and prose, including letters—to give the essence of a writer's work and thinking. Where appropriate, texts have been tactfully modernized and all are complemented by essential Notes, an Introduction, Chronology, and suggestions for Further Reading.

'The Oxford Authors series can always be relied upon to be splendid—with good plain texts and helpful notes.' Robert Nye, *Scotsman*

OSCAR WILDE

Edited by Isobel Murray

The drama of Oscar Wilde's life has for years overshadowed his achievement in literature. This is the first large-scale edition of his work to provide unobtrusive guidance to the wealth of knowledge and allusion upon which his writing stands.

Wilde had studied Greek and Latin and was familiar with American literature, while he was as well read in French as he was in English, following Gautier and Flaubert as well as Pater and Ruskin. Through her Notes Isobel Murray enables the modern reader for the first time to read Wilde as such admiring contemporaries as Pater, Yeats, and Symons read him, in a rich, shared culture of literary and visual arts.

This edition underlines the range of his achievement in many genres, including *The Picture of Dorian Gray, Salome, The Importance of Being Earnest, The Decay of Lying*, and *The Ballad of Reading Gaol*. The text is that of the last printed edition overseen by Wilde.

Also in the Oxford Authors:

Sir Philip Sidney
Ben Jonson
Byron
Thomas Hardy

OXFORD LETTERS AND MEMOIRS

Letters, memoirs, and journals offer a special insight into the private lives of public figures and vividly recreate the times in which they lived. This popular series makes available the best and most entertaining of these documents, bringing the past to life in a fresh and personal way.

RICHARD HOGGART

A Local Habitation
Life and Times: 1918–1940

With characteristic candour and compassion, Richard Hoggart evokes the Leeds of his boyhood, where as an orphan, he grew up with his grandmother, two aunts, an uncle, and a cousin in a small terraced back-to-back.

'brilliant . . . a joy as well as an education' Roy Hattersley

'a model of scrupulous autobiography' Edward Blishen, *Listener*

A Sort of Clowning
Life and Times: 1940–1950

Opening with his wartime exploits in North Africa and Italy, this sequel to *A Local Habitation* recalls his teaching career in North-East England, and charts his rise in the literary world following the publication of *The Uses of Literacy*.

'one of the classic autobiographies of our time' Anthony Howard, *Independent on Sunday*

'Hoggart [is] the ideal autobiographer' Beryl Bainbridge, *New Statesman and Society*

Also in Oxford Letters and Memoirs:

My Sister and Myself: The Diaries of J. R. Ackerley
The Letters of T. E. Lawrence
A London Family 1870–1900   Molly Hughes

OXFORD LIVES

Biography at its best—this acclaimed series offers authoritative accounts of the lives of men and women from the arts, sciences, politics, and many other walks of life.

STANLEY

Volume I: The Making of an African Explorer
Volume II: Sorceror's Apprentice

Frank McLynn

Sir Henry Morton Stanley was one of the most fascinating late-Victorian adventurers. His historic meeting with Livingstone at Ujiji in 1871 was the journalistic scoop of the century. Yet behind the public man lay the complex and deeply disturbed personality who is the subject of Frank McLynn's masterly study.

In his later years, Stanley's achievements exacted a high human cost, both for the man himself and for those who came into contact with him. His foundation of the Congo Free State on behalf of Leopold II of Belgium, and the Emin Pasha Relief Expedition were both dubious enterprises which tarnished his reputation. They also revealed the complex—and often troubling—relationship that Stanley has with Africa.

'excellent . . . entertaining, well researched and scrupulously annotated' *Spectator*

'another biography of Stanley will not only be unnecessary, but almost impossible, for years to come' *Sunday Telegraph*

Also available:

A Prince of Our Disorder: The Life of T. E. Lawrence
John Mack
Carpet Sahib: A Life of Jim Corbett   Martin Booth
Bonnie Prince Charlie: Charles Edward Stuart   Frank McLynn

OPUS

General Editors: Walter Bodmer, Christopher Butler,
Robert Evans, John Skorupski

OPUS is a series of accessible introductions to a wide range of studies in the sciences and humanities.

METROPOLIS

Emrys Jones

Past civilizations have always expressed themselves in great cities, immense in size, wealth, and in their contribution to human progress. We are still enthralled by ancient cities like Babylon, Rome, and Constantinople. Today, giant cities abound, but some are pre-eminent. As always, they represent the greatest achievements of different cultures. But increasingly, they have also been drawn into a world economic system as communications have improved.

Metropolis explores the idea of a class of supercities in the past and in the present, and in the western and developing worlds. It analyses the characteristics they share as well as those that make them unique; the effect of technology on their form and function; and the problems that come with size—congestion, poverty and inequality, squalor—that are sobering contrasts to the inherent glamour and attraction of great cities throughout time.

Also available in OPUS:

The Medieval Expansion of Europe J. R. S. Phillips
Metaphysics: The Logical Approach José A. Benardete
The Voice of the Past 2/e Paul Thompson
Thinking About Peace and War Martin Ceadel

HISTORY IN OXFORD PAPERBACKS

Oxford Paperbacks' superb history list offers books on a wide range of topics from ancient to modern times, whether general period studies or assessments of particular events, movements, or personalities.

THE STRUGGLE FOR
THE MASTERY OF EUROPE 1848–1918
A. J. P. Taylor

The fall of Metternich in the revolutions of 1848 heralded an era of unprecedented nationalism in Europe, culminating in the collapse of the Hapsburg, Romanov, and Hohenzollern dynasties at the end of the First World War. In the intervening seventy years the boundaries of Europe changed dramatically from those established at Vienna in 1815. Cavour championed the cause of *Risorgimento* in Italy; Bismarck's three wars brought about the unification of Germany; Serbia and Bulgaria gained their independence courtesy of the decline of Turkey—'the sick man of Europe'; while the great powers scrambled for places in the sun in Africa. However, with America's entry into the war and President Wilson's adherence to idealistic internationalist principles, Europe ceased to be the centre of the world, although its problems, still primarily revolving around nationalist aspirations, were to smash the Treaty of Versailles and plunge the world into war once more.

A. J. P. Taylor has drawn the material for his account of this turbulent period from the many volumes of diplomatic documents which have been published in the five major European languages. By using vivid language and forceful characterization, he has produced a book that is as much a work of literature as a contribution to scientific history.

'One of the glories of twentieth-century writing.' *Observer*

Also in Oxford Paperbacks:

Portrait of an Age: Victorian England   G. M. Young
Germany 1866–1945   Gorden A. Craig
The Russian Revolution 1917–1932   Sheila Fitzpatrick
France 1848–1945   Theodore Zeldin

WOMEN'S STUDIES FROM
OXFORD PAPERBACKS

Ranging from the *A–Z of Women's Health* to *Wayward Women: A Guide to Women Travellers*, Oxford Paperbacks cover a wide variety of social, medical, historical, and literary topics of particular interest to women.

DESTINED TO BE WIVES
The Sisters of Beatrice Webb
Barbara Caine

Drawing on their letters and diaries, Barbara Caine's fascinating account of the lives of Beatrice Webb and her sisters, the Potters, presents a vivid picture of the extraordinary conflicts and tragedies taking place behind the respectable façade which has traditionally characterized Victorian and Edwardian family life.

The tensions and pressures of family life, particularly for women; the suicide of one sister; the death of another, probably as a result of taking cocaine after a family breakdown; the shock felt by the older sisters at the promiscuity of their younger sister after the death of her husband are all vividly recounted. In all the crises they faced, the sisters formed the main network of support for each other, recognizing that the 'sisterhood' provided the only security in a society which made women subordinate to men, socially, legally, and economically.

Other women's studies titles:

A–Z of Women's Health   Derek Llewellyn-Jones
'Victorian Sex Goddess': Lady Colin Campbell and the Sensational Divorce Case of 1886   G. H. Fleming
Wayward Women: A Guide to Women Travellers
Jane Robinson
Catherine the Great: Life and Legend   John T. Alexander